SAP® BW Performance Optimization Guide

 **PRESS**

SAP PRESS is issued by
Bernhard Hochlehnert, SAP AG

SAP PRESS is a joint initiative of SAP and Galileo Press. The know-how offered by SAP specialists combined with the expertise of the publishing house Galileo Press offers the reader expert books in the field. SAP PRESS features first-hand information and expert advice, and provides useful skills for professional decision-making.

SAP PRESS offers a variety of books on technical and business related topics for the SAP user. For further information, please visit our website: *www.sap-press.com*.

Thomas Schneider
SAP Performance Optimization Guide
2006, 522 pp., ISBN 1-59229-069-8

N. Egger, J.-M. R. Fiechter, J. Rohlf
SAP BW Data Modeling
2005, 437 pp., ISBN 1-59229-043-4

N. Egger, J.-M.R. Fiechter, R. Salzmann, R. P. Sawicki, T. Thielen
SAP BW Data Retrieval
Mastering the ETL Process
2006, 552 pp., ISBN 1-59229-044-2

Armin Kösegi, Rainer Nerding
Change and Transport Management
2005, 744 pp., ISBN 1-59229-059-0

Thomas Schröder

SAP® BW Performance Optimization Guide

SAP PRESS

Translation Lemoine International, Inc.,
Salt Lake City, UT
Copy Editor Nancy Etscovitz, UCG, Inc.,
Boston, MA
Cover Design Nadine Kohl
Printed in Germany

ISBN 1-59229-080-9
ISBN 13 978-1-59229-080-2
1st edition 2006

Contents

6 The SAP BW Data Model 89

7 Analyzing the Database, Memory, and Hardware 117

8 Analyzing the System Load 155

9 Indices and Database Statistics 189

10   Reporting Performance   243

11   Aggregates   301

1   Introduction and Overview

When SAP first marketed a proprietary data warehouse solution in 1998 (i.e., SAP Business Information Warehouse, SAP BW), established competitors were rather skeptical about this new system—the first marketable version thought to be capable of handling only small reporting applications and small data quantities. Since then, their initial assessment has proven to be utterly wrong. Today, SAP BW is one of the most widespread business intelligence platforms used to map the most complex analytical reporting requirements.

I became motivated to write a book on optimizing performance in SAP BW because I found that performance is a recurrent topic in each data warehousing project, and ultimately, it is the deciding factor for a system's acceptance by users. For example, no user wants to wait minutes or even hours for report queries, since the query results should be available in real time.

Background

Yet, what does "in real time" actually mean and how can we define a high-performing system? Although the term "performance" is commonly used, it is difficult to describe. When we use the term in this book, we mean a system behavior that enables users to perform their work well and in a motivated manner under accepted conditions. This description tells us that there is no such thing as an absolute performance, but that performance itself represents the ability to achieve acceptable response times or a certain data throughput under certain conditions. Long-lasting report or data update runtimes can ultimately hinder the usability of the system to such an extent that the availability of business-critical information in real time can no longer be guaranteed. In that case, not only would users not accept the system, but they would even reject using it.

Performance

In many data warehousing and SAP BW implementation projects, I discovered that system performance was either insufficiently accounted for, or not accounted for at all during the design and implementation phases. Oftentimes, the response behavior of the applications is not checked until a performance test is run just before the system goes live. If, at that time, response times are determined to be unacceptable, case studies are conducted that can lead to a change of data models or report definitions. This causes an unnecessary increase in the costs and runtimes of the Business Intelligence (BI) application implementation. For this reason, performance must be taken into account as early as the design phase, but no later than the implementation phase. However, you should note that not

Considering performance aspects at an early stage

everything that a user considers necessary or possible can be implemented with acceptable response times. Therefore, you should ensure that all decisions regarding the design of BI applications are assessed at an early stage so their effects on system performance are known from the start.

Target audience When I tried to narrow down the specifics of performance optimization in SAP BW, it became readily apparent that the target audience for such a book consists of many different interest groups, each responsible for certain aspects of performance — design, development, and operation of SAP BW systems.

On the one hand, this book is intended for SAP BW consultants and developers whose main tasks include the design and implementation of BI applications. The book will support them in assessing the effects of the design and implementation measures at an early stage, in running a systematic performance analysis, and in optimizing the SAP BW system.

On the other hand, this book is intended for all those folks who are responsible for ensuring the smooth operation of an SAP BW system. This group of people often represents the first point of contact for raising complaints about the system's poor performance during the running operation. Because the usage profile and load behavior of an SAP BW system differ from that of an SAP R/3 system, this book provides this group of users with the basic principles and specific characteristics of the SAP BW system, as well as its optimization options.

1.1 Structure of the Book

The book is divided into three main sections:

1. Description of the theoretical basics required to understand the functionality of the SAP BW system and technical principles for performance optimization

2. Introduction of methods and tools to be used for a systematic performance analysis

3. Detailed description of performance optimization measures including tips for the design

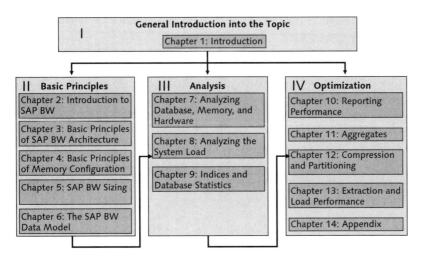

Figure 1.1 Structure of the Book

Chapter 2 describes the basic principles of the data warehouse concept in general, as well as the structure of SAP BW.

Chapter 3 provides the basic principles of the SAP BW architecture with regard to the software components of the SAP BW system and of the SAP Basis system.

Chapter 4 introduces you to the basics of SAP memory configuration in the SAP BW application server. The chapter describes the most important SAP memory areas and provides information on configuring the SAP BW system.

Chapter 5 describes the SAP BW sizing process. Correct sizing is the basis for an adequate system performance. The chapter describes the basic principles and computing models used for sizing SAP BW and it introduces SAP Quick Sizer, a tool used for sizing SAP systems.

Chapter 6 introduces you to the SAP BW data model. Understanding the structure and functionality of the SAP BW data model is integral to analyzing and finding the causes of BW performance problems, as well as learning how to optimize the SAP BW reporting applications.

Chapter 7 introduces you to the analysis of the database, memory, and hardware of an SAP BW system. The chapter describes the SAP performance monitors and provides information on configuring an SAP BW system.

Chapter 8 describes the use of the system load monitor for analyzing the R/3 and BW system load.

Chapter 9 shows you how to analyze and manage indices and database statistics. Indices and database statistics must be up-to-date to ensure a high-performing system.

In Chapter 10, you'll learn about design and optimization measures that help you to improve the reporting performance. This chapter describes the SAP BW system settings for the online analytical processing (OLAP) processor and the query monitor, and it explains how you can optimize the query settings.

Chapter 11 focuses on the creation and administration of aggregates, which is one of the most important performance measures for optimizing response times in reporting. This chapter describes the basic principles of SAP BW aggregates and methods for developing adequate aggregates.

Chapter 12 describes the various methods available for compressing and partitioning InfoCubes in SAP BW, which represent an optimization measure for reducing the dataset in SAP BW.

Chapter 13 examines the performance aspects pertaining to the extraction and load processes. It describes the usage of the load monitor, as well as available options for optimizing the extraction and load performance.

Chapter 14 (the appendix) contains a list of the most important performance-relevant SAP notes that provide further details on performance. Furthermore, the appendix describes essential SAP BW system tables and provides a sample design that you can use to optimize the reporting performance of SAP BW workbooks.

1.2 How to Use This Book

This book is intended to support you in your daily work. It is therefore not necessary to read the book from cover to cover. Instead, you can read the individual chapters as needed, depending on your current level of knowledge and information requirements.

Readers who want to learn the basic principles of the SAP BW system, however, should start with Chapter 2, *Data Warehousing and SAP BW— An Introduction*, then read Chapter 3, *Basic Principles of the SAP BW Architecture*, and then move on to Chapter 6, *The SAP BW Data Model*.

Those of you who are already familiar with the SAP BW system and want to analyze the system performance right away should begin with Chapter 7, *Analyzing Database, Memory, and Hardware*, and Chapter 8, *Analyzing the System Load*.

And finally, those readers who have already localized the weak points of their system and are now looking for the right measures to support their performance optimization efforts should jump to Chapter 10, *Reporting Performance*, Chapter 11, *Aggregates*, Chapter 12, *Compression and Partitioning*, and Chapter 13, *Extraction and Load Performance*.

The world of SAP and SAP terminology change rapidly. The latest version of the "classical," transactional SAP system is called *mySAP ERP 2005*, and the application core of this system is referred to as *SAP ECC* (Enterprise Core Component). For the sake of simplicity and also because most of you are probably using older systems that still have *R/3* as part of their names, I will use *R/3* consistently throughout this book when I refer to SAP online transaction processing (OLTP) systems.

Terminology used in this book

1.3 Acknowledgements

This book would not have been possible without the support and contribution of many people, friends, and colleagues. At this time, I would like to acknowledge the following people for their cooperation, constant support, and help, but most of all for their patience.

First, a special thank you to Florian Zimniak and everyone at SAP PRESS for their professional support that they provided me from the conception to the final production of this book. It was truly a collaborative effort.

A special thank you goes to SAP AG, and, in particular, to Gerhard Beck and Dr. Thomas Schneider. Gerhard Beck showed great patience in critically reviewing this book and provided numerous suggestions for improvement and valuable advice that contributed enormously to its quality. Dr. Thomas Schneider is a proven SAP performance expert whose book on SAP performance, *SAP Performance Optimization Guide*, which is currently available in its fourth edition, has inspired me to write this book.

Thanks also to my boss and mentor, Reinhard Härle, who manages the SAP NetWeaver BI team that I have been working with for several years now, and who enabled me to write this book by keeping me free of ties to other projects.

A big thank you goes to all my coworkers in the SAP BI team at Capgemini,[1] in particular, to Tanja Heckert and Adrian Blockus for their inspiring discussions and questions that essentially fostered the success of this book.

But, above all, my very special thanks goes to my wife, Anja Keßler, who had to spend many weekends and long evenings without me in the past year. Her love, care, and incessant patience have always given me the necessary support, strength, and confidence to finish this book. Therefore, I dedicate this book to her.

Bargfeld-Stegen, May 2006
Thomas Schröder

---

1 Capgemini is a global leader in consulting, technology, outsourcing, and local professional services. The company is headquartered in Paris, France, and operates in more than 30 countries, with nearly 60,000 people in North America, Europe, and the Asia Pacific region.

2   Data Warehousing and SAP BW

SAP Business Information Warehouse (SAP BW) is a compre-
hensive data warehousing solution that can be used for data
extraction, data storage, and data analysis. This chapter pro-
vides an overview of the data warehousing technology and
SAP BW.

When SAP introduced SAP Business Information Warehouse in 1998, it
provided a data warehousing solution that met the technological requirements of decision-oriented information systems. The vocabulary for all
the concepts used in the data warehousing and SAP BW areas is volumi-
nous. For this reason, this chapter introduces you to only the most important terms and characteristics of the data warehousing concept. It
describes the structure of data warehousing systems, as well as the most
important differences between data warehousing systems and operational systems.

In the second half of this chapter, you're introduced to the structure of
SAP BW and the terminology used to describe these structural concepts.
Here, the components used for data extraction, data storage, and data
analysis/data presentation are described, as well as the most important
terms used in the SAP BW environment.

2.1   Introduction to Data Warehousing

The *data warehousing* concept was coined in the mid 1980s to define the
technological solution for the decision-oriented collection, preparation,
and retrieval of business-relevant information.

The main task of a data warehouse is to collect data from different operational systems, store it over a specific period of time, and format it for
data analysis and information retrieval purposes. Regardless of whether
the data originates from different source systems, the different datasets
are merged in the data warehouse in such a way that an integrated, sub
ject-oriented, and historical view of the information is made possible.
Data warehousing systems are designed for storing and analyzing large
data quantities, which is enabled by an adequate transformation and
aggregation of the data.

B. Inmon,[1] who is often referred to as the inventor of the data warehouse, defined the typical characteristics of data warehousing systems as follows:

Subject orientation Data warehousing systems are subject-oriented. This means that the data of a data warehouse is combined according to certain points of view across the company (for example, products, customers, suppliers, sales and marketing, and so on), and that it is not structured according to operational tasks such as purchase order entry, retail, or invoicing. The subject-oriented combination of different data therefore causes a "disentanglement" of the data from its operational sources so as to merge it into an integrated view along the value chain of the company.

Integrated data basis A data warehousing system combines data from different heterogeneous source systems. Each of these source systems stores the data in its purpose-oriented, local structure. Therefore, material or customer master data, for example, can differ among heterogeneous source systems in different locations. The combination of the different data in the data warehouse requires a harmonization of the data, in particular, with regard to different data formats, field lengths, and so on, before it can be transferred into a consistent schema within the data warehouse.

Historical The data of a data warehouse is stored over a longer period of time, sometimes even for several years. The data warehouse therefore enables you to keep *historical records* of the data statuses in a company, even for periods in which the source data of the operational systems has already been deleted. In each import cycle such as a day, a week, or a month, new data is stored in the data warehouse, and like a camera snapshot, this data represents the current data status. The storage of data over a long period of time enables you to perform the time series analyses that is a typical characteristic of data warehouse applications; however, it places very high requirements on the data storage capacity and analysis performance.

Non-volatility The data in a data warehouse is non-volatile, that is, once this data has been stored in the data warehouse, its contents won't change and it won't be deleted. Contrary to operational systems that sometimes change their data every second to present the current status, the data that's stored in the data warehouse will no longer change, except for necessary corrections; for example, when a data load is incorrect because of wrong update rules. The requirement for data consistency is based on the denormalized data storage that is typical of data warehouse applications,

---

1 B. Inmon: *Building the Data Warehouse*. John Wiley 1992.

and which makes it very difficult to change data at a later stage due the data redundancy. However, the requirements that modern data warehousing systems must meet, such as real-time reporting even on operational data, somewhat undermine the data consistency requirement because different data storage mechanisms such as operational data stores (ODS) can be used.

In the context of data warehousing, you often hear about the term *OLAP*. This abbreviation stands for *Online Analytical Processing* and describes the analysis technique that's typically implemented in data warehouse applications.

OLAP

The OLAP data storage can best be described as a Rubik's cube.

▶ The qualitative evaluation views of the analysis are mapped along the axes or dimensions of the cube. These views can represent characteristics such as time, product, customer, or region.

▶ The intersections of the axes contain the quantities to be measured. These values are key figures such as revenues, sales volumes, quantity, and so on.

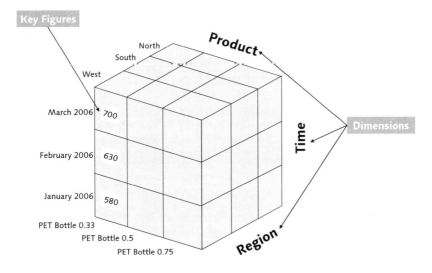

Figure 2.1 OLAP Cube Model

Of course, the cube model is only a metaphorical depiction of the data storage and analysis techniques. In real life, data can be analyzed in more than three dimensions, which however cannot be illustrated. Still, the data cube concept has prevailed. In SAP BW, we use the term *InfoCube* when referring to multidimensional data storage.

The OLAP technology enables you to flexibly analyze data according to different points of view ("What were our revenues with product XY in January 2006?").

2.2 Differences Between Operational and Decision Support Systems

The requirements for a data warehousing system differ from those for operational systems, especially when you look at usage behavior and the associated load profiles. Whereas operational systems—*Online Transaction Processing* (OLTP)—provide support for purpose and transaction-oriented data processing in the company (for example invoicing tasks), decision support systems—*Online Analytical Processing* (OLAP)—enable a flexible data analysis and provide support in the decision-making process. Table 2.1 lists the most important differences.

Requirements	Operational systems (OLTP)	DWH systems (OLAP)
Data structures	Flat tables, normalized (low data redundancy)	Multidimensional structures, denormalized (high data redundancy)
Typical operations	Frequent accesses, small data quantities; read, write, change, delete	Mainly read accesses (except for planning systems); analysis of large data quantities
Changes	Very often, transaction-oriented	Periodic
Up-to-date history	Always up-to-date, only short history (several months only)	Often up-to-date, long history (sometimes several years)
Data granularity	Detailed	Detailed and aggregated (depending on the requirements)
Complexity of queries	Low	High; complex database queries
Flexibility of queries	Low; often inflexible query forms	Highly flexible; freely selectable, spontaneous queries possible
Data sources	Often only one	Several to many
Number of users	Often high	Low to medium

Table 2.1 Comparison of Operational and Decision Support Systems

Requirements	Operational systems (OLTP)	DWH systems (OLAP)
Optimization requirements	High availability and stability, high data throughput, very short response times (milliseconds to seconds)	Management of large data quantities (up to terabytes), short to medium response times in reporting (seconds to minutes)

Table 2.1 Comparison of Operational and Decision Support Systems (cont.)

The main differences between operational systems and data warehousing systems can be found in the type of data storage used, the data quantities to be stored, and the usage profile of the system:

▶ The data models in operational systems are characterized by a low data redundancy. Those data models are often created in a normalized form and enable a fast update of data using simple database operations. The normalization in operational, relational databases causes a disintegration of data relationships into several relations to avoid redundancies (i.e., repeated information and the associated risk of data anomalies). Data warehousing systems, however, store data as highly redundant for the purpose of query optimization.

▶ Operational systems frequently have a very limited data history of only a few months. For this reason, their data storage capacity is smaller than that of data warehousing systems whose data capacity can increase enormously due to the storage of data that can be up to several years old.

▶ The usage profile of OLTP systems is often characterized by simple, repeated read and write accesses in which small volumes of data are added, changed, or read. OLAP systems are designed for a flexible analysis of very large data quantities, which involves complex data queries.

2.3 Structure of Data Warehousing Systems

The generic structure of data warehousing systems can be divided into the following three areas:

▶ Data retrieval
▶ Data storage
▶ Data presentation/data analysis

Figure 2.2 shows the structure of a data warehousing system, which can be used to describe the basic principles of the data warehouse architecture.

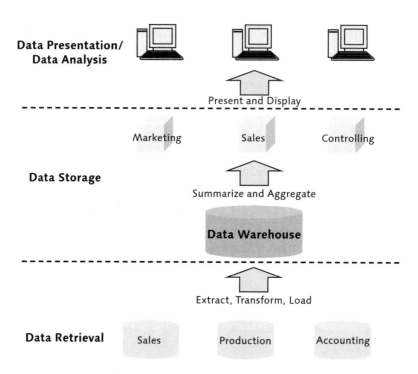

Figure 2.2 Structure of a Data Warehousing System

Data retrieval
The data retrieval process involves the transfer of data from the heterogeneous source systems into the data warehouse. This process is also referred to as the *Extraction, Loading, and Transformation* (ETL) process, because it contains the three process steps of extracting data from the source systems, transforming the data, and finally loading the data.

The data extraction process consists of selecting and filtering the data required for the analysis from the operational systems.

The transformation, the standardization, the cleansing, and the quality assurance of the data all occur prior to the data being transferred into the data warehouse.

During the loading process, the just formatted data is imported into the data warehouse and stored in its inbound layer. The inbound layer is often an exact copy of the source data, which precedes the subsequent aggregation of the data in data cubes and aggregates.

Data storage
The data storage process consists of storing the data in a format that is optimized for the data analysis. The data is frequently stored and aggregated in the data cubes (InfoCubes in SAP BW) according to specific sub-

jects and evaluations. Because data warehousing systems must store large data quantities—of up to several terabytes due to the storage of historical data—the database and the type of data storage must meet very high requirements in terms of performance and scalability. For this reason, the data storage process in a data warehouse involves special techniques for optimizing database queries. In the following sections, we'll describe some optimization options only briefly, since we will address them in much greater detail later on in this book.

To optimize the queries, data is stored in data cubes and in *aggregates*. **Aggregates** Aggregates are a type of data storage in which the data is stored in a lower granularity. The subsequent loss of information that must be tolerated here improves query performance due to the smaller data quantities that need to be handled. When new data is loaded into the data warehouse, aggregates require additional disk space and system performance for calculation and adjustment due to the redundant data storage.

Partitions are the reason for dividing a dataset into smaller data subsets. **Partitions** The partitions help to optimize the performance, because, unlike partitioned datasets, smaller database areas must be searched during the data analysis. You can create partitions physically in the database of the data warehousing system, if the database is well suited for that. Another option that you can try is the logical partitioning at the application level, in which the dataset of a data cube is divided into small, separate sub-cubes.

Indices are another means of improving read access in databases. You can **Indices** compare indices to the table of contents of a book or to the sorting of a phone directory by names. If you search the phone number of a specific person, only a few "read accesses" in the family name are necessary to obtain the required information. At the database level, the relationships between the primary keys of a table and the foreign keys of each data record in an external table, for example, are stored in an index to accelerate the access to the data records required for the analysis. Because indices are additional tables, they require additional disk space and system performance for calculation and adjustment purposes, when new data is loaded into the data warehouse.

The data presentation and data analysis layer is the interface between the **Data presen-** user and the system. This layer displays the output of the data selected by **tation/data** the user as predefined reports or flexible ad-hoc analyses on the client **analysis** computer of the user. The user doesn't need to have any specific knowledge in database query languages or table structures, because the analysis and display of data is mainly performed by query tools or data warehouse frontends, which enable a clear presentation of business information and an easy operation of the data analysis.

2.4 Overview of SAP BW

SAP BW is a comprehensive data warehousing solution that provides all tools, functions, and components of decision support systems. These tools, functions, and components include the following:

▶ Tools for administration, customizing, modeling, controlling, and monitoring

▶ Functions for data extraction, transformation, and loading

▶ Data storage components

▶ Metadata management tools

▶ Analysis and reporting tools

Figure 2.3 displays the integration of the individual components and functional areas in SAP BW.

Each of the following sections introduces the most important areas of SAP BW. They describe the tools and functional areas integrated in SAP BW, as well as the most important concepts.

Figure 2.3 Data Warehouse Architecture of SAP BW

2.4.1 Administration and Customizing

The initial point of entry for administrating and customizing SAP BW is the Administrator Workbench that can be called via Transaction RSA1. The Administrator Workbench is the "control center" of SAP BW. From here, you can carry out the modeling tasks and make the customizing settings, call process and job control functions, monitor the loading processes, call the Metadata Repository (see also Section 2.4.4), and import the business content.

Business content consists of predefined analytical applications provided by SAP in the standard SAP BW version that can be installed if required. The business content comprises the entire data process in SAP BW for many different evaluation scenarios. This means that predefined programs are available for data extraction, as well as data models for data storage, and predefined reports that can be used for data analysis. Business content enables you to quickly implement preconfigured evaluations. In addition, you can use the business content as a basis for your own enhancements and extensions to meet customer-specific analysis requirements.

Business content

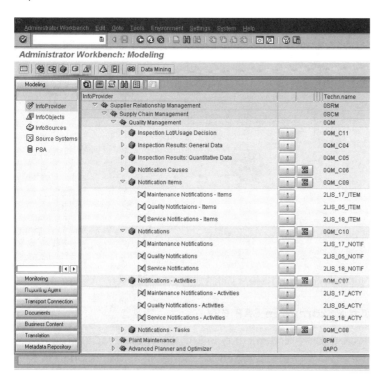

Figure 2.4 Administrator Workbench (AWB)

2.4.2 Data Extraction in SAP BW

The extraction of data for SAP BW can occur from almost any data source, both for R/3 and non-SAP systems.

SAP source systems The integration of data from SAP systems occurs via application-specific extractors that must be installed as plug-ins in the SAP source system. In addition to the data extraction programs, the plug-ins also contain application-specific extraction structures for various SAP modules. Those structures are provided as business content by SAP. The extractors can be extended according to customer-specific requirements that have been created for instance in R/3 Customizing.

Non-SAP source systems SAP BW provides several interfaces for extracting data from non-SAP systems. For example, you can import data from relational and multidimensional databases using DB Connect or UD Connect. In addition, you can import XML data and flat files and integrate third-party applications or data extraction tools via the Business Application Programming Interface (BAPI).

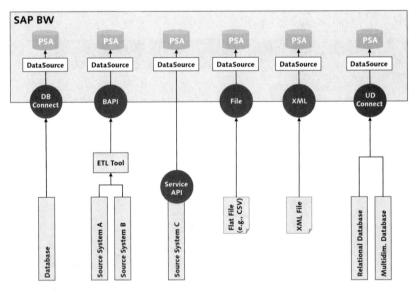

Figure 2.5 Integrating Source Systems with SAP BW

2.4.3 Data Storage in SAP BW

The smallest business-related entity in SAP BW is the *InfoObject*. InfoObjects are the "building blocks" used for modeling all data models in SAP BW.

InfoObjects can be divided into characteristics and key figures:

▶ *Characteristics* are business-related reference values such as customers, products, company codes, or distribution channels on which you can classify key figures. In addition to the business-related characteristics, SAP BW also contains units such as currency and quantity units, time characteristics like the calendar day or month, and technical characteristics such as the request number used to identify a loading process.

If characteristics have attributes, text, or hierarchies, that is, master data, they are referred to as *master data-bearing characteristics*.

▶ *Key figures* are metrical units such as quantities, amounts, and numbers of pieces that enable arithmetic operations.

InfoObjects can be modeled in the **InfoObjects** menu of the Administrator Workbench.

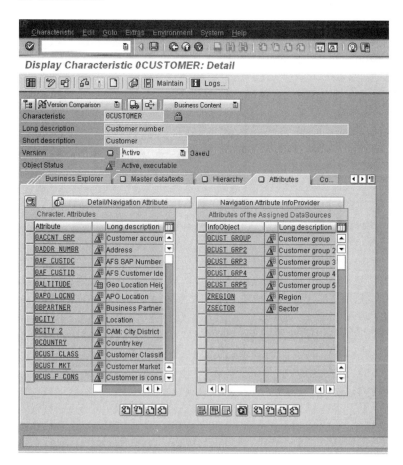

Figure 2.6 Modeling InfoObjects

InfoProviders   All objects in SAP BW that can be used for reporting are referred to as *InfoProviders*. The data of an InfoProvider can be analyzed using the standard BW reporting tool, SAP Business Explorer Analyzer (SAP BEx Analyzer).

The InfoProviders in SAP BW can be divided into two different areas:

▶ *InfoProviders that contain data* and that are stored in physical tables in SAP BW and complemented with new data in periodic loading processes. This group of InfoProviders includes InfoCubes, operational data store (ODS) objects,[2] and master data-bearing InfoObjects that are declared as InfoProviders and therefore, can also be used for reporting.

▶ *InfoProviders without a physical data storage* that represent a logical view of data. This group of InfoProviders includes VirtualProviders (SAP RemoteCubes, RemoteCubes, and RemoteCubes with service), InfoSets, and MultiProviders.

Figure 2.7 Presentation of the InfoCube Data Model in the AWB

---

2   The term ODS object was changed to *DataStore object* with the introduction of SAP NetWeaver 2004. However, since ODS object is still widely used, we will also use this term in this book.

SAP BW InfoCubes consist of relational tables that are structured according to the *star schema*. The key figures are stored at the center of a large fact table, around which the analysis views of the dimension tables are grouped including the respective characteristics. The data is physically stored in the InfoCube tables and can be analyzed using a BEx query.

InfoCubes

ODS objects are flat, transparent database tables that physically store master data and transaction data at the document level (basic level), if possible. ODS objects consist of data record keys (for example, a document number), as well as data and value fields. Because the data is stored in a flat structure, it doesn't contain any dimension or fact tables. You can use ODS objects for reporting; however, as is the case with InfoCubes, their performance optimization options are rather limited.

ODS objects

InfoObjects of the *character* type can also be declared as InfoProviders, if they contain master data (i.e., master data-bearing InfoObjects). Such InfoObjects/InfoProviders are available for data analysis purposes in reporting.

InfoObjects as InfoProviders

VirtualProviders don't contain any data by themselves, but for reporting, they read additional data that can be stored in SAP BW and in other SAP systems and non-SAP systems. The VirtualProviders can be divided into three different types:

VirtualProviders

▶ VirtualProviders whose transaction data is read directly from an SAP system via a DataSource, or an InfoProvider in reporting (SAP RemoteCube)

▶ VirtualProviders whose transaction data is read from external systems via a BAPI program interface in reporting (RemoteCube)

▶ VirtualProviders whose transaction data is read via customized function modules in reporting (RemoteCube with service)

An InfoSet is a semantical view that summarizes ODS objects, InfoCubes, and master data-bearing InfoObjects via a join operation. *InfoSet queries* can be created for reporting on the basis of InfoSets.

InfoSets

MultiProviders are InfoProviders that combine data from several InfoProviders and then make it available for reporting. A MultiProvider doesn't contain any data by itself, but it represents a logical access view that summarizes the underlying InfoProviders using a UNION operation. Chapter 12 contains detailed information on the properties of MultiProviders and how they can be used in performance optimization.

MultiProviders

2.4.4 Metadata Management

All SAP BW objects defined in SAP Business Information Warehouse, such as InfoProviders, queries, InfoObjects, and so on, are managed in a central Metadata Repository (see Figure 2.8). Basically, metadata is information on data that describes the properties of objects such as the technical name, description, field type, and field length, as well as the interrelationships between these objects.

All SAP BW objects are differentiated by object types in the Metadata Repository (for example, query, InfoCube, MultiProvider), and can be called via hyperlinks.

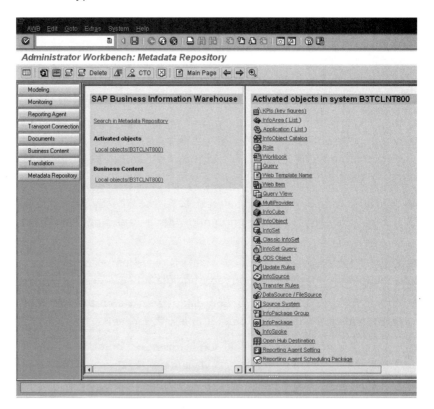

Figure 2.8 Metadata Repository in SAP BW

2.4.5 Analysis and Reporting

The data that is stored in SAP BW can be analyzed using various reporting tools. You can use either SAP Business Explorer (SAP BEx), which is integrated in SAP BW, or third-party reporting tools.

SAP Business Explorer is the business intelligence suite of SAP BW that consists of different components with reporting and analysis functions:

SAP Business Explorer (SAP BEx)

▶ The *BEx Query Designer* is the development environment for creating queries and reports in SAP BW.

▶ The *BEx Analyzer* is the reporting and analysis tool for Microsoft Excel-based queries in SAP BW. Because the tool is based on an MS Excel add-in, the reporting and analysis functions are completely available in MS Excel.

▶ The *BEx Web Application Designer* is a desktop development environment for web-based queries. You can use this tool to publish queries, which have been created in the BEx Query Designer, as reports on the web.

▶ The *BEx Web Analyzer* is a web-based application that enables you to run queries on the web and to create new queries. The BEx Web Analyzer is available as of SAP BW 3.5.

▶ *Information Broadcasting* enables you to provide a wide range of users with objects containing business intelligence content, which are both time- and event-driven.

SAP BW also enables you to perform data analysis using various third-party tools, which are referred to as *data warehouse frontends*. In this case, the tools do not directly access the InfoProviders in SAP BW; instead, they access the QueryCubes, which must be explicitly generated in SAP BW. The following three interfaces are currently provided by SAP for integrating third-party tools:

Third-party tools

▶ The ODBO interface (OLE DB for OLAP)

▶ The OLAP (Online Analytical Processing) BAPI interface (Business Application Programming Interface)

▶ The XMLA interface (XML for Analysis)

The ODBO interface is based on Microsoft's interface specification OLE DB for OLAP and was initially implemented in SAP BW 1.2. From SAP BW 2.0 onward, it was extended by additional SAP-proprietary functions.

The OLAP BAPI interface is a platform-independent program interface developed by SAP, which has been available for the integration of third-party tools since SAP BW Release 2.0.

The XMLA interface was introduced by Microsoft and Hyperion in 2001. XML for Analysis is a Simple Object Access Protocol (SOAP) based, standardized program interface used for data access by OLAP providers on the web.

Table 2.2 lists some third-party reporting and analysis tools, which have been certified for use in SAP BW. Please note that this list is not exhaustive.

Manufacturer	Product	Interface
Actuate	e.Reporting Suite	OLE DB for OLAP
	Actuate	OLAP BAPI
Applix	TM1	OLE DB for OLAP
arcplan Information Services AG	dynaSight	OLE DB for OLAP
		OLAP BAPI
Business Objects SA Europe	BusinessObjects BW Connect	OLE DB for OLAP
	BusinessObjects Integration Kit	OLAP BAPI
	Crystal Enterprise Enhanced SAP Edition	OLAP BAPI
Codec	Codec BWeb	OLE DB for OLAP
Cognos	Cognos PPDS ODBO Interface for SAP BW	OLE DB for OLAP
	Cognos Driver for BAPI	OLAP BAPI
Comshare	Comshare Decision	OLE DB for OLAP
CorVu North America	CorVu	OLE DB for OLAP
Cubeware	Cubeware Analysesystem	OLE DB for OLAP
humanIT	InfoZoom(R) Connect for SAP BW	OLE DB for OLAP
Hyperion Solutions	Hyperion Intelligence	OLE DB for OLAP
	Hyperion SQR	OLAP BAPI
Information Builders	WebFOCUS for SAP BW	OLE DB for OLAP
		OLAP BAPI
Macnica	B3 Smart	OLAP BAPI
MicroStrategy	Microstrategy	OLAP BAPI
MIK Management Information Kommunikation	MIK-ONE	OLE DB for OLAP

Table 2.2 Reporting Frontends for SAP BW

Manufacturer	Product	Interface
MIS	MIS Alea	OLE DB for OLAP
	MIS onVision WebServices	OLE DB for OLAP
	MIS Plain WebExtension	OLE DB for OLAP
	OnVision	OLE DB for OLAP
mSE GmbH Management Consultation and System Engineering	PointOut for BW	OLE DB for OLAP
ORBIS	iControl	OLE DB for OLAP
Samsung SDS	EasyBase	OLE DB for OLAP
	REQUBE	OLE DB for OLAP
SAS Institute	Enterprise Guide®	OLE DB for OLAP
Temtec International	Executive Viewer	OLE DB for OLAP
TONBELLER	Qubon	OLE DB for OLAP
Viador	E-Portal Suite	OLE DB for OLAP

Table 2.2 Reporting Frontends for SAP BW (cont.)

3 Basic Principles of the SAP BW Architecture

This chapter introduces the basic principles of the SAP BW architecture. It describes the individual components of an SAP BW system and provides useful information on how to configure those components.

Like an R/3 system or other SAP components, SAP Business Information Warehouse (SAP BW) is based on the SAP Basis system. The SAP Basis system provides various standard programs developed in ABAP, as well as basic tools such as the ABAP Workbench, the Computer Center Management System (CCMS), system administration tools, and communication and database interfaces. Since the release of Version 6.10, with its new features like the integration of HTTP services into the SAP Basis system for example, this Basis system has been generally referred to as the *SAP Web Application Server*.

3.1 Software Components of an SAP BW System

The SAP BW system consists of different software components. A software component contains a number of software objects that are provided together. Each software component has its own release statuses that are adjusted separately by using support packages.

The most important software components of an SAP BW system are as follows:

▶ SAP_BASIS (formerly SAP Basis, today SAP Web AS)

▶ SAP_ABA (application interface)

▶ PI_BASIS (Basis plug-in)

▶ SAP_BW (SAP Business Warehouse)

▶ BI_CONT (Business Intelligence Content)

▶ SAP Kernel (at OS level)

▶ SAP GUI (frontend user interface)

▶ ST-PT (SAP Solution Tools plug-in, optional for Early Watch Service)

You can view the list of software components installed in your SAP BW system including their currently installed release and patch statuses in the

SAP Easy Access menu by selecting the following path: **System · Status · Component information** (see Figure 3.1).

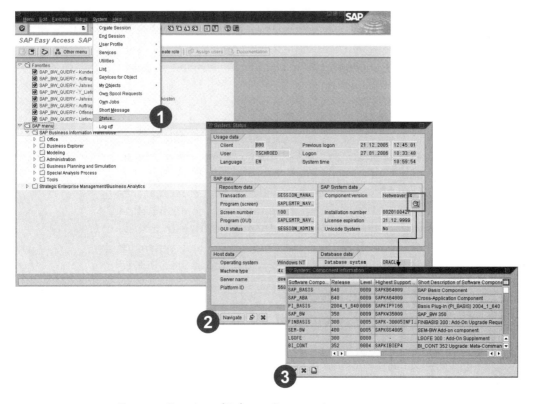

Figure 3.1 Overview of Software Components

Support packages   Support packages are used to adjust the SAP system by correcting software components and installing the required adjustments. A support package is valid for exactly one release status and can only be installed in the system, if all support packages of the previous release statuses are also available in the system in the correct order. You should note that an upgrade to a new release status automatically contains all support packages of the previous release statuses.

Support package
stacks   In 2003, SAP changed its support strategy for the distribution of packages in such a way that it now delivers support package stacks (SP stacks) for some product versions.

SP stacks are a combination of mandatory and recommended support packages and patch statuses of the components of a product version that must be commonly installed in the system. The SP stacks strategy ensures that all involved components have the minimum required status so that the packages can be installed in the most useful combination.

The Support Package Manager, which can be called, using Transaction SPAM, provides an overview of all support packages that have been installed in your system (see Figure 3.2). When you call this transaction, the system displays all support packages for each software component, including the patch number, installation status, and the date of the installation.

Support Package Manager

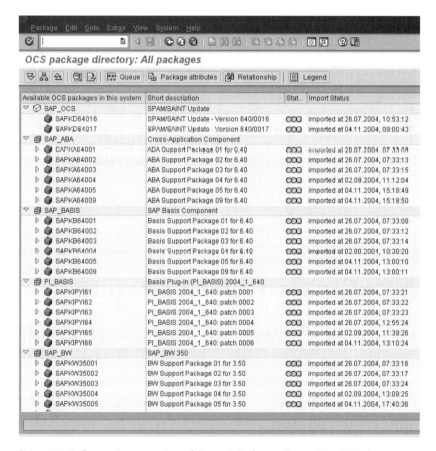

Figure 3.2 Software Components and Support Packages (Transaction SPAM)

To ensure a trouble-free and high-performing operation of your SAP BW system, you should regularly install the latest support packages. To check for the availability of new support packages, go to SAP Service Marketplace (*http://service.sap.com*) and then to the **Software Distribution Center** (*/swdc*) or to the **SAP Business Intelligence** area (*/bi*).

Figure 3.3 SAP Service Marketplace—Software Distribution Center

3.2 Overview of the SAP BW Architecture

The architecture of SAP BW is based on a multilevel client/server architecture that consists of the presentation, application, and database layers.

Presentation layer

The presentation layer contains the user interface of the SAP BW system. Typically, SAP GUI is installed on the client computer as a user interface for SAP BW and the reporting component applications that may contain different analysis tools such as the SAP BEx Analyzer add-in for Excel (generally referred to as SAP BEx Analyzer), a web browser, or third-party tools. You must install SAP GUI for Windows, SAP BEx Analyzer, and any other third-party frontend tools on the client computer; however, do not install any reporting tool on the client computer, if you want to use reports on the web whose queries are published using SAP Web Application Designer, since those reports can be accessed using the web browser.

Application layer

The application layer contains the actual SAP BW system. The system consists of the SAP Web Application Server (SAP Web AS since SAP Basis

6.10, previously SAP Basis) and the SAP BW application logic, which comprises the customer-specific BW applications for data management, data storage, and reporting. The application layer can be distributed to several application servers. During the logon process, a user is assigned to exactly one application server. In this way, you can distribute the system load equally across several application servers.

The database layer represents the core of an SAP BW system. It stores the data that is extracted from the source systems and optimized for the data analysis. The database assumes a key role in SAP BW systems, because the requirements it must meet—in terms of the data quantity to be stored, and the load it has to bear due to the number of read accesses during a data analysis—are incomparably higher than they are in R/3 systems. It is therefore advisable to install the database on a separate database server instead of operating it with the application server on one machine. That way, you can ensure that sufficient resources are available for the database.

Database layer

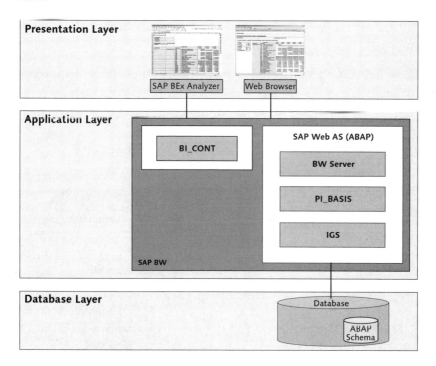

Figure 3.4 Layers of an SAP BW Client/Server Architecture

SAP Web Application Server (SAP Web AS)

SAP Web Application Server (SAP Web AS) is an advanced development of the SAP_BASIS component. Since the integration of HTTP services in Version 6.10, the SAP Basis system has been referred to as *SAP Web Application Server*. The SAP Web AS enables both the server-side and client-side implementation of web applications. Depending on the installation you choose, the SAP Web AS can run ABAP-based and Java-based programs, and it supports client communications via HTTP, HTTPS, and SMTP protocols, as well as the SAP-proprietary DIAG protocol.

You can configure SAP Web AS as a (web) server and as a client. If you configure it as a server, the Internet Communication Manager (ICM) is responsible for receiving inbound requests, which it redirects to the SAP system for processing in the SAP Web AS. If you set up SAP Web AS as a client, the ICM redirects incoming requests to another server for further processing.

The Internet Communication Framework (ICF) is an integral part of the SAP Web AS because it is responsible for processing HTTP requests in the ABAP work processes of the SAP system.

Figure 3.5 shows the most important SAP Web Application Server components, which will be briefly described in the following section.

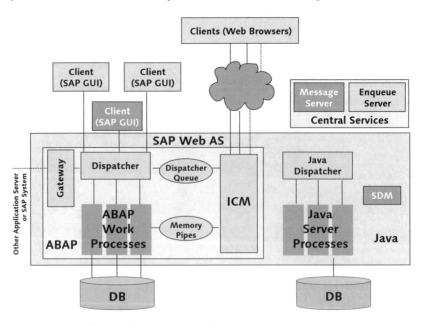

Figure 3.5 SAP Web Application Server Architecture

The *Internet Communication Manager* (ICM) is a component of the SAP Web Application Server that enables the communication between the SAP system and the Internet. Incoming requests from the web such as the call of a web query, and outgoing requests like the return of a query result to the web browser are received by the ICM, or returned to the client computer respectively via the HTTP, HTTPS, or SMTP protocols.

The ICM identifies incoming requests on the basis of the URL and the port, and then uses request handlers to redirect them for further processing. You can use the profile parameters of the ICM to define which URL prefixes are to be processed by which handlers. You can configure the following handlers in the ICM:

▶ **Logging handler**
The logging handler records all inbound and outbound requests.

▶ **Server cache handler**
The ICM has a cache that controls the read and write accesses to the SAP Web Application Server.

▶ **File access handler**
The return of files, such as images from a file system for example, is handled by the file access handler. The ICM parameter `icm/HTTP/file_access_<xx>` is used to define the URL prefixes for which a data access is supposed to occur.

▶ **Redirect handler**
The redirection of HTTP requests to another HTTP server (HTTP redirect) is handled by the redirect handler. The ICM parameter `icm/HTTP/redirect_<xx>` defines the destination to which the ICM is supposed to redirect specific URL prefixes.

▶ **SAP R/3 handler**
The SAP R/3 handler redirects requests to the SAP system and, in turn, receives them from the SAP system. This is the only handler that establishes a user context in the work process.

▶ **J2EE handler**
The J2EE handler redirects requests to an integrated SAP J2EE application server.

A request handler can only be called by a URL that has been entered in a browser, if the handler is integrated in an Internet Communication Framework service (ICF service). Several ICF services are available for SAP BW. They can be called in the ICF service hierarchy under the node

default_host · bw, or in the ICF service maintenance using Transaction SICF (see Figure 3.6).

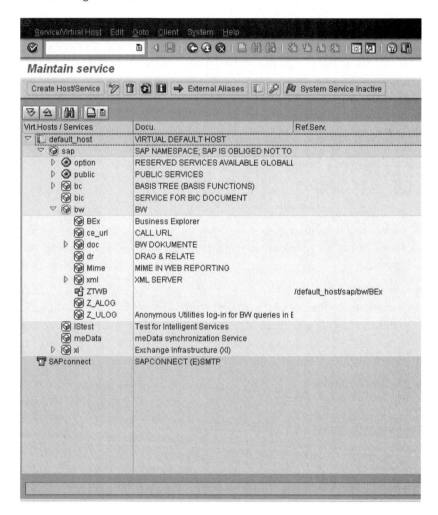

Figure 3.6 ICF Service Maintenance (Transaction SICF)

You can only run an ICF service, if it has been activated. The activity status of a service can be checked via the context menu of a service component. If the service is active, the menu item **Activate service** is disabled.

The ICF services enable you to display or exchange SAP BW data via a URL. The URL of an SAP BW ICF service is structured as follows:

<Protocol>://<Server>:<Port>/sap/bw/<Service>

with

- ▶ <Protocol> = http or https
- ▶ <Server> = URL path of the message server
- ▶ <Port> = port of the message server
- ▶ <Service> = name of the service in the service tree (Transaction SICF, Figure 3.6)

You can determine the URL prefix of your SAP BW system by using the ICM parameters in the ICM monitor via the following menu path (see Figure 3.7, Step 1): **Goto · Parameters · Display**.

ICM profile parameters

Figure 3.7 Displaying the ICM Profile Parameters

The host name of your computer that runs the ICM is specified in the profile parameter `icm/host_name_full`.

You should pay special attention to the configuration of the parameter `icm/keep_alive_timeout` when maintaining the general profile parameters (Transaction RZ11) since that parameter is required for running web queries. It specifies the number of seconds after which an existing connection times out, if no communication takes place through this connection. The default setting for this value is 60 seconds, which, in general, is too low for SAP BW web reporting. So, if you experience too many connection timeouts, you should increase this value.

ICM monitor   The ICM monitor is used to administer and monitor the ICM. You can call the ICM monitor using Transaction SMICM (see Figure 3.8).

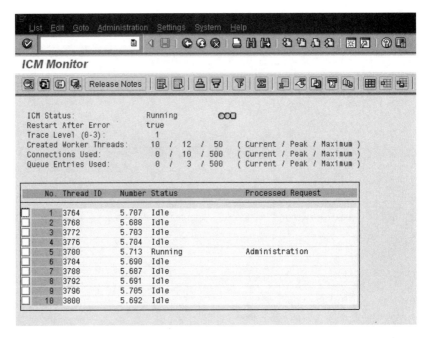

Figure 3.8 ICM Monitor (Transaction SMICM)

The structure of the ICM monitor is similar to that of the work process monitor. The initial screen displays a list of worker threads including the activity of the individual threads. The worker threads handle the inbound and outbound requests of a connection. Table 3.1 describes the individual ICM monitor fields:

Field	Description
No.	Number of the thread
Thread ID	ID of the thread. Like the process ID (PID) in the work process monitor, this ID is assigned by the operating system.

Table 3.1 Fields in the ICM Monitor

Field	Description
Number	Number of requests that have been handled by the thread since the last startup of the ICM.
Status	Current status of the thread. The following statuses are possible:
	free: The thread is free and is waiting for a request
	running: The thread is currently handling a request
Request handled	Specification of the request type that is currently handled by the thread. The following types are possible:

Blank field	No activity
Administration	Activity that triggers Transaction SMICM. When Transaction SMICM is called, this means that a thread is always assigned administration tasks.
Read request	Request is being read (server)
Write response	Response is being written (server)
Write request	Request is being written (client)
Read response	Response is being read (client)
Open connection	A connection to the server is being established.
Close connection	A connection to the server is being closed.
Accept connection	A connection to a client is being accepted.
Time-dependent action	Time-dependent events are being carried out.
Shut down	Terminates ICM
Wait for response (SERV)	SAP Web AS is a server and is waiting for a response from the application server.
Wait for response (CLNT)	SAP Web AS is a client and is waiting for a new request from the application server.

Table 3.1 Fields in the ICM Monitor (cont.)

4 Basic Principles of SAP Memory Configuration

This chapter contains information on SAP Memory Management and SAP Memory Configuration. It describes the most important memory areas of your SAP system and provides useful tips for configuring the SAP memories of an SAP BW system.

This chapter examines the SAP memory areas that must be configured for an SAP instance. The memory areas of an SAP instance are not SAP BW-specific, because the architecture of the basic SAP Business Information Warehouse (SAP BW) system was adopted from the SAP Basis system Release 6.10. For this reason, the technology and administration of the SAP memory areas in an SAP BW system are not different from those in an SAP R/3 system. What is different, however, is the configuration of the memory areas, because SAP BW applications exhibit a different usage and load behavior than do R/3 applications.

Therefore, this chapter is intended for SAP BW administrators and customizers who should be familiar with SAP Memory Management in order to carry out a performance analysis. Furthermore, the chapter provides useful information for SAP Basis administrators who are responsible for a SAP BW-specific configuration of the SAP memory areas.

First, we'll describe the terminology used in this book. To make a clear distinction between memory management at the operating-system (OS) level and at the SAP level, we'll use the prefix "SAP" whenever we refer to SAP memory areas.

4.1 Terminology Definitions

The SAP memory areas include SAP Buffer, SAP Roll Memory, SAP Extended Memory, SAP Heap Memory, SAP Paging Memory, and the local memory of the SAP work processes.

Let's take a closer look at the memory areas at OS level. Here we distinguish between two types of memory—the *local memory* and the *shared memory*. The local memory is always assigned to exactly one (local) OS process. This means that only this one process can write data into the local memory and read data from it. The shared memory, on the other hand, can be used by several OS processes for read and write actions.

Local versus shared memory

Virtual versus physical memory	Both the local and the shared memory use the *virtual memory*. Basically, you can allocate more virtual memory in an operating system than is physically available, because the virtual memory is managed both in the *physical memory* (main memory RAM) and in the *swap memory*. The maximum available virtual memory is determined by two values:

▶ The total amount of physical main memory plus available swap memory. Both values are physically limited by the hardware that is used.

▶ The maximum available memory area that can be addressed. This memory area is referred to as the address space and is limited by the operating system. Theoretically, this limit is $232 = 4$ GB in a 32-bit operating system. However, in real life, the actual value for the address space is somewhere between 2 to 3.8 GB. In a 64-bit operating system, the theoretical limit is $264 = 16.7$ million TB.

4.2 Basic Principles of SAP Memory Management

For a better understanding of the SAP memory areas, we'll first describe some basic principles of SAP Memory Management.

When an SAP work process is triggered, an ABAP program, such as a transaction, is generally executed, and it requires process memory, which is made available by SAP Memory Management.

User context
: Any time a user launches an SAP transaction, user-specific and authorization-specific data related to this transaction, such as variables, authorizations, and so on, is written into the *user context*, which is stored in the application server memory. All user contexts can be stored in the SAP Extended Memory, the SAP Roll Memory, or in the SAP Heap Memory.

Mode context
: In addition to the user-specific area, each user context contains a *mode context* for the SAP mode. Each user can open up to six external modes **(System · Generate mode)**. When a new mode is opened, a new user context is generated. The different modes behave like independent logons to the R/3 system and are located in different memory areas. A mode that is explicitly generated by a user is referred to as an *external mode*. But a mode can also be implicitly opened from a program. It is then referred to as an *internal mode*. Each external mode can manage several internal modes.

Figure 4.1 shows a simplified diagram of the relationship between the user context, the mode context, and the internal mode.

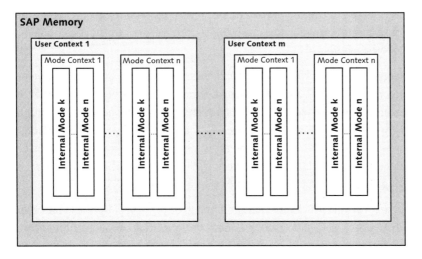

Figure 4.1 User Context, Mode Context, and Internal Mode

The SAP Memory Management system assigns the necessary memory to a work process. Three different types of memory exist, which are described in the following sections.

The user context of a work process is first stored in the local *SAP roll area*. The roll area is always the first memory that's assigned to a work process. Each SAP work process can only access its own roll area, because it is a local memory.

Local SAP roll area

The roll area consists of two segments: roll segment 1, whose storage capacity is defined using the parameter ztta/roll_first, and roll segment 2, whose storage capacity equals the difference between the parameters ztta/roll_area and ztta/roll_first. The ztta/roll_first parameter determines the volume of the roll area in terms of bytes, which is initially allocated by a dialog process before SAP Extended Memory is assigned. The memory of roll segment 2 is available for dialog processes, if no additional extended memory can be assigned to the user context.

ztta/roll_first and ztta/roll_area

During a context change for the work process, for example, if a user leaves the work process at the end of a transaction step so that another user can use the work process, the data from the local roll area is copied to the shared roll area. The shared SAP roll area is either memory space in the shared memory of the application server, which is referred to as the *SAP roll buffer*, or a file on the hard disk of the application server (SAP roll file), or a combination of the two. The process of copying data from the

Shared SAP roll area (roll buffer)

local roll area to the shared roll area is referred to as a rollout, whereas the reverse case of copying data from the shared roll area to the local roll area is called a roll-in.

SAP Extended Memory

A large portion of the user context data is stored in the *SAP Extended Memory*. During a context change (roll-in), the user context that is located in the extended memory is not copied to the local memory, but is assigned to changing work processes via address-mapping operations, which are also referred to as *pointers*. Because it is not the data itself that's copied, the roll process is very fast and the quantity of data copied during a roll-in and rollout is rather small.

em/initial_size_ MB and ztta/roll_ extension

The size of the SAP Extended Memory is determined by the parameter em/initial_size_MB. The extended memory that can be occupied by a user context is limited by the parameter ztta/roll_extension. This parameter ensures that a single user or only a few users cannot utilize the entire extended memory. If the limit of the allocated extended memory is exceeded and the roll memory is also fully utilized, additional local memory must be allocated.

Heap memory

Like the SAP roll area, *SAP Heap Memory* is a local memory that is allocated by a work process when the user context exceeds a certain size and no more SAP Extended Memory is available. Because SAP Heap Memory is a local memory, it cannot be used by other work processes. The work process is assigned to exactly one user context and therefore is not available to other user contexts. The work process is operated in the *PRIV mode* (private mode) and is reserved for processing the current user context until the work process is released.

abap/heaplimit

If a work process requires more heap memory than is defined in the abap/heaplimit parameter, it is restarted when the dialog step is completed, so that the local memory is available to other processes again.

abap/heaparea_ (non)dia

The SAP Heap Memory that is available for a dialog work process is determined by the parameter abap/heap_area_dia, while the parameter abap/heap_area_nondia determines the available heap memory for non-dialog work processes. If the heap memory utilization exceeds the limits defined by the parameters, the user context that is currently being processed terminates. By setting these parameters, you can prevent a single work process (i.e., a single user context) from occupying the entire local memory of the application server. All work processes of an application server can consume only as much local memory as is defined in the abap/heap_area_total parameter.

Swap space is storage space on the hard disk to which unused data from the main memory is temporarily stored so that there is more memory space available in the main memory for the currently running program. Objects are stored in the swap space when the buffer is full and the SAP system must load more objects into the buffer. If that occurs, those objects, which have not been accessed for the longest period of time, are removed. In this context, swapping means that the objects, which have been removed from the buffer, are lost and can only be replaced via another expensive access to the database. The **Swaps** column in the Memory Management Monitor (Transaction ST02) displays the number of objects that have been removed from the buffer since the last system startup. Note that the number displayed in the **Swaps** column represents the total number of swaps since system startup. If your system has been running for a long time, the number of replaced objects can become very large.

The use of swap space is very important for SAP application servers. If the swap space of a computer is fully utilized, you can encounter serious system problems. As a rule of thumb, the size of the swap space should be three times the size of the main memory or at least 3.5 GB to attain optimal system performance.

Figure 4.2 displays the SAP memory areas that can be assigned to dialog processes, as well as the related SAP profile parameters.

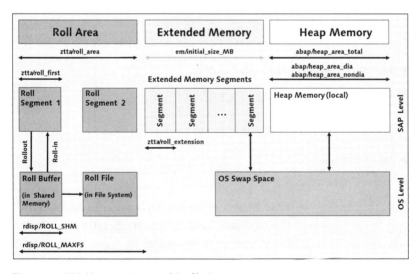

Figure 4.2 SAP Memory Areas and Profile Parameters

SAP Paging Memory *SAP Paging Memory* is another memory area. The SAP Paging Memory is used to allocate memory for the current internal mode by temporarily storing memory pages. It enables the extension of the SAP roll area at ABAP runtime, if large data quantities are processed, for example, large internal tables. The SAP Paging Memory contains only objects from ABAP data clusters, which are saved using the ABAP statements `IMPORT/EXPORT... TO MEMORY`, as well as data extracts that are generated using the ABAP statement `EXTRACT`.

The SAP Paging Memory consists of a memory area in the shared memory of the application server (SAP paging buffer) and an SAP paging file on the hard disk of the application server. The size of the SAP paging buffer is defined using the SAP profile parameter `rdisp/PG_SHM`, while the size of the SAP paging file is determined by the SAP profile parameter `rdisp/PG_MAXFS`.

SAP buffers SAP buffers are another memory area for each SAP instance. SAP buffers use individual segments of the shared memory that are available to all work processes, and local memory areas of the respective work processes.

The SAP buffers store frequently used data to reduce the number of database accesses and the workload that is put on the database server, when different work processes access the same information. For example, the buffers contain ABAP programs, ABAP screens, and ABAP Dictionary data.

The SAP buffers in the shared memory can be divided into six areas:

- ▶ repository buffers (nametab buffers)
- ▶ program buffers
- ▶ SAP GUI buffers
- ▶ calendar buffers
- ▶ table buffers
- ▶ import/export buffers

Repository buffers (nametab buffers) The repository buffer (also known as the nametab buffer or ABAP Dictionary buffer) contains the table and field definitions that are active in the SAP system. Every time a user uses the ABAP Dictionary (Transaction SE11) to call a table, an entry is generated in the repository buffer or the information on the respective table is read from the repository buffer.

The program buffer (also referred to as the SAP Executable buffer or ABAP buffer) stores the compiled executable versions of the ABAP programs. Each time a Business Explorer (BEx) query is run, a program that is stored in the program buffer is generated.

The SAP GUI buffer consists of two types of buffers: the presentation buffer (also referred to as the screen buffer or dynpro buffer) and the menu buffer or Central User Administration (CUA) buffer. The screen buffer stores the generated screens or dynpro loads, while the CUA buffer stores objects from SAP GUI, such as menus and button definitions.

The SAP calendar buffer stores the factory and public holiday calendars that are defined in the SAP system.

The table buffer consists of two types of buffers: the partial table buffer (also known as the partial buffer or single record table buffer) and the generic table buffer (also referred to as the generic key buffer or resident table buffer). The partial table buffer contains individual data records and the corresponding field values. For example, SAP BW master data table entries are stored in the partial table buffer. The generic table buffer stores several data records including the corresponding field values. It can even store complete tables. Most BW-specific tables and RS* tables[1] are stored in the generic key buffer.

The import/export buffer, which is also referred to as the shared buffer, stores data that is required by more than one work process. The buffer is used to store data in the shared memory and is addressed by using the ABAP commands `EXPORT TO/IMPORT FROM SHARED BUFFER` and `DELETE FROM SHARED BUFFER`. Buffer objects of the BW Online Analytical Processing (OLAP) cache are stored in the shared buffer.

Program buffers

SAP GUI buffers

Calendar buffers

Table buffers

Import/export buffers

4.2.1 Sequence of Memory Usage

The SAP Memory Management system allocates memory from the *SAP Roll Memory*, *SAP Extended Memory*, and *SAP Heap Memory* (process local memory) areas to the user contexts. The sequence in which the memory is allocated depends on whether the user context is executed in a dialog work process or in a non-dialog work process.

In terms of memory allocation, the three memory types have the following properties:

Memory area properties

---

1 Resource system tables of R/3 or BW.

Memory type	Memory area	Properties
SAP Roll Memory	Shared memory (roll buffer, roll file)	Sequential memory allocation to several work processes in slow copy processes, because the data must be completely copied.
SAP Extended Memory	Shared memory	Sequential memory allocation to several work processes in a fast allocation process. If more memory is needed, swap space is allocated.
SAP Heap Memory	Local memory	Memory allocation is linked to a single work process (PRIV mode). If more memory is needed, swap space is allocated.

Table 4.1 Memory Area Properties

Memory allocation for dialog work processes

1. The first memory is allocated from the roll area. For technical reasons, the first 100 to 250 KB (depending on the operating system) are allocated in this memory area even if the SAP profile parameter `ztta/roll_first` is set to 1, as recommended.

2. If more memory is needed than can be allocated in the first roll area, memory from the SAP Extended Memory is made available. SAP Extended Memory can be made available until

   ▶ The work process has reached the work-process-specific limit of the SAP Extended Memory, which is determined by the profile parameter `ztta/roll_extension`

   ▶ The SAP Extended Memory, whose size is determined by the profile parameter `em/initial_size_MB`, is completely utilized

   The extended memory is the memory area that dialog processes use most.

3. If the SAP Extended Memory is completely utilized and more memory is needed, additional memory from the roll area is made available until the limit `ztta/roll_area` is reached.

4. If the user context needs additional memory, it is allocated process local memory (heap memory). Heap memory has the particular characteristic that it is a local memory, which means that it cannot be copied or rolled into a shared memory. The user context cannot be transferred to another work process, because the work process is exclusively assigned to the user (PRIV mode).

5. If the limit of the process local memory for dialog work processes, `abap/heap_area_dia`, or the limit of the entire process local memory

of all work processes of an application server, abap/heap_area_ total, is reached, or if the swap space is completely utilized, the program terminates.

Figure 4.3 shows an overview of the memory allocation sequence for dialog work processes.

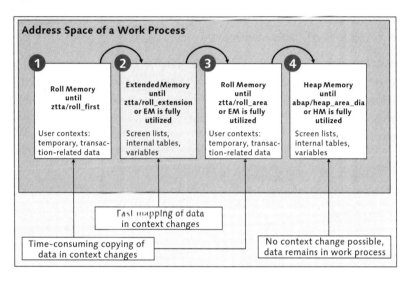

Figure 4.3 Memory Allocation Sequence for SAP Dialog Work Processes

In contrast to dialog work processes that mainly use the shared extended memory, non-dialog work processes allocate primarily local SAP Heap Memory. The reason for this is that non-dialog work processes don't need to exchange the user contexts since batch, update, and spool requests are always completely assigned to one work process. This means that the sequence of memory allocation for non-dialog work processes is the reverse opposite of what it is for dialog work processes:[2]

Memory allocation for non-dialog work processes

1. First the memory is taken from the roll area until the limit of the profile parameter ztta/roll_area is reached (blocks 1 and 3 in Figure 4.3).

2. If the memory in the roll area is completely utilized, heap memory, in other words process local memory, is allocated to the work process (block 4 in Figure 4.3).

---

2 In this context, Windows NT is an exception. On Windows NT, the allocation sequence of non-dialog work processes is the same as that for dialog work processes. Allocation sequence: Roll (up to ztta/roll_first) → Extended Memory → Roll (rest up to ztta/roll_area) → Heap Memory.

3. If the limit of the process local memory for non-dialog work processes, `abap/heap_area_nondia`, or the limit of the entire process local memory of all work processes of an application server, `abap/heap_area_total`, is reached, or if the swap space is completely utilized, a non-dialog work process can use the SAP Extended Memory (block 2 in Figure 4.3).

4.2.2 SAP Profile Parameters

Table 4.2 contains a list of the SAP profile parameters described in Section 4.2, which can be used to configure the SAP memory areas. The specifications in the "Recommended setting" column represent the settings in a sample Oracle-based SAP BW system for approximately 75 parallel users.[3]

	Profile parameter	Description/type	Recommended setting	Goal
SAP Roll Memory	`ztta/roll_first`	Size of the local SAP roll area at initial allocation before extended memory is allocated	1 (for technical reasons, approximately 100 KB is initially allocated)	Optimal and early utilization of the fast extended memory
	`ztta/roll_area`	Size of the local SAP roll area	6,500,000 bytes	Minimum data transfer during context change; the value should be increased if the system resorts to OS paging
	`rdisp/ROLL_SHM`	Size of the SAP roll buffer in blocks of 8 KB	15,000 (approximately 120 MB)	Minimum amount of time for context changes
	`rdisp/ROLL_MAXFS`	Size of the entire SAP roll area (roll buffer plus roll file) in blocks of 8 KB	30,000 (approximately 235 MB)	Minimum amount of time for context changes

Table 4.2 Overview of SAP Profile Parameters for SAP Memory Areas

---

3 Please refer to SAP Note 192658, which contains detailed information on setting the basic parameters of an SAP BW system.

	Profile parameter	Description/type	Recommended setting	Goal
SAP Extended Memory	em/initial_size_MB	Size of the SAP Extended Memory that is allocated at the startup of the SAP instance The value must be an integral multiple of (em/blocksize_KB divided by 1024).	3,000 to 4,000 MB	Fast context changes of all users. Ideally the extended memory contains all user contexts.
	em/blocksize_KB	Size of a segment from the SAP Extended Memory	1,024 KB	
	ztta/roll_extension	Maximum size of a user context in the SAP Extended Memory	500,000,000 to 1,000,000,000 bytes | (4 MB to 1 GB)	Minimization of the work processes in PRIV mode, equal distribution of extended memory across all users
SAP Heap Memory	abap/heap_area_dia	Maximum size of the SAP Heap Memory that can be allocated by a single dialog work process	800,000,000 to 1,500,000,000 bytes (480 MB to 1.4 GB) The value must be smaller than abap/heap_area_total.	Avoidance of swap space bottleneck for large user contexts
	abap/heap_area_nondia	Maximum size of the SAP Heap Memory that can be allocated by a single non-dialog work process (update, spool, batch work process)	800,000,000 to 1,500,000,000 bytes (480 MB to 1.4 GB) The value must be smaller than abap/heap_area_total.	Avoidance of swap space bottleneck for large user contexts
	abap/heap_area_total	Size of the SAP Heap Memory that can be allocated by all work processes together	1,500,000,000 bytes (approximately 1.4 MB)	Avoidance of swap space bottleneck for large user contexts

Table 4.2 Overview of SAP Profile Parameters for SAP Memory Areas (cont.)

Profile parameter	Description/type	Recommended setting	Goal
`abap/heaplimit`	Amount of memory in terms of bytes. If this value is exceeded, a work process is restarted after completing the dialog step.	40,000,000 bytes (approximately 38 MB)	If possible, work processes shouldn't be restarted often, and swap space bottlenecks be avoided.

Table 4.2 Overview of SAP Profile Parameters for SAP Memory Areas (cont.)

Figure 4.4 once again illustrates the memory areas of an SAP system.

Maintaining SAP profile parameters You can maintain the SAP profile parameters using Transaction RZ10. After entering the name of the instance profile, the SAP profile parameters can be changed in the menu path **Basic Maintenance · Change · Memory Management**. Figure 4.5 displays the individual memory profile parameters and their technical names.

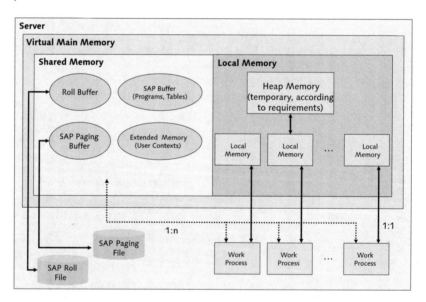

Figure 4.4 Memory Areas of an SAP System

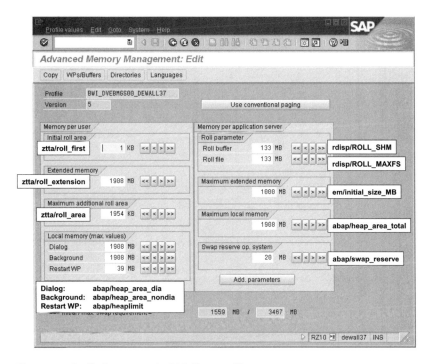

Figure 4.5 Profile Parameters in SAP Memory Management

You can call an overview of the configuration of all SAP profile parameters that are valid in the running system using the report RSPARAM. To do that, run the program RSPARAM in Transaction SE38 under **Program · Run · Directly**.

Report RSPARAM

The report indicates the settings of the parameters. The first column of the table displays the parameter name, the second column displays the value that is set by the user, and the third column contains the default value. If the second column is left blank, the default value is active.

If you're interested in additional detailed information on SAP memory configuration, please refer to the book by Thomas Schneider, *SAP Performance Optimization*.[4]

---

4 Thomas Schneider: *SAP Performance Optimization*, 4th edition, SAP PRESS 2005.

5 SAP BW Sizing

The correct calculation of hardware resources is integral to getting a good performance out of your SAP BW system. To help you better determine your available resources and the resources you'll need, this chapter provides information on the SAP BW sizing process. It describes methods and provides examples that enable you to forecast the hardware resources required for the system's memory, CPU, and database.

One task that you should undertake very early on in the lifecycle of your SAP Business Information Warehouse (SAP BW) project is the sizing of your system. By sizing or hardware sizing, we mean a calculation and forecast of the required hardware resources to enable a high-performing operation of your SAP BW applications for the system users. Correct hardware sizing is imperative to achieve a high system performance.

Calculating the sizing requirements of an SAP BW system can be much harder than forecasting the hardware requirements for an R/3 system. On the one hand, the SAP BW system is a collection of different applications and tools that supports the entire operation of a data warehouse—from data extraction to data storage to data preparation and presentation in the form of reports. Here, the sizing process depends on different factors, such as the following:

▶ The initial data volume

▶ Data volume increase due to periodic loads

▶ Preparation of data in the form of InfoCubes, ODS objects, and aggregates

▶ Timeframe for data administration like extraction, change run, and aggregate calculations

▶ Number of users and user profiles

▶ Number and complexity of queries and workbooks

Moreover, the usage behavior of the system users, for whom an acceptable system operation must be ensured both at average system load and at peak loads. For this reason, company-specific, as well as technical aspects, must both be the object of interest in each sizing process. In other words, a relationship must be established between the data quantities to be processed and the number of end users, including how they use the SAP BW applications.

The following sections describe the hardware sizing process in the lifecycle of an SAP BW project. SAP provides support in various phases of the hardware-sizing project, up to and including the system go-live. Another section describes how you can create an initial calculation for forecasting the hardware requirements of your SAP BW system. Several methods and sample calculations are provided to show you how to forecast the hardware requirements of your SAP BW system in terms of database memory, main memory, and CPU resources. You should note that all the descriptions and calculations that are used here are only initial approximate calculations, and therefore, cannot replace a detailed sizing calculation that you should carry out in collaboration with your hardware supplier.

5.1   The SAP Sizing Process

SAP systems are sized according to a standardized procedure, which involves SAP experts and a certified hardware partner at an early stage of the project. For this purpose, SAP provides a process that is synchronized between the hardware partner, the customer, and SAP. Based on various parameters (including the number of system users and quantity structures, the number and structure of data targets, and the structure of the staging processes), this process calculates an initial sizing that must be verified by SAP or its service partner prior to the system go-live. Figure 5.1 displays a sample sizing process.

SAP Quick Sizer   The sizing process of the SAP system usually begins with the quick sizing. For a first rough sizing of the CPU, main memory and hard disk capacity, SAP provides the *SAP Quick Sizer* at SAP Service Marketplace under *http://service.sap.com/quicksizer*. Once you have entered several project parameters regarding the size and usage behavior of SAP BW applications in a web-based questionnaire, the tool uses detailed empirical values on the memory and CPU usage to calculate the hardware requirements forecast. Section 5.7 contains more information on SAP Quick Sizer and the specifications you must enter in it.

Sizing performed by the hardware partner   The results of the SAP Quick Sizer can be made available to the hardware partner on the Internet. For this purpose, you must create a sizing project in SAP Quick Sizer, which must be accessible by hardware partners to whom you want to submit a hardware offer. Based on the specifications entered in SAP Quick Sizer, the hardware partners create a detailed hardware offer. The hardware suppliers are ultimately responsible for sizing the hardware in your project, because they can only guarantee the performance of their own systems.

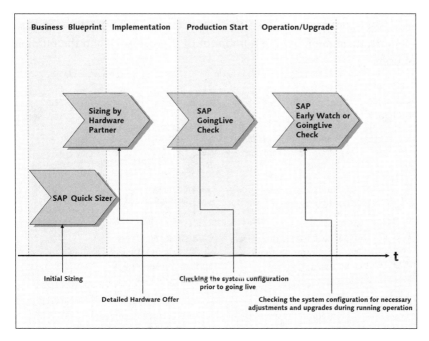

Figure 5.1 Sizing Process in the Lifecycle of an SAP Project

In the context of an SAP software agreement, SAP offers the *SAP GoingLive Check* to its customers. During the course of this service, SAP employees or employees of a service partner verify the sizing by remotely logging on to the customer system and performing several tests. The SAP GoingLive Check detects changes in the system requirements and in the configuration of applications (ABAP programs, user exits, data models, and so on) in real time prior to going live, and can validate the system suggestions made by the hardware supplier. Consequently, the GoingLive Check generates an evaluation of the system as to whether the existing hardware can manage the expected load. You can find more information on the SAP GoingLive Check in SAP Service Marketplace at *http://www.service.sap.com/goinglivecheck*.

SAP GoingLive Check

5.2 Size Categories of SAP BW Systems

A first approach to establishing a possible size category of your future SAP BW system, or of a future extension of an existing SAP BW system, is referred to as *T-shirt sizing*, which has been developed by SAP. The name of this sizing approach originates from the classification of a SAP BW system into five size categories that remind you of T-shirt sizes. The system classes that are divided into those size categories differ depending on the hardware configuration (one-tier, two-tier, multi-tier), the database memory, main memory, the number of CPU processors, and the number of users.

SAP BW Category	Configuration	Hardware	Number of Users
XS	DB and application server configured on one host	>= 1 GB RAM, >= 2 CPUs, DB 30–50 GB	1–10
S	DB and application server configured on one host	>= 4 GB RAM, >= 2–4 CPUs, DB 50–100 GB	10–20
M	DB and application server configured on separate hosts	>= 4 GB RAM, >= 4 CPUs for DB and application servers, DB 100–200 GB	20–50
L	DB and application server configured on separate hosts	>= 4 GB RAM and >= 4 CPUs for DB server >= 2 GB RAM and >= 2 CPUs for application server, DB 200–1,000 GB	50–150
XL	One DB instance, multiple application servers	>= 4 GB RAM and >= 8 CPUs for DB server >= 4 GB RAM and >= 4 CPUs for application server, DB >1,000 GB	> 150

Table 5.1 SAP BW T-Shirt Sizing (Source: SAP AG)

The sample configurations listed in Table 5.1 are based on typical SAP BW installations and empirical values provided by SAP. You should think of these sample configurations as a guide to help you determine the size category of your system.

5.3 Sizing Hard Disk Capacity

The required quantity of hard disk capacity depends primarily on the number and size of the InfoCubes, ODS objects, PSA tables, and aggregates. The following sections describe a calculation schema for estimating the hard disk requirements for the aforementioned data objects. The calculation schema is based on SAP Quick Sizer. Section 5.7 describes the use of SAP Quick Sizer in greater detail.

5.3.1 Calculating InfoCubes

When calculating InfoCubes, the size of the fact table determines 80% to 90% of the size of the InfoCubes. The most important parameters for the calculation of an InfoCube are the number of data records that must be stored in the InfoCube, and the record length of the data records to be stored.

The number of data records depends on the following factors:

▶ Number of data records in the initial filling
▶ Number of data records in the delta filling
▶ Number of delta fillings per time unit

The length of data records depends on the following factors.

▶ Number of dimensions of the InfoCube
▶ Number of key figures

In the following section, we'll create a sample calculation schema for calculating the size of the business content InfoCube 0SD_C01 (*Sales analytics—SAP R/3 SD: Customer*).

In the first step, we have to determine the number and size of the dimension tables. InfoCube 0SD_C01 contains eight dimensions including the dimensions "time," "data package," and "unit." Next, we need to estimate the size and number of data records for each dimension table. To estimate the size of a data record in a dimension table, we total the number of characteristics in the dimension table. In doing so, we estimate an average data record length of 6 bytes per characteristic and an additional 4 bytes for the key in the dimension table. The disk space requirement of a dimension table can be calculated according to the following formula:

> [number of characteristics × Ø byte length per characteristic + byte length per key] × (initial) number of data records

Our estimate for the calculation of the dimensions of InfoCube 0SD_C01 is as follows:

Dimension tables

Dimension	Number of characteristics	Ø Byte length per characteristic	Byte length per key	Number of data records	Total (bytes)
Customer	1	8	4	10,000	120,000
Material	1	8	4	1,000	12,000
Sales area	3	8	4	150	4,200
Version	1	8	4	2	24
Value type	1	8	4	3	36
Time	5	8	4	365	16,060
Data package	3	8	4	300	8,400
Unit	2	8	4	20	400
Total (bytes)	**161,120**				

Table 5.2 Calculating the Disk Space Requirements of Dimension Tables

Fact table
In the next step, we'll calculate the size of the fact table of InfoCube OSD_C01. For this purpose, we must determine the number of key figures of the fact table, which we assume to be 16. For each key figure, we'll calculate a record length of 10 bytes. Each dimension table contains a foreign key in the fact table whose record length we estimate to be 4 bytes. Moreover, we must estimate the number of data records in the initial filling of the InfoCube, and we assume that to be two million data records. The disk space requirement of the fact table can be calculated according to the following formula:

[number of key figures × 10 bytes + number of dimensions × 4 bytes] × (initial) number data records

Our estimate for the calculation of the dimensions of InfoCube OSD_C01 is as follows:

[16 key figures × 10 bytes + 8 dimensions × 4 bytes] × 2,000,000 records = 366 MB

Data volume increase
The preceding calculations for the fact table and dimension table sizes that are forecast don't include the increase in the data volume for the InfoCube. If you want to include this increase, you must consider the average number of data records for each delta load, as well as the number of periodic delta loads (for example, once per day) in the calculation. Then, you have to calculate the number of data records using the following formula:

total number of data records = (initial) number of data records + (peri-odic) number of data records × number of periods

5.3.2 Calculating ODS Objects

Operational Data Store (ODS) objects must be subdivided into transactional ODS objects and standard ODS objects. Transactional ODS objects are mainly used in planning tools that write data into the ODS object; standard ODS objects are used in the staging process for updating and analyzing data. We'll focus on describing standard ODS objects here. Transactional ODS objects and standard ODS objects contain the same data model, however, a standard ODS object enables a parallel data update from several DataSources, as well as the determination of delta information.

Standard ODS objects contain the following three different types of tables: the activation queue, the change log, and the table that contains active data, whereas transactional ODS objects consist of only the table containing active data.

The activation queue is a transparent table whose structure matches the data model of the ODS object, which means that key fields and data fields are specified during the definition of the ODS object. Before data is loaded into an ODS object, data requests (including their request IDs) are written to the activation queue. The activation queue key consists of the request ID, the data package number, and the data record number.

Activation queue

The data is not yet available for further updating or analysis in the ODS object, since it must first be activated so that it can be transferred into the ODS object. At the start of the activation, the activation queue data is sorted by data package numbers and data record numbers. Data records that have identical data package numbers are activated in the same data package. When the ODS data is activated, the data is deleted from the activation queue.

During the activation process, changes between the activation queue and the active data of the ODS object are identified and stored as delta information in the change log. The change log is a persistent staging area (PSA) table that is generated for each ODS object. The change log is not automatically deleted and it contains the complete history of all data activations for the ODS object, unless you explicitly delete data from the change log. To enable the updating of delta information from the change

Change log

log into the ODS object, you must first perform a delta initialization for the ODS object during which the object's active data is read.

Active data
The actual data that is to be updated into other data targets such as InfoCubes, or is to be used for data analysis, is stored in the active data table. This table does not contain a request ID as a key; instead, it contains the semantic key and data fields that have been defined for the ODS object.

Therefore, to calculate the size of an ODS object, you must consider the following two tables: the active data table and the change log.

The data record length of the ODS table containing active data can be estimated by totaling the record lengths of the fields of the corresponding InfoSource. As is the case with InfoCubes, the disk space requirement is the product of the total of data record lengths of all InfoObjects of the ODS object and the number of data records. If you don't know the exact structure of the ODS object, you can estimate the size of the active data table at an average data record length of 8 bytes per InfoObject.

For the change log table, you must add 48 bytes for the request ID, in addition to the ODS object fields. The number of data records of the change log—and therefore the disk space requirement— depends on the average number of ODS object updates and on the delta changes. The size of the change log table should be at least the size of the active data table.

5.3.3 Calculating PSA Tables

The calculation of PSA tables is similar to the calculation of disk space requirements for the change log table of the ODS object. You must build the total of field lengths for all objects of the corresponding InfoSource, plus 48 bytes for the request ID. The disk space requirement results from the product of the total of data record lengths of all InfoObjects of the InfoSource and the number of data records.

Table RSTSODS
The disk space requirement of PSA tables can increase very fast, if you don't delete the PSA tables routinely. When estimating the disk space requirement, you should simply assume that a request in the PSA is approximately four times the size of a request in the InfoCube. You can use the transparent table RSTSODS (ODS for the transfer structure) to determine the technical PSA table in the database that corresponds to an InfoSource. To do that, you must enter the technical name of the PSA object into the **ODSNAME** field in the data browser (Transaction SE16).

The technical table name of the corresponding PSA table is displayed in the **ODSNAME_TECH** field (naming convention: /BIC/B*).

5.3.4 Calculating the Total Hard Disk Capacity

For the calculation of the total hard disk capacity, you must calculate the disk capacities for aggregates, indices, and master data, in addition to the data targets discussed in Sections 5.3.1 to 5.3.3.

You can use the following calculations for an initial estimate of the disk space requirement:

Size of InfoCube	see also Section 5.3.1
+ size of ODS	see also Section 5.3.2
+ size of PSA	see also Section 5.3.3
+ 100% for aggregates	
+ 100% for Indices	
+ 10% for master data	
+ 2 × disk space requirement of the largest fact table or at least 10 GB	temporary database cache (for example, Tablespace PSAPTEMP)

Table 5.3 Calculating the Total Disk Space Requirement

5.4 CPU Sizing

The CPU load of an SAP BW system is influenced by different factors. On the one hand, the CPU usage is determined by the modeling of data targets and by the data staging. These include:

▶ The number and size of InfoProviders (InfoCubes, ODS objects, and so on)
▶ The data volume that must be periodically loaded for extraction and loading processes
▶ The number of aggregates
▶ The frequency and scope of roll-ups and change runs

On the other hand, the CPU usage is determined by the users who use queries to retrieve data from the system. These include:

▶ The number of InfoProviders
▶ The number of queries

▶ The complexity of the queries (navigation through reports, slicing & dicing, and so on)

▶ The usage behavior of the users, for example, simple queries versus detailed analyses

▶ The number of concurrent system users

SAP benchmarks (SAPS)
To evaluate the CPU performance of a system, we must first introduce a measurement item that enables us to describe the system performance. For this purpose, SAP provides *SAP Application Performance Standard* (SAPS). SAPS is a hardware-independent measurement item that describes the performance of an SAP client/server environment consisting of a server, a relational database system, and the SAP software. The SAP Standard Application Benchmarks have been available since R/3 software Release 1.1H (April 1993). Today, you can get SAP benchmarks for different R/3 modules and mySAP applications. Benchmarks are only comparable within the same module or mySAP application. For example, you cannot compare the benchmark values of a Sales and Distribution (SD) benchmark with the values of a Materials Management (MM) benchmark.

The SAPS measurement item is a standardized value that derives from the SD Standard Application Benchmark in which 100 SAPS are defined as 2,000 completely processed request items per hour in the system. This system performance corresponds to 6,000 dialog steps (screen changes) with 2,000 updates or 2,400 SD transactions per hour. The SAPS value of a system is therefore a throughput measurement value that describes the performance of a system, independent of the hardware configuration; in other words, the SAPS value is the "kilowatt performance" of a system. SAPS values are always specific to the version of the tested SAP component. In each SAP benchmark, the tested hardware is certified for the SAPS number that has been reached.

BW benchmark
In addition to various R/3 modules and applications, a benchmark test is also available for SAP BW. The BW benchmark consists of the following three test steps:

1. Step 1 measures the data throughput (number of records per hour) for loading master data from a flat file into master data tables, as well as for loading transaction data from a flat file into the persistent staging area (PSA) and an InfoCube. In addition, it measures the data throughput for aggregate roll-ups and the calculation of database statistics and indices.

2. Step 2 measures the data throughput for loading and activating data from the PSA into an ODS object.

3. Step 3 focuses on testing the query performance. It measures the navigation steps per hour for various query actions (selections and drill downs) on an SD InfoCube.

5.4.1 CPU Sizing for Loading and Data Staging Processes

The certified SAPS value provides information on the hardware performance. To calculate the CPU resources required for loading processes, we use a measurement value that specifies the data throughput per time unit.

The loading performance of a system is supposed to be measured as the number of data records per hour. To obtain information on how much SAPS performance the system requires in order to master the required data throughput, we must convert the data throughput per time unit into an SAPS value.

Number of data records per hour

As with most models, the model calculation described here, which was developed by SAP on the basis of several BW benchmarks, is predicated on several assumptions and therefore can only approximate reality. The model is supposed to help you translate the SAPS value specified by your hardware partner into data throughput performance.

Model calculation

Our model is based on the following assumptions:

▶ The system can load 750,000 data records per hour and job.

▶ We don't use any complex transformation, transfer, and update rules.

▶ The data is loaded into the PSA and updated into an ODS object, an InfoCube, and 10 aggregates.

▶ The loading process consists of loading the data, aggregate roll-ups, a change run, index restructuring, and the calculation of statistics.

▶ The data can be loaded in several requests, and a job is required for each data request.

▶ The average CPU utilization during the loading process is 65%.

▶ A job requires 350 SAPS.

The SAPS performance of a system can be estimated for the loading processes using the following calculation formula:

$$SAPS = number\ of\ jobs \times 350\ SAPS / 0.65$$

with

> *number of jobs = (total (number of data records per delta upload) / time (h)) / 750,000*

These calculation formulas enable you to convert the SAPS value for a system into a probable data throughput performance and to forecast the SAPS requirement for a probable data throughput. Table 5.4 contains a list of some sample calculations.

Delta/h	Number of Jobs	SAPS
100,000	0.1	72
250,000	0.3	179
500,000	0.7	359
750,000	1.0	538
1,000,000	1.3	718
5,000,000	6.7	3,590
10,000,000	13.3	7,179
15,000,000	20.0	10,769

Table 5.4 Calculating SAPS Values

5.4.2 CPU Sizing for Queries

To facilitate the calculation of the CPU performance for running queries, we must introduce another performance value that enables us to forecast the query performance.

Number of navigation steps per hour

We want to measure the value for evaluating the query performance of CPU resources as navigation steps per hour. For example, a navigation step can be the call of a query, the selection of a characteristic, or a drill-down by rows or columns within the query navigation characteristics. In addition to the influencing factors described in Section 5.4 we'll use the usage behavior of the end users and the query type as the basis for calculating the query performance in our simplified model.

This model which was developed by SAP is based on the following assumptions:

The model contains three types of users who use the system by running queries at different intensities. The user types described here are based on the user typology of the Early Watch report.

User types

▶ The *low user* uses the system at irregular intervals with predefined, mainly static reports. By using the reports, this user generates *one navigation step per hour* on a weekly average.

▶ The *medium user* uses the system regularly. Navigating the reports of this user is more complex (drilldown, slicing & dicing[1]), and the reports are frequently supported by aggregates. By using the reports, this user generates *eleven navigation steps per hour* on a weekly average.

▶ The *high user* uses the SAP BW system intensely. As a data analyst, this user runs ad-hoc queries for which often no aggregates have been defined. With the analyses, this user generates *33 navigation steps per hour* on a weekly average.

In addition to the user types, the model contains three query (report) types that generate different system loads when a query is run. The report types are different with regard to complexity and system load. The different system loads generated by the query are considered by using a weighting factor. The weighting factor specifies by what factor one query type requires more (or less) resources compared to another query type:[2]

Query types

▶ *Easy queries* consist of prdefined standard reports for which optimal aggregates are available. The weighting factor is 1.

▶ *Medium queries* are reports in which you can navigate using drilldown and slice and dice techniques. The navigation in the reports is mainly supported by different aggregates. The weighting factor is 1.5, which means that this query type requires 1.5 times more CPU resources than the easy query type.

▶ *Heavy queries* are ad-hoc reports containing flexible, unpredictable navigation paths. The reports are used to analyze detail data at the document and item levels and are not supported by precalculated

---

1 These terms originate from OLAP technology: "Drilldown" refers to a mechanism that converts an aggregated set of data into a higher level of detail by successively dissolving the aggregation along the aggregation structure. "Slicing & dicing" describes a complex data analysis functionality—the "cutting out" of slices or sub-cubes from an InfoCube by restricting one or more dimensions to a value or value range.

2 The weighting factors in the model are based on SAP BW benchmarking scenarios. If you use different query types, you should adjust the factors.

aggregates. The weighting factor is 5, which means that this query type requires 5 times more CPU resources than the easy query type.

Report distribution The distribution of report types to user types represents another operand in the model. The distribution specifies the frequency at which a user uses a specific report type in terms of percentages. Table 5.5 shows a sample report type distribution that you can adjust according to your own model calculations.

	Easy Query (1)	Medium Query (1.5)	Heavy Query (5)
X low users (1 nav. / h)	80%	20%	0%
Y medium users (11 nav. / h)	50%	50%	0%
Z high users (33 nav. / h)	0%	0%	100%

Table 5.5 Percentage of Report Type Distribution

The values in Table 5.5 tell us that, for instance, half of the reports a medium user uses are simple standard reports while the other half are reports with navigation options. This model matrix now enables us to calculate the system load caused by queries.

The system load which is measured as navigation steps per hour can be calculated on the basis of the matrix shown in Table 5.5 and the previously described report types, according to the following formula:

$$Number\ of\ nav\ /\ h = \quad X \times (0.8 \times 1 + 0.2 \times 1.5 + 0 \times 5) \times 1\ +$$
$$Y \times (0.5 \times 1 + 0.5 \times 1.5 + 0 \times 5) \times 11\ +$$
$$Z \times (0 \times 1 + 0 \times 1.5 + 1 \times 5) \times 33$$

This formula enables you to calculate the probable system load in terms of navigation steps per hour. Table 5.6 contains a list of some calculations that depend on the number of users:

Total Number of Users	Low User X	Medium User Y	High User Z	Nav. / h
30	10	10	10	1,799
40	10	10	20	3,449
40	10	20	10	1,936

Table 5.6 Query System Load Depending on the Number of Users

Total Number of Users	Low User X	Medium User Y	High User Z	Nav. / h
40	20	10	10	1,810
150	80	60	10	2,563

Table 5.6 Query System Load Depending on the Number of Users (cont.)

The system load calculated in Table 5.6 shows that the number of high users significantly determines the total system load due to the more complex reports and the associated system load increase. For example, a duplication of the number of high users almost doubles the system load, whereas if you double the number of medium or low users, you would observe an increase of the system load of only 7 or 8 percent. The calculations also show that the decisive factor that determines the system load is not the total number of query users, but the distribution of user types. A system with 40 users, 20 of which are high users, can generate more system load through running queries than a system with 150 users, 10 of which are high users.

To determine the SAPS performance of a system that is required to manage the forecasted query system load (in terms of navigation steps per hour), the query system load is converted into the SAPS performance according to the following formula:

SAPS performance

$$SAPS = (nav. / h \times 1.33 \times 2.28 \times 9 / 60) / 0.65$$

The components of this formula have the following meaning:

Component	Meaning
1.33	Correction factor
2.28	Conversion factor between SD benchmark and BW benchmark
9	Number of dialog steps per query navigation step[3]
60	Conversion factor hours to minutes
0.65	Assumed CPU utilization of 65%

Table 5.7 Components Used for Converting Query System Load to SAPS Performance

---

3 The number of dialog steps represents the number of process steps in the SAP system. The exact meaning of a process step depends on the task type. Query calls are processed in the DIALOG task type. A dialog step corresponds to a request, which the R/3 system handles for a user.

For the query system loads that depend on the user distribution, as listed in Table 5.6, we can therefore calculate the following SAPS performance requirements:

Total Number of Users	X / Y / Z	Nav. / h	SAPS
30	10 / 10 / 10	1,799	1,259
40	10 / 10 / 20	3,449	2,414
40	10 / 20 / 10	1,936	1,355
40	20 / 10 / 10	1,810	1,267
150	80 / 60 / 10	2,563	1,794

Table 5.8 Number of Users, Query System Load, and SAPS Performance

The SAPS values shown in Table 5.8 represent only the calculative SAPS performance requirements of an SAP BW system for managing the system load generated by queries. They do not include any other system loads that are generated by loading processes, aggregate structuring, and statistical and index calculations.

5.4.3 CPU Load Distribution

In the calculations of the CPU resources that are required for the query operation and loading processes, we purposefully did not distinguish between the CPU resources required on the application server and those required on the database server. Such a differentiation isn't necessary in a two-tier architecture, which contains the database and application servers on one hardware unit, because, in that case, no physical separation of the CPU resources exists, and therefore no differentiation of CPU capacities between the database server and the application server is required.

In a three-tier or multi-tier architecture, you can separate the CPU resources with regard to the load profiles of the database and application servers. Based on our experience, an SAP BW system usually contains a load distribution between the presentation server, the application server, and the database server, as shown in Table 5.9.

Layer	CPU Load Distribution	Distribution of CPU resources (SAPS)
Presentation	5–10%	
Application server	30–80%	Data staging: 50% Queries: 80%
Database server	20–50%	Data staging: 50% Queries: 20%

Table 5.9 Distribution of CPU Load and Resources

The values in Table 5.9 tell us that 20 to 50% of the CPU load in an SAP BW system is used on the database server, 30 to 80% on the application server, and approximately 5 to 10% for the graphical display. Therefore, the processes on the application server account for most of the CPU load. In a three-tier architecture, in which the database and application servers are installed on physically separate hosts, the calculated SAPS resources for loading processes should be 50% for the application server and 50% for the database server; the CPU resources for queries should be at 80% on the application server and 20% on the database server.

5.5   Memory Sizing

The memory requirement of an SAP BW system is determined by many different factors. As with CPU capacity requirements, the loading and data staging processes determine the memory requirement. The main factors that determine the memory requirement are:

▶ The number of parallel jobs, for example, loading jobs

▶ The number of data records that are loaded within a data package

▶ The complexity of transfer and update rules in data staging processes

▶ The degree of parallelization of database processes in the relational database system

▶ The configuration of the SAP BW memory areas such as SAP Roll Memory, SAP Extended Memory, and SAP buffers of the application server (see also Chapter 4)

▶ The configuration of the memory areas of the relational database system such as the data buffer shared pool and log buffers (see also Chapter 7)

On the other hand, the memory utilization is determined by the users who run database queries on the system. The main factors that determine memory usage are:

▶ The number of report users logged on to the system (SAP BEx and Web services)

▶ The quantity of data selected by queries

The calculation of the memory requirement is also based on model calculations, which, in turn, fall back on empirical SAP BW benchmark values. The requirement of main memory for data staging processes and queries is calculated separately according to memory requirement for the application server and for the database server.

5.5.1 Memory Sizing for Loading and Data Staging Processes

To simplify the model calculation for the main memory size, we once again make the following assumptions.

General assumptions:

▶ The number of data records for each data package is 50,000.

▶ We don't use any complex transformation, transfer, and update rules.

▶ The data is loaded into the PSA and updated into an ODS object, an InfoCube, and 10 aggregates.

Assumption for the application server:

▶ A loading job requires 300 MB of extended memory.

▶ The minimum size of the SAP buffers is 500 MB (table buffers, program buffers, export/import buffers, and so on)

Assumptions for the database server:

▶ The minimum size of the database buffers is 700 MB.

▶ Additional 10 MB of main memory is required for every one million data records of an InfoCube.

▶ Each dialog or batch process requires 120 MB of main memory.

▶ The relational database system requires [2 × number of jobs] times the time for parallel processes.

For data staging processes, the memory requirement for the application server can be calculated according to the following formula:

Memory requirement for the application server

SAP BW main memory = number of jobs × 300 MB + 500 MB

The number of jobs can be calculated according to the following formula:

number of jobs = (total (number of data records per delta upload) / time (h)) / 750,000.

These formulas enable you to calculate the probable requirement of main memory for the SAP BW application server depending on the data throughput. Table 5.10 contains a list of some sample calculations.

Delta/h	Number of Jobs	Main Memory (MB)
100,000	0.1	540
250,000	0.3	600
500,000	0.7	700
750,000	1.0	800
1,000,000	1.3	900
5,000,000	6.7	2,500
10,000,000	13.3	4,500
15,000,000	20.0	6,500

Table 5.10 Calculating the Main Memory Requirement of the SAP BW Application Server for Data Staging Processes

For data staging processes, the memory requirement for the database server can be calculated according to the following formula:

Memory requirement for the database server

RDBMS main memory = 700 MB + max (number of records per InfoProvider and fact table) / 1 million × 10 MB + number of jobs × 120 MB + 2 × number of jobs × 120 MB

The number of jobs can be calculated according to the following formula:

number of jobs = (total (number of data records per delta upload) / time (h)) / 750,000.

These formulas enable you to calculate the probable requirement of main memory for the SAP BW database server depending on the data throughput. Table 5.11 contains a list of some sample calculations.

The calculations in Tables 5.9 and 5.10 show that based on the above assumptions the total requirement of main memory for the application and database servers for data staging processes is at least approximately 1.3 GB, even in small SAP BW installations (250,000 data records in the largest fact table, 100,000 delta records per hour).

Delta/h	Number of Jobs	Number of Fact Table Records	RDBMS Main Memory (MB)
100,000	0.1	250,000	751
250,000	0.3	500,000	825
500,000	0.7	1,000,000	950
750,000	1.0	5,000,000	1,110
1,000,000	1.3	10,000,000	1,280
5,000,000	6.7	50,000,000	3,600
10,000,000	13.3	100,000,000	6,500
15,000,000	20.0	200,000,000	9,900

Table 5.11 Calculating the Main Memory Requirement of the SAP BW Database Server for Data Staging Processes

5.5.2 Memory Sizing for Queries

To simplify the model calculation for the main memory size, we once again make several assumptions. The model calculations described here refer to SAP web query users.

Assumptions for the application server:

▶ The query user is connected via the SAP Web Application Server (SAP Web Queries).

▶ The keep-alive timeout of the Internet Communication Manager (ICM) is 60 seconds.[4]

▶ Each user needs 30 MB of extended memory.

▶ The minimum size of the SAP buffers is 500 MB (table buffers, program buffers, export/import buffers, and so on)

---

4 This parameter ensures that the ICM keeps an existing connection open, if new data is transferred through the network connection within the next 60 seconds. If no communication occurs over a longer period of time through an existing connection, the ICM closes that connection. This technique avoids the time-consuming establishment and deestablishment of network connections.

Assumptions for the database server:

▶ The minimum size of the database buffers is 700 MB.

▶ Additional 10 MB of main memory is required for every one million data records of an InfoCube.

▶ Each dialog process requires 120 MB of extended memory.

▶ A dialog process can simultaneously process one high user, two medium users, or five low users.

▶ Queries are not processed in parallel.

For the running of queries, the memory requirement for the application server can be calculated according to the following formula:

Memory requirement for the application server

SAP BW main memory = 500 MB + number of connected users × 30 MB

with

number of connected users = (X + Y + Z) / 3,600 × keep_alive[5]

These formulas enable you to calculate the probable requirement of main memory for the SAP BW application server for the execution of queries. The memory usage on the application server is determined primarily by the total number of query users. Table 5.12 contains a list of some sample calculations.

Total Number of Users	Main Memory (MB)
20	510
30	515
50	525
100	550
150	575

Table 5.12 Calculating the Main Memory Requirement of the SAP BW Application Server for Queries

For the running of queries, the memory requirement for the database server can be calculated according to the following formula:

Memory requirement for the database server

RDBMS main memory = 700 MB + max (number of records per InfoProvider and fact table) / 1 million × 10 MB + number of concurrent users × 120 MB

---

5   X = number of low users, Y = number of medium users, Z = number of high users.

with

> *number of concurrent users = (X/5 + Y/2 + Z) / 3,600 × keep_alive × 120 MB*

These formulas enable you to calculate the probable requirement of main memory for the SAP BW database server for the execution of queries. The memory usage on the database server depends on the distribution of the user profile and the size of the fact table of the InfoCubes. Table 5.13 lists some sample calculations based on an assumed user distribution.

Total Number of Users	X / Y / Z	Number of Fact Table Records	RDBMS Main Memory (MB)
20	10 / 5 / 5	250,000	722
30	10 / 10 / 10	250,000	737
50	30 / 10 / 10	250,000	745
100	50 / 30 / 20	250,000	793
150	80 / 40 / 30	250,000	835
20	10 / 5 / 5	500,000	724
30	10 / 10 / 10	500,000	739
50	30 / 10 / 10	500,000	747
100	50 / 30 / 20	500,000	795
150	80 / 40 / 30	500,000	837
20	10 / 5 / 5	1,000,000	729
30	10 / 10 / 10	1,000,000	744
50	30 / 10 / 10	1,000,000	752
100	50 / 30 / 20	1,000,000	800
150	80 / 40 / 30	1,000,000	842
20	10 / 5 / 5	10,000,000	819
30	10 / 10 / 10	10,000,000	834
50	30 / 10 / 10	10,000,000	842
100	50 / 30 / 20	10,000,000	890
150	80 / 40 / 30	10,000,000	932

Table 5.13 Calculating the Main Memory Requirement of the SAP BW Database Server for Queries

The calculations in Tables 5.11 and 5.12 show that—based on the above assumptions—the total main memory requirements for the application and database servers to run queries is at least 1.2 GB, even in small SAP BW installations for a maximum of 20 users.

5.5.3 Summary

The sizing of your SAP BW system, that is, the adequate capacity planning for the required system resources, is integral for the success of your SAP BW project in order that you can avoid having to deal with bad response times and system operation errors. A correctly dimensioned system is the basis for a good system performance.

During the sizing process, it is often difficult to estimate the volume requirements for the system at a very early stage of the project whose final number of users (or quantity structures) is still inexact. You should therefore take your time to quantify the system capacity requirements together with the end users, as your calculations can only be as exact as your input values.

Specifying volume requirements

The methods and model calculations described in this chapter are based on SAP's experience and are supposed to help you differentiate between the influencing factors relevant to the sizing of hardware resources, and to create initial approximations for your system's size categories. The models are partly based on ideal-world assumptions, especially for cases in which the influence of custom developments, as in transfer and update rules (for ABAP programs, for example), can hardly be assessed. Poor custom developments can significantly affect the system performance.

Model calculations

Your hardware partner is responsible for the correct sizing of the hardware. For this reason, you should work closely with the sizing experts of your hardware partner and of SAP during the sizing process. The model calculations do not replace the sizing process carried out by your hardware partner. But they are supposed to help you specify the influencing factors relevant for your hardware partner's calculations and to better understand the system suggestion made by your hardware partner.

Sizing by hardware partners

Table 5.14 contains a summary of the described model calculations, influencing factors, and forecast results.

Model Calculation	Influencing Factors	Results
Sizing RDBMS Disc Space (Section 5.3)	▶ # initial load records ▶ # delta load records ▶ # InfoCubes ▶ # ODS objects ▶ # InfoCube dimensions ▶ # characteristics/ key figures	Quantity structures for ▶ InfoCubes ▶ ODS objects ▶ PSA tables ▶ aggregates ▶ indices ▶ master data
CPU sizing for data staging (Section 5.4.1)	▶ # delta load records	▶ Data throughput/h ▶ # SAPS
CPU sizing for queries (Section 5.4.2)	▶ # low users ▶ # medium users ▶ # high users ▶ % easy queries ▶ % medium queries ▶ % heavy queries	▶ # Navigation steps/h ▶ # SAPS
Memory sizing for data staging (Section 5.5.1)	▶ # delta load records ▶ # fact table records	▶ MB of database server main memory ▶ MB of application server main memory
Memory sizing for queries (Section 5.5.2)	▶ # connected user application servers ▶ # concurrent users on database server	▶ MB of database server main memory ▶ MB of application server main memory

Table 5.14 Model Calculations and Influencing Factors in SAP BW Sizing

5.6 Operation Mode and Load Distribution

The sizing procedures and calculation models described in Sections 5.3 through 5.5 are supposed to help you forecast the required hardware resources, depending on the described system loads such as data throughput and the number of users. The total calculation for main memory and CPU resources must always be viewed in connection with the load distribution within a system architecture, and with the system operation.

User times in system operation

When calculating the total hardware resource requirements, you should consider whether it makes sense to separate the operation of the loading processes from that of the read processes. If the system is used for loading data during the night and for reporting operations during the day, you can use the system resources, which are reserved for the loading opera-tion, for reporting operations during the day. In any case, you should cal-culate the resource requirements for reporting and loading processes sep-arately to ensure that the operation time and mode, which is more resource-intensive, determines the minimum system capacity.

For a system with a load profile described below, we assume that the sys-tem is available for reporting operations during the day, whereas, the sys-tem resources are required for loading data during the night.

Load Parameter	Value
Delta/h	1,000,000 data records
Total number of users	150
Number of low users X	80
Number of medium users (Y)	40
Number of high users (Z)	30
Number of fact table records	100,000,000

Table 5.15 Load Profile

Figure 5.2 shows the CPU and main memory capacities needed for the load profile specified in Table 5.15.

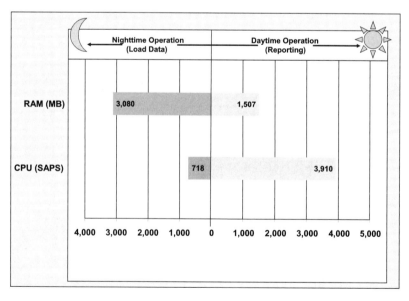

Figure 5.2 Main Memory and CPU Capacity Depending on the Operation Mode

If the operation modes "Load data" and "Reporting" can, for the most part, be separated between daytime and nighttime operations of the system, the total requirement of main memory and CPU capacity results from the maximum resource driver in each operation mode. For the load profile described in Table 5.15, this means a CPU capacity of 3,910 SAPS, and 3,080 MB RAM can be calculated.

5.7 SAP Quick Sizer

SAP Quick Sizer is a tool that enables you to roughly estimate the size of the required hardware in terms of CPU, main memory, and disk capacity. Based on historical values regarding memory and CPU utilization of different SAP applications and the web-based questionnaires on throughput and user numbers filled out by the user, the tool calculates the required main memory, the CPU capacity, and the hard disk volume.

SAP Quick Sizer provides values for the minimum and the optimal main memory size for the database and all SAP instances. All resource requirement values are hardware-independent and are made in the SAP-specific metrics, SAPS.

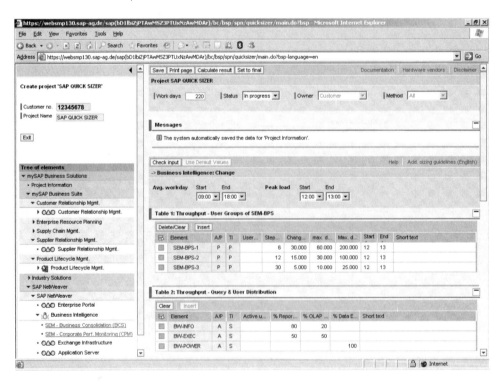

Figure 5.3 SAP Quick Sizer (I)

SAP Quick Sizer was developed in 1997 in cooperation with hardware manufacturers and is now available for many SAP applications including SAP BW. You can call the tool in SAP Service Marketplace from *http://service.sap.com/quicksizer*. There you can also find a user manual for SAP Quick Sizer.

Once you have started SAP Quick Sizer, you can create a sizing project. You can start the sizing calculation by entering the installation number and a name for the sizing project.

Creating a sizing project

In the subsequent screen, you can then enter the data required for the sizing calculation, for example the number of reporting users and the distribution of report types ❶ in terms of percentages, or you can enter details on the initial size and the delta loads of the InfoCubes ❷.

Entering the sizing data

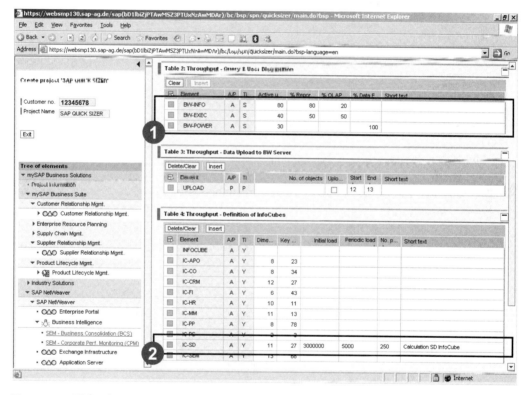

Figure 5.4 SAP Quick Sizer (II)

The sizing calculations are triggered by clicking on the **Calculate Sizing** button.

Starting the sizing calculation

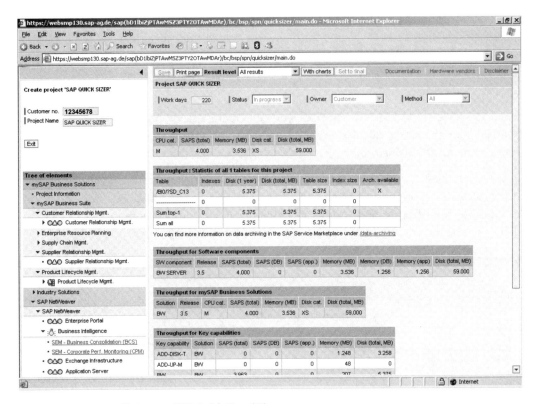

Figure 5.5 SAP Quick Sizer (III)

Hardware vendors The **Hardware Vendors** button enables you to provide different hardware vendors with access to your sizing data in the SAP Service Marketplace by entering the SAP customer number and the name of the sizing project. The hardware partner will then create a concrete hardware offer based on your specifications.

You should always have the hardware partner evaluate the hardware performance in terms of SAPS, because that is the only way in which you can clearly compare the hardware offers.

6   The SAP BW Data Model

Understanding the SAP BW data model is essential to opti-
mizing the performance of SAP BW applications. This chapter
describes all the basic principles of the data model for Info-
Cubes and operational data stores (ODS) objects, and pro-
vides design-related tips for different aspects of performance.

The design of the SAP Business Information Warehouse (SAP BW) data
model plays an integral role in the creation of a BW application. On the
one hand, you must be able to use the data model to map the reporting
requirements of the users. This involves making decisions on data granularity, key figures, and characteristics in the data targets, as well as determining the format of the reports. On the other hand, the data model
must enable you to implement the data targets based on your knowledge
of the memory requirements for the data quantities, the data staging and
processing during operations, and ultimately the performance requirements. You won't be able to implement all reporting requirements without compromising the performance of an application. For this reason, the
design of a good data model will only be achieved by an early evaluation
process that considers both analysis and performance requirements.

Many performance problems in SAP BW reporting applications are
caused by data models with poorly or insufficiently designed data storage
areas. Because of this, the data model of the underlying InfoProviders
must always undergo performance analysis and, if necessary, optimization. The following sections describe the basic principles of SAP BW data
storage and explain how performance is intrinsically dependent on data
design.

6.1   The Star Schema Data Model

The *star schema* is one of the basic data models of reporting applications,
especially of data warehousing applications. The name of this data model
originates from the star-shaped arrangement of several (small) dimension
tables that store the characteristics of the InfoCube, around a central
(large) fact table, which stores the key figures of the InfoCube. A typical
characteristic of this data model is the denormalized data storage in the
dimension tables where the data is stored redundantly and optimized for
queries.

The characteristics and key figures are stored in InfoObjects. Across the entire system, each InfoObject has a unique technical name (for example, 0COSTCENTER) and can be identified by a description (for example, cost center). All InfoProviders in SAP BW are based on those InfoObjects.

Dimension tables The dimension table is an organizing principle that contains objects whose contents are interrelated. For example, the dimension "customer" should contain all characteristics that describe the customer, such as the customer number, customer name, ZIP code, and the place of residence.

Dimension and fact tables are relational database tables that are linked to each other via key relationships (DIM IDs). The dimension key identifies a row in the corresponding dimension table and links the data record with a record in the fact table.

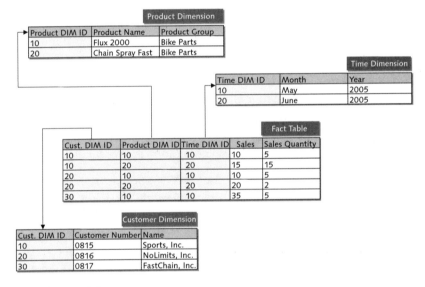

Figure 6.1 Star Schema

SID key The inclusion of characteristic values in the dimension tables shown in Figure 6.1 has been implemented in a modified form in the data model of the SAP BW InfoCube. All characteristic values of a dimension are linked with the attributes via an SID key (surrogate ID, also referred to as a master data ID). The SID is a 4-byte integer key that links the dimension tables with the master data of the characteristics.

6.2 The SAP BW Data Model

Although the SAP BW InfoCube data model is more complex than the classic star model, the concept of the SID keys has some advantages in data modeling.

Depending on the reporting requirements, the SID-key concept allows for a flexible modeling of the relationships between characteristics and attributes within a dimension table. It also enables you to gradually implement complex changes to objects in dimensions, which map historical data combinations. Dimensions that are affected by changes over a period of time are referred to as *slowly changing dimensions*.[1] The SAP BW master data of a reporting characteristic can be made available in the current dataset at any time by using the link with the SID table. The master data of an InfoObject is located outside of the InfoCube, and therefore, does not need to be modeled separately in the InfoCube. In addition, you can use the SID table of the InfoObject simultaneously in several Info-Cubes.

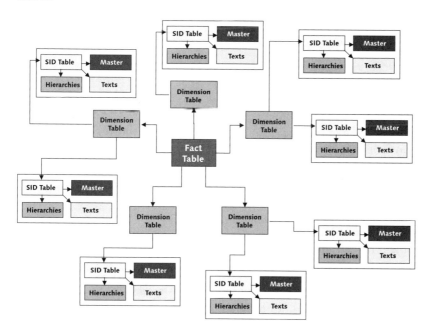

Figure 6.2 SAP BW Data Model

---

1 Kimball, Reeves, Ross, Thornthwaite: *The Data Warehouse Lifecycle Toolkit: Expert Methods for Designing, Developing, and Deploying Data Warehouses*. Wiley 1998, p. 360f.

The following sections describe the meanings of the different table types in the SAP BW data model.

6.2.1 Fact Tables in SAP BW

In the SAP BW data model, the fact table of an InfoCube is structured in the same way as the fact table in the standard star schema. The foreign keys of the fact table are either the keys (prefix name KEY_<InfoCube>) that are contained in the dimension table columns (DIM IDs), or the SID keys if line item dimensions are used. Each row in the fact table can be uniquely identified by the combination of all dimension IDs of the dimension tables or by the combination of the SID keys of the SID tables.

Since SAP BW Release 2.0B, each InfoCube has two fact tables. The F fact table contains uncompressed data including the request IDs of the loading processes. Individual load requests can be separately administrated via the request ID; for example, to delete erroneous load requests from the InfoCube. The E fact table contains the compressed data records. During compression of the InfoCube, the request IDs are deleted from the F fact table, while the compressed load requests are moved to the E fact table.

6.2.2 Dimension Tables in SAP BW

Characteristics whose contents are related to each other are grouped in a dimension table. The characteristics can be stored directly in the dimension table, or the master data of the characteristics can be imported via the SID key relationship. The type of modeling depends on the reporting requirements, which appear in the same chronological order as the data it corresponds to.

An SAP BW basic InfoCube can contain a maximum of 16 dimension tables, 13 of which can be freely defined, because the *Package*, *Time*, and *Unit* dimensions are predefined for each basic InfoCube.

Package dimension · The package dimension can be used with the request ID to manage each load request of an InfoCube separately. This may be necessary if, for example, you have to delete certain data requests from the InfoCube.

Time dimension · The time dimension contains all characteristics that refer to the time-related metrics of the fact table.

Unit dimension · The unit dimension contains a metrical unit for all key figures that represent a quantity or amount.

Each dimension table can contain 248 InfoObjects so that each InfoCube can contain 3,968 (i.e., 16 × 248 = 3,9468) InfoObjects, plus the attributes of each InfoObject.

The columns of the dimension table don't contain the characteristic values, but the SID keys of the characteristic or its attributes. The DIM ID that links the dimension tables with the fact table via a 4-byte integer key is the primary key of the table.

Dimension Table "Material"

DIM ID	Material SID
1	111
2	222
3	333
4	444
5	555

Figure 6.3 Dimension Table "Material" (I)

The terms *characteristic* and *attribute* are often used in different ways. We will use these terms here to differentiate among the storage locations within a dimension. Whenever the object is a component of the dimension table, we'll refer to it as a characteristic. If the object is part of the master data of a characteristic, we'll refer to it as an attribute.

Characteristic and attribute

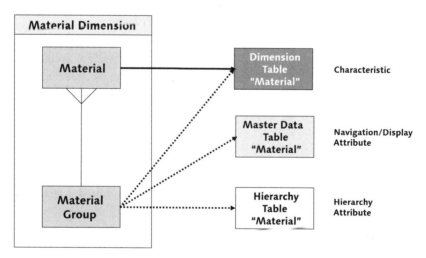

Figure 6.4 Dimension Table "Material" (II)

Figure 6.4 illustrates the relationship of the objects *Material* and *Material Group* in the *Material Dimension* table. A 1:n relationship exists between the objects *Material Group* and *Material*. The relationship to the InfoObject *Material Group* can be modeled in different ways:

▶ As a characteristic in the dimension table *Material*

▶ As an attribute in the master data table of the InfoObject *Material*

▶ As a hierarchy node in the hierarchy table of the InfoObject *Material*

The modeling type depends on the reporting requirements.

Historical presentation The inclusion of the *Material Group* object in the dimension table enables you to display the data collectively at an historical point in time ("What was the material group at that time?"), because by including the attribute in the dimension table, the current relationship to the characteristic is lost.

Current presentation If the material group is modeled as a master data attribute of the *Material* object, the dataset displayed is for the current point in time ("Which is the material group of the material today?"). In order to display the current values of the master data attributes for a characteristic, the modeling must display the current master data attribute, or the navigation attribute for the respective InfoObject.

Date-based presentation If you want to display the attribute values for a specific date, the material group must also be modeled as a master data attribute for the relevant InfoObject. In that case, a validity period for the attribute values is additionally stored (see also Sections 6.2.3 and 6.2.4).

Contrary to navigating in the dimension tables via attributes, executing a query with navigation attributes in the master data tables requires an additional JOIN operation. To optimize performance, we therefore recommend that you model the attributes in the dimension tables (historical presentation). In addition, you must customize aggregates with navigation attributes in the change run after each master data load (see also Section 11.4.6, Hierarchy and Attribute Changes).

For performance reasons, you should avoid using time-dependent attributes for a date-based presentation of the attribute values, since time-dependent master data tables can increase dramatically, and the administration of aggregates containing time-dependent attributes can become very complex (see also Sections 6.2.3 and 6.2.4).

Line item dimension If dimension tables contain only one InfoObject, SAP BW allows you to establish a link with the InfoCube's fact table—directly through the

4-byte integer SID keys of the characteristic instead of via the dimension tables' DIM keys. These dimensions are referred to as *line item dimensions*. Because of the direct inclusion of the SID keys in the fact table, a dimension table is not necessary.

In SAP BW, line item dimensions are primarily intended for improving system performance when using large dimensions. You should use line item dimensions when a dimension table contains only one InfoObject, or approximately as many data records as the fact table.

If possible, try to model large dimensions with only one InfoObject so that you can create a line item dimension. If a dimension table of your data model contains over 20% of the data records of the fact table, you should model the dimension as a line item. This simplification of the data model, which is made possible by using line item dimensions, enables you to establish a better read and load performance.

6.2.3 Master Data Tables in SAP BW

The SAP BW master data concept enables you to display a date-based or up-to-date presentation of characteristic attributes. You can import the master data attributes from the R/3 system, or maintain them directly in SAP BW. The master data of a characteristic includes the following:

▶ Texts

▶ Master data

▶ Hierarchies

In SAP BW, texts contain descriptive information on characteristic values such as country, product, or customer names. With regard to their length, texts can be stored in a short form (20 characters), medium form (40 characters), and long form (60 characters). Texts for characteristics can be language-dependent or time-dependent. If language dependency is activated, an additional column is created in the text table of the InfoObject. This column contains the language-dependent code.

Texts

To ensure performance, you should check the use of language dependency since the data records in the text table are duplicated for each stored language.

In addition to the language dependency, you can also model a time dependency for the texts. If the texts are not time-dependent, the system always displays the currently valid, recently loaded texts in reporting. However, if you want to display texts for a specific date in reporting, the texts must be time-dependent. If time dependency is activated, two additional columns are inserted into the text table of the InfoObject. These columns are used to maintain the validity period of the text according to a VALID FROM—VALID TO logic.

When using time-dependent texts, you should know that a new validity period is added with each loading process of the master data. For this reason, the valid-from date of the texts is determined by the loading time, not by the change date in the source system. Depending on the loading cycle, the number of data records in the text table can quickly multiply.

The texts are maintained in the administration of the InfoObject, in the **Master data/texts** tab (see Figure 6.5).

When the InfoObject master data is activated, a transparent table that references the name of the InfoObject is generated:

InfoObject type	Technical name of the table
Standard InfoObject	/BIO/T<tech. name of InfoObject>
Non-standard InfoObject	/BIC/T<tech. name of InfoObject>

Table 6.1 Naming Conventions for Text Tables

Master data The master data concept in SAP BW allows you to store additional attributes for a characteristic. Contrary to texts, those attributes are also available as navigation and filter objects in reporting.

Like the texts, the master data of a characteristic is set in the InfoObject maintenance on the **Master data/texts tab** (see Figure 6.5). If you activate the **With master data** option, several tables are generated that differ in their attribute settings for an InfoObject. You can generate the following attribute types for a characteristic:

▶ Time-constant attributes

▶ Time-dependent attributes

▶ Navigation attributes

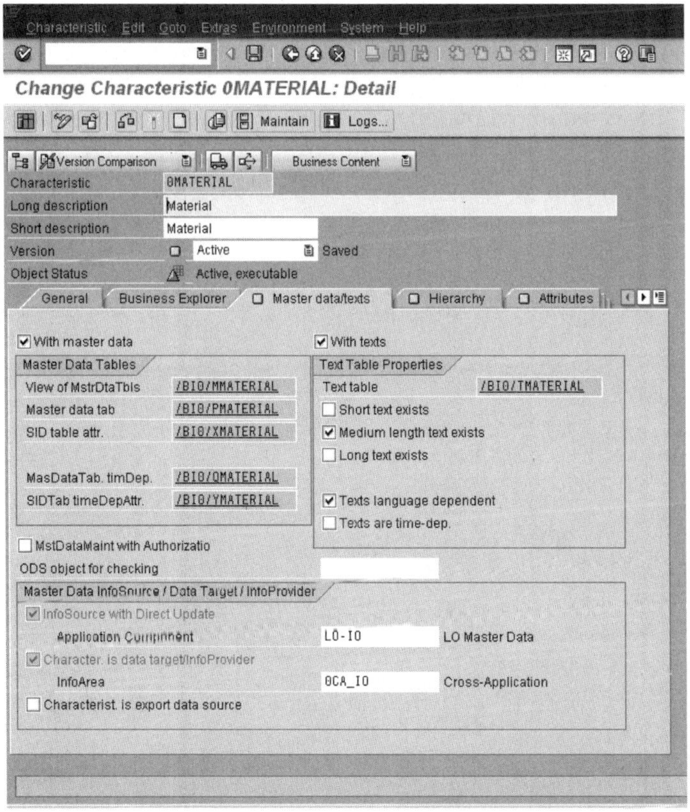

Figure 6.5 Texts of an InfoObject

Time-constant attributes are simply additional information on a characteristic. This information is intended only for display in reporting and does not provide any navigation or filter options (for example, last name, first name, and ZIP code for a customer number). This type of attribute is also referred to as a *display attribute*. The characteristic values of the time-constant attributes are always available in the current form of the dataset for the InfoObject and are therefore not time-dependent. They are not stored as an SID key in the table, but in their actual form.

Time-constant attributes

Master Data Table /BIO/PMATERIAL

MATERIAL	MATL_TYPE
101091	100
101092	200
101093	100
101094	100

Figure 6.6 Master Data Table for a Time-Constant Attribute

For example, Figure 6.6 shows the master data table /BIO/PMATERIAL of InfoObject 0MATERIAL. All characteristic values are directly stored in the table. The display attribute *Material type* (MATL_TYPE) for the *Material* characteristic is stored in the master data table. If the material type for a characteristic value changes, the previous attribute value is overwritten, because historical attribute values of a characteristic are not stored when there are time-constant display attributes.

You can set the characteristic attribute values in the InfoObject maintenance on the **Attributes** tab (see Figure 6.7).

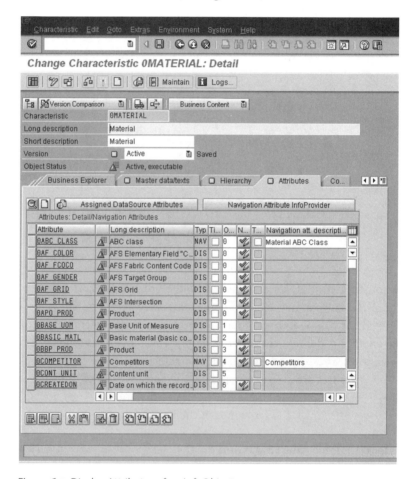

Figure 6.7 Display Attributes of an InfoObject

Table 6.2 shows the naming conventions for time-constant display attributes:

InfoObject type	Technical name of the table
Standard InfoObject	/BIO/P<tech. name of InfoObject>
Non-standard InfoObject	/BIC/P<tech. name of InfoObject>

Table 6.2 Naming Conventions for a (Time-Constant) Master Data Table

The time-constant storage of a characteristic's display attributes is not sufficient for reporting requirements that demand a date-dependent display of valid attribute values. For this reason, SAP BW allows for a time-dependent storage of attributes and texts. You can manage the time dependency in the InfoObject maintenance by activating the **Time dependency** option in the **Attributes** tab (see Figure 6.7). Note that you can activate the time dependency of the attribute values separately for each characteristic attribute.

Time-dependent attributes

As for the texts, the validity period of the attribute values is encoded in two additional columns according to the VALID FROM—VALID TO logic.

Master Data Table /BIO/QMATERIAL

MATERIAL	VALIDFROM	VALIDTO	MATL_GRP
AAA	01/01/1000	12/31/9999	Y
BBB	01/01/1000	07/31/2005	Y
BBB	08/01/2005	12/31/9999	X
CCC	01/01/1000	12/31/9999	X

Figure 6.8 Master Data Table for a Time-Dependent Attribute

Figure 6.8 shows an example of the master data table /BIO/QMATERIAL of the InfoObject 0MATERIAL. The display attribute *material group* (MATL_GRP) is time-dependent here. In this sample table, the material *BBB* is assigned the attribute *material group* with the value *Y* for the period from 01/01/1000 to 07/31/2005. On 08/01/2005, the material *BBB* is assigned material group *X*, which generates a new data record in the table (VALIDFROM = 08/01/2005). The previous attribute value won't be overwritten, but the period closes on the final date of the validity period (VALIDTO = 07/31/2005). As is the case with time-constant attributes, characteristic and attribute values are not stored as an SID key in the table, but with their actual values.

Table 6.3 shows the naming conventions for time-constant display attributes:

InfoObject type	Technical name of the table
Standard InfoObject	/BIO/Q<tech. name of InfoObject>
Non-standard InfoObject	/BIC/Q<tech. name of InfoObject>

Table 6.3 Naming Conventions for a (Time-Dependent) Master Data Table

When using time-dependent attributes in reporting, you should note that a single query can initiate the display of only one valid characteristic attribute value for a specific date. The valid date must be set in the query properties.

In SAP BW, the access to data of time-constant and time-dependent attributes does not occur directly in the two master data tables P and Q, but rather through a view that is automatically created by SAP BW. Table 6.4 shows the naming conventions for this view:

InfoObject type	Technical name of the table
Standard InfoObject	/BIO/M<tech. name of InfoObject>
Non-standard InfoObject	/BIC/M<tech. name of InfoObject>

Table 6.4 Naming Conventions for the Master Data Table View

The following list summarizes the main points of modeling display attributes and texts of a characteristic:

▶ Display attributes and texts of master data enable the display of current, but not of historical attribute values.

▶ The characteristic and attribute values are not stored via an SID key in the master data tables. Instead, the values are stored directly in the tables.

▶ Texts and attributes can be stored as time-dependent.

▶ The time dependency of the attribute values can be activated separately for each attribute.

▶ The modeling of the time dependency of attributes and texts enables the display of valid attribute values for a specific date.

▶ Display attributes and texts cannot be used for navigation and filtering purposes in reporting.

- From a technical point of view, the following two master data tables exist if a characteristic contains time-constant and time-dependent attributes:

  - A master data table /BIC/P<techn. name of InfoObject> for custom objects or /BIO/P<techn. name of InfoObject> for standard objects for time-constant attributes

  - A master data table /BIC/Q<techn. name of InfoObject> for custom objects or /BIO/Q<techn. name of InfoObject> for standard objects for time-dependent attributes

- The master data tables for time-dependent attributes contain additional columns that store information on the validity period of the attributes based on the VALID FROM—VALID TO logic.

- A query can display only one valid attribute value for a specific date.

6.2.4 SID Tables in SAP BW

You cannot use the attributes described in Section 6.2.3 for navigation or filtering purposes in reporting, because they are to be used for only supplementary information for a characteristic. If you need specific navigation or filtering attributes in reporting, you can define them in SAP BW. For performance reasons, the attribute values stored in the master data tables for the attributes are not suitable for navigation, because the attribute values themselves are stored in the tables. In SAP BW, navigation is implemented via the SID key concept, and therefore, the navigation attribute values are encoded in separate master data tables in the form of a 4-byte-integer SID key.

The SID tables in SAP BW can be divided into the following three types:

- Standard SID tables
- SID tables for time-constant navigation attributes
- SID tables for time-dependent navigation attributes

The standard SID table is generated for each InfoObject that is not an explicit display attribute. An SID table is also generated for attributes for which the **Attribute only** option is activated in the **General** tab of the InfoObject maintenance, however, this table does not contain any data.

Standard SID tables

Standard SID Table /BIO/SMATERIAL

SID Material	MATERIAL
0001	AAA
0002	BBB
0003	CCC
0004	DDD
0005	EEE

Figure 6.9 Standard SID Table for InfoObject 0MATERIAL

The sample SID table for the 0MATERIAL characteristic shown in Figure 6.9 is accessed whenever a query uses a navigation attribute, or a characteristic without an attribute, for an InfoCube or an ODS object.

Table 6.5 shows the naming conventions for the standard SID table:

InfoObject type	Technical name of the table
Standard InfoObject	/BIO/S<tech. name of InfoObject>
Non-standard InfoObject	/BIC/S<tech. name of InfoObject>

Table 6.5 Naming Conventions for Standard SID Tables

Time-constant navigation attributes For time-constant navigation attributes for a characteristic, a table, which is an extension to the standard SID table, is generated. In addition to the characteristic value and its SID key, the SID key of the associated attribute is stored in the SID table.

SID Table /BIO/XMATERIAL

SID Material	MATERIAL	SID MATL_GRP
0001	AAA	110
0002	BBB	110
0003	CCC	120
0004	DDD	110
0005	EEE	120

Figure 6.10 SID Table for Time-Constant Navigation Attribute

The sample SID table of the InfoObject 0MATERIAL shown in Figure 6.10 contains the time-constant navigation attribute *material group* (MATL_GRP) in the form of an SID key.

If you want to use the material group navigation attribute for navigation or filtering purposes in reporting, the navigation attribute must be activated in the corresponding InfoCube maintenance menu for navigation attributes (see ❶ and ❷ in Figure 6.11). Otherwise, the navigation attribute is not available.

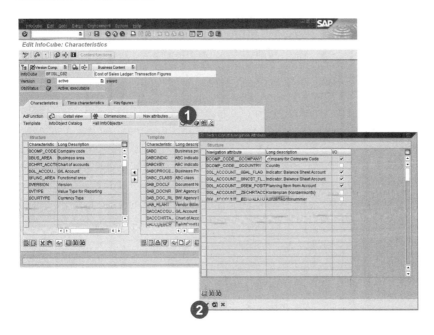

Figure 6.11 Managing Navigation Attributes in an InfoCube

Table 6.6 shows the naming conventions for the SID table for time-constant navigation attributes:

InfoObject type	Technical name of the table
Standard InfoObject	/BI0/X<tech. name of InfoObject>
Non-standard InfoObject	/BIC/X<tech. name of InfoObject>

Table 6.6 Naming Conventions for an SID Table for Time-Constant Navigation Attributes

An additional SID table for time-dependent navigation attributes of a characteristic is generated. This table contains two additional columns that store the validity period of the attribute values based on a VALID FROM—VALID TO logic.

Time-dependent navigation attributes

SID Table /BI0/YMATERIAL

SID Material	MATERIAL	VALIDFROM	VALIDTO	SID MATL_GRP
0001	AAA	01/01/1000	12/31/9999	110
0002	BBB	01/01/1000	07/31/2005	110
0002	BBB	08/01/2005	12/31/9999	120
0003	CCC	01/01/1000	12/31/9999	120
0004	DDD	01/01/1000	12/31/9999	110

Figure 6.12 SID Table for a Time-Dependent Navigation Attribute

The sample SID table of the InfoObject 0MATERIAL shown in Figure 6.12 contains the time-dependent navigation attribute *material group* (MATL_GRP) in the form of an SID key. This example uses the *BBB* material to illustrate the time change in the assignment of the navigation attribute *material group* to the *material* characteristic. During the period from 01/01/1000 until 07/31/2005, the material *BBB* was part of the material group *110*. From 08/01/2005 onward, the material is assigned to material group *120*.

The necessity of time-dependent navigation attributes should be assessed carefully, because these attributes can become an administrative nightmare when it comes to performance optimization. When using time-dependent navigation attributes, you can only use aggregates if these aggregates are calculated for a specific key date. Frequent changes of the key date therefore require expensive and regular adjustments of the aggregates.

Table 6.7 shows the naming conventions for the SID table for time-dependent navigation attributes:

InfoObject type	Technical name of the table
Standard InfoObject	/BIO/Y<tech. name of InfoObject>
Non-standard InfoObject	/BIC/Y<tech. name of InfoObject>

Table 6.7 Naming Conventions for an SID Table for Time-Dependent Navigation Attributes

The SID tables are automatically updated during the master data-loading processes, therefore, they don't require any separate administration. During the update of data in InfoCubes, SID keys are automatically generated from the transaction data, regardless of whether no master data exists for the navigation attributes of the loaded records. For this reason, you must activate the option **Always update data, even if no master data exists** in the InfoPackage maintenance. Otherwise, the transaction data will not be loaded.

6.2.5 External Hierarchies in SAP BW

The tree-like structure of attribute values that are stored as *characteristics hierarchies* in separate tables is referred to as an external hierarchy in SAP BW. The characteristics hierarchies are defined for exactly one InfoObject and can be used like master data in the InfoProviders. Examples include the hierarchy of cost centers that are summarized into cost center groups, or the hierarchy of sales locations that are summarized in regions

In addition, there are other options for creating a hierarchy: For example, when hierarchical structures are determined in the InfoCube modeling, the InfoObjects 0CALDAY, 0CALMONTH, and 0CALYEAR already form a hierarchy in the time dimension. In the InfoObject maintenance, a hierarchy can be mapped in the characteristic attributes; for example, the InfoObjects 0MATERIAL, 0MATL_GROUP, and 0MATL_TYPE. Those hierarchies are referred to as *internal hierarchies*. In the following sections, we'll describe only external characteristics hierarchies.

Each hierarchy consists of a hierarchy root and subordinate hierarchy nodes and hierarchy leaves. The hierarchy nodes contain the different characteristic values and can be divided into chargeable and non-chargeable hierarchy nodes:

▶ Non-chargeable hierarchy nodes determine the structure of the hierarchy and represent a kind of "container" for the characteristic values.

▶ Chargeable hierarchy nodes comprise the attribute values of the characteristic itself.

You can define the structure of non-chargeable nodes as per your requirements, so the branches of the hierarchy can have different depths and the node descriptions can be unique or ambiguous. Non-chargeable nodes can be created as *text nodes* and the node name can be defined

Non-chargeable nodes

with a text of your choice. Moreover, you can also use the texts of InfoObjects to describe the nodes. This way the node descriptions always contain the current master data texts. For this purpose, you must integrate *external characteristic nodes* in the hierarchy maintenance, and assign an InfoObject and text to each hierarchy node.

Chargeable nodes Chargeable nodes of a hierarchy structure contain the characteristic attribute values themselves. The lowest level of a branch is referred to as a *hierarchy leaf*, which represents the end point of the tree that is loaded with data. The structure of the chargeable nodes and leaves determines the totaling process in the nodes.

Hierarchy intervals In addition to posting individual values to nodes and leaves, you can define value intervals for a node in a hierarchy; for example, to map number ranges of attribute values. If you activate the **Intervals in Hierarchies** option, the system generates a separate hierarchy intervals table.

Versions of hierarchies You can simultaneously define several versions of the same hierarchy, which can be useful in reporting for displaying the data in different hierarchy versions for comparisons.

Time dependency of hierarchies Like master data of a characteristic, you can also store hierarchies for a characteristic as time-dependent. In this case, a validity period is determined for the hierarchy. The time dependency of hierarchies can be divided into the time dependency of the entire hierarchy and the time dependency of the hierarchy structure.

The time dependency of the entire hierarchy defines the validity period for the hierarchy root and all subordinate nodes and leaves. The SAP BW system creates hierarchy versions for time-dependent entire hierarchies. These versions are valid for one time interval. A valid hierarchy can be uniquely identified by the technical name and a from-to date. In reporting, you can determine the valid hierarchy by using the query key date.

In time-dependent hierarchy structures, the validity period is defined for one node of each hierarchy. You can use this type of modeling to map time-dependently changing relationships within a structure, for example, if sales employees are responsible for different sales regions over a period of time. In reporting, you can determine the valid hierarchy for the current key date or the key date defined in the query.

To ensure performance, you should note that when using time-dependent hierarchies, you could use precalculated hierarchy aggregates for specific hierarchy levels only in time-dependent entire hierarchies, but not in time-dependent hierarchy structures.

Figure 6.13 illustrates the basic structure of a simple hierarchy.

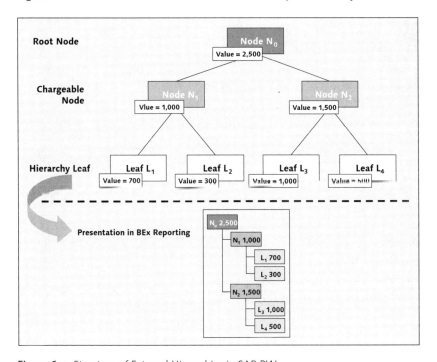

Figure 6.13 Structure of External Hierarchies in SAP BW

You can configure the following hierarchy settings for an InfoObject in the **Hierarchy** tab of the InfoObject maintenance (see Figure 6.14):

▶ Set if the InfoObject has hierarchies

▶ The version dependency of hierarchies

▶ The time dependency of the entire hierarchy or hierarchy structure

▶ The permission of intervals for hierarchy nodes

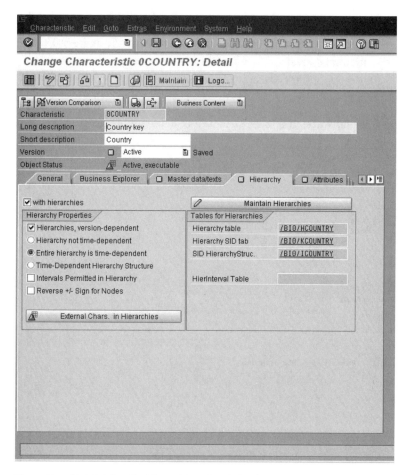

Figure 6.14 Maintaining the Hierarchies of an InfoObject

Table 6.8 lists several transparent tables that are generated during the creation of hierarchies.

	Standard InfoObject	Non-standard InfoObject
Name of InfoObject	0<InfoObject>	<InfoObject>
Hierarchy table (hierarchical relationship of characteristic values)	/BIO/H<InfoObject>	/BIC/H<InfoObject>
Hierarchy SID table (translation of characteristic values in SID keys)	/BIO/K<InfoObject>	/BIC/K<InfoObject>

Table 6.8 Naming Conventions for Hierarchy Tables

	Standard InfoObject	Non-standard InfoObject
SID structure of hierarchy nodes	/BIO/I<InfoObject>	/BIC/I<InfoObject>
Hierarchy intervals	/BIO/J<InfoObject>	/BIC/J<InfoObject>

Table 6.8 Naming Conventions for Hierarchy Tables (cont.)

Let's use the simple example of the "Country" hierarchy to illustrate how the hierarchy tables can be linked with each other.

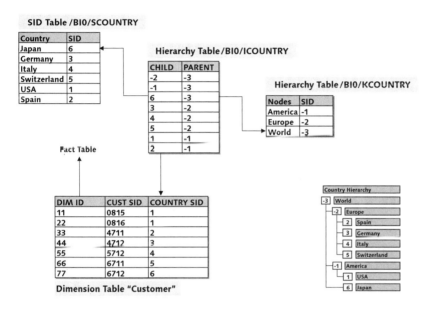

Figure 6.15 Linking the Hierarchy Tables

Figure 6.15 shows that the *Customer* and *Country* characteristics are included in the dimension table *Customer*. A hierarchy has been created for the *Country* characteristic so that the SID key of the *Country* characteristic in the dimension table branches into the hierarchy inclusion table /BIO/ICOUNTRY, which stores the hierarchy structure as SID keys. The inclusion table is the link between the hierarchy table /BIO/KCOUNTRY that stores the translation of the hierarchy nodes and their SID keys and the SID table of the *Country* characteristic, which stores the SID keys and attribute values of the characteristic. In contrast to SID tables of characteristics the SID IDs are negative in hierarchy tables.

6.2.6 Summary

The SAP BW data model provides extensive and flexible modeling options, but its structure is very complex. A profound understanding of the SAP BW data model is indispensable to examine performance analysis and achieve optimization.

Table 6.9 once again lists all tables with BW master data, texts, and hierarchies:

	Standard InfoObject	Non-standard InfoObject
Name of InfoObject	0<InfoObject>	<InfoObject>
Text table	/BIO/T<InfoObject>	/BIC/T<InfoObject>
Master data table with time-constant attribute	/BIO/P<InfoObject>	/BIC/P<InfoObject>
Master data table with time-dependent attribute	/BIO/Q<InfoObject>	/BIC/Q<InfoObject>
Master data view	/BIO/M<InfoObject>	/BIC/M<InfoObject>
Standard SID table	/BIO/S<InfoObject>	/BIC/S<InfoObject>
SID table for time-constant navigation attribute	/BIO/X<InfoObject>	/BIC/X<InfoObject>
SID table for time-dependent navigation attribute	/BIO/Y<InfoObject>	/BIC/Y<InfoObject>
Hierarchy table (hierarchical relationship of characteristic values)	/BIO/H<InfoObject>	/BIC/H<InfoObject>
Hierarchy SID table (translation of characteristic values in SID keys)	/BIO/K<InfoObject>	/BIC/K<InfoObject>
SID structure of hierarchy nodes	/BIO/I<InfoObject>	/BIC/I<InfoObject>
Hierarchy intervals	/BIO/J<InfoObject>	/BIC/J<InfoObject>

Table 6.9 Overview of SAP BW Master Data Tables

Example For a better understanding of the SAP BW data model, we'll now use a sample query to illustrate the interaction between the different tables. Let's suppose that the *material group* shown in Figure 6.16 is a time-constant navigation attribute of the *Material* characteristic in the master data table of the characteristic. The simplified query

Sales revenues for material groups X and Y

is supposed to show the interaction of the different tables in the Info-Cube query.

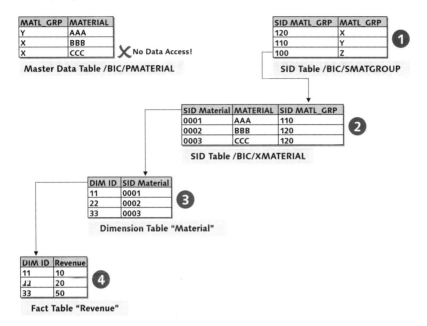

Figure 6.16 InfoCube Query

The query shown in Figure 6.16 can be divided into the following steps:

1. Access to SID table *Material group* /BIC/SMATGROUP and selection of SID keys *110* and *120* for material groups *X* and *Y*.

2. Access to SID table *Material* /BIC/XMATERIAL with time-constant navigation attribute *Material group*, and selection of material SID keys *0001*, *0002*, and *0003* for the material group SID keys *110* and *120* selected in Step 1.

3. Access to dimension table *Material* of the corresponding InfoCube using the SID keys *0001*, *0002*, and *0003* selected in Step 2, and selection of the corresponding DIM IDs *11*, *22*, and *33*.

4. Access to the fact table of the InfoCube using the DIM ID keys *11*, *22*, and *33* selected in Step 3, and aggregation of the *Revenue* key figure for the material groups *X* (= 70) and *Y* (= 10).

The data access occurs in the same way for dimension tables, which are typically involved in a query. The selection of the data from the fact table results from the combination of external key relationships between the DIM IDs.

The query illustrated in Figure 6.16 does not involve any access to the master data table /BIC/PMATERIAL, because the selection occurs through the material group navigation attribute and not through the display attribute, which cannot be used for navigation and filtering processes.

6.3 Performance-Relevant Modeling Aspects

The design decisions made in the InfoCube and query modeling phase can substantially affect the loading and reporting performance. When creating the data model, you should therefore consider both the reporting requirements and performance aspects. The following list provides an overview of performance-critical design decisions you should take into account when modeling data models in SAP BW.

Large dimension tables When modeling dimension tables, you should ensure that separate characteristics with a strong data growth that are related to each other in m:n relationships are modeled in separate dimension tables (for example, *Customer* and *Product*). The maximum number of data records in a dimension table should not exceed the size of the fact table by more than 10 percent. If possible, dimensions with a strong growth in data should be modeled as line item dimensions. If you use line item dimensions, the SID key of the dimension characteristic is directly included in the fact table, and which negates the need for a table join for queries. Line item dimensions require the inclusion of only one characteristic into the corresponding dimension table.

In general, we recommend that you create many small dimension tables rather than just a few big tables. For big dimension tables, you should check whether you can separate the characteristics and attributes into several dimension tables. For example, it is advisable to separate a dimension table containing the characteristic *Material* and the attribute *Material Group* into two dimension tables if *Material* and *Material Group* contain many values, and also if many queries need only one of the two objects.

Large fact tables *Large fact tables* that contain several millions of data records can dramatically affect the performance of certain queries. If you use such fact tables, you should check if you can improve the query runtimes by using aggregates (see also Chapter 11), or by partitioning the fact table. For very large InfoCubes, it may also be prudent to distribute the data into different InfoCubes (logical partitioning, see Chapter 12).

You can define a size category for each table in the SAP BW system, including the fact and dimension tables. The size category determines the anticipated space requirements of a table in the database. A specific, fixed size of a storage area in the database is defined for each category. A standard SAP BW system contains size categories from 0 to 4; as of SAP BW 3.0B SP11, you can use size categories of up to and including 9. Table 6.10 lists the size categories and the number of data records to be expected:

Size category	Number of data records
0	0 to 76,000
1	76,000 to 300,000
2	300,000 to 1,200,000
3	1,200,000 to 4,900,000
4	4,900,000 to 19,000,000
5	19,000,000 to 39,000,000
6	39,000,000 to 78,000,000
7	78,000,000 to 150,000,000
8	150,000,000 to 310,000,000
9	> 310,000,000

Table 6.10 Size Categories for SAP BW Tables

When you create a table, an initial space is reserved in the database. As the table grows, the additional storage space is added for the corresponding size category.

In general, the predefined values are sufficient for the fact and dimension tables (size category 0 for dimension tables, size category 4 for fact tables). If the size categories in your SAP BW system are not sufficient, you can use the following customization options:

1. **Partitioning the fact table**
   If possible, you should partition the fact table because the settings of the size category apply to each partition, which means you can increase the size category of the fact table by a multiple.

2. **Changing the size category (locally)**
   If the predefined size category is insufficient, you can change the size category of the fact table (data type DFACT) and of the dimension

tables of the relevant InfoCube (data type DDIM) in the **Extras · Maintain DB storage parameters** menu of the InfoCube maintenance. However, prior to changing the size category, you must ensure that the InfoCube doesn't contain any data, which may require the InfoCube to be emptied first.

3. **Changing the size category (globally)**
   If you want to use a different size category than the default setting for defining fact and dimension tables, Transaction SE13 enables you to change the size category of fact tables in the transparent table RSDM-FACTAB, and to change the size category of dimension tables in the transparent table RSDMDIMTAB. The default values set in those tables are then used for all fact and dimension tables. Since these changes modify the system, you must re-enter the settings when the system is upgraded.

Non-cumulative key figures

Non-cumulative key figures are key figures that cannot be totaled and are based on one or more objects that are always displayed with a time relation. The non-cumulative key figure always requires the existence of a chronological reference characteristic to perform an exception aggregation. Examples of non-cumulatives include the headcount, the account balance, and the material stock. Non-cumulative key figures are not stored in the InfoCube; instead, they are calculated on the basis of non-cumulative deltas or goods received, and goods issued quantities that are stored in the fact table. The actual non-cumulative can then be calculated based on an opening non-cumulative that is stored as a *marker* at a specific point in time and the changes in stock are displayed as non-cumulative deltas or incoming and outgoing stocks. The calculation of the non-cumulative based on stock changes occurs at query runtime, which may cause longer query runtimes. You can improve the runtime for InfoCubes that contain non-cumulative key figures by compressing the InfoCube, because, with each compression, the current non-cumulative is stored as a marker in the fact table so that less stock changes must be read for new non-cumulative calculations.

Cardinality of characteristic values

If the characteristic of a dimension table contains many different characteristic values (high cardinality), the size of the dimension can increase rapidly. In this case too, you should model a line item dimension. As of SAP BW 3.x, whose database system is based on Oracle, you can set the index type of external keys in the fact table to the B*-tree index, which is recommended for characteristics with a high cardinality.

To ensure a good query performance, you should not use the **High Cardinality** setting. If an index is set to B*-tree, it can no longer be used in a star join, although it is usually the most selective of all indices. This automatically causes longer query runtimes.

If you have to map frequently changing attribute relationships in your data model, you shouldn't model the attributes as master data. Frequently changing attribute relationships are often found in status attributes that describe the status of a characteristic depending on time or other attributes. An example of this is the PR status of a product that can be advertised in different campaigns (flyers, email, phone, TV, and so on). The historical mapping of the promotion status—by including the promotion status as an attribute of the product in the product master data table—can result in an extreme increase of the master data table, which, in turn, causes performance problems.

Status attributes

You should therefore map frequently changing attribute relationships in dimension tables. In this context, the status attribute (here the *promotion status*) is modeled in a separate dimension table. This means that the size of the dimension table remains manageable, which would not be the case if the attribute was modeled as master data. Moreover, you can increase the query performance if you use the status attribute as a filtering or navigation object in a query.

Navigation attributes are part of the "extended star schema" and require additional JOIN operations in a query, as opposed to characteristics in a dimension that are also available for navigation and filtering purposes in reporting. Due to the more simple JOIN operations, dimension characteristics have a performance advantage over navigation attributes. When modeling your data, you should therefore carefully check whether navigation attributes are required for your reporting purposes. Not only do navigation attributes cause a bad query performance, you also have to adjust aggregates containing navigation attributes in a change run after each master data load.

Navigation attributes

Time-dependent navigation attributes store a validity period in addition to the attribute values. The valid attribute value is determined on the basis of a key date during the query run. If you want to use aggregates for the query, you must calculate the aggregates in relation to a key date so that the query can use the aggregate. You should carefully check whether the use of time-dependent navigation attributes is really necessary, because regular changes of the key date or the validity period of naviga-tion attributes require regular adjustments of the aggregates.

Hierarchies If you use hierarchies, you should check whether you can use internal hierarchies within a dimension table (e.g., 0COUNTRY → 0REGION → 0CITY). These hierarchies usually show a better performance when com-pared with external hierarchies, because they don't require any additional JOIN operations through tables of the extended star schema. As is the case with attributes in dimension tables, you can only model the histori-cal presentation for hierarchies in dimension tables. When creating aggre-gates for dimension hierarchies, you should note that you can use aggre-gates for hierarchy levels with a higher degree of aggregation only if the aggregates have been included in the aggregate calculation. For example, queries that accumulate data at the 0COUNTRY level cannot use any aggregates that summarize data at the subordinate hierarchy level 0REGION. For this reason, you should include all hierarchy levels when creating an aggregate so you can use the aggregates as much as possible.

When using external hierarchies, you can only use aggregates if the read mode of the query is set to **Read upon navigation/hierarchy drills** (see also Section 11.1.3). You can define hierarchy aggregates for a hierarchy node or for an entire hierarchy. If you use time-dependent hierarchies, you should note that you can use hierarchy aggregates only for time-dependent entire hierarchies, but not for time-dependent hierarchy structures.

For very large hierarchies (several thousands of leaves) with different nodes, or if you use many different hierarchies, you should check whether the size of the hierarchy table buffer is sufficient. The hierarchy table buffer stores hierarchy nodes that have already been calculated in separate tables, which are administrated in the buffer table RSDRHL-RUBUFFER. If you use very large hierarchies or many different hierarchies, the buffer entries can be removed so that the hierarchy nodes must be recalculated. You can check the buffer table using Transaction SE16. SAP recommends an increase of the table buffer if more than 170 entries exist, or if the timestamp of more than 90% of the entries shows the cur-rent date or the current date -1. You can use Report SAP_RSADMIN_ MAINTAIN (Transaction SE38) in Table RSADMIN to change the buffer size. The RSDRH_BUFFER_SIZE object determines the number of entries in the buffer. By default, this value is set to 200 entries. The parameter value is factored when the number of 200 entries is exceeded. According to SAP, the value should be between 200 and 1,000 entries.

7 Analyzing the Database, Memory, and Hardware

This chapter shows you how to systematically analyze the database, memory, and hardware in SAP systems. You'll learn about methods for monitoring database and storage parameters, as well as options for identifying performance problems.

When analyzing SAP BW systems, you should always consider the database, memory, and hardware on which the SAP system is based. By analyzing these areas, you'll get an insight into how your SAP BW system uses the available memory, database, and hardware resources, and where resource bottlenecks can occur.

Because using an SAP BW system differs from using an online analytical processing (OLTP) system (R/3) when it comes to memory and database usage, this chapter will indicate, wherever possible, how you can set parameters for a BW system regarding memory, database, and hardware resources. The stated values are only a rough approximation and should therefore be treated as initial settings before production startup. For that reason, you should correct the parameterization of your system after production startup, if necessary, and adapt it to the actual requirements.

In particular, the system values described here do not replace the SAP support services, such as the GoingLive Check or the Early Watch contract for SAP BW systems!

The performance analysis tools introduced in this chapter are part of the SAP performance monitors. All SAP performance monitors can be called using Transaction STUN. Figure 7.1 gives you an overview of the most important analysis tools.

SAP performance monitors

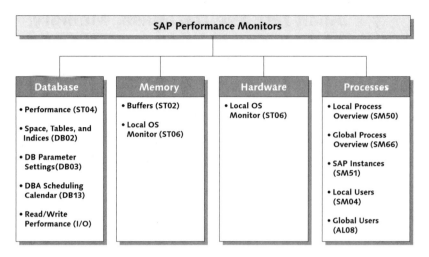

Figure 7.1 SAP Performance Monitors

7.1 Analyzing the Database

Before we start dealing with the analysis of database parameters, we will first explain the terminology used in this context.

7.1.1 Terminology Definitions

The terms computer, application server, database server, SAP instance, and database instance are used in this book as follows:

A *computer* is the physical machine (= physical hardware) with CPU and memory.

An *application server* is a computer running one or more SAP instances.

A *database server* is a computer running one or more database instances.

An *SAP instance* is a self-contained administrative unit on a computer, which is accessed by work processes and consists of work processes, dispatchers to manage the work processes, and SAP buffers in the computer's shared memory.

A *database instance* is a self-contained administrative unit on a computer that enables database access and consists of database processes and database buffers in the computer's shared memory. A computer that runs one or more database instances is referred to as a *database server*. A database and an SAP instance can also run concurrently on one computer.

SAP BW can be run on different relational database systems. Eight database systems are supported currently—Oracle, Informix, MS SQL Server, MaxDB (previously SAP DB), IBM DB2 UDB for UNIX and Windows, IBM DB2/400, and IBM DB2/390. Although the architectures of the database systems vary, the SAP system underlying the SAP BW system provides a central database monitor that enables you to analyze the performance data of the underlying database system. On the one hand, the database monitor uses performance data—created by the database system—that can also be accessed via the database-specific monitoring tools. On the other hand, a portion of the performance data is collected directly by the SAP system.

The database monitor can be called via Transaction ST04 (see Figure 7.2). The database parameters are explained using an Oracle database system as an example; the terminology might differ from other database systems.

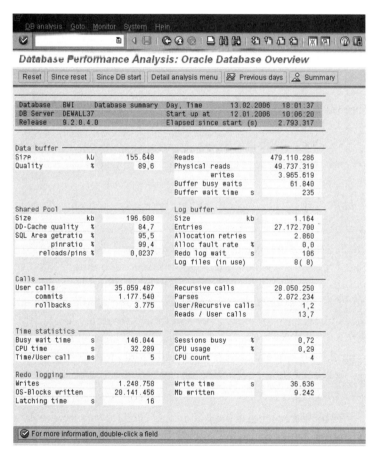

Figure 7.2 Database Performance Monitor (Transaction ST04)

7.1.2 Analyzing the Database Buffers

Database buffers are memory areas where data that has already been selected (table contents, indices, etc.) is kept in readiness in the main memory. When this data is accessed again, you don't need to read it from the disk system; it can be retrieved from the database buffer instead. Database buffers therefore reduce the number of necessary disk accesses and accelerate data access, because the access to an object that is persistent in the main memory is approximately 10 to 100 times faster than the read access to the disk system of the database server.

The buffer names of a database system vary depending on the manufacturer. The memory areas described below are explained using the example of the Oracle database system. The Oracle database system distinguishes between shared memory, a memory area that can be addressed by all Oracle processes, and process local memory that is assigned to exactly one process.

System Global Area

The *System Global Area* (SGA) is a memory area in the shared memory that is allocated during the startup of the database instance in the main memory of the database server. The most important memory areas of SGA are:

▶ The *data buffer* (also called buffer pool or data cache) where the data blocks are buffered

▶ The *shared pool* (also called shared SQL area, shared cursor cache, or library cache) where parsed SQL statements and Oracle DDIC information are stored

▶ The *log buffer* (also called a redo buffer) where the redo log files are stored

Program Global Area

Besides the System Global Area, there is another memory area, the Program Global Area (PGA), which provides process local memory that can be assigned to only one database process. The most important memory area in the PGA is the *sort buffer* (also called *sort and hash area*) where sortings, hash joins, bitmap operations, and other temporary local memory requests are processed (e.g., when parsing SQL statements). The sort buffer is critical for the query performance and should therefore be set to a sufficient size, because many sorting processes have to be carried out during query execution.

Data buffer

The *data buffer* (or data cache) is the buffer area used for caching the data blocks of database tables that were recently read from the hard disk and their respective indices. An SAP work process does not read the data directly from the hard disk but from the data buffer. Therefore, all data read from the database is first written into this buffer area. The data buffer stores data in so-called *blocks* or *pages* that are sized between 2 KB and 32 KB, depending on the database and operating system. The data is always read from the hard disk in blocks or pages, respectively. The data buffer memory is managed via the so-called *Least Recently Used* (LRU) algorithm. This algorithm ensures that the most frequently used data blocks are retained in the memory.

To determine the quality of the data buffer, you use the number of data blocks that can be read directly from the data buffer without accessing the hard disk. The number of read accesses from the data buffer is called *reads*. Whenever a work process requests a data block that is already stored in the data buffer, a *hit* is registered for the buffer. If the requested data block is not stored in the data buffer, it must be read from the hard disk. The database blocks that are physically read from the disk are referred to as the *physical reads*.

The *hit ratio* is therefore calculated as follows:

Hit ratio (%) = (reads / (reads + physical reads)) x 100

The higher the number of read accesses from the data buffer (*reads*) in relation to the physical read accesses (*physical reads*), the better the buffer quality. A hit ratio of 100% indicates that all read accesses could be answered from the main memory of the database instance and did not have to be read from the disk.

For the data buffer, you can determine the following parameters using Transaction ST04 (see Figure 7.2 using the example of an SAP BW system based on the Oracle database system):

▶ The size of the database buffer is 155.6 MB. The size of the data buffer is calculated by multiplying the block size (db_block_size) with the number of database block buffers (db_block_buffers) specified in the parameter file *init<SID>.ora*. In most Oracle-based SAP BW systems, a default size of 8,192 bytes is used for the block size, which must be determined when creating the database and cannot be changed at a later stage. The size of the database block buffer can be adapted to meet the operation requirements at any time. In SAP BW 3.x systems, the database block buffer should never be smaller than 9,000 blocks (approximately 70 MB). As of SAP Release 6.40 and Oracle 9i, the db_cache_size parameter is used as the default instead of db_block_buffers. In these cases, db_block_buffer may no longer be used.[1] The `db_cache_size` parameter should not be smaller than 70,000,000 bytes.

▶ The data buffer quality is 82.3%. In a productive SAP BW system, the data buffer quality should not be lower than 95%. To properly evaluate the buffer quality, the database should have run for an adequate period of time after the last startup. The buffer quality may be temporarily low in the SAP BW system, because numerous full table scans (e.g., due to hash joins) can lead to a reduced block hit ratio, a problem that cannot be solved by simply enlarging the buffer.

▶ Since the last startup of the database instance, 76,495,753 blocks have been read from the data buffer.

▶ 13,523,920 blocks had to be read from the hard disk.

▶ 1,288,126 blocks were written to the hard disk by the write process.

▶ In 15,786 cases, there were wait situations when accessing the data blocks.

▶ Altogether, the waiting time amounted to 40 seconds.

The size of the data buffer usually has the greatest impact on database performance. Therefore, you must ensure that the data buffer pool is sufficient in size to keep the number of time-consuming disk accesses as low as possible. For a productive SAP BW system with 200 to 500 users, the data buffer size should be at least 2 GB.

Shared pool As the name implies, the shared pool is a shared memory area containing structures of the data dictionary cache and the shared SQL area (also called the library cache). The data dictionary cache stores information about recently used database objects (tables, views, etc.) that are required by administrators, users, and the database system itself. The shared SQL area (also called the shared cursor cache or shared SQL area) stores the SQL text, the parse trees of SQL statements, and the execution plans.

For the shared pool, you can determine the following parameters by using Transaction ST04 (see Figure 7.2 using the example of an SAP BW system based on the Oracle database system):

---

1 Up to and including Oracle8i (8.1.7.x), the size of the memory areas available in the SGA was fixed (= static) at the start of the instance. The database had to be restarted after the SGA configuration had been changed. Since Oracle9i, most of the buffer areas in the SGA can be dynamically changed at runtime without stopping the database instance. Please refer to SAP Note 617416 for more information on this topic.

- The size of the shared pool is 197 MB. SAP recommends a setting of >= 400 MB for the shared pool. The size of the shared pool is determined by the *init<SID>.ora* parameter `shared_pool_size`.

- In the example shown in Figure 7.2, the data dictionary cache quality is 90.3%; this indicates how often the Oracle data dictionary must be accessed when SQL commands are being processed. In an SAP BW production system, the data dictionary cache quality should always exceed 90%, if possible.

- The quality of accesses to SQL applications in the shared SQL area is measured using the **SQL Area getratio** and **SQL Area pinratio** parameters. Reusing identical SQL applications reduces the system load caused by parsing and loading SQL applications in the memory. While the **SQL Area getratio** parameter determines the number of object requests in the library cache, the **SQL Area pinratio** parameter measures the number of object executions in the library cache. In a productive SAP BW system, this value should be close to 99%.

Please note that the values stated here always apply to a system that has been running for some time and can vary after restarting the system. Therefore, you should check whether the following parameters have been met in a system that is stable:

- DD Cache Quality > 80%
- pinratio >= 95
- reloads/pin <= 0.04
- User/recursive calls >= 2

If these values are not met, the shared pool may be too small and should be increased. For a productive SAP BW system with 200 to 500 users, the shared pool size is approximately 800 MB to 1 GB.

Log buffer

The log buffer (also called the redo log buffer) is the buffer area where all changes to the database are logged. Every data change generates a redo entry in the log buffer that enables you to restore the data changes to an earlier stage when recovering the data. When loading data in SAP BW, for example, a lot of redo entries are generated.

In the example illustrated in Figure 7.2, the size of the redo log buffer is 1,164 KB. The default setting for R/3 systems is usually 320 KB (327,680 bytes); in SAP BW systems, a higher value must be chosen. When setting this parameter, you have to consider that the value must be a multiple of `db_block_size` (default size is 8,192 bytes). The default setting of an R/3 system is therefore 40 × 8,192 bytes = 320 KB. For a productive SAP BW system, the startup configuration should be approximately 150 to 200 times the value of `db_block_size`.

The **Allocation retries** parameter shows the number of failed allocation retries of space in the redo log buffer. This case occurs whenever the Oracle log writer process (LGWR) could not immediately write redo log entries from the buffer to the hard disk, but had to wait for a redo log file change in order to allocate the space.

The **Alloc fault rate** specifies the ratio between the failed allocation retries and the total number of entries in the redo log buffer. This value should not exceed 1%.

Calls **Calls** refer to the total number of queries received by the kernel of the database system since the database instance was started. In Figure 7.2, the following parameters are shown in the **Calls** category:

▶ Since the database instance was started, 8,216,733 calls have been received by the Oracle kernel (**user calls**).

▶ 347,714 **commits** (transactions with Commit) were completed. In case of a commit, all changes made by a transaction are permanently stored in the database instance. Transactions completed with a commit cannot be undone via a **rollback**.

▶ 1,287 rollbacks (rolled back transactions) occurred since the database instance was started. In a rollback, all changes carried out by a transaction are undone in the database instance. Rollbacks are triggered by program errors, application locks, or other application terminations.

▶ **Recursive calls** are SQL statements from the database system that need to be issued, in addition to the SQL statements from the user. To answer the database calls, the system requires administrative information from the database cache. If this information is not available in the database cache, it must be reloaded from the disk using a **recursive call**. Recursive calls can be triggered in the data directory cache by *misses*, for example, and can adversely affect the performance of the database system.

▶ The ratio of recursive calls to user calls is calculated in the **User/Recursive calls** parameter. The number of recursive calls should not exceed the number of user calls. A higher value indicates a bad data buffer hit ratio. The ratio should therefore not fall below a value of 2:1. In most cases, you can resolve the problem by increasing the *init<SID>.ora* parameter `shared_pool_size`.

When evaluating the ratio of recursive calls to user calls, you should note that the value of recursive calls is usually high immediately after starting the database instance, because the data dictionary cache is initially empty and all requests for filling the cache are recursive.

A SQL statement is first parsed before it is executed. During this process, the access strategies are determined and a check is carried out to determine whether the used tables and columns actually exist in the database. The result of the check is stored in the shared cursor cache. When the query is executed again, it will access only this information. The **Parses** value counts how often SQL statements had to be parsed. The ratio of *parses to user calls* specifies the average parsing rate and should not exceed 25%. High parsing rates indicate a problem with retaining the cursor in the shared cursor cache (shared SQL area). In this case, you should check the data dictionary cache quality and increase the size of the shared pool, if necessary.

Parses

The **Reads/User Calls** parameter is the ratio of the blocks read from the data buffer to the total number of database calls since the database instance has been started. It specifies how many blocks have to be read from the data buffer on average in order to answer a database call. In the example shown in Figure 7.2, nine data blocks are read from the data buffer on average to answer a call to the database. The **Reads/User Call** ratio indicates whether the shared SQL area should be analyzed any further. A high value (> 30) suggests expensive and complex queries/SQL statements that should be investigated (see Section 7.1.3).

Reads/User calls

7.1.3   Analyzing the Shared SQL Area

The statistical data in the shared SQL area may, for instance, contain information about the number of executions of a SQL statement or the number of logical and physical reads per SQL statement. The SQL statements are stored in the shared SQL area. To analyze the statistical data of the shared SQL area, start the main screen of the database monitor (Transaction ST04) and follow the **Detail analysis menu · SQL request menu**.[2]

---

2 The term *SQL Request* is used in the Oracle database system and can be different in other databases.

After you confirm the following screen in which you can set more restrictions, a list of SQL statements, for which the database has been keeping statistics in readiness since the database has been started, is displayed (see Figure 7.3).

Figure 7.3 Analyzing Statistical Data of the Shared SQL Area (Oracle) (I)

For every SQL statement, the list contains, among others, the following fields (Table 7.1):

Monitor Column	Description
Executions	Number of executions of the SQL statement since the database has been started
Disk Reads	Total number of physical reads that were required for all executions of the SQL statement
Reads/Exec	Average number of physical reads that were required for one execution of the SQL statement
Buffer Gets	Total number of logical reads that were required for all executions of the SQL statement
Bgets/Exec	Average number of logical reads that were required for one execution of the SQL statement

Table 7.1 Fields in the Database Monitor of the Shared SQL Area (Oracle)

Monitor Column	Description
Rows/Proc	Number of rows that were read for all executions of the SQL statement
Rows/Exec	Average number of rows that were read for one execution of the SQL statement
CPU Time	Total CPU time in microseconds that was required for all executions of the SQL statement
CPU Time/Exec	Average CPU time that was required per execution of the SQL statement
Program Name	Name of the program that executed the SQL statement

Table 7.1 Fields in the Database Monitor of the Shared SQL Area (Oracle) (cont.)

For a complete detail view of a SQL statement, double-click on the statistical data record. SQL statements with high CPU or I/O usage can be identified by their high number of logical or physical read accesses. For this purpose, sort the list in descending order by **Buffer Gets** or **Disk Reads** to identify the CPU or I/O-intensive statements. Performance-intensive SQL statements are those that cause more than 5% of all logical or physical reads. You can determine which proportion of all logical or physical accesses are performed with a SQL statement by dividing the **Buffer Gets** of a SQL statement in the shared SQL area by the **Reads** in the main screen of the database monitor, or by dividing the **Disk Reads** of a SQL statement in the shared SQL area by the **Physical Reads** in the main screen of the database monitor.

Performance-intensive SQL statements

If performance-intensive SQL statements are identified they should be examined further. Double-click on the row with the SQL statement (see Figure 7.4).

Using the **DDIC Info** buttons in the detail view you can display information about the viewed dictionary object (table, view), **Explain** lets you view the access strategy, and **ABAP display** shows the source text of the last ABAP program.

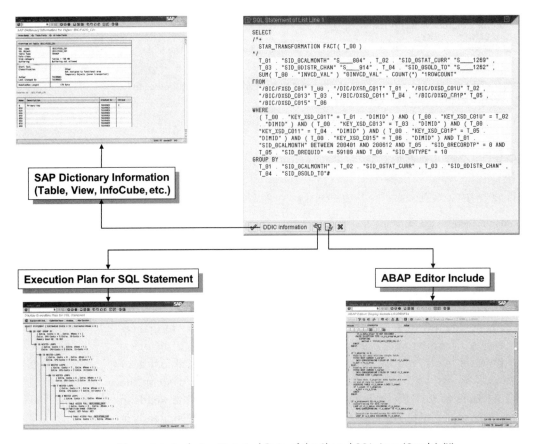

Figure 7.4 Analyzing Statistical Data of the Shared SQL Area (Oracle) (II)

7.1.4 Analyzing the Table Scans

The database performance monitor (Transaction ST04) enables you to monitor the table access methods. Under the **Table Scans** category you can check how many complete table scans (*full table scans*) have been carried out since the start of the database instance. A full table scan is always required when the entire table is read, instead of using an index to find the requested data.

Short/long tables When monitoring table accesses, the database performance monitor distinguishes between short and long tables. *Short tables* are tables with a depth of less than five data blocks; *long tables* comprise five Oracle data blocks and more.

The **Short table scans** value shows the total number of full table scans performed in short tables. For very short tables, a full table scan is often preferable to searching via an index, because at least two tables need to be read during an index search (index table and data table).

The **Long table scans** value specifies the number of full table scans for tables with five or more data blocks. For long tables, searching via an index is usually preferable to doing the full table scan, so this value should be as low as possible.

The total of both values (*short table scans + long table scans*) specifies the total number of full table scans since the database instance has been started. The share of the long table scans in all table scans (*long table scans/(short table scans + long table scans) × 100*) should not exceed 1% in a production system. A large portion of long table scans can indicate faulty or missing indices, which should be investigated further.

7.1.5 Analyzing the Sorting Processes

Certain SQL statements within a query force the sorting of table data. These include the SQL operations ORDER BY, GROUP BY, and SORT MERGE JOIN. The creation of an index also requires that the data be sorted. In the database performance monitor, you can check the number of sorting processes.

The **Memory** parameter specifies the number of sorting processes that could be performed in memory since the database was started. The **Disk** parameter can be used to determine how many sorting operations had to be performed on the disk system. The memory portion for sorting operations is determined by the *init<SID>.ora* parameter sort_area_size. The memory set in this parameter is assigned to every database process that carries out a sorting operation. Therefore, the memory requirements in production systems can increase very quickly. Sorting operations requiring more memory than is available are performed in a temporary segment on the hard disk. SAP systems use the PSAPTEMP tablespace for these segments.

Memory/Disk sort

Sorting the data in memory is a lot faster than sorting the data on the hard disk. This is why the ratio of disk sortings (**Disk**) to memory sortings (**Memory**) should not exceed five percent. Because SAP BW queries can consume a large amount of process local memory for sorting operations, you must ensure that the *init<SID>.ora* parameter sort_area_size is sufficiently sized for high-performing queries. An initial start value should not be lower than 10 MB.

The most important database parameters of the System Global Area and the Program Global Area are listed in Table 7.2. The recommended settings are based on the Oracle database system and should be regarded as initial start values. Please note that a hardware sizing of your system is always required before production startup to determine the values of the parameters `db_block_buffers` and `shared_pool_size`. To set more database parameters of an SAP BW system, you should also refer to the SAP Notes listed in the Appendix (see Chapter 14).

Memory area	DB parameter	Typical setting
System Global Area	DB_BLOCK_BUFFERS	>= 2 GB
	DB_CACHE_SIZE[3]	>= 70,000,000
	SHARED_POOL_SIZE	>= 400 MB
	LOG_BUFFER	1,048,576 (= 1 MB)
Program Global Area	SORT_AREA_SIZE	10,485,760 (= 10 MB)
	HASH_AREA_SIZE	2 × SORT_AREA_SIZE
	BITMAP_MERGE_AREA_SIZE	33,554,432 (= 32 MB)
	CREATE_BITMAP_AREA_SIZE	33,554,432 (= 32 MB)
	PGA_AGGREGATE_TARGET[4]	20% of the main memory of the database server (40% for a standalone database server). Under NT or W2K, respectively, not more than 600 MB.

Table 7.2 BW Settings of Some DB Parameters

7.1.6 Analyzing the Database Buffers

The various buffers of a database store user data (table contents) and administrative information of the database in the main memory to reduce disk access. Since accessing objects in the main memory is approximately 10 to 100 times faster than accessing the hard disk, the analysis of data buffers should be part of every performance analysis.

Information about monitoring the database buffers can be retrieved via the database monitor (Transaction ST04). The database monitor shown in

---

3 Please also refer to Footnote 1 in Section 7.1.2 and SAP Note 617416 when using the dynamic SGA.
4 Please also refer to SAP Note 619876 when using the automatic PGA management.

Figure 7.2 is based on the Oracle database system. The database buffer terminology can differ from other database systems.[5]

An Oracle database instance allocates memory in the following areas:

▶ In the *data buffer* (Data Buffer: Size field) that is allocated as shared memory

▶ In the *shared pool* (Shared Pool: Size field) that is allocated as shared memory

▶ In the *log buffer* (Log Buffer: Size field) that stores redo log entries of the database

▶ Program Global Area (PGA) where process local memory is allocated that can be assigned to only one database process. The most important memory area in the PGA is the sort buffer (also called *sort and hash area*) where sortings, hash joins, bitmap operations, and other temporary local memory requests are processed (e.g., when parsing SQL statements).

The memory requirements of the database instance can be determined using the database monitor (Transaction ST04) as described in the following. The following rule applies to an Oracle database system:

Memory requirements of the database instance

Virtually required memory =

> *data buffer: size*
> *+ shared pool: size*
> *+ log buffer: size*
> *+ 5 MB × number of work processes in the entire system*
> *+ 50 MB*

7.1.7 Analyzing Memory, Tables and Indices

Information about the population level of the database and about the data objects (tables and indices) can be accessed using Transaction DB02.

The performance values displayed via Transaction DB02 in the example illustrated in Figure 7.5 are based on the statistical data from the database. The time of the last statistics analysis can be obtained from the DB performance monitor. The statistics can be updated using the **Refresh** button. In the shown example there are seven tablespaces set up on the

---

5 You can find an overview of the database buffers of the most commonly used database systems in *SAP Performance Optimization* (4th edition, SAP PRESS 2005) by Thomas Schneider.

Oracle database system. The memory used by the tablespaces amounts to 84,633,600 KB (= 80.71 GB), 6% of free memory capacity (or 5,425,152 KB = 5.17 GB) is still available in the database. The allocation of the disk capacity by the individual tablespaces can be called using the **Current Sizes** button (see Figure 7.6).

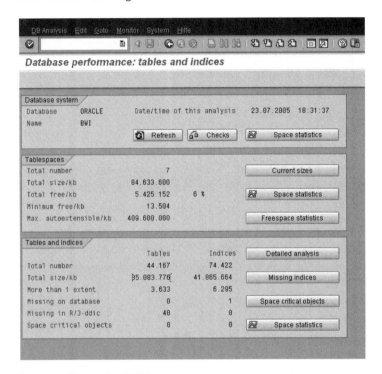

Figure 7.5 Transaction DB02

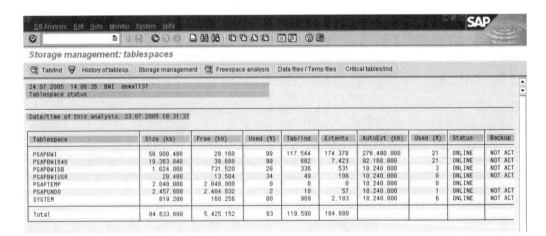

Figure 7.6 Memory Requirements of the Tablespaces

The tablespaces storage management view shown in Figure 7.6 contains the following parameters (see Table 7.3):

Field	Description
Tablespace	Name of the tablespace
Size (kb)	Memory occupied by the tablespace
Free (kb)	Free memory in the tablespace
Used (%)	Percentage of memory occupied by the tablespace
Tab/ind	Number of tables/indices in the tablespace
Extents	Number of extents. Extents are consecutive sets of data blocks grouped in segments.
AutoExt (kb)	Size of the AutoExtend functionality. As of Oracle 8, tablespaces can be set to **autoextensible**. The tablespaces are increased automatically, if necessary. The specified size is the maximum size in KB up to which a tablespace can be extended.
Used (%)	Percentage of memory occupied by the **autoextensible** tablespaces
Status	Status of the tablespace (ONLINE/OFFLINE)
Backup	Setting that determines whether the backup function for the tablespace is enabled.

Table 7.3 Parameter Storage Management of Tablespaces

You should pay special attention to the PSAPTEMP tablespace. Massive I/O operations are executed in this tablespace when running queries and database operations like sorting and aggregation. The need for additional temporary tablespace increases when running parallel processes such as the parallel processing of multiprovider queries or the parallel building of aggregates. The temporary tablespace should be at least twice as large as the largest fact table and no smaller than 2 GB. If the planned database exceeds 50 GB, the temporary tablespace should be able to hold at least 10 GB. Depending on the number of key figures, the need for temporary tablespace can increase considerably and amount to a size that far exceeds the fact table.

Tablespace PSAPTEMP

You can also analyze the memory requirements of individual tables and their indices on the database using Transaction DB02. In the view shown in Figure 7.7, the **Tab/Ind** button can be used to determine the size of a table as well as its indices ❶.

Analyzing individual tables and indices

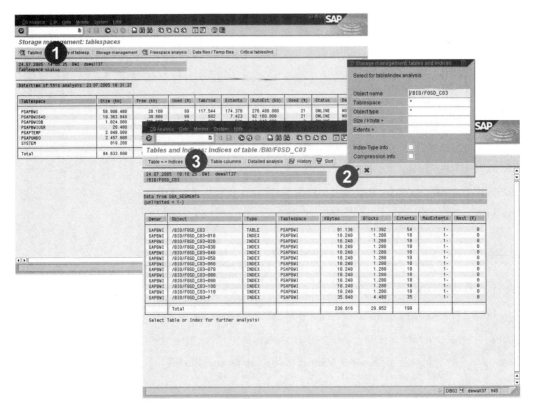

Figure 7.7 Analyzing the Memory Requirements of Tables and Indices

Using the **Tab/Ind** button ❶, the input mask for selecting a table in the tablespace is called ❷. After the technical name of the table has been entered, the size of the table is returned in KB. Via the **Table <-> Indices** button ❸ the size of the table and its indices is listed.

Analyzing the indices The status of the indices created on the database or defined in the ABAP dictionary, respectively, can also be accessed via Transaction DB02. After the transaction has been called, the **Tables and Indices** category in the screen shown in Figure 7.8 displays the number of tables and indices created on the database, the size in KB, and the number of missing indices on the database or in the ABAP dictionary, respectively. Missing indices are a scenario that should be analyzed immediately, because they can be a significant reason for bad system performance.

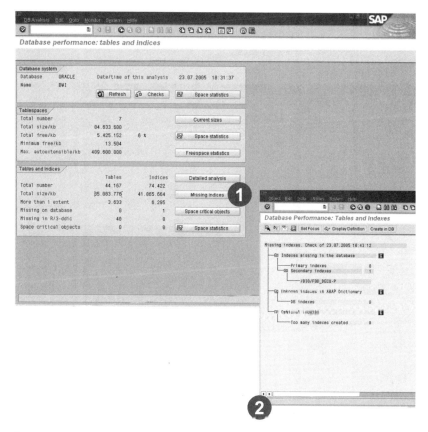

Figure 7.8 Analyzing Missing Indices

The analysis of missing indices is started using the **Missing Indices** button (❶ in Figure 7.8). The following screen lists the indices missing on the database or in the ABAP dictionary ❷. Please note that the indices status displayed in Transaction DB02 is always based on the last database check, the date that appears in the upper part of the screen. If a current database status is required, the Refresh function can be run to check the statistics data of the database. For more information on analyzing and repairing indices, see Section 9.4.1.

7.1.8 Checking the DB Parameters

The configuration of all database parameters can be checked using Transaction DB03 (see Figure 7.9).

Figure 7.9 Checking the DB Parameters (Transaction DB03)

After calling Transaction DB03, all active database parameters of the system are listed together with their settings on the system. The **History of file** button ❶ lets you determine the change date and the previous system value of the DB parameters ❷. The same can be achieved via the **Select Period** function, which you can use to determine the changed DB parameter values starting from a key date to be entered. To set the DB parameters, also read SAP Note 567745 and the SAP Notes for setting the DB parameters listed in the appendix of this book.

7.1.9 DBA Planning Calendar

The DBA Planning Calendar enables you to control and automate regular database administration actions. For example, you can schedule database backups and the creation of database statistics and run them automatically via the DBA Planning Calendar. To set up an automatic execution of the administration jobs, you must set the start time and the specific task required in the calendar.

The DBA Planning Calendar is part of the Computing Center Management System (CCMS) and can be called via Transaction DB13 (see Figure 7.10).

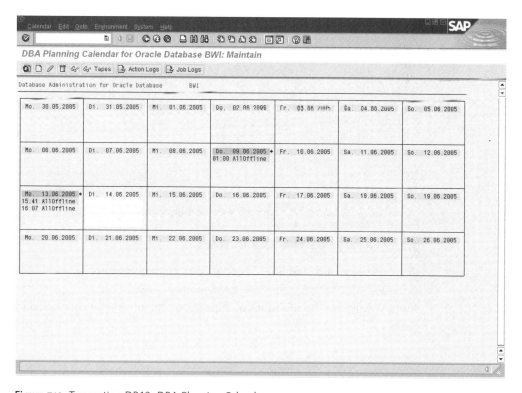

Figure 7.10 Transaction DB13: DBA Planning Calendar

For more information on the DBA Planning Calendar, see Section 9.7.4.

7.2 Analyzing the SAP Memory Areas

The SAP memory areas can be monitored via the SAP memory management monitor. The SAP memory management monitor is started via Transaction ST02. The main screen **Tune Summary** is displayed (see Figure 7.11).

The main screen of the SAP memory management monitor shows information about the configuration and usage of the SAP buffers, the SAP roll area, the SAP paging area, and the extended memory and heap memory areas. Note that all data specified in the monitor has been valid since the start of the SAP instance.

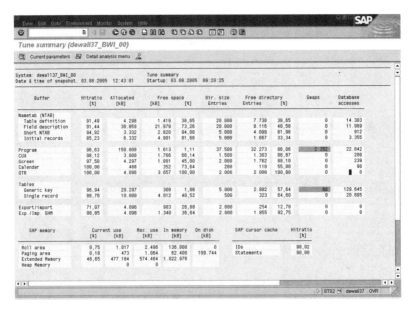

Figure 7.11 SAP Memory Management Monitor Main Screen (Tune Summary)

7.2.1 Analyzing the SAP Buffers

The main screen of the SAP memory management monitor (Figure 7.11) provides information about the configuration, utilization, and quality of the SAP buffers. The monitor columns show the information specified in Table 7.4.

Monitor Column	Description
Buffer	Name of the SAP buffer
Hitratio [%]	Hit ratio of the buffer. Measurement for the buffer quality, that is, how often data could be retrieved from the buffer. Identical to the definition of the database buffer described in Section 7.1.2.
Allocated [KB]	Memory of the respective buffer that is allocated when the SAP instance is started. In reality, the memory that can be occupied is smaller than the allocated memory due to the space necessary for managing the buffer.

Table 7.4 Columns in the SAP Memory Management Monitor

Monitor Column	Description
Free Space	Free space in the respective buffer. This is the difference between **Available** and **Used** in the detail analysis of the respective buffer.
Dir. size Entries	Maximum number of entries in the buffer
Free directory Entries	Number of free buffer entries
Swaps	Number of swaps from the buffer to the swap space
Database accesses	Number of database accesses for populating the respective buffer

Table 7.4 Columns in the SAP Memory Management Monitor (cont.)

A detail analysis can be called for every buffer by double-clicking on the buffer or by clicking on the **Detail analysis menu** button (see Figure 7.12).

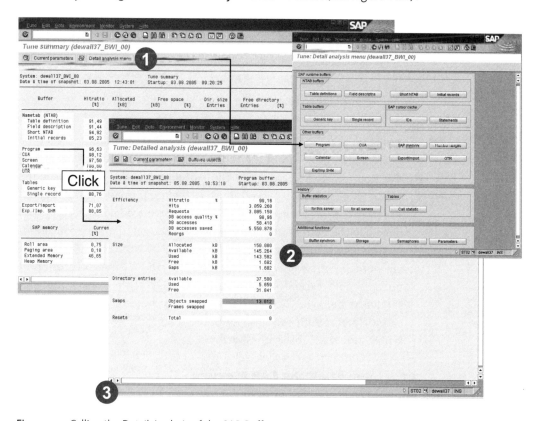

Figure 7.12 Calling the Detail Analysis of the SAP Buffer

The SAP buffer quality (**Hit ratio**) should always reach a certain level to enable a high-performing and stable operation. Buffers that are too small cause frequent swaps of the buffer objects, which leads to time-consuming read processes on the database and unnecessary performance problems.

SAP buffer quality When analyzing the SAP buffers, you should consider the following:

▶ The buffer quality (**Hit ratio**) should always be higher than 98% in a production system. Exceptions are the export/import buffer, the program buffer, and the single-record buffer. For these buffers, the hit ratios may be lower.

▶ Ideally, swaps should not occur in a production system. If swaps are detected, the buffer or the maximum number of buffer entries should be increased. In an SAP BW system, an exception to this rule is the program buffer, for which a higher number of swaps can be tolerated and seldom avoided, because the reusability of information stored in the program buffer is clearly lower than it is in an R/3 system. Up to 5,000 swaps per day are acceptable.

▶ The program buffer in SAP BW 2.x and 3.x systems should be set to a minimum of 300 MB and not be smaller than 200 MB.

▶ The export/import buffer is intensely used in SAP BW systems. If you're working with complex hierarchies in BW, the buffer should be clearly increased beyond the recommended size of 40 MB (as of SAP BW 3.x). As of Release 4.6B, the ABAP List Viewer (ALV) uses the export/import buffer for optimizing the performance. The objects stored in the export/import buffer are not removed automatically, but remain in the buffer until the system is shut down. If other applications use the export/import buffer, or if the buffers are too small, an increasing number of swaps can occur. The hit ratio of the export/import buffer should exceed 80%. If possible, 10% of the total buffer size should be free, and 10% of free directories should be available. If the export/import buffer swaps a lot (more than 1,000 swaps per day), the buffer should be enlarged as well.

7.2.2 Analyzing the SAP Memory

In the main screen of the SAP memory management monitor (Figure 7.4), in the **SAP Memory** section, you can find information about the SAP memory areas **roll area**, **paging area**, **extended memory**, and **heap memory**. The meaning of each column is listed in Table 7.5.

Monitor Column	Description
Current Use	Size of the currently used memory in KB or %
Max. use	Maximum size of the used memory in KB since the SAP instance has been started (high water mark)
In Memory	Size of the allocated memory (= SAP roll buffer or SAP paging buffer for the roll or paging area, respectively)
On disk	Size of the SAP roll file and SAP paging file on the hard disk of the application server

Table 7.5 Columns in the SAP Memory Management Monitor

When analyzing the SAP memory areas, you should determine two important key figures for evaluating the memory situation of the SAP instance:

1. Ratio between **max. use** and **in memory** of the **roll area**: The **max. use** value should be smaller than the **in memory** value, that is the roll file should not be used (on disk = 0).

2. Ratio between **max. use** and **in memory** of the **extended memory**: The **max. use** value should be at least 20% smaller than the **in memory** value, that is even at peak times there should be 20% of extended memory available. If both values have almost the same size the extended memory must be enlarged (profile parameter `em/initial_size_MB`).

If the role memories or the SAP extended memory reach or exceed the configured memory size, you can increase the values of the SAP profile parameters `rdisp/ROLL_SHM` or `em/initial_size_MB`. For setting the SAP memory and SAP buffer, please also read the SAP Notes 192658 and 103747. Generally, the system should provide sufficient main memory reserves; otherwise, there is the risk of a memory bottleneck. A description of all profile parameters and default values, as well as the admissible minimum and maximum values can be called via Transaction RZ11, or by using the **Current Parameters** button in the SAP memory management monitor.

7.2.3 Analyzing the Allocated Memory and the Main Memory

When analyzing the main memory, you should check the ratio between the memory allocated by the SAP system and the main memory (RAM) that is physically available.

You can obtain an overview of the memory usage via the SAP memory management monitor (Transaction ST02) using **Detail analysis menu · Storage**. The **Storage usage and requirements** screen is displayed (see Figure 7.13).

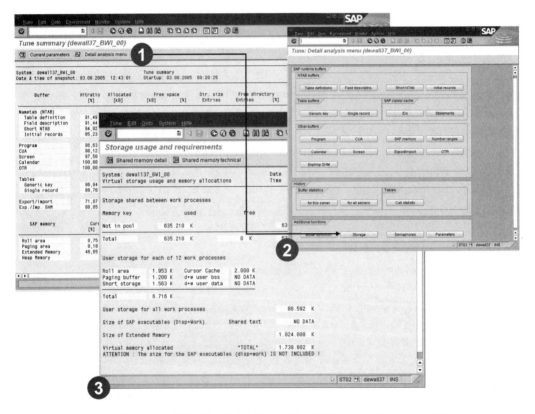

Figure 7.13 Calling the Detail View of the SAP Memory Management Monitor

The total memory allocated on the computer can be calculated by adding up the following memory areas:

1. Virtual memory allocated: This is the memory allocated by an SAP instance during system startup (see Figure 7.13). If several SAP instances reside on one computer, the values of every SAP instance need to be added up.

2. Virtual database memory if a database is stored on the computer (see Section 7.1.6)

3. Main memory requirements of the operating system, which can be roughly calculated as approximately 100 MB

Compare the sum of the allocated memory to the physically existing memory (RAM). Information about the main memory can be found in the main screen of the operating system monitor (Transaction ST06) in the **Memory** section (**Physical Mem avail Kb** field, see Figure 7.14):

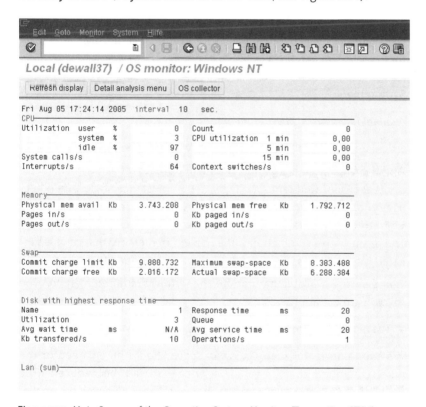

Figure 7.14 Main Screen of the Operating System Monitor (Transaction ST06)

In this comparison, you'll usually find that the allocated memory is somewhat larger than the physically existing memory. As long as the allocated memory is not more than 50% larger than the physical memory, this proportion is non-critical.

7.2.4 Analyzing the Swap Space

In another step, you can use the operating system monitor to determine whether your system has a sufficient amount of swap space.

In the **Swap** section (**Configured Swap Kb** or **Commit charge llmit Kb** field under Windows NT), you can find the currently allocated swap space. Generally, the swap space should be approximately three times as large as the physical main memory and at least 3.5 GB.

Your system should always have enough swap space; otherwise, there is always the risk that the system will run into a memory bottleneck that will cause serious program terminations.

To check whether your system has enough swap space, you can do the following:

1. Calculate the available memory: Add up the physically available main memory (RAM) and the available swap space. Both values can be found in the main screen of the operating system monitor via Transaction ST06 (Figure 7.14).

   Available memory = physical memory + swap space

2. Calculate the virtually required memory as described in Section 7.2.3.

3. Add the **Maximum heap area for all work processes** value (main memory that is allocated temporarily by the SAP instance at startup, if necessary) to the virtually required memory. This value is identical to the SAP profile parameter `abap/heap_area_total` (see also Section 4.2). The result of this summation is the maximum memory that can be allocated by the SAP system, the database, and the operating system.

4. Compare the available memory to the virtually required memory. The following must apply:

   Virtually required memory < available memory (RAM + swap space)

If this condition is not met, the swap space should be enlarged or the required memory `abap/heap_area_total` should be reduced. The `abap/heap_area_total` parameter, however, should never be smaller than 600 MB.

7.3　Analyzing the Hardware

The main screen of the operating system monitor (Transaction ST06, Figure 7.14) lets you determine the most important parameters about the CPU and main memory utilization.

The operating system monitor data is collected via the operating system collector SAPOSCOL. SAPOSCOL is a standalone program running in the operating system background and collecting data about operating system resources like:

Operating system collector SAPOSCOL

▶ Usage of virtual and physical memory
▶ CPU utilization
▶ Utilization of physical disks and file systems
▶ Resource usage of running processes

By default, the data is collected and recorded by SAPOSCOL every 10 seconds. In addition, the program records the hourly average values of the last 24 hours.

The **CPU** section of the operating system monitor provides information about the user, the system, and about periods during which the CPU has no task to execute or is waiting for input/output (*idle*).

Analyzing the CPU utilization

The information available in the CPU section is listed in Table 7.6.

Monitor Column	Description
Utilization user	Percentage of CPU used by user processes (SAP system, database, etc.)
Utilization system	Percentage of CPU used by the operating system
Utilization idle	Percentage of free CPU capacity waiting for input/output
Count	Number of CPUs (processors)
CPU utilization (Load average)	Average number of waiting processes during the last minute, the last five minutes, and the last fifteen minutes. This is the number of processes per CPU that reside in a queue before being assigned to a free CPU.
Physical mem avail Kb	Physically available main memory (RAM)

Table 7.6 Fields of the Operating System Monitor

7.3.1 Analyzing CPU or Main Memory Bottlenecks

To analyze a CPU bottleneck, you should first observe the CPU utilization of the last 24 hours. Using the **Detail analysis menu · Previous 24 hours: CPU** button, you can obtain an overview of the CPU utilization during the previous 24 hours (see Figure 7.15).

Local (dewall37) / CPU Last 24 Hours

Graphics by column

Mon Feb 13 17:58:35 2006

Hour	CPU utilization in %			Interrupts	System calls	Context switches
	User	System	Idle	/h	/h	/h
17	2	3	95	232.186	0	0
16	2	3	96	235.800	0	0
15	2	3	95	232.213	0	0
14	2	3	95	234.000	0	0
13	2	3	95	232.200	0	0
12	2	3	95	233.972	0	0
11	2	3	96	235.813	0	0
10	2	3	95	232.213	0	0
9	2	3	95	233.972	0	0
8	2	3	96	235.800	0	0
7	2	3	95	234.027	0	0
6	2	3	95	232.186	0	0
5	2	3	96	235.800	0	0
4	2	3	95	232.213	0	0
3	2	3	95	233.972	0	0
2	2	3	96	235.800	0	0
1	2	3	95	234.027	0	0
0	2	3	95	232.186	0	0
23	2	3	96	235.800	0	0
22	2	3	95	232.200	0	0
21	2	3	96	235.800	0	0
20	2	3	95	232.213	0	0
19	2	3	95	233.972	0	0
18	2	3	96	235.800	0	0

Figure 7.15 CPU Utilization During the Last 24 Hours

On an hourly average, the available CPU capacity **CPU utilization idle** should be at least 20%. Over a longer period, no less than 20% free CPU capacity should be available. The current CPU utilization can be obtained via the **Detail analysis menu · CPU** button. If you observe a high CPU utilization, you should use the operating system monitor to identify the programs that cause the highest CPU load. The overview of operating system processes can be displayed via **Detail analysis menu · Top CPU**. This overview shows the currently active processes and their resource utilization. SAP work processes can be identified by the command name "disp+work" (Windows NT) or "dw_<instance>" (UNIX). Database processes can usually be identified by the database name (Oracle, Informix, etc.) within the command name.

If you observe an SAP work process causing a high CPU load over a longer period, you should also start the SAP work process monitor (Transaction SM50) to identify the program name and the user (see also Section 7.4). If a database process shows a high CPU utilization over a longer period, you should start the database process monitor to identify the SQL statement causing this utilization.

With regard to the average number of waiting processes per CPU (**CPU utilization**, **Load average**) you should be aware that a CPU resource bottleneck might be impending if there are three processes on average per available CPU. A high **CPU utilization** combined with a high CPU usage can indicate that too many processes are active on the server. Along with a low CPU usage, a high CPU utilization can indicate that the main memory is too small. In this case, the processes are waiting due to a high paging rate.

CPU utilization

In addition to the CPU capacity you should also observe the paging rate of the physical main memory. For this purpose, in the **Detail analysis menu · Previous 24 hours: Memory** detail view, compare the paged in and paged out rates (KB/h) to the available physical main memory. Usually, the paging is non-critical if less than 20% of the physical main memory is paged per hour. If you observe very high paging rates, you should calculate the main memory allocated by the SAP instances and the database (see Section 7.2.3, *Analyzing the Allocated Memory and the Main Memory*).

Paging rate

> Note that in contrast to UNIX-based systems, Windows-based systems page preemptively, even if there are still resources available in memory. Therefore, for Windows-based systems, the page-in rates are relevant, while for UNIX-based systems, the page-out rates should be considered when evaluating paging rates.

7.3.2 Analyzing I/O Problems

Information about disk utilization can be found in the operating system monitor (Transaction ST06) under **Detail analysis menu · Disk**. The individual disks are listed along with the information described in Table 7.7. A double-click on a single line lists the average response times of the selected disk during the previous 24 hours.

Monitor Column	Description
Disk	Device name of the disk
Resp.	Average response time of the disk in milliseconds (ms)
Util.	Percentage of the time during which the disk is busy
Wait	Wait time of the disk in milliseconds (ms) while a request remains in the queue
Serv.	Service time in milliseconds (ms) for an input/output
Kbyte	Kilobytes transferred per second
Oper.	Number of disk operations per second

Table 7.7 Disk Monitor Information

The disk with the highest response time is also displayed in the main screen of the operating system monitor together with the information listed in Table 7.7.

I/O bottleneck A potential I/O bottleneck exists when individual disks are experiencing an average utilization of more than 50% (**Util.** > 50%) over a longer period. The high utilization is critical particularly when these disks contain data files that are frequently used. These files include the operating system swap space, as well as the database logging; for example, the redo log files in the Oracle database system. Ideally, the disk response time should not exceed 10 milliseconds, or not considerably exceed this value over a longer period. If this occurs, the hardware partner should be asked to check the disks and the disk controller.

7.4 Analyzing the SAP Work Processes

Most of the processes executed by an SAP system are carried out via SAP work processes. A work process is a process that executes an application written in ABAP as a component of an application server. To process requests from several frontends, the SAP requests are collected by the dispatcher of the SAP application server and transferred to the appropriate work processes for processing.

The following types of work processes exist:

Work Process Type	Description
DIA	Work process for executing dialog processes like SAP BW query execution and delta loads
UPD	Work process for processing update requests
BTC	Work process for processing background jobs (batch jobs) like SAP BW data import processes, data deletion, aggregation, and request compression
ENQ	Work process for executing lock operations (enqueue)
SPO	Work process for processing spool jobs like print formatting
UP2	Work process for processing V2 update requests

Table 7.8 SAP Work Process Types

The work processes can be devoted to individual application servers. Via Transaction SM51, you can list all SAP servers set up on the computer. By double-clicking on the server, you can open the SAP work process monitor (Transaction SM50, see Figure 7.16).

Figure 7.16 Overview of SAP Servers (Transaction SM51) and SAP Work Processes (Transaction SM50)

For the entire runtime of the SAP system, every work process remains logged on to the database system as a user. For the duration of a dialog step, ABAP programs are assigned one work process each. Additionally, the dispatcher tries to process as many dialog steps of *one* user as possible within *one* work process to avoid having to reload the roll area of the user.

The SAP work process monitor (Transaction SM50) always shows a snapshot of the current state of the work processes on the SAP application server to which you are logged on. The display can be updated using the **Refresh** function (F8), which gives you a quick overview of the utilization and the state of the work processes configured on the SAP system.

The work process monitor provides the following information:

Work Process Monitor Column	Description
No.	Internal work process number. This number is also stored in the list of system logs so that there is a unique reference to a work process.
Type	Work process type. See also Table 7.8.
PID	Work process ID in the operating system.
Status	Current status of the work process. The system distinguishes between the following status types: ▶ **Running**: Job is being processed. ▶ **Waiting**: Process is waiting for a job and is available. ▶ **On hold**: Process is being held for a single user; the work process can serve only a single user. Many processes with this status affect the system performance. ▶ **Terminated**: Process was terminated due to an error.
Reason	This field indicates the reason why a work process is on hold. If this column shows the PRIV entry, the workspace is reserved for a specific user (see also Section 4.2).
Start	This field specifies if the process is to be restarted after it was prematurely terminated.
Err	This field specifies how often the work process was cancelled.
Sem	This field specifies the number of the semaphore for which the work process is waiting.
CPU	Cumulative CPU time in seconds and hundredths of a second since a work process has been started. The CPU time must be called via the **CPU** button.
Time	This field specifies how much time a work process already spent on a dialog step that is being processed (current runtime of a job in seconds).

Table 7.9 Contents of the Work Process Monitor

Work Process Monitor Column	Description
Report	Name of the ABAP report or program currently run by the work process.
Client	Client of the session that is currently run.
User	Name of the user whose requests are currently processed.
Action	Name of the action currently performed by the work process.
Table	Name of the database table being accessed.

Table 7.9 Contents of the Work Process Monitor (cont.)

When analyzing the work process monitor, you should first observe the work processes over a period of time (**Refresh** button) to discern whether all work processes of one type (for example, dialog) are busy (**Running** status). See Figure 7.17.

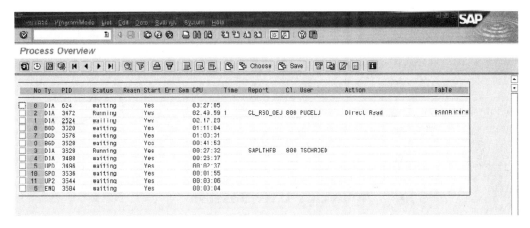

Figure 7.17 Sorting of Work Processes

Check that the value of the dialog work process that is least utilized tends to equal zero seconds, so that at least one work process is always available. Additionally, the batch work processes regarding the CPU time should not have the same size, if possible.

If they do have the same size, or if all dialog work processes have a CPU time of more than two minutes, you should consider setting up more work processes on the system.

Additionally, you should always configure at least one dialog work process so the number of dialog work processes exceeds the number of work processes. For example, if you have 15 work processes, you should configure at least eight work processes as dialog work processes.

Setting up additional work processes The setup of further work processes does not automatically result in a better performance: Generally speaking, countless SAP work processes permit a simultaneous processing of many user jobs. This, however, can cause wait situations in the operating system queue if there is not enough CPU capacity, and if expensive context changes at operating-system level additionally strain the CPU resources and therefore slow down system performance by switching the processors between the SAP work processes. As a rule, a maximum of five work processes per CPU is recommended.[6]

An example of a work process configuration for an SAP BW server with four CPUs, as well as a database and an application server on one computer, is shown in Table 7.10:

Work Process Type	Number
DIA	12
BTC	5
ENQ	1
SPO	1
UPD	1

Table 7.10 Example of a Work Process Configuration

7.5 Analyzing User Sessions

Transaction SM04 (see Figure 7.18) displays all active system users who are logged on to the application server. The normal view shows the logged-on users who can be identified by the SAP user name and the name of the computer that they use. Additionally, the view can present you with RFC logons and system sessions like updates or background processes on the server that are represented by the user *SAPSYS*.

---

6 See also SAP Note 9942 on configuring work processes.

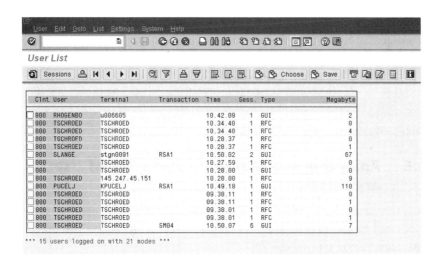

Figure 7.18 Analyzing User Sessions (Transaction SM04)

The information available In the user monitor is listed in Table 7.11.

User Monitor Column	Description
Client	SAP client to which the user is logged on
User	SAP user name of the user logged on to the server
Terminal	Name of the terminal that is being used so the user can log into the SAP system. On a UNIX frontend, the terminal name corresponds to the display variable of the frontend process; on a Windows frontend , the terminal name corresponds to the name of the computer on which the frontend has been started.
Transaction	Name of the transaction code of the SAP transaction that was last executed
Time	Last time a user sent input to the system
Sessions	Number of external sessions of the user session opened by the user. A user can open up to six sessions (see also Section 4.2). To obtain information about the session of a user, select the user and press the **Sessions button**.
Type	Connection types: ▶ **GUI**: Dialog session ▶ **RFC**: RFC connection ▶ **Plugin**: Logon of the user via a plug-in, e.g. an HTTP request ▶ **System**: System connection, e.g. update or background processes

Table 7.11 Contents of the User Monitor

User Monitor Column	Description
Megabyte	Size of the memory allocated for the user in MB. The allocated memory comprises the memory types roll, page, extended, and heap memory and is a summation across all external sessions of a user. For information about memory types see also Section 4.2.

Table 7.11 Contents of the User Monitor (cont.)

7.6 Analyzing the Memory Utilization of Users and Sessions

A user's memory utilization of the roll, page, extended, and heap memory types can be called from the user list (Transaction SM04) via the **Goto · Memory** button (see Figure 7.19).

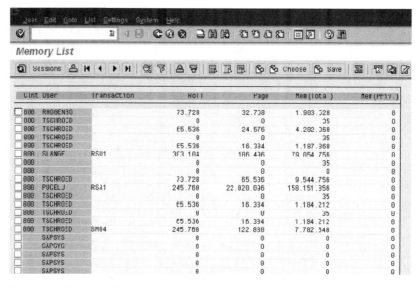

Figure 7.19 Memory Utilization of a User

Memory utilization by user

In the memory list shown in Figure 7.19, the memory utilization of a user is displayed across all external sessions for the roll (**Roll** column), page (**Page** column), extended (**Mem (Total)** column), and heap (private memory, **Mem (Priv.)** column) memory types.

Memory utilization by user and session

If you need to differentiate the memory utilization by session you can select a user and then display the memory utilization of the user per session and memory type via the **Goto · Memory List (Session Details)** button.

8   Analyzing the System Load

The analysis of the system load on an SAP system is a central element of every performance analysis. The SAP system provides the workload monitor—a powerful tool for analyzing the system load of SAP and SAP BW systems. This chapter provides all the information you need for a structured analysis of the load on your SAP BW system.

The SAP workload analysis provides you with information on the throughput, load, and response times of the SAP system and its components. Before you begin your analysis of performance problems, you should always analyze the system load, because it gives you an overview of the areas that display signs of performance problems. Knowing where performance problems exist is essential before you undertake detailed and more focused analyses to determine the causes of these problems.

An analysis of the system load in SAP BW distinguishes the general system load from the SAP BW system load. An analysis of the general system load provides information on the load distribution for applications in the SAP system, according to programs, transactions, function modules, and so on. Statistical data on every transaction step in the system, which enables statements about response times, memory use, database time, and CPU time, is collected. The statistical data is condensed into load profiles that the workload monitor can examine. See Sections 8.1 through 8.3 for an introduction to terminology and to learn about the execution of the general workload analysis. We recommend the book *SAP Performance Optimization*[1] to readers who are interested in getting a comprehensive introduction to workload analysis with SAP systems.

General system load

SAP BW system load is a special load profile of the system load caused by running SAP BW queries and SAP BW loading processes. In this area, the objects critical to performance that must be examined are the queries run in the database and on the application server. You use them to determine how strong a load SAP BW reports put on the system during the period under examination. The analysis identifies the performance-critical queries for the database, the online analytical processing (OLAP) cache runtimes, and the frontend runtimes—the objects of further optimization

SAP BW system load

---

1   Thomas Schneider: *SAP Performance Optimization Guide*, SAP PRESS, 4th edition, 2005.

measures. See Section 8.4 for more information on performing system load analyses for SAP BW.

8.1 Basic Principles and Terms

Before we describe the use of the Workload Monitor, we should discuss the basic principles and terms pertaining to the processing of transaction steps in the SAP BW system and the times measured during processing.

8.1.1 Processing a Transaction Step in the SAP System

A user entry in the SAP system triggers a transaction step. Each screen change in the system corresponds to a transaction step in a dialog work process. For update or spool work processes, every task is counted as a transaction step. Background processes can consist of one or more transaction steps.

At the end of the user entry, the presentation server sends the request to the *dispatcher* of the application server (see ❶ in Figure 8.1). The dispatcher is a process that coordinates the work within an SAP instance. Each SAP instance has exactly one dispatcher. The dispatcher checks the availability of the required type of work process (dialog, batch, update, and so on) and directs the request to the work process. If all the work processes of the required type are busy, the request is placed into the dispatcher queue ❷, where it waits until a work process is released. When an appropriate work process is released, the request is transferred to it for processing ❸. The time between the transfer of the request to the dispatcher on the application server and the return of data to the presentation server is referred to as the average response time. The time that a request sits in the dispatcher queue is called the average wait time.

Roll-in and rollout
The data needed for a transaction—user entries, variables, internal tables, and so on—is called the user context. Several dialog work processes usually process the steps of a transaction, so that the user context must be exchanged among the work processes. The exchange occurs by rolling the user context into the local memory of the work process (roll-in) ❹. When the transaction step is completed, a rollout is performed: the current user data is saved in the SAP Roll Memory ⓬. The length of a roll-in is called the *roll-in time*; the length of a role-out is called the *rollout time*.

Roll wait time
The *roll wait time* differs from the roll-in and rollout times. With remote function calls (RFC), the work process rolls out the user context and waits

for the end of the RFC in the roll area. The wait time until the dialog step continues is called the *roll wait time*.

The ABAP programs and dynpros required to run the transaction steps must be present in the buffers of the application server. The loading or generation of the programs is referred to as the average load and generation time (**Av. load+gen time**).

Load time

Reading data from or writing data to tables in the database requires time, called the average database request time (**Av. DB request time**). During a query of data in database tables, an initial check is performed to determine whether the query can be answered from the SAP R/3 table buffers. If the required data objects are present in the SAP R/3 buffers, they're accessed directly ❺. This approach is up to 100 times faster than a database access. Buffer accesses are not posted as database time. If the query cannot be answered completely from the SAP R/3 table buffers, it is transferred to the database server ❻. Another check is performed on the database server to determine whether the data objects can be read from the database buffer ❼. If the database buffer does not contain the required data blocks, they are read from the database and loaded into the database buffer ❽. The SAP work process does not read the data directly from the hard drive, but from the database buffer, which is why all the data read from the database is first written to the buffer area. The database buffer is managed by the *least recently used* (LRU) algorithm. The algorithm ensures that the memory contains the most frequently used data blocks and that unnecessary data blocks are purged from the buffer ❾.

Database time

The database time lasts from the transfer of the query to the database server, until the end of the transfer to the application server. Accordingly, the transfer time in the network is contained in the database runtime, which is why an increased database time reflects network problems.

The results of the query are then transferred to the application server ❿. The buffered table contents are modified ⓫ as appropriate, based on changes in the database.

The transaction step ends with the rollout of the user context from the local memory of the work process and saving the data in the SAP roll buffer.

The results of the user query are then transferred to the presentation server. The GUI time is the average response time between the dispatcher and the GUI during the roundtrip. Roundtrips are communication steps

GUI time

between SAP systems and the frontend during a transaction step (see also Section 10.7).

Enqueue time If the SAP enqueue process sets a lock (an *SAP enqueue*) during a work process, the length of the locking procedure is called the *enqueue time*. SAP enqueues are locking mechanisms of the SAP system. They work independently of database locks to lock data objects within ABAP programs to ensure the consistency of data across multiple transaction steps. At the latest, all SAP enqueues are released at the end of the SAP transaction.

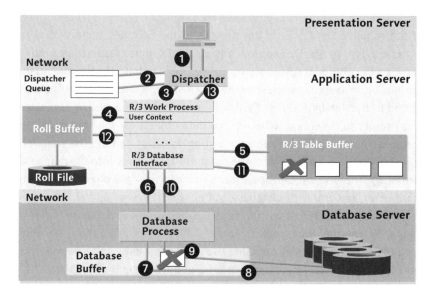

Figure 8.1 SAP Transaction Steps (Source: SAP AG)

The following section describes the flow of a transaction step in the SAP system (see also Figure 8.1):

❶ The user query is transmitted to the application server.

❷ The user query is placed into the dispatcher queue if all SAP R/3 work processes are busy.

❸ The user query is assigned to an SAP R/3 work process.

❹ The user context is rolled into the SAP R/3 work process.

❺ The system tries to answer the SQL statement from the SAP R/3 table buffers.

❻ The SQL statement is transmitted to the database server.

❼ A check determines whether the SQL statement can be answered from the database buffer.

❽ Missing data blocks are loaded into the database buffer from the database.

❾ The data blocks are purged from the database buffer.

❿ The results of the SQL statement are transmitted to the application server.

⓫ The buffered table contents are modified.

⓬ The user context is rolled out of the SAP R/3 work process.

⓭ The results of the user query are transferred to the presentation server.

8.1.2 Distributing the Response Times

The response time is defined as the time from the receipt of a user query until the transmission of a reply, as measured on the application server. That figure does not include the network transmission time between the presentation server and the application server.

The response time of an SAP system consists of the following components:

Response time = execution time + processing time

The execution time consists of the following components:

▶ **Dispatcher wait time**
The time that the user query waits in the dispatcher queue

▶ **Roll-in**
The time needed to copy the user context to the SAP R/3 work process

▶ **Load time**
The load and generation time of repository or dictionary objects

▶ **Enqueue time**
The time from transmitting a lock request to the SAP R/3 enqueue server until the receipt of the results

▶ **Database time**
The time between the execution of a SQL statement until the receipt of the results (but this time does not contain the network transmission time between the application sever and the database server)

> ▶ **Roll wait time**
> The time after an RFC during which the user query is not processed in a work process

> ▶ **Rollout**
> The time needed to copy a user context into the roll buffer

CPU time The SAP work process determines execution times directly on the application server. Besides the execution times, an additional time, the CPU time, is measured simultaneously. The operating system defines the CPU time. At the end of a transaction step, the SAP work processes queries the CPU time from the operating system. Unlike the wait time, the roll-in time, the load time, and the database time, the CPU time does not add to the response time. Figure 8.2 shows the relationship between the response time and the CPU time.

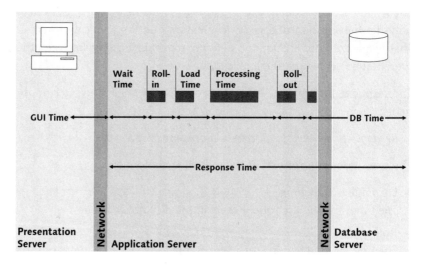

Figure 8.2 CPU Time and Components of the Response Time (Source: SAP AG)

Processing time The difference between the measured response time and the execution time (except for the GUI time) is the processing time, which essentially covers the processing of programs. The processing time therefore also consumes CPU time.

8.2 The Workload Monitor

The Workload Monitor is called with Transaction ST03N. It is the central tool for monitoring the system load of your SAP system. It is a component of the Computer Center Management System (CCMS) and offers a complete interface for evaluating GUI, frontend, network, and RFC times.

For the analysis of SAP BW system loads, the Workload Monitor contains a monitoring tool to analyze the system load caused by SAP BW queries and load processes, based on the statistical data recorded by the SAP BW server.

The Workload Monitor helps analyze the log files recorded on response times, memory use, database accesses, and so on by the SAP kernel for each transaction step. This data can be analyzed for each SAP instance and for the overall system. Figure 8.3 illustrates the various screen elements of the Workload Monitor.

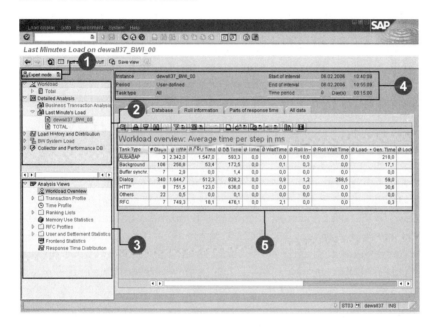

Figure 8.3 Screen Elements of the Workload Monitor

After starting the Workload Monitor, you can select the user mode ➊. The user mode defines the view of statistical data. Note the following three user modes:

User mode

▶ **Administrator mode**
This is the standard user mode. It enables access to the system load statistics of the current day and provides an overview of the system load distribution.

▶ **Service engineer mode**
This mode provides a detailed analysis of the system load of the current day and the previous week. It also gives an overview of the load history and distribution.

► **Expert mode**

This mode contains all the functions available in the System Load Monitor. It can display all the available data on the system load: daily, weekly, and monthly data. You must select the expert mode to analyze the SAP BW system load (see Section 8.4).

Functions of the Workload Monitor

In the menu window ❷, you can control various functions of the Workload Monitor. For example, you can select an analysis of the entire SAP system (**Total**) or of a specific SAP instance. Data on the system load is normally taken hourly from the performance database, MONI. Accordingly, current statistical data is available only hourly. If you want to monitor the current changes in system performance, you must select the **Last Minute's Load** function. You can access the statistics files of individual instances and display the system performance for a period. The menu window ❷ is also the starting point for analyzing the SAP BW system load under menu entry **BW System Load**. See Section 8.4 for more details.

Analysis views of the Workload Monitor

In the menu window ❸, you can set the analysis views of the Workload Monitor. The views let you display statistical data by users, transaction steps, memory usage, and so on. The starting point of your analysis should first be the analysis view, **Workload Overview**. It enables a display of load distribution to individual types of tasks. You can use other analysis views for detailed analyses, such as the temporal distribution of transaction steps over a day or the 40 transaction steps with the longest response time and database times. The analysis views depend on the selection of the user mode. Most analysis views are available in the expert mode.

Header data of the Workload Monitor

Menu area ❹ contains entries for the selected instance, the period of the analysis, and the task type selected for data analysis.

Analysis data

Menu window ❺ displays the statistical data of the selected analysis view. The output area uses an ALV grid control. You can adjust the display of the selected view according to your requirements. When you select the **Workload Overview**, the statistical data for response times and throughput figures is displayed according to the various types of tasks. The task types are subdivided analogously to the work process types: **Dialog**, **Update**, **Update2**, and **Background**. The *dialog* type of work process is subdivided into the following task types: **Dialog**, **RFC**, **AutoABAP**, and **Buffer synchr**. The data of most analysis views is also grouped in the results area by topical tabs.

8.3　SAP System Load Analysis

The SAP system load analysis provides you with a general overview of the distribution of response times on the database, hardware, and SAP Basis. You can also get a summary of the response times in transactions and programs. Here, you'll learn about performance in terms of database time, CPU time, and memory management. The SAP System Load Monitor is a powerful tool for analyzing the performance of your SAP system and localizing performance problems. You should consult with your SAP system administrator for a detailed analysis of system performance and an exact delimitation of performance problems. Because this book focuses on the analysis and correction of performance problems specific to SAP BW, Section 8.4 describes the use of the System Load Monitor to analyze the SAP BW system load in detail. This section can serve only as a general introduction to the use of the Workload Monitor to analyze SAP system load.[2] Please consult the SAP online documentation for a detailed description of working with the System Load Monitor.

8.3.1　Analyzing the System Load Overview

Start the Workload Monitor using Transaction ST03N. To analyze the general system load, select the **Workload Overview** analysis view. The workload overview is available in the following user modes: **administrator**, **service engineer**, and **expert**. If you want to create a load overview for a specific day and period, you must select the **Expert** mode and then the **Last Minute's Load** option in the **Detailed Analysis** menu.

To begin an evaluation of the system performance, first analyze the number of transaction steps and the average response time per transaction step. As the threshold for good system performance in an SAP R/3 system, an average dialog response time of one second is appropriate. This value can be higher for SAP BW. To obtain an overview of the system performance, you should first examine the statistical data in the **Dialog** task type in more detail. It is difficult to give benchmarks for response times in dialog processing, because the load on the system depends to a great extent on the applications developed in SAP BW. Nonetheless, Table 8.1 lists the most important measurements, their significance, and benchmarks. Please note that they can deviate considerably, depending on the use of applications.

Response time per transaction step

2　For a detailed description of the use of the Workload Monitor for SAP system load analysis, see Thomas Schneider: *SAP Performance Optimization Guide*, SAP PRESS, 4th edition 2005.

Parameter	Description	Benchmark	Problem indicator
Average response time	Average amount of time from the transfer of the request in the dispatcher to the transfer to the presentation layer	< 1,000 up to a maximum of 2,000 ms (dialog)	General performance problem
Average CPU time	Average amount of time that a work process utilizes the CPU	< 40% of the average response time	CPU bottleneck
Average wait time	Average amount of time an unprocessed dialog step spends in the dispatcher queue to wait for a free work process	Between 1 and 10% of the average response time	General performance problem
Average load and generation time	Average amount of time to load and generate programs and objects	< 10% of the average response time	Program buffer is too small or CPU bottleneck
DB time	Average amount of time from transmitting a SQL statement to receiving the results (including the network time between the application server and the DB server)	Approximately 40% of the response time	Database problem, network problem, or CPU bottleneck in the database server
GUI time	Average communication time between the dispatcher of the application server and the GUI	< 200 ms	Network bottleneck or hardware problem on the presentation server

Table 8.1 Interpretation of Average Response Times Determined for the Dialog Task Type

8.4 Analysis of SAP BW System Load

In addition to the analysis of the general SAP R/3 system load, SAP BW allows you to analyze the system load caused by SAP BW queries and loading processes. With an analysis of the SAP BW system load, you can examine individual queries to identify performance problems that occur when running queries. The following sections describe how you can analyze the statistical data of the online analytical processing (OLAP) processor, how you can use the SAP BW System Load Monitor to examine the runtime of SAP BW queries in detail, and how you can use the technical content to set up reporting for ongoing analysis of SAP BW loading processes and of SAP BW reporting.

8.4.1 BW Statistics

SAP BW statistical data, usually abbreviated as BW statistics, is the foundation for an analysis of the performance of queries and processes of warehouse management, such as loading processes and aggregations.

With BW statistics, SAP BW logs all steps during the running of queries and the processes of warehouse management. The log records of BW statistics are stored in various transparent tables in SAP BW. During the running of queries, data of the OLAP processor and accesses to the database are captured and stored at the end of each navigation step. Additional statistical data is collected during the filling and rollup of aggregates, and after loading data in warehouse management. To be able to record statistical data, you must enter the InfoCubes to be monitored for statistics recording.

Set the InfoCubes to be included in the logs in the Administrator Workbench (**Tools · BW Statistics for InfoProviders**, see Figure 8.4). Statistics data is recorded only for InfoCubes; ODS objects, InfoSets, and InfoObjects are not even considered.

Entering InfoCubes in statistics recording

Figure 8.4 Switching On BW Statistics Log Reporting for InfoCubes

During the creation of an InfoCube, its log recording is deactivated as a whole, so that log recording must be switched on specifically for each new InfoCube. BW statistics distinguish two types of log recording: logging by warehouse management (WHM) and logging by the OLAP processor. You can use the statistics of warehouse management to log the runtimes of loading processes and the aggregate change run. The log recordings of the OLAP processes are relevant to the evaluation of query runtimes. The log records are stored in the transparent table RSDDSTAT.

Aggregates cannot be included in log recording. If you use aggregates when running a query, the OLAP processor automatically accounts for the runtimes.

Queries on Multi-Providers

To record the runtimes of queries on MultiProviders, you must also switch on log recording for the MultiProviders involved. Switching on log recording of only the basic InfoCubes will not suffice. But, MultiProvider queries don't resolve the statistics data for the basic InfoCubes that make up the query. You can thus determine the total running time of the query on the MultiProvider, but not the runtime of the individual basic Info-Cubes.

When you include InfoProviders in BW statistics, the log files are stored in various transparent tables. The following list provides an overview of all tables involved in the log recording of statistics data of the OLAP processor and of warehouse management.

Table	Description	Log type
RSDDSTAT	Statistical BW data for aggregate selection and accounting	OLAP
RSDDSTATAGGR	Statistical BW data for aggregate selection and accounting	OLAP
RSDDSTATAGGRDEF	Statistical OLAP data: Navigation step for each aggregate definition	OLAP
RSDDSTATBCACT	BW statistics: business content activation	WHM
RSDDSTATCOND	BW statistics data on InfoCube compression run	WHM
RSDDSTATDELE	Data on data deletions in the InfoCube	WHM
RSDDSTATEXTRACT	BW statistics extractor: time of last delta load	WHM

Table 8.2 Transparent Tables of SAP BW System Load Analyses

Table	Description	Log type
RSDDSTATLOG	BW statistics: sequence of events for DEBUG user	WHM
RSDDSTATWHM	BW statistics data for warehouse management	WHM

Table 8.2 Transparent Tables of SAP BW System Load Analyses (cont.)

You should also refer to the Appendix for a description of the most important tables for analyzing the statistical data of queries or the warehouse management processes. The storage space for statistical data that is required by the tables listed in Table 8.2 can become quite large. We therefore recommend that you delete data at regular intervals. You can delete selected data records of the tables in the entry mode of BW statistics (see Figure 8.4) for any period with the delete function (F7).

The statistical data of Table RSDDSTAT is used to analyze query runtimes. You can analyze Table RSDDSTAT using various transactions and programs:

Table RSDDSTAT

▶ Transaction SE16

▶ Transaction ST03N

▶ Function module RSDDCVER_RFC_BW_STATISTICS (Transaction SE37)

▶ Technical Content

Transaction SE16 enables a direct analysis of the log recordings In transparent table RSDDSTAT using the table browser. Transaction ST03N calls the System Load Monitor, which you can use to monitor the SAP BW system load. With function module RSDDCVER_RFC_BW_STATISTICS, you can include an analysis of the most important statistical parameters of Table RSDDSTAT in your own programs. The technical content provides an easy way to install complete reporting for the analysis of OLAP log recording.

The following table describes each field of Table RSDDSTAT in more detail.

Field	Description
STATUID	Primary table key, link in RSDDSTAT_V view
SESSIONUID	Identification of the frontend call. All data of a frontend session (between the start and end of the frontend) is compounded with this unique GUID.
NAVSTEPUID	Number of a navigation step in a frontend session.
INFOCUBE	Technical name of the InfoCube that the query is run on.
HANDLE	Sequential number (ID) of an embedded query in the frontend. If web queries are run, ID "9999" is set.
QUERYID	Technical name of the query that is run.
PAGEID	Technical name of the web query HTML page.
UNAME	System name of the user.
QAGGRUSED	Name of the aggregate used by the OLAP processor. It is left blank if no aggregate was used.
QNACHLESEN	Read mode of the query: ▶ H = query reads upon navigation or expansion of the hierarchy ▶ X = query reads upon navigation ▶ A = query reads all data at once
OLAPMODE	Operation mode of the OLAP processor: ▶ 000 = no OLAP activity ▶ 001 = run query or navigation step ▶ 002 = batch printing ▶ 003 = rolling up an aggregate ▶ 004 = warehouse management ▶ 005 = ODBO interface ▶ 006 = query on the web ▶ 007 = database interface (ListCube)
DBSELTP	Database read mode ▶ 000 = not assigned ▶ 001 = cumulative value ▶ 002 = non-cumulative value, reference points ▶ 003 = non-cumulative value, delta
QNAVSTEP	Sequential numbering of navigation steps within a query session.

The rows above are grouped under the side label: Administrative information on the query

Table 8.3 Fields of Table RSDDSTAT

	Field	Description
Quantity specifications for the query	QDBSEL	Number of records that had to be read from the database.
	QDBTRANS	Number of records transferred from the database to the server.
	QNUMCELLS	Number of cells transferred to the frontend.
	QNUM-RANGES	Number of formats transferred to the frontend.
	RECCHAVL-READ	Quantity of master data to be read.
Runtime environment of the query	QRUNTIME-CATEGORY	Time required for a navigation step (QTIMEOLAPINIT + QTIMEOLAP + QTIMEDB + QTIMEEXCEL + QTIMECHAVL-READ), rounded up to the next decimal power (1, 10, 100, 1000, and so on, in seconds). As of Release 1.2B, rounded to 1, 2, 3, ... 10, 20, 30, ... 100, 200, 300 and so on, in seconds.
	QNUMOLA PREADS	Number of read processes per navigation step in the OLAP processor.
	QTIMEOLAP-INIT	Time required for initializing the query. To load the query in OLAP for compilation, if necessary, for example
	QTIMEOLAP	Time used by the OLAP processor to run the query.
	QTIMEDB	Time used by the database and network to select and transfer the transaction data.
	QTIMEVARDP	Time needed by the user for entering the variables ("time to think it over" for the user).
	QTIMEUSER	Time needed by the user between the navigation steps.
	QTIMECLIENT	Time needed for data preparation in the frontend. This time value includes the transport of data through the network and the output in the frontend.
	TIMECHAVL-READ	Time needed for reading master data
	TIMEAUTH-CHECK	Time needed to perform an authorization check
	TALERTMON	Time needed to read the alert monitor.
	TIMEREST	Remaining time, without any specific assignment.
	DMTDBBASIC	Time needed to read data from a BasicCube.

Table 8.3 Fields of Table RSDDSTAT (cont.)

Field	Description
DMTDBRE-MOTE	Time needed to read data from a RemoteCube.
DMTDBODS	Time needed to read data from an ODS object.
STARTTIME	Long form of UTC timestamp.
TIMEFRONT-PROC	Time needed for the processing in the frontend.

Table 8.3 Fields of Table RSDDSTAT (cont.)

8.4.2 Analysis of Statistical Data with Transaction SE16

You can analyze the transparent table RSDDSTAT using Transaction SE16 (data browser), as shown in Figure 8.5.

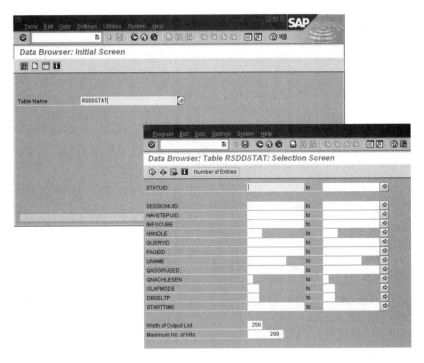

Figure 8.5 Analysis of Table RSDDSTAT Using Transaction SE16 (Data Browser)

You can use the data browser to select specific queries, InfoCubes, users, or flexible periods. You can display or hide various fields of Table RSDDSTAT with **Settings · Selections**. You can adjust the display of the results as per your requirements with **Settings · User Parameters** (see Figure 8.6).

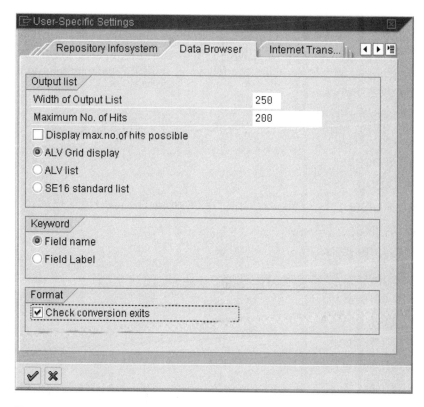

Figure 8.6 User-Specific Settings for the Display of Results in Transaction SE16

To display the name of the query, the **Check conversion exits** flag must be set. If the flag is not set, the internal, 25-character SAP BW name of the query is displayed.

You can select a period in the **STARTTIME** field. **STARTTIME** is standardized to the high-resolution UTC timestamp (10^{-7} seconds). UTC stands for *Universal Coordinated Time*. It is equivalent to the old standard, *Greenwich Mean Time* (GMT) that is used worldwide as a unique reference time. The UTC timestamp is logically subdivided into a date and time portion in the following format: <YYYYMMDDhhmmss.xxxxxxx>, with seven decimal places.

When using Central European Time, for example, the local time in the **STARTTIME** field is one to two hours behind UTC. Note the difference when analyzing Table RSDDSTAT using Transaction SE16.

Table RSDDSTAT provides comprehensive information for analyzing the statistical data of the OLAP processor. To obtain an initial overview of the most important runtime and quantity entries in the queries run by the system, you should combine the following statistical parameters into a new table layout:

► SESSIONUID
► NAVSTEPUID
► INFOCUBE
► HANDLE
► QUERYID
► UNAME
► QAGGRUSED
► QDBSEL
► QDBTRANS
► QRUNTIMECA
► QTIMEOLAP
► QTIMEDB
► QTIMECLIENT
► STARTTIME

Figure 8.7 shows how you can change the columns to be displayed in the data browser with **Settings · Layout · Change ❶** after you have selected Table RSDDSTAT, by selecting the columns to be displayed from the columns available in the configuration menu ❷. You can then save the new table layout and can call it for additional queries with **Settings · Layout · Select ❸**.

Every query call, navigation step, drilldown, and so on creates a new entry in Table RSDDSTAT. When you use MultiProviders, each navigation step creates only one table entry, because statistical data for the Multi-Provider is recorded and the log files are not broken down by the corresponding basic InfoCubes. For additional comments on the interpretation of statistical data and procedures to identify performance-critical queries, see Section 8.4.3.

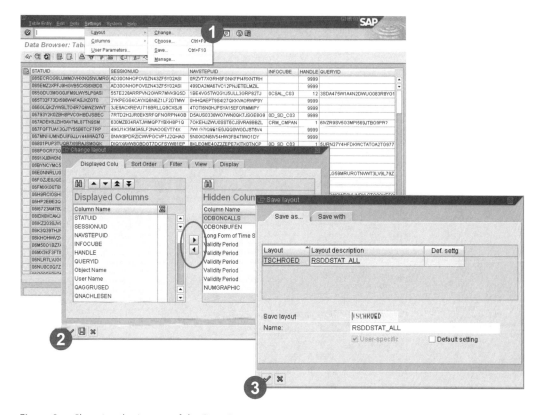

Figure 8.7 Changing the Layout of the Data Browser

8.4.3 Analyzing Statistical Data Using the System Load Monitor (ST03N)

You can use the System Load Monitor (described in Section 8.3.1) for an easy analysis of the log recordings of the OLAP processor to evaluate the load on the SAP BW system. Start the System Load Monitor using Transaction ST03N (see Figure 8.8), select the **Expert** mode, and then expand the **BW System Load** menu.

You can select predefined analyses of query runtimes for various periods from the **BW System Load** menu entry (see Figure 8.9). For example, you can retrieve daily, weekly, and monthly statistics. If you want to define a different period—say the runtimes for a few hours within a given day—use the menu entry **Last Minute's Load**, where you can define a period by day and time.

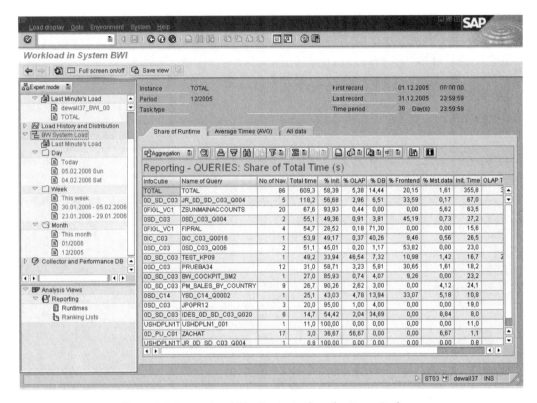

Figure 8.8 System Load Monitor to Analyze the Query Performance

You can display a summary of the runtime analyses you have called based on the queries and InfoCubes run in the system. The conversion to summary form works from the **Aggregation** menu. When you select the **InfoCube** option, all statistical data is summarized according to InfoCubes. When you select the **Query** option, the statistical data is displayed according to the queries run in the analysis period. All entries in the System Load Monitor are based on the log recordings in Table RSDDSTAT and are determined for the SAP BW application areas—database, OLAP processor, and frontend.

You can examine an individual query call or query navigation only with the detailed data of Table RSDDSTAT. The statistical parameters of the SAP BW System Load Monitor contain absolute values on runtimes and data quantities, along with key figures to calculate the average and portion.

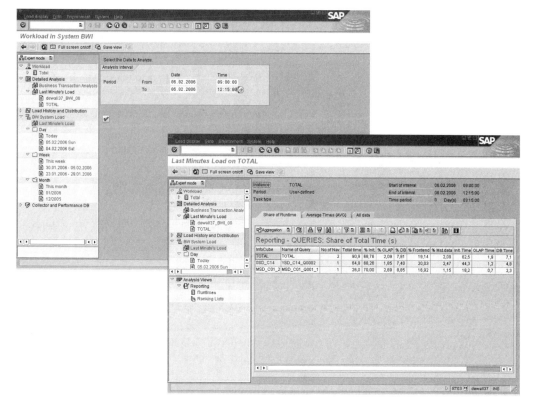

Figure 8.9 Analysis of Query Runtimes for Freely Selected Periods

Table 8.4 lists the most important statistical parameters on query performance.

Column	Description
InfoCube	Technical name of the InfoCube
Name of the Query	Technical name of the query
No. of Nav.	Number of navigation steps or calls of the query. A navigation step is run for each query or drilldown into the data view.
Total time	Total time of the query in seconds = initialization time + OLAP runtime + frontend runtime + master data runtime + database time
% Init	Portion of the initialization time of the query in the OLAP processor in percent (loading the query definition)

Table 8.4 Statistical Parameters of the System Load Monitor to Evaluate the SAP BW System Load

Column	Description
% OLAP	Portion of the processing of the query in the OLAP processor in percent
% DB	Portion of the runtime needed to read transaction data from the database, in percent
% Front end	Portion of the runtime used in the frontend and network, in percent
% Mst. data	Portion of the time to read master data and texts from the database, in percent
Init. Time	Initialization time of the query in the OLAP processor, in seconds (loading the query definition)
OLAP Time	Time to process the query in the OLAP processor, in seconds
DB Time	Database runtime needed to read transaction data from the database, in seconds
Front-End Time	Runtime used in the frontend and network, in seconds
Master Data Time	Time to read master data and texts from the database, in seconds
Ø Init	Average time of the query in the OLAP processor, in seconds (loading the query definition)[3]
Ø OLAP	Average time to process the query in the OLAP processor, in seconds
Ø DB	Average database runtime needed to read transaction data from the database, in seconds
Ø Frontend	Average runtime used in the frontend and network, in seconds
Ø Master Data	Average time to read master data and texts from the database, in seconds
Selected	Number of data records selected in the database
Transferred	Number of data records transferred to the application server
Select./Transf.	Relationship of the number of selected data records to the number of transferred data records
DB/Record	Database time for each selected record, in milliseconds

Table 8.4 Statistical Parameters of the System Load Monitor to Evaluate the SAP BW System Load (cont.)

---

3 The average time determined from the absolute time divided by the number of navigation steps.

For a more detailed analysis of individual queries and their navigation steps, you can go to Table RSDDSTAT from the System Load Monitor. Simply go to the **Query** aggregation level, and select the **All data** tab of the System Load Monitor (see Figure 8.10). Double-click on the table entry ❶ to open the individual records view of the selected query ❷. Use the function button in the upper left to switch between **Standard Info** ❷ and **RSDDSTAT Info** ❸ on the individual query records of the System Load Monitor.

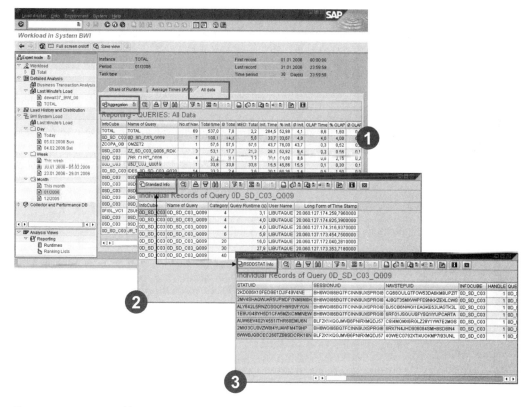

Figure 8.10 Going To Table RSDDSTAT for Analyses of Individual Queries

In the **Analysis Views** menu, you can use the **Ranking Lists** submenu for query runtimes to display the top runtimes according to Overall, Database, OLAP, and Frontend runtime. You can use the **Number of Entries** button to list the top 10, top 40, or any number of (top n) entries (see Figure 8.11).

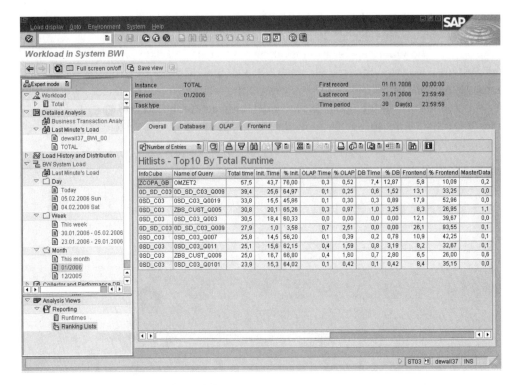

Figure 8.11 Analysis of the Top 10 Runtimes

8.4.4 Interpreting Statistical Data

The statistical data provided by Table RSDDSTAT and the System Load Monitor is quite comprehensive. The goal of analyzing the load on the SAP BW system should be to obtain a quick overview of the critical Info-Cubes, queries, and runtimes.

Average general runtime
Accordingly, we recommend examining the average general runtime for each navigation step first. From here, you can determine the average runtime used for a call or navigation step of a query. However, you should note that the value you determine also contains calls from the OLAP cache. The initial call of a query can last significantly longer. Sorting the average runtime from highest to lowest will determine the critical, long-running queries.

DB runtimes
In the next step, you can examine the runtimes for the database, the OLAP processor, and the frontend. For high database runtimes (> 30% of the general runtime or > 60 s), you should determine whether an aggregate is appropriate to shorten the database runtime. For such queries, check the number of selected data records (DBSEL) and the ratio of the

selected data records to the transferred data records (DBTRANS). The ratio of DBSEL to DBTRANS indicates how many data records on the database were selected in terms of the number of data records transferred to the application server. If the ratio is > 10, you should use aggregates to support such queries. Long runtimes for queries often result from missing aggregates. You should also consider using aggregates when a very large number of data records has been selected in the database (DBSEL > 10,000) and the database runtime is > 30% (see also Chapters 11 and following). The average database runtime for each query call or navigation should not be above 60 seconds, because users find a response time of more than one minute disruptive. If aggregates are already available for a query, check the correct use of the aggregates in Table RSDDSTAT, Column QAGGRUSED (see Section 11.3.3 on the where-used list for aggregates). You should also check the availability of current database statistics for the InfoCube or aggregate (see Section 9.7.2) and ensure that the read mode of the query is set as recommended to option **H: read query upon navigation or hierarchy expansion**.

For repeated, identical query calls, the database runtime should be at zero seconds, because repeated query calls with the same navigation should be run in the OLAP cache. Select the analysis period, go to the **Ranking Lists** view, and check the database runtimes. A large portion of database runtime must always be examined in the context of the OLAP runtime. If repeated calls of a query with the same navigation steps use the greatest portion of the runtime in the database and the portion of the OLAP runtime is near 0%, the query runs involve continual initial calls that cannot be stored in the OLAP cache. The causes for this situation require a detailed study (see Section 10.2 and following). **Identical query calls**

You can select initial query calls from Table RSDDSTAT using Transaction SE16 by limiting the field DBSEL ≠ 0, because the repeated query calls should be answered with the same navigation from the OLAP cache and no selection occurs in the database (DBSEL = 0). **Initial query calls**

For high OLAP runtimes, you should first check whether a large number of cells was selected (**Cells** column in the **All data** view). If a large number of cells is always selected, the cause can be separate OLAP processing. You should therefore use Transaction RSRT to check the technical properties of the query to verify whether separate OLAP processing (exception aggregation or calculation before aggregation) is present. Additional reasons for high OLAP runtimes can include the use of a user exit or a complex hierarchy. **OLAP runtimes**

Frontend runtimes When you interpret the frontend runtimes, note that the percentage of the frontend runtime of the general runtime becomes higher as the OLAP and database runtime portions become smaller. A runtime portion of the frontend of 90% or higher does not automatically mean a bad network connection. For high frontend runtimes, verify whether many cells and formats were transferred to the frontend (columns QNUMCELLS and QNUMRANGES in Table RSDDSTAT). You should also be using the recommendations on hardware resources for frontend PCs (CPU and RAM, see Section 10.7).

Please note that statistical data for a query call or query navigation is collected for all runtime entries in Table RSDDSTAT. No data is captured for the call of a workbook. If you use workbooks that contain multiple queries, the runtime of the workbook consists of the runtimes of all the queries contained in the workbook.

Table 8.5 lists some findings from the analysis of BW statistical data and possible causes in the form of a checklist.

Finding	Possible causes	Section
High DB runtime for a query?	Aggregates unavailable or unused	11.3.3
	Calculation of DB statistics for the InfoCube or aggregate not up-to-date	9.7.2
	Calculation of DB statistics for the InfoCube or aggregate not up-to-date	9.4.1
	Read mode of the query is not optimal	10.4.1
High DB runtime for all queries?	Calculation of DB statistics not current	9.6
	Missing indices in the database	9.4
	Database parameters not set optimally	7.1.8
	Buffer, I/O, CPU, and memory on the DB server exhausted	7.1 to 7.3
High OLAP runtime for a query?	A high number of transferred cells, because the read mode of the query is not optimal	10.4.1
	Separate OLAP processing (calculation before aggregation, for example): check using Transaction RSRT	10.8.5
	User exits used when running a query	
	Use of large hierarchies	

Table 8.5 Findings and Causes During Analysis of SAP BW Statistical Data

Finding	Possible causes	Section
High front-end run-times?	Transfer of a large number of cells and formats to the frontend (columns QNUMCELLS and QNUMRANGES in Table RSDDSTAT)	10.7
	Insufficient hardware resources on the frontend PC	10.7
	Insufficient WAN or LAN resources	10.7

Table 8.5 Findings and Causes During Analysis of SAP BW Statistical Data (cont.)

8.5 Technical Content

The procedures described in Section 8.4 enable a differentiated and rapid analysis of the load on the BW system caused by queries and warehouse management processes. If you want to analyze the load behavior of your SAP BW system regularly and over a longer term, we recommend that you install the *technical content*. With the technical content, SAP provides comprehensive business content in SAP BW. This content appears as Info-Providers, queries, predefined workbooks, extraction, update, and transfer rules, which you can use to implement user-friendly reporting for regular and long-term analysis of the load on the SAP BW system.

If log recording and statistics are activated (see Figure 8.4 earlier in this chapter), the system load data on queries, load processes, rollups, and compression runs are recorded. You can analyze the data using the queries and workbooks of the technical content.

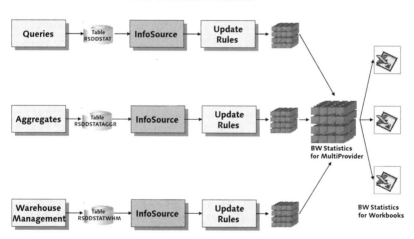

Figure 8.12 Technical Content of SAP BW

As of SAP BW 3.0B, technical content is subdivided into three topical areas:

▶ *BW statistics* to analyze and optimize the processes of warehouse management and OLAP reporting

▶ *BW data slice* to analyze the data in InfoCubes

▶ *BW technical content FC1* (feature characteristics) to analyze and test loads of master data attributes, texts, and master data maintenance

You use the technical content of *BW statistics* to analyze the system load caused by loading and reporting processes, as described in more detail below.

BW statistics are provided as part of the technical content and include a MultiProvider, six InfoCubes, and several queries to analyze the load on the SAP BW system. Table 8.6 summarizes the InfoProviders of BW statistics.

InfoProvider	Description
0BWTC_C10	MultiProvider of BW statistics
0BWTC_C02 (OLAP)	This InfoCube contains the log data created when running queries. Reporting on this InfoCube also lets you analyze how often specific InfoCubes or queries were used and the runtime consumed.
0BWTC_C03 (OLAP, detailed navigation)	Reporting on this InfoCube enables analysis of selection conditions and the definition of the underlying aggregate and its use by a query. SAP BW uses this InfoCube for suggesting aggregates.
0BWTC_C04 (Aggregates)	This InfoCube contains the log data created during filling and rolling-up data in an aggregate. Reporting on this InfoCube shows you how often data was loaded into an aggregate, how long the fill or rollup lasted, and whether the reading or writing of the data required more time.
0BWTC_C05 (WHM)	This InfoCube contains the log data created by running a process in warehouse management. This InfoCube lets you analyze the source system of data requests, the InfoSource, the transfer method, and the time of a specific process.
0BWTC_C09 (Compression of InfoCubes)	This InfoCube contains the log data created when compressing the data requests of an InfoCube. You can use this InfoCube to analyze the number of data records to be processed for compressing an InfoCube and the runtime of the compression.

Table 8.6 InfoCubes of BW Statistics (Technical Content)

InfoProvider	Description
0BWTC_C11 (Deletion of data from InfoCube)	This InfoCube contains the log data created when deleting data from an InfoCube. Reporting on this InfoCube provides information on the use of the selected deletion mode.

Table 8.6 InfoCubes of BW Statistics (Technical Content) (cont.)

Figure 8.13 illustrates the data flows of the InfoProviders of BW Statistics.

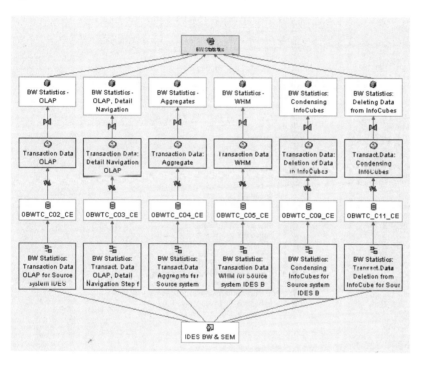

Figure 8.13 Data Flow of BW Statistics (Technical Content)

8.6   Transferring Technical Content

You can transfer the technical content from the SAP BW business content. If you don't want to transfer all of the technical content, you can install individual areas of the extraction and the SAP BW objects. The transfer occurs separately according to technical content for extraction and SAP BW objects.

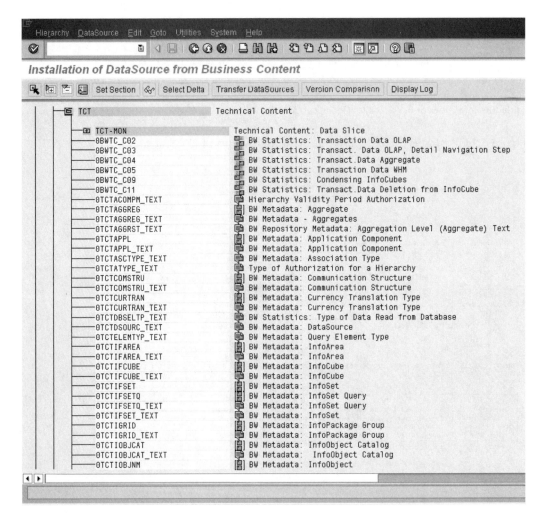

Figure 8.14 Transferring the DataSources of the Technical Content

8.6.1 Technical Content for Extraction

The technical content for extraction contains the DataSources for master and transaction data that are used in the SAP BW system to read the statistical data of the OLAP processor and the staging engine from the transparent tables of log recording. The DataSources and technical content are found in application component TCT (0BWTC* and 0TCT*): you can use Transaction RSA5 to install them. The DataSources are in the SAP BW system, but are not automatically available.

After you install the DataSources from the business content, you must replicate them in the source system, "SAP BW" (see Figure 8.15).

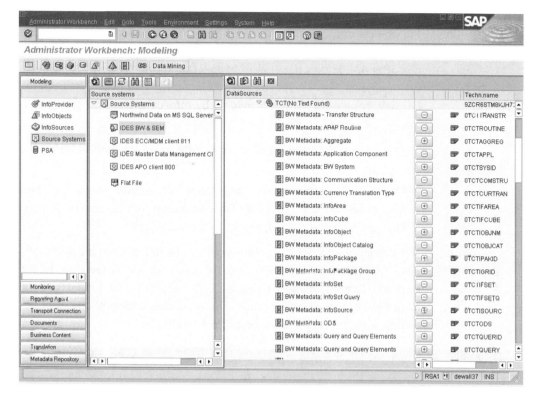

Figure 8.15 Source System Tree with DataSources of the Technical Content

8.6.2 Technical Content for SAP BW Objects

After you install the DataSource of the technical content for extraction of the log data and master data of BW statistics, you can install the SAP BW objects of the technical content that contain the InfoProviders, InfoObjects, InfoSources, queries, and workbooks.

Before the installation of the SAP BW objects of the technical content, you should determine whether your SAP BW system is marked as active in the list of source systems. If it isn't, you cannot collect DataSources, transfer rules, and InfoPackages.

You have several options to transfer the SAP BW objects of the technical content. If you want to transfer only individual objects (queries, Info-Cubes, transfer rules, and so on), from the business content, you can use the **Business Content** menu in the **InfoProviders by InfoAreas** view of the Administrator Workbench to transfer the InfoProviders to be installed selectively from the **Technical Content (0BWTCT)** InfoArea. The InfoProviders of BW statistics are located in InfoArea **0BWTCT_STA**. If you trans-

Transfer of individual objects

fer the business content with the **Data flow before and after** grouping, all
the objects of the entire data flow (with the exception of the InfoPackageGroups) are automatically transferred. Select the **Data flow before
and after** option only if you want to collect and transfer only a small number of objects. If you want to transfer a larger number of objects from the
business content in the **InfoProviders by InfoAreas** view, proceed as follows:

1. First select the **Required objects only** grouping and transfer the
   objects.

2. Once you have transferred the objects successfully, select the **Data
   flow before** grouping and then **Data flow after** for the same InfoCubes.
   That captures the related queries and InfoSources.

Transferring
the role
Transferring the technical content with the **Technical Content** role (SAP_
BW_TCONT) is particularly user-friendly. Go to the **Roles** view in the
Business Content menu (see Figure 8.16) and collect the objects in the
Data flow before grouping mode. The InfoCubes and InfoSources of the
technical content are then collected automatically.

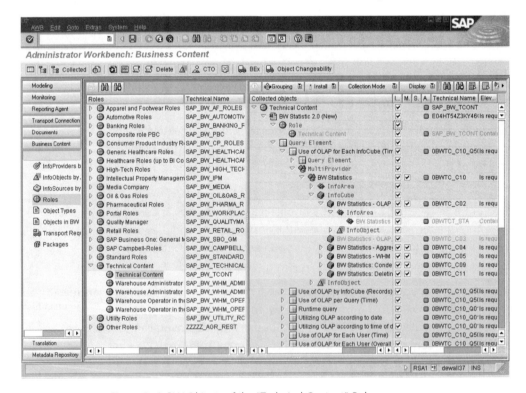

Figure 8.16 BW Objects of the "Technical Content" Role

Even after the initial transfer of the technical content, you might have to compare the InfoObjects to be transferred with the InfoObjects already present. The reason is that the technical content also uses objects that are also present in other application components (time characteristics, for example) or InfoObject 0TCTUSERNM (the system user name of a user) that also occurs in the InfoSources of CRM organizational data and in cost center accounting (in InfoSource 0CRM_HR_PA_OS_1 or 0CO_OM_CCA_P_HR, for example).

The procedure described here transfers the InfoPackages, but not the InfoPackageGroups that group logically related InfoPackages. To remedy the situation, go to the **Object Types** view in the **Business Content** menu and select the **BW statistics** entry from the **InfoPackageGroup** object type. The InfoPackageGroups for master data, master data texts, and transaction data of the technical content must be transferred specifically from the business content.

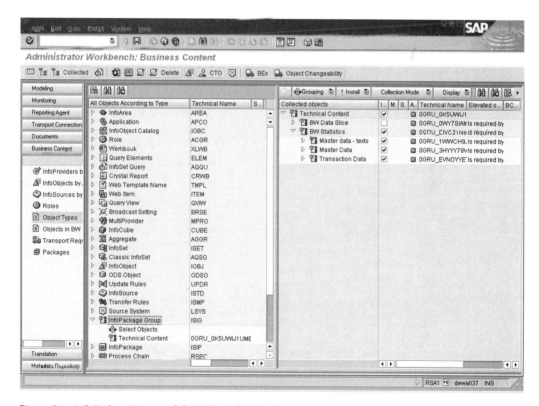

Figure 8.17 InfoPackageGroups of the Technical Content

9   Indices and Database Statistics

Correct database statistics and indices are prerequisites for high performing read and load processes. This chapter first explains the basics of RDBMS and then shows you how to work with these database elements to best meet your needs.

Database statistics and indices of a database can be compared to a map. Consider the following scenario: You know the destination; but there are several different routes to choose from that will get you there. The same applies to querying data from a relational database system. The SQL query language, on which all queries on relational data targets in SAP BW are based, collects the data requested via a query. In this respect, the SQL statement recognizes the data targets (i.e., data objects), but it doesn't know the best route to take to expedite the data search and collection and thereby achieve a quick response time. To find the most favorable access and reading paths, the database needs a map to direct it to the data. This is where the database statistics and indices come in — by helping the database find the quickest way to the data.

9.1   Principles

To find the most favorable search strategy for a database query, the database system uses a *database optimizer*. The optimizer is part of the database program and determines the access route that is used to collect the data. In the database system, the access route is called an *execution plan* and is created by the database optimizer. To understand the functionality of the optimizer, you first need to understand the basics of database management and organization in relational database systems.

Introductory Example

A very simple but realistic example is provided here to describe the basics of data organization in a relational database system.

A table with employee data is created in a database using the structure shown in Figure 9.1.

Last Name	First Name	Department	Location	Street	Phone No.
Wolk	Tom	Controlling	Chicago	71 Monroe Street	312-332-7005
...					
Hunt	David	Consulting	Seattle	2379 Eastlake Av.	206-325-0081
...					
Kennedy	Debbie	Controlling	Seattle	2379 Eastlake Av.	206-325-0081
...					
Malone	Sarah	Consulting	Minneapolis	1300 Nicollette Av.	612-333-2277
...					
Hunt	Nancy	Facility Mngmt.	Minneapolis	1300 Nicollette Av.	612-333-2277
...					

Figure 9.1 Employees Example Table

The table entries are not sorted, because relational database systems usually don't store the data in a sorted way: Newly added data is inserted at the end of the list, or in places that are currently free. For data to be found in a data table, all rows of the table are marked with a *row ID*. This row ID uniquely identifies every data record in a table and gives the database the exact position of the row. If you now wanted to select a specific employee in the *Employees* table shown in Figure 9.1, every record of the table would have to be read sequentially for every query. This read access would be very inefficient and could result in long read times depending on the table size.

Primary index To prevent this, a *primary index* exists for the unsorted table to make the search more efficient. An index is a database structure that contains a sorted value list with pointers to the data records and helps the database to quickly find a row in a table. Indices support various database operations. These include

▶ SELECT...WHERE <tablecolumn> = <value>

▶ UPDATE...WHERE <tablecolumn> = <value>

▶ DELETE...WHERE <tablecolumn> = <value>

▶ Table Joins (<table1.column1> = <table2.column2>)

In the *Employees* example table, the primary index would be a list sorted alphabetically by last name and first name. In this list, the exact position of the data record in the table is stored for every last and first name. For the data to be found in the table, all rows are uniquely identified by a row ID. In this example, "Last Name" and "First Name" are the index fields, and the position number is the row ID.

In R/3 tables, primary indices are always *unique indices*, which means that there is a unique table entry for every combination of index fields. You can omit this requirement for the *Employees* example table, since several entries with the same last and first names can, of course, exist in the employee table. The fact table of a BW InfoCube has no unique index, because its dimension key IDs are indexed as foreign keys of dimension tables via a P index that is *non-unique* (see also Section 9.3).

If you wanted to select all employees of the Seattle location in another query, you could not use the primary index for a quick search, because the "Location" field is not included in the index. To avoid having to read all of the table records sequentially, you can support the query with a *secondary index*. A secondary index contains one or several table fields and a reference to the row ID or the primary key of the table. In the *Employees* example table, a secondary index on the "Location" field would be appropriate to support a query of all employees at the Seattle location. Secondary indexes are usually not unique; several table entries can exist for one index entry.

Secondary index

In the example of the *Employee* table, all employees named Hunt at the Seattle location are to be selected in another query. The database could run these queries using various search strategies:

Execution plan

1. Sequentially search the entire table.

2. Search using the primary index using the "Last Name" and "First Name" fields.

3. Search the secondary index using the "Location" field.

The search strategy to be used is determined by the *database optimizer*. The chosen access path is called the *execution plan*. The execution plan of a query can be viewed in the query monitor of the BW system (Transaction RSRT) via the **Execute + Debug · Display Run Schedule** function (see Figure 9.2).

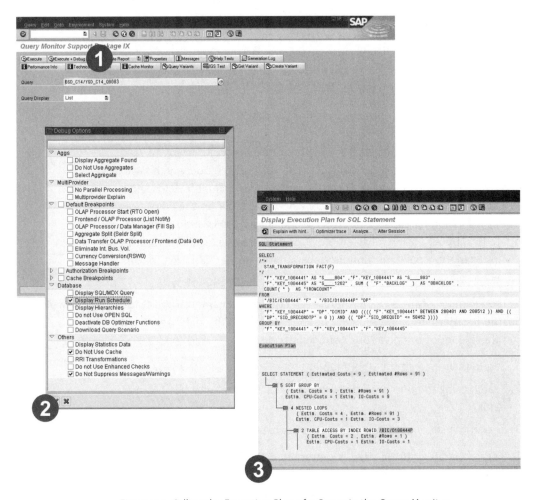

Figure 9.2 Calling the Execution Plan of a Query in the Query Monitor

Using the above example, the different access options can be regarded in more detail. The terminology, *full table scan, index unique scan*, and *index range scan*, refers to the Oracle database system and can be different for other database systems.

Full table scan   A full table scan, that is, the sequential search of the entire table, must be performed by the database system whenever no index can be applied, because the selected search fields are not included in any index. A SQL query for the *Employees* table could read as follows:

```
SELECT * FROM TABLE Employees WHERE Department =
'Controlling'.
```

There is no index for the "Department" field in the *Employees* table. The search can therefore not be supported by any index and the table must be read record by record. A full table scan is very unfavorable for large tables due to the long read times. For small tables, however, the full table scan can be more appropriate than the data access via an index. The database optimizer decides on the best search strategy.

The index unique scan is performed when all fields of the primary index are specified with an equal-to condition in the WHERE clause of the SQL statement. An example for the *Employees* table could look as follows:

```
SELECT * FROM TABLE Employees WHERE Name = 'Hunt' AND
First Name = 'David' .
```

Because the primary index is always a unique index, the index unique scan will never return more than one data record.

Although there is a search index in an index range scan, the search restriction in the WHERE clause is not unique. In the following SQL statement

```
SELECT * FROM Employees WHERE Name = 'Hunt'.
```

the primary index can be used for the search. However, the WHERE clause does not specify a unique data record in the primary index, but all data records of the name Hunt (more precisely, all row IDs of the records with the name Hunt). Because this index range needs to be read record by record, this is called an index range scan. Via a secondary index, the system always performs an index range scan because it is not unique. An index range scan always needs to be performed whenever not all index fields (in this case Last Name and First Name) in the WHERE condition are specified with "=". The database optimizer then needs to search an index area to determine the data records of the table.

One of the algorithms used when searching data in database tables is the *binary search*. The binary search works in a similar way to guessing numbers. In a sorted value list, the searched value is first searched for in the middle of the list. If the found value is not the searched value, the search continues in the same way, either before or behind the found element, depending on whether the searched value is higher or lower than the found value. The search ends when the searched element has been found, or when there is no area that remains to be searched.

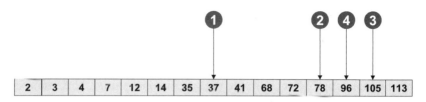

Figure 9.3 Binary Search

The binary search algorithm is illustrated in Figure 9.3. The number to look for is 96. The search algorithm first starts searching in the middle of the list and finds the value 37 ❶. The searched value is higher than the found value, so the search is continued in the middle of the right part of the list. The found value is 78 ❷. The searched value is higher than the found value, so the search is continued in the middle of the remaining right part of the list. The found value is 105 ❸. The searched value is smaller than the found value, so the search is continued in the left area. The found value is 96 ❹. The searched value is found and the search is over. The example in Figure 9.3 shows that the binary search is a very efficient search algorithm, because only four read accesses are necessary to find the searched value. If the sorted list was searched sequentially, element by element, 13 read accesses would be required.

9.2 Structure Types of the Indices

The BW system distinguishes between two types of indices: The table index and the bitmap index.

The *table index* stores the indexed value fields of a table row together with the physical position of the row (row ID). The index can be created on one or several columns. The index entries are stored in the so-called B-tree structure. The B-tree is an index structure that can be derived from binary trees and that ensures short access paths to the key values, while requiring a minimum number of I/O operations.

Binary tree   In the binary tree, every node contains a value entry that is assigned exactly two nodes (hence "binary"). The left pointer always points to a node with a smaller value, while the right pointer always points to a node with a higher value (see Figure 9.4).

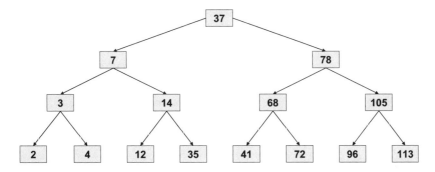

Figure 9.4 Binary Tree

The number of entries per node is referred to as *ranking*. Therefore, a binary tree always has a ranking of 2. The number of access operations required to find the searched value is referred to as the *depth* of the binary tree.

The *B-tree* structure is a generalized form of the binary tree, because it can contain more than one value entry per node, and consequently, more than two pointers per node. A node in a B-tree of the ranking d can contain up to 2d value entries and 2d+1 pointers, where at least d elements must be contained in the node so that every node is 50% populated.

B-tree

Figure 9.5 shows a B-tree index of the ranking 2 with four values per node and five pointers.

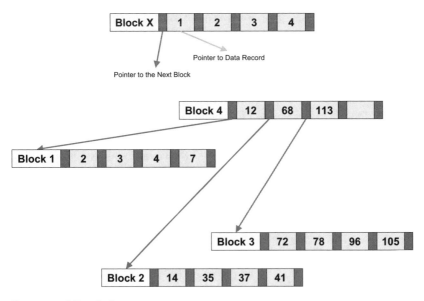

Figure 9.5 B-Tree Index

In a B-tree structure, all paths have the same length from the root node to the leaves, which is also referred to as *balanced structure*. The value entries in the nodes are sorted; every node has a number of entries between n and a maximum of 2n, and the root node can have between 1 and 2n entries. The search of values in the B-tree index is carried out according to the binary search algorithm described in Figure 9.3. The search costs in a B-tree index are better than in a binary tree, because the B-tree is completely balanced and can accept more than two value entries per node so that fewer nodes need to be searched.

Inserting new values The insertion or deletion of elements in the B-tree index must again produce a balanced tree. If a new element is added, whether this element already exists in the tree is always checked first. For the data record to be inserted, the correct block is then searched and the value is written in the block. If the block is already complete, the content is split in two new blocks, where the smaller entries with the new value are written to the left block; the next higher value is written as a node to the superior block; and the remaining values are written to the right block. If the superior parent block is also full, the block must be split again. The depth of the tree increases only if the splitting process needs to be continued up to the root node.

The process of inserting new values is shown in Figure 9.6. The value 15 is to be added to Block 2. Since Block 2 was previously completely populated (see Figure 9.5), the block must be split. The items up to the new value remain in Block 2 (items 14 and 15), the next higher value 35 is inserted in the superior Block 4 node, and the remaining elements 37 and 41 from Block 2 are assigned to the new Block 5.

B*-tree index A special form of the B-tree index is the B*-tree index that is used in most of the commercial relational database systems. The B*-tree index requires that two thirds of each node must be filled. The lower tree depth leads to a higher memory utilization and faster searches compared to the standard B-tree index. However, the cost for reorganizing (deleting and inserting) the data is more expensive for the B*-tree index than it is for the standard B-tree due to the population grade of 66%.

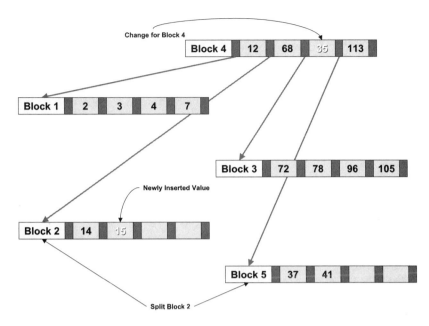

Figure 9.6 B-Tree Index – Inserting New Values

A normal B*-tree index is a tree built of blocks with one to five levels. The top level consists of one single block called the *root block*, which is the starting point for every index access. The lowest level consists of a potentially very large number of blocks called *leaf blocks* that contain the actual data (values of the indexed columns and row ID for accessing the corresponding table entry) in sorted order from left to right. These entries are referred to as *leaf rows*. Leaf rows also include previous entries that were not physically removed from the index, but just marked with a flag as deleted. These leaf rows are called *deleted leaf rows*.

Depending on the index size, there can be more index levels with *branch blocks* between the root and the leaf blocks. These blocks contain control data for quickly finding the relevant data in the index. If an index consists of only one level, the root block is identical to the leaf block and contains the actual data. If an index consists of several levels, the root block is comparable to the branch blocks and contains information about index navigation.

The bitmap index is particularly useful for values with low cardinality, that is, few possible characteristic values. The *gender* characteristic, for example, can take on two values (m/f). Characteristic values like these are not very selective. Bitmap indices therefore accelerate search processes

Bitmap index

where non-selective columns are used for reducing rows from the number of returned rows.

In a bitmap index, a bitmap field is created for every characteristic value. This field gets a value of 1 when the indexed characteristic has the characteristic value; otherwise, the bitmap field contains a value of 0. If the bitmap index contains many "1s," this is referred to as a dense population of the bitmap index. For the *Gender* characteristic, the population rate would be 50%.

The example of a table with holidays—shown in Figure 9.7—contains two bitmap indices, one bitmap index for the *Public Holiday (y/n)* characteristic and one bitmap index for the *Month* (month 1 to 12).

#	Holiday	Public Holiday (y/n)?	Bitmap Index y	Bitmap Index n	Month	1	2	3	4	5	6	7	8	9	10	11	12
1	New Year's Day	y	1	0	January	1	0	0	0	0	0	0	0	0	0	0	0
2	Martin Luther King Day	y	1	0	January	1	0	0	0	0	0	0	0	0	0	0	0
3	Valentine's Day	n	0	1	February	0	1	0	0	0	0	0	0	0	0	0	0
4	Washington's Birthday	n	0	1	February	0	1	0	0	0	0	0	0	0	0	0	0
5	May Day	n	0	1	May	0	0	0	0	1	0	0	0	0	0	0	0
6	Mother's Day	n	0	1	May	0	0	0	0	1	0	0	0	0	0	0	0
7	Memorial Day	y	1	0	May	0	0	0	0	1	0	0	0	0	0	0	0
8	Independence Day	y	1	0	July	0	0	0	0	0	0	1	0	0	0	0	0
9	Labor Day	y	1	0	September	0	0	0	0	0	0	0	0	1	0	0	0
10	Columbus Day	y	1	0	October	0	0	0	0	0	0	0	0	0	1	0	0
11	Halloween	n	0	1	October	0	0	0	0	0	0	0	0	0	1	0	0
12	Veterans Day	y	1	0	November	0	0	0	0	0	0	0	0	0	0	1	0
13	Thanksgiving Day	y	1	0	November	0	0	0	0	0	0	0	0	0	0	1	0
14	Christmas Day	y	1	0	December	0	0	0	0	0	0	0	0	0	0	0	1

Figure 9.7 Bitmap Index with "Public Holiday" and "Month" Characteristics

Bitmap indices enable a quick read performance with low memory requirements (approximately 5 to 10% of the memory requirements of normal indices). However, the performance cost is high during the update. Bitmap indices should only be implemented for columns with low cardinality (non-selective columns) that are used in WHERE conditions.

For comparison, Table 9.1 lists the differences between B-tree index and bitmap index:

	B-tree index	Bitmap index
Cardinality	Appropriate for characteristics with high cardinality	Appropriate for characteristics with low cardinality
Number per table	Typically one index per table	Several indices per table

Table 9.1 Comparison of B-Tree Index and Bitmap Index

	B-tree index	Bitmap index
Space requirements	Space requirements independent of number of different values	Space requirements depend on cardinality of the characteristic, usually lower than for B-tree indices
Reorganization	Lower cost due to efficient algorithms	Expensive for INS/DEL
Access type	Single record accesses, expensive intersection	MultipleRecord accesses, fast AND/OR links

Table 9.1 Comparison of B-Tree Index and Bitmap Index (cont.)

9.3   Indexing Schema in SAP BW

In SAP BW, tables of the InfoCube facts and dimensions are automatically indexed and usually don't need to be created or extended. The indexing schema of the database tables of an InfoCube is explained using the following example of the SAP CO-PA Demo (0D_COPA) InfoCube.

InfoCubes in SAP BW are built according to the *star schema*. The star schema owes its name to the star-shaped arrangement of the dimension tables around the fact table of the InfoCube. The dimension tables represent the actual evaluation views of characteristics like *customer*, *article*, *day*, and so on. The master data tables contain the characteristic values like *price* or *color* of a product, while the fact table includes the metric key figures like *turnover*, *sales*, *revenue*, and so forth. All database tables of an InfoCube can be called via Transaction LISTSCHEMA (see Figure 9.8).

The following example will discuss where the fact table of the 0D_SD_C03 InfoCube intersects with the *Material* dimension table and the master data tables of the *Material* characteristic in more detail.

Figure 9.9 illustrates the tables of the 0D_SD_C03 InfoCube. The fact table /BIO/F0D_SD_C03 contains the key figures and the foreign keys of the dimension tables listed in Figure 9.8. The example shows the key relationship of the fact table to the *Material* dimension table (/BIO/D0D_SD_C033), to the *Material* master data characteristic (/BIO/XD_MATERIAL), and to the material group (/BIO/SD_MTLGROUP).

Per InfoCube dimension, the fact table contains one column with foreign keys and one column per key figure.

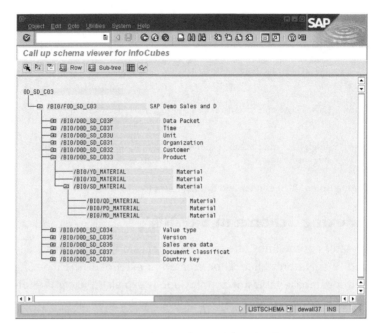

Figure 9.8 Transaction LISTSCHEMA Demo Cube 0D_SD_C03

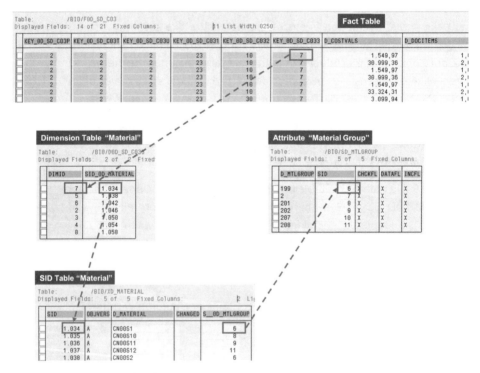

Figure 9.9 InfoCube 0D_SD_C03

Every dimension table includes one column with a dimension ID (DIMID) that contains the primary key of the table, as well as one column per characteristic in the dimension. The SID keys of the corresponding characteristics are written to these columns. In Figure 9.9, the *Material* dimension table (/BIO/D0D_SD_C033) contains the primary key of the table (DIMID) as well as an SID key to the corresponding tables of the *Material* characteristic.

The tables corresponding to the SID key can be different tables: the default S table /BIO/SMATERIAL that stores the relationship between SID keys of the dimension and the characteristic, the X table /BIO/XMATERIAL that stores the relationship between SID keys of the dimension and the SID keys of the time-independent navigation attributes, or the Y table /BIO/XYMATERIAL that stores the relationship between SID keys of the dimension and the SID keys of the time-independent navigation attributes.

The SID keys of the attribute SID Table for InfoObject Material (table /BIO/XD_MATERIAL, column S_0D_MTLGROUP) branch to the default S table of the navigation attribute Material Group (table /BIO/SD_MTL-GROUP).

9.3.1   Indexing the Fact Table in Standard InfoCubes

In the SAP BW releases BW 2.x and 3.x, two fact tables are used per Into-Cube. The F fact table contains the uncompressed data requests (Request Package IDs > 0); the E fact table contains the compressed data requests (Request Package IDs = 0). If an InfoCube is compressed, the data records are condensed via the request ID, deleted from the F fact table and copied to the E fact table.

The index schema is identical for both table types. In general, all columns with a foreign key of a dimension table (KEY_ prefix) in Oracle databases are indexed using a bitmap index. This does not apply to dimensions with characteristics for which the **High Cardinality** flag is enabled. For these characteristics, the foreign keys in Oracle database systems are indexed using a B*-tree index (see also Section 9.3.5). These secondary indices created by the BW system have a prefix of the format /BIC/F<Info-Cube>~010, ~020, and so on. The indices on the dimension keys of the fact table support read accesses by queries.

Oracle index schema

Both fact tables have no unique index defined via the primary key of the table. Besides the secondary indices, there is a composite index across all columns of the DIM Ids: the *P index* (prefix /BIC/F<InfoCube>~P). In Oracle database systems, the P index exists only on the E fact table in order to accelerate the compression process.

In DB2/400-based BW systems, there are secondary indexes for every column of the dimension foreign key: a *radix index* that corresponds to a binary tree. This index is the main index that you should use for accessing the fact table. These secondary indices have a prefix of the form /BIC/F<InfoCube>+10, +20, and so on. Up to SAP BW 2.0B SP22, 2.1C SP14, and 3.0A SP06, there still was the *encode vector index* (EVI), which is a DB2/400-specific bitmap index. It is required for dynamic bitmap indexing as it occurs, for example, in a star join. These indices were named like the corresponding radix index; only the number was higher by 500, for example /BIC/F<InfoCube>+510, +520, etc. Since it turned out that the database optimizer did not use EVI, because dynamic bitmap indexing was evaluated as being too expensive, EVI was removed from the general index schema of the specified support packages.

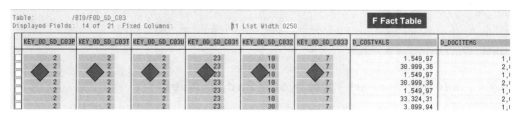

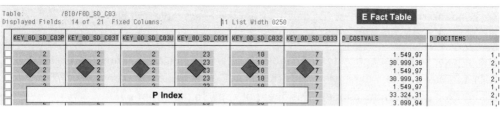

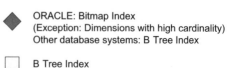

Figure 9.10 Index Schema Fact Table of Standard InfoCubes

Usually, dimension keys of the fact table are indexed using a non-unique P index (/BIC/F<InfoCube>~P or /BIC/E<InfoCube>~P, respectively). In

Oracle- and Informix-based BW-systems, only the E fact table is indexed using the P index. In MS SQL Server, the E fact table is indexed using a unique 0 index. In DB2-UDB-based BW systems, the P index is created as a clustering index on the E and F fact tables. A clustering index sorts all data records of a table physically in the database. This accelerates read and delete accesses (see Figure 9.10)

9.3.2 Indexing the Dimension Tables

In the dimension tables, the primary key of the DIM IDs is generally indexed using a unique B-tree index. These indices have prefixes of the format /BIC/D<InfoCube><#>~0 (# represents the number of the Info-Cube dimension), or the suffixes P (package dimension), U (unit dimension) or T (time dimension). Except for Oracle and DB2/AS400 database systems, all single columns of the SID keys are additionally indexed via non-unique B-tree secondary indices to accelerate the load processes. Typically, the first SID column does not need an index, because it is the first column in the index across all SID columns.

In Oracle and DB2/AS400 database systems, SID keys in the dimension table are indexed using a composite non-unique B-tree index (prefix /BIC/D<InfoCube><#>~010). See Figure 9.11.

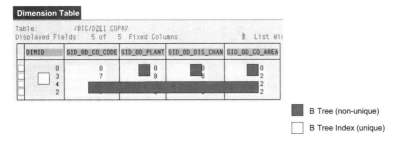

Figure 9.11 Indexing Schema for Dimension Tables

9.3.3 Indexing the Master Data Tables (X/Y Tables)

The master data tables of the navigation attributes are only indexed via the primary key (prefix /BIC/X~0 or /BIC/Y~0). SAP BW does not usually create indices on the columns of the characteristic values and navigation attributes. When using navigation attributes in queries, you need to consider that navigation attributes require an additional join in the extended star schema, compared to a query using the same object as a characteristic. When using restrictions on values of the navigation attribute in a query, we therefore recommend that you manually create additional indices on the master data tables of the navigation attribute.

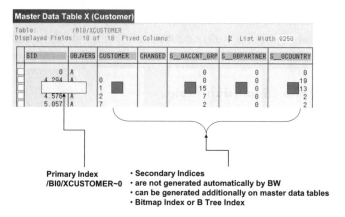

Figure 9.12 Indexing Schema in Master Data Tables

Typical scenarios for this are, for example, queries with navigation attributes on large master data tables (> 20,000 data records) with restrictions on the navigation attribute or, in the F4 input help, on such navigation attributes.

You can check the access to large master data tables in the execution plan via Transaction ST05, or in the query monitor (Transaction RSRT). In the example shown in Figure 9.12, an additional index on the *business partner* (S__OBPARTNER) navigation attribute can improve the query response time for a numerous entries in the master data table of the OBPARTNER object when the navigation attribute is used. In any case, the gain in performance should be verified after additional indices on master data tables have been created, because additional indices can negatively affect the load performance of master data and the attribute change run due to the required maintenance effort. If the navigation attribute to be indexed only has a few characteristic values (a low cardinality), the bitmap index should be chosen in Oracle-based BW systems due to its quick read performance.

9.3.4 Indexing the SID Tables

The SID tables of a characteristic have two unique B-tree indices—one primary index on the value column of the characteristic (prefix /BIC/S<characteristic>~0) and one secondary index on the SID column (prefix /BIC/S<characteristic>~001).

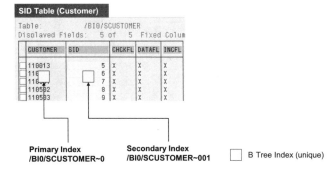

Figure 9.13 Indexing Schema in SID Tables

The condition of a unique index on the SID column is an additional protection mechanism that prevents the insertion of duplicate SID keys. Both indexes accelerate the frequently used function of translating an SID key to the characteristic value and vice versa.

9.3.5 Indices for Dimension Tables with High Cardinality

By default, SAP BW creates a single-column bitmap index on the columns of the dimension keys in the fact table of an InfoCube (see Figure 9.10). For large dimensions and attributes with high cardinality, the bitmap index is not appropriate, because the reorganization of bitmap indices due to data changes (inserts, deletes) is more expensive than B-tree indices, and the space requirements of the bitmap index depend on the attributes' cardinality. During the maintenance of dimensions, SAP BW therefore enables you to convert the bitmap index, which is created by default into a B-tree index.

By enabling the **High Cardinality** flag, the bitmap index is changed to a B-tree index (see Figure 9.14). As of BW 3.0, you can maintain this conversion separately by setting the line item dimension.

The bitmap indices created by default by SAP BW in the columns of the dimension keys of the fact table are the only indices that can be used for the star query join. Therefore, you should not enable the High Cardinality flag to create B-tree indices in Oracle-based BW systems, because the B-tree index is not used in the star query join on Oracle databases.

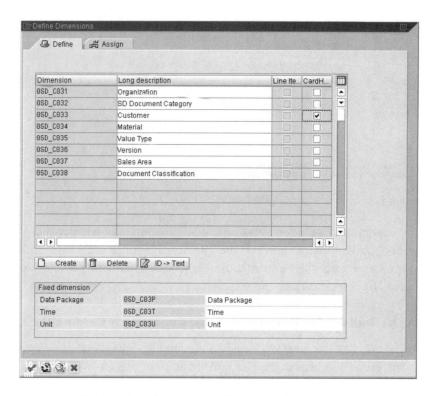

Figure 9.14 Administration of an Index with High Cardinality

Theoretically, Oracle could also use the B-tree index; however, the database optimizer would then have to convert the index to a bitmap index at runtime. This property was *explicitly* disabled by SAP, because it resulted in incorrect data. The option is maintained by the B_TREE_BITMAP_PLANS database parameter, which has the default setting *FALSE*.

You can check the amount of fact tables, dimension tables, and data records that exist by using Transaction RSRV (see Figure 9.15).

For this purpose, the elementary test **Database Information about Info-Provider Tables** must be selected in the **Database** category via the context menu ❶ along with the InfoCube to be checked ❷. After the test has been executed ❸, you check the number of data records and dimension tables in the test log using the specification of the fact table size, for example, "Size corresponds to 0% of the InfoCube") ❹.

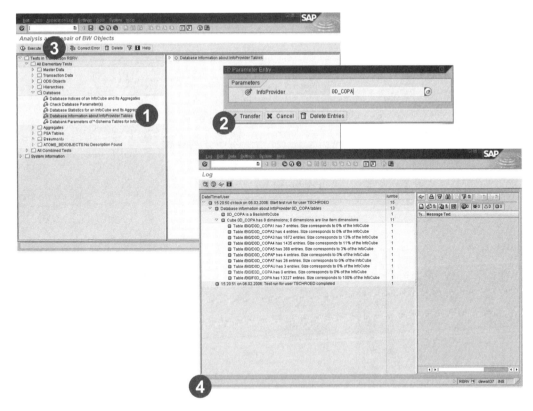

Figure 9.15 Transaction RSRV—Checking the Fact and Dimension Tables

9.3.6 Star Join Execution Plan

The use of indices during the execution of a query can be viewed via the execution plan in SAP BW. For this purpose, in the query monitor (Transaction RSRT, see Figure 9.16) from the **Debug Options ❶** window, select the **Display Run Schedule** setting ❷.

Figure 9.17 shows the execution plan of a query. The execution plan describes the steps that are performed by the database when the query is executed.

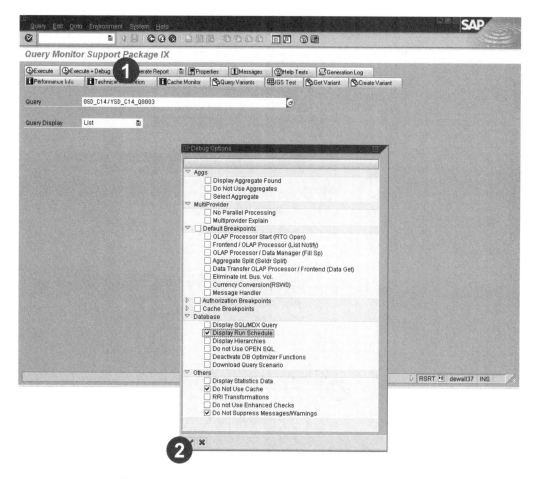

Figure 9.16 Query Monitor—Display of the Execution Plan

Using the execution plan, you can check the use of the indices. For every table called in the execution plan, the indices and additional information about table size and statistics calculation can be retrieved (see also Section 9.4).

The reading and interpreting of execution plans generally requires some practice and is usually left up to the experienced database administrator. Additionally, the terminology shown in the execution plan is determined by the database system and varies among the different database system providers.

On the one hand, the execution plan provides the objects involved in a query like tables and indices that are identified by the key words TABLE and INDEX. On the other hand, the execution plan shows the access types and join operations chosen by the database optimizer that are identified by key words like TABLE ACCESS FULL or MERGE JOIN.

Structure of the execution plan

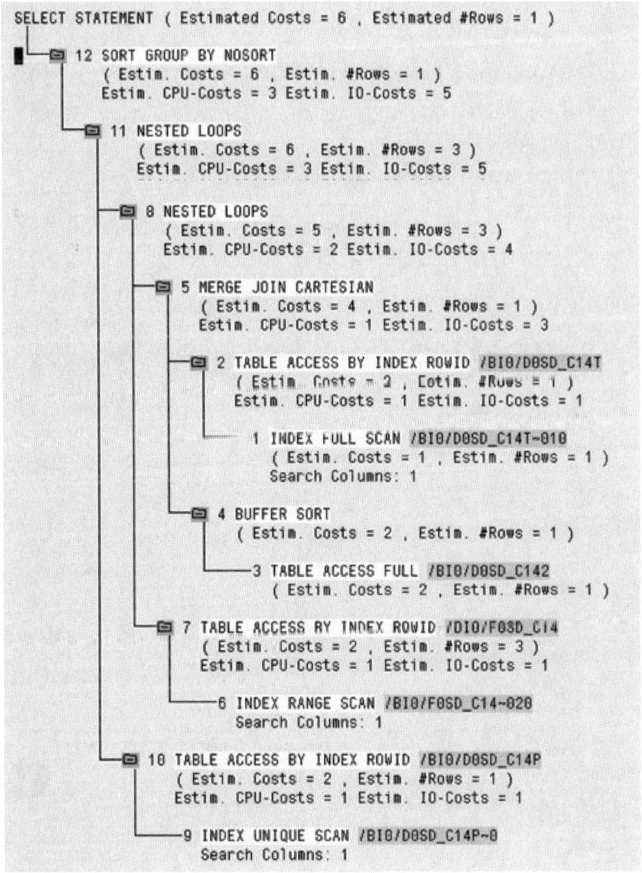

```
SELECT STATEMENT ( Estimated Costs = 6 , Estimated #Rows = 1 )
 └─🖵 12 SORT GROUP BY NOSORT
         ( Estim. Costs = 6 , Estim. #Rows = 1 )
         Estim. CPU-Costs = 3 Estim. IO-Costs = 5

      └─🖵 11 NESTED LOOPS
            ( Estim. Costs = 6 , Estim. #Rows = 3 )
            Estim. CPU-Costs = 3 Estim. IO-Costs = 5

         └─🖵 8 NESTED LOOPS
               ( Estim. Costs = 5 , Estim. #Rows = 3 )
               Estim. CPU-Costs = 2 Estim. IO-Costs = 4

            └─🖵 5 MERGE JOIN CARTESIAN
                  ( Estim. Costs = 4 , Estim. #Rows = 1 )
                  Estim. CPU-Costs = 1 Estim. IO-Costs = 3

               └─🖵 2 TABLE ACCESS BY INDEX ROWID /BI0/D0SD_C14T
                     ( Estim. Costs = 2 , Estim. #Rows = 1 )
                     Estim. CPU-Costs = 1 Estim. IO-Costs = 1

                  └─ 1 INDEX FULL SCAN /BI0/D0SD_C14T-010
                        ( Estim. Costs = 1 , Estim. #Rows = 1 )
                        Search Columns: 1

               └─🖵 4 BUFFER SORT
                     ( Estim. Costs = 2 , Estim. #Rows = 1 )

                  └─ 3 TABLE ACCESS FULL /BI0/D0SD_C142
                        ( Estim. Costs = 2 , Estim. #Rows = 1 )

            └─🖵 7 TABLE ACCESS BY INDEX ROWID /DI0/F0SD_C14
                  ( Estim. Costs = 2 , Estim. #Rows = 3 )
                  Estim. CPU-Costs = 1 Estim. IO-Costs = 1

               └─ 6 INDEX RANGE SCAN /BI0/F0SD_C14-020
                     Search Columns: 1

      └─🖵 10 TABLE ACCESS BY INDEX ROWID /BI0/D0SD_C14P
            ( Estim. Costs = 2 , Estim. #Rows = 1 )
            Estim. CPU-Costs = 1 Estim. IO-Costs = 1

         └─ 9 INDEX UNIQUE SCAN /BI0/D0SD_C14P-0
               Search Columns: 1
```

Figure 9.17 Execution Plan

In general, the following types of operations listed in Table 9.2 can be distinguished in an execution plan (extract from the Oracle database system example):

Operation Type	Examples
Basic operation (Statement)	SELECT, UPDATE, INSERT, DELETE
Access types	INDEX UNIQUE SCAN, INDEX RANGE SCAN, INDEX FULL SCAN TABLE ACCESS FULL, TABLE ACCESS BY INDEX ROWID, TABLE ACCESS CLUSTER
Join operations	HASH JOIN, HASH JOIN SEMI, HASH JOIN ANTI, MERGE JOIN MERGE JOIN OUTER, MERGE JOIN ANTI, MERGE JOIN SEMI, MERGE JOIN CARTESIAN, NESTED LOOPS, NESTED LOOPS OUTER
Sort operations	SORT UNIQUE, SORT JOIN, SORT ORDER BY, SORT GROUP BY SORT AGGREGATE, BUFFER SORT
Filter operations	FILTER
Set operations	INTERSECTION, MINUS, UNION, CONCATENATION

Table 9.2 Operation Types in Execution Plans

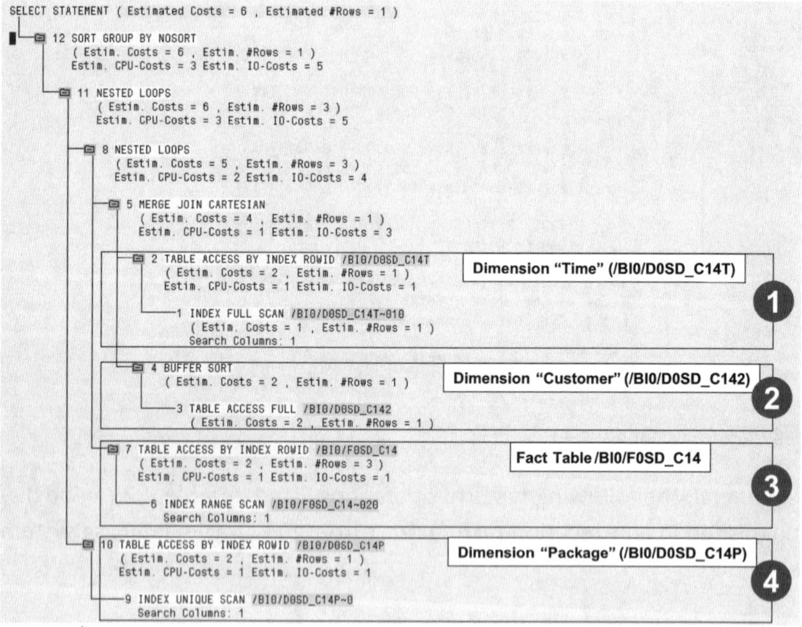

Figure 9.18 Structure of an Execution Plan

To read the execution plan in a structured way, we recommend that you first divide the execution plan into blocks, containing the tables involved in the query, and read the plan starting from the outside to the inside, that is, in the order of table accesses that can be identified using the numbering of operation steps. Figure 9.18 illustrates this concept.

Reading the execution plan

In the example query, data is selected from the fact table /BIO/FOSD_C14 of the InfoCube 0SD_C14 (Backorders business content cube). The data in the fact table is narrowed down using the dimensions *time* (table /BIO/D0SD_C14T), *customer* (table /BIO/D0SD_C142), and *package* (table /BIO/D0SD_C14P).

Block 1 in the execution plan:

Index full scan

```
INDEX FULL SCAN /BIO/D0SD_C14T~010
(Estim Costs = 2, Estim #Rows = 1)
Search Colums: 1
```

In Block 1, the database optimizer first selects the INDEX FULL SCAN type of access to the ·010 index of the time dimension table /BIO/D0SD_C14T. In Oracle database systems, the SID keys in the dimension table are indexed using a composite non-unique B-tree index. (For information about the index schema of dimension tables, see also Section 9.3.2.) Whenever an index scan is performed, data is read from an index to find the keys (row IDs) of the required data records. In an INDEX FULL SCAN, the Oracle process searches the index tree using its logical sorting. The result is a sorted result set.

```
TABLE ACCESS BY INDEX ROWID /BIO/D0SD_C14T
(Estim Costs = 2, Estim #Rows = 1)
```

The TABLE ACCESS BY INDEX ROWID access type uses the physical address (row ID) that was previously read via the index scan to determine the block to read and the number of the data record. The access via the row ID allows the data record to be read more quickly from the table.

The result of the operation in the first block is a selection of a data record in the *time* dimension, because the SAP Business Explorer (BEx) query contains the time characteristic 0CALMONTH as a selection parameter.

Block 2 in the execution plan:

Full table scan

```
TABLE ACCESS FULL /BIO/D0SD_C142
(Estim Costs = 2, Estim #Rows = 1)
```

In Block 2 of the execution plan, the entire *customer* dimension table (/BIO/DOSD_C142) is being searched (full table scan). In a full table scan, all blocks of the table are read into the block buffer where the individual rows are further processed using the WHERE condition or other accesses. A full table scan is often considered to be a very slow access type. For small tables, however, a full table scan is often the preferable when compared to using the index. When searching large tables with small result sets, the full table scan indicates the lack of indices. Subsequently, the result of the table access is sorted in the data buffer (process step 4: BUFFER SORT). The result sets from Blocks 1 and 2 are then linked via a *cartesian join* (process step 5: MERGE JOIN CARTESIAN). In a cartesian join, all data records of the first result set (Block 1) are linked with all data records of the second result set (Block 2), because both result sets from Block 1 and Block 2 each contain only one data record.

Index range scan

Block 3 in the execution plan:

```
INDEX RANGE SCAN /BIO/FOSD_C14~020
Search Columns: 1
```

In Block 3, the ~020 index of the /BIO/FOSD_C14 fact table of the OSD_C14 InfoCube is accessed via the index range scan access type. The ~020 index is the foreign key of the *time* dimension in the fact table, which is indexed via a bitmap index. (For information about the index schema of fact tables, see also Section 9.3.1.) In an index range scan, the optimizer finds a record set of several row IDs in the index. The data in the table is subsequently accessed again via the physical address of the data records (process step 7: TABLE ACCESS BY INDEX ROWID).

The result set from Block 3 is linked to the join result from Blocks 1 and 2 via the join operation NESTED LOOPS in process step 8. In a nested loop, the entire second result set is searched for every record set from the first result set. If both result sets are very small, or if there is a cartesian product (where every record is linked to every other record), the nested loop is usually the most favorable join variant. If both result sets are very large, the nested loop is the least favorable join variant. In the example shown in Figure 9.18, both result sets are very small, which is why the join variant of the nested loop is chosen.

Index unique scan

Block 4 in the execution plan:

```
INDEX UNIQUE SCAN /BIO/DOSD_C14P~0
Search Columns : 1
```

In Block 4, the scan is performed via the ~0 index of the primary key of the /BIO/D0SD_C14P table (*package* dimension table). In dimension tables, the primary key of the DIM IDs is generally indexed via a unique B-tree index. (For information about the index schema of dimension tables, see also Section 9.3.2.) The index unique scan is used when the WHERE condition uses a column with a unique index. The index blocks are then read from the root block to the leaf block. Again, the actual data access takes place via the physical address of the data record (TABLE ACCESS BY INDEX ROWID) in the /BIO/D0SD_C14P table of the *package* dimension. (For information about the *package* dimension, see also Section 6.2.2.)

The result set from Block 4 is again linked to the result set from Block 1+2 and 3 via a nested loop.

This method of reading execution plans helps you to understand and interpret most of the execution plans in SAP BW. The join operations and access types of the Oracle database system illustrated in the example shown in Figure 9.18 represent only a small portion of the available process steps. The most important join operations and access types are therefore listed and described in Table 9.3:

Operation Type	Process Step	Contents
Join operations	NESTED LOOP	Searches the entire second result set for every data record of the first result set.
	SORT MERGE JOIN	Joins two same-level result sets. This is very efficient for result sets of roughly the same size that were previously sorted.
	HASH JOIN	Reads the smaller result set into memory and calculates a table of hash keys for the join criterion that enable quicker access to the result set than the index access.
	ANTI JOIN	Reads the data records for which there are no corresponding data records (e.g., for NOT IN clauses).
	OUTER JOIN	Creates a union of two datasets even if there are no corresponding records.
	CARTESIAN JOIN	Joins all records of the first result set to all records of the second result set (cross product).

Table 9.3 List of Oracle Join Operations and Access Types

Operation Type	Process Step	Contents
Access types	FULL TABLE SCAN	Searches an entire table. Very efficient for small tables. Not effective for large tables with small result sets (potential indication of a lack of indices).
	TABLE ACCESS BY INDEX ROWID	Determines the number of the data record via the physical address (row ID) of the data block. The row ID is usually determined via an index scan.
	INDEX UNIQUE SCAN	Index scan for columns with a unique index, for example, for primary keys. One row is returned at a time.
	INDEX RANGE SCAN	Index scan for a value range in the index tree. Returns a row range (LIKE, BETWEEN, ORDER BY).
	INDEX FULL SCAN	Searches the index tree until all matching values are found. Returns a sorted result set.
	FAST FULL INDEX SCAN	Reads all blocks of an index without reading the data blocks of the table itself. Very efficient if all data required in the WHERE condition exists in the index.

Table 9.3 List of Oracle Join Operations and Access Types (cont.)

9.3.7 Index Schema for Transactional InfoCubes

Transactional InfoCubes are primarily used in SAP Strategic Enterprise Management (SAP SEM) applications, where the data is written to and read from the transactional cube by usually different users. SAP SEM is the planning tool of the SAP BI range of products for planning, consolidation, and corporate performance management. It enables writing and reading data in transactional InfoCubes of SAP BW.

The volatility of data in SEM InfoCubes requires a different indexing schema of the fact table than basic InfoCubes of BW. The bitmap index that is normally used on the dimension key columns of the fact table of an InfoCube is usually not appropriate for tables for which a lot of insert, update, and delete operations are run. Bitmap indices on tables with few selective values contain a reference to the row IDs. Because bitmap indices do not support row-level locking, data changes and an update of bitmap indices would lead to locking that would considerably affect the performance during update operations due to deadlocks.

In Oracle database systems, the dimension keys in the fact table of transactional InfoCubes are not indexed using the bitmap index, but the B-tree index instead, because this index type has a more cost-effective reorganization algorithm for data changes than does the bitmap index.

9.3.8 Index Schema for Partitioned InfoCubes

In partitioned InfoCubes, the data of the F fact table is physically distributed to several partitions of the database. The data distribution is effected using a partitioning characteristic that must be defined in the basic Info-Cube as a time characteristic. In SAP BW, currently only the 0CALMONTH and 0FISCPER time characteristics can be set as partitioning characteristics. Partitioning is only performed on the compressed E fact table. In the F fact table, another bitmap index is therefore inserted on the column of the partitioning characteristic that corresponds to the related column of the partitioning characteristic in the E fact table (prefix /BIC/F<InfoCube>~900). Using the index on the partitioning characteristic in the E fact table, the database optimizer recognizes the right partition on the database in the compressed E fact table.

9.3.9 Indices on ODS Objects

No indices are created automatically by SAP BW in ODS objects. Depending on the query requirements, the indices must be created manually during the maintenance of the ODS object (see Figure 9.19).

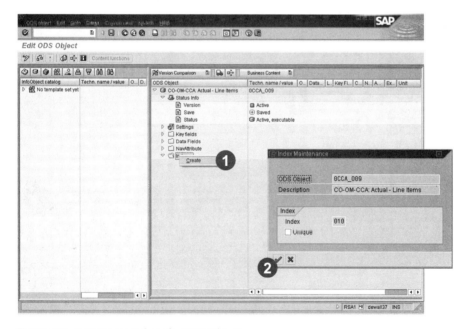

Figure 9.19 Maintaining Indices for ODS Objects

9.4 Administration of Indices

Using the SAP BW administration tools, indices can be created, checked, and deleted. The administration of indices using database tools is not necessary for this purpose. The indices are largely created automatically when creating tables in SAP BW (for example, indices on foreign keys of the fact table of an InfoCube). In some cases, it can be useful to create secondary indices in addition to the existing indices. The creation of additional indices or the deletion of indices should always take place using the administration tools provided by SAP BW, because the index tables are then automatically made known to the Data Dictionary.

9.4.1 Checking Indices

For an InfoCube, you can check the status of the secondary indices of the E and F fact tables. The primary index of the fact table and user-defined indices (for example, indices with prefixes of the format /BIC/F<Info-Cube>~A10) are not included in this check.

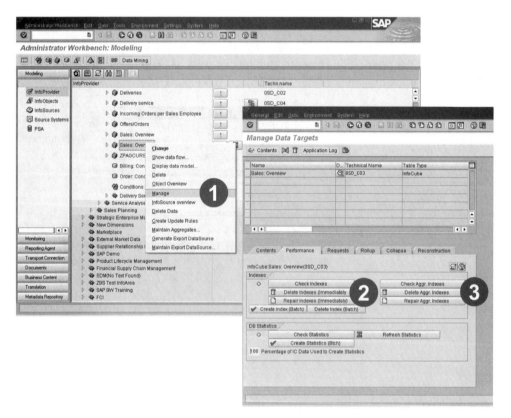

Figure 9.20 Checking Indices of InfoCube and Aggregates

Via the context menu in the InfoCube maintenance (❶ in Figure 9.20), the **Performance** tab provides various index administration functions. These include checking the status of the indices, deleting indices, and repairing indices ❷. For the aggregates corresponding to the InfoCube, the same functions are provided for the indices of all aggregate fact tables ❸.

Using the **Check Indexes** button, you can verify whether indices already exist and whether the index type is correct (bitmap or B-tree index): If the status is **green,** there are indices in the correct index type. If the status is **yellow,** indices exist with the wrong index type. If the status is **red,** there are either no indices or they are defective.

Checking Indices

You can also check the index status via using Transaction RSRV (see Figure 9.21). For this purpose, you need to use the context menu to select the elementary test **Database Indices of an InfoCube and Its Aggregates** from the **Database** category ❶ and then specify the InfoCube to be checked ❷. After the test has been executed ❸, the status of the database indices of the InfoCube fact table and all related aggregates can be checked in the test log ❹.

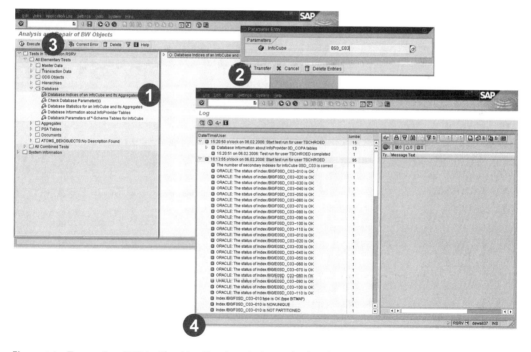

Figure 9.21 Transaction RSRV—Checking Database Indices of InfoCube and Aggregates

Missing indices Missing indices can also be checked via Transaction DB02 using the **Missing Indexes** button (see Figure 9.22).

Please note that indices are automatically deleted and recreated when InfoCubes are loaded in order to accelerate the load process. If you notice that indices are missing on InfoCube fact tables, you should first check whether the InfoCube was being loaded at the time of the index check.

The **Missing indexes** function ❶ performs a consistency check for primary indices and secondary indices on the database. Missing primary indices should be regarded as highly critical, because data consistency can no longer be granted in such a case and there is the risk of duplicate key entries. Additionally, the performance of database accesses is very low due to the lack of a primary index.

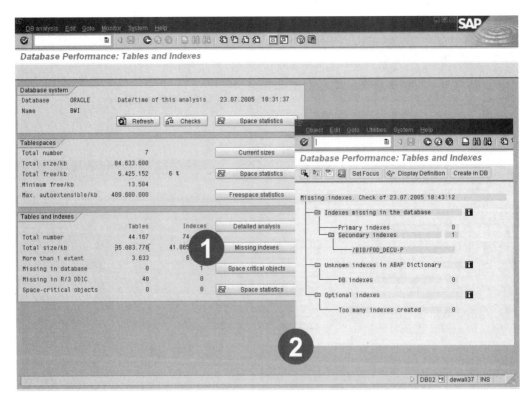

Figure 9.22 Transaction DB02 — Checking Missing Indices

The result log of the **Missing indexes** function ❷ distinguishes among these three index categories:

1. Indices that are defined in the ABAP Dictionary, but are missing on the database

2. Indices that have been found on the database, but are not known to the ABAP Dictionary

3. Indices that are defined as optional indices in the ABAP Dictionary

Missing database indices that are defined in the ABAP Dictionary can result if the index was deleted using a database-specific tool. To avoid inconsistencies, a permanent deletion of indices should always be done via the ABAP Dictionary.

Indices in the ABAP Dictionary

Indices found on the database that are not known to the ABAP Dictionary might also have been created using a database tool. Provided that you have adhered to the SAP naming convention for indices and the index resides in the customer namespace, you can create these indices at a later time in the ABAP Dictionary. Otherwise, you should delete the index from the database and recreate it using Transaction SE11.

Indices on the database

Depending on the database system, optional indices let you specify whether an index defined in the ABAP Dictionary should be created on the database. You can choose to permanently create those indices that are defined in the ABAP Dictionary, or to create the indices only on selected database systems, or not to create the indices on the database. This category of the consistency check displays those indices that were created on the database, even though, according to the definition in the ABAP Dictionary, they should not have been created on the given database. The check also displays indices that are missing on the database, but that should have been created for the database system according to the ABAP Dictionary.

Optional indices

When checking inconsistencies between the ABAP Dictionary and the database catalog, Transaction DB02 uses the internal table DBDIFF. The DBDIFF table stores exceptions for tables and indices where an *accepted inconsistency* exists between the ABAP Dictionary and the database catalog. The objects stored in the DBDIFF table can be fact tables without primary index or temporary objects like temporary tables, views, or triggers. Transaction DB02 considers the objects stored in the DBDIFF table and does not report any consistency errors for these objects.

Checking inconsistencies

If temporary objects are reported as inconsistent objects in Transaction DB02, you should execute the ABAP report SAP_UPDATE_DBDIFF, which updates the DBDIFF table and adds the temporary objects to the table. After updating the results in Transaction DB02, no inconsistency errors will be reported for these objects.

Suppressing inconsistency warnings

To suppress inconsistency warnings for an object, you can also manually create entries in the DBDIFF table to generate exception rules. Transaction SM30 provides the DBDIFFVIEW maintenance view for this purpose. User-defined entries to the DBDIFF table should be created only for objects like temporary tables that exist on the database, but not in the ABAP Dictionary.

If Transaction DB02 reports missing indices in the result log shown in Figure 9.22, these indices can be created directly from the transaction (see Figure 9.23).

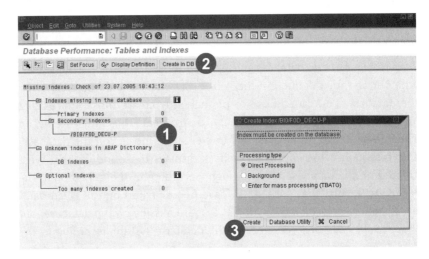

Figure 9.23 Creating Indices from TA DB02

For this purpose, the missing index must first be marked ❶ and then created on the database ❸ via the **Create in DB** button ❷.

Deleting indices

By using the **Delete Indexes** button in the InfoCube *Administration* on the **Performance** tab, you can delete the indices of the InfoCube. You should delete the InfoCube indices particularly if delta uploads of large data quantities (more than a million records) cause the indices to be deleted and completely rebuilt after the rollout, instead of being adapted during rollup for performance reasons.

Indices are reorganized using the **Repair Indexes** button. This function Reorganization of indices restores deleted indices and corrects defective indices. The deletion and reorganization of InfoCube indices can be automated using the InfoCube settings (see Figure 9.24).

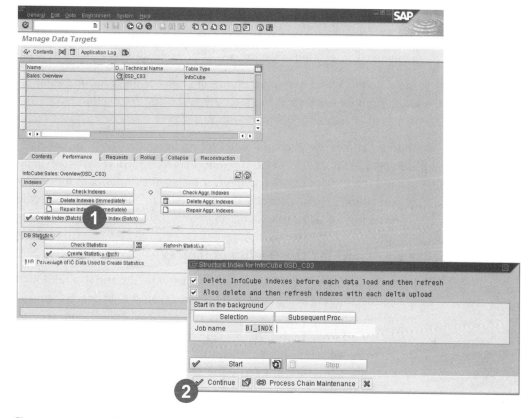

Figure 9.24 Settings for Deleting/Reorganizing InfoCube Database Indices

Using the **Create index (Batch)** function ❶ you can preset the automatic deletion and reorganization of indices for every load process ❷.

Although the procedure of automatically deleting indices before every load process and reorganizing them after the load process is completed accelerates the load process, it can substantially slow down simultaneous read processes on an InfoCube. Therefore, if you apply this procedure, you should ensure that no queries are executed on the InfoCube while data is being loaded.

The reorganization of indices can result in locking conflicts with the automatic InfoCube compression and rollup, because no requests in the aggregate can be rolled up or compressed during index reorganization (see also Section 11.4.1, Table 11.3). It is therefore recommended that you schedule the index jobs via process chains. If an automatic request processing has been set for the InfoCube, however, this setting is not considered when process chains are used. In this case, the automatic processes must be additionally integrated in the process chain as process types.

The scheduling and execution of indexing jobs of the InfoCube administration can be checked in the job overview using Transaction SM37. The names of all indexing jobs start with BI_INDX.

You can also repair the InfoCube indices using the ABAP report SAP_ INFOCUBE_INDEXES_REPAIR. This report corrects missing secondary indices and the P index of the F and E fact tables of all InfoCubes in the BW system. Because you cannot explicitly select an InfoCube, you should schedule this job as a background process.

9.4.2 Checking the Quality of Indices

In particular cases, the performance might still be dissatisfying, although the correct index is being used. If this occurs, you should check the quality of the index. A bad index quality can occur whenever data records were deleted from a table. In this case, the data record is deleted from the index as well. The space in the index tree remains empty until a new data record is inserted in exactly the same place. If there are many of these empty spaces, more blocks need to be read to find all matching data records when accessing the index.

Index fragmentation

This is referred to as index fragmentation. The degree of fragmentation indicates how well the space in the index blocks is used: The smaller the space that is actually used, the more fragmented the index. The index is then also referred to as unbalanced or degenerated. Index fragmentation usually occurs in tables with high data fluctuation.

The storage quality of the index can be checked in the following way:

First-level analysis of the index quality

1. In Transaction DB02, use the **Detailed Analysis** button to display to the input mask for selecting the table to be analyzed and enter the table name.

2. In the displayed screen, use the **Table <-> Indices** button to list the indices of the table, and select the index to be analyzed.

3. Using the **Detailed Analysis** button, go to the detailed analysis of the index.

4. The index quality can be retrieved via the **Analyze index · Storage quality** menu (❶ in Figure 9.25).

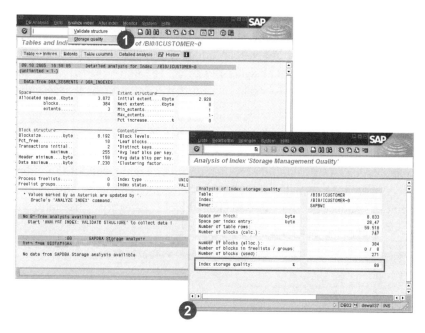

Figure 9.25 Storage Quality of the Index (I)

In the associated screen ❷, a percentage of the index quality is given in the **Index storage quality** row. If the specified percentage is < 70, we recommend that you reorganize the index. For very small indices, the calculated percentage might be too small, although the index has been reorganized. In this case, you should also check the **Number of blocks (used)** value. If this value is < 10, we recommend that you use the method described in the following sections to determine the storage quality.[1]

1. In Transaction DB02, use the **Detailed Analysis** button to display the screen for selecting the table to be analyzed and enter the table name.

> Detailed analysis of the index quality

2. In the displayed screen, use the **Table <-> Indices** button to list the indices of the table, and select the index to be analyzed.

---

1 SAP also provides ABAP Report RSORATAD, which can be called via Transaction SE38. You can use this report to carry out the described procedure for a first-level analysis of the index quality.

3. Using the **Detailed Analysis** button, go to the detailed analysis of the index.

4. Start calculating the index quality via the **Analyze index · Validate structure · Dialog** menu (see Figure 9.26).

Using this last function, the current statistics are determined from the index_stats system table. You should note that running **Validate structure**—just like **Analyze index**—can affect system performance, because parts of the index are locked against updates. Therefore, do not run these commands when there is the likelihood that many users will access the index_stats system table!

After running **Validate structure**, call the **Detail Analysis** screen again to check the **Used in tree … without del. rows** value in the **Analysis of B*-tree** category. This value reflects the current storage quality of the index and should not be smaller than 70%. Additionally, check the **entries** and **deleted** values in the **B*-tree leaf blocks** category. The ratio of **deleted/entries** should be smaller than 25%.

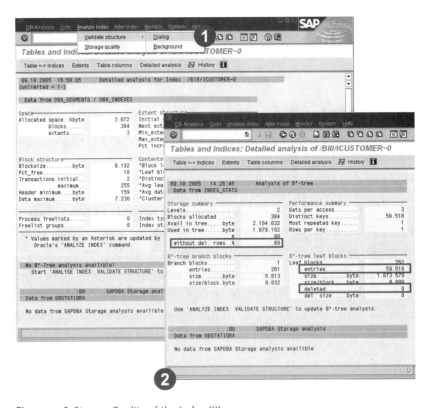

Figure 9.26 Storage Quality of the Index (II)

If the index parameters to be checked are not within the specified range, you should ask the database administrator to reorganize the index. For information about reorganizing the indices of an InfoCube, see Section 9.4.1.

Index reorganization

9.4.3 Creating New Indices

Indices can significantly improve the load and read performance; however, incorrect indices or a plethora of indices can also drastically deteriorate performance. Therefore, you should be very careful when creating new indices and always check how creating new indices impacts performance.

The following example shows the creation of an index for a navigation attribute in the master data table of the underlying characteristic. Sometimes, you may have to create additional indices on master data tables when using navigation attributes of large master data tables in queries. In these cases, restrictions to specific values of the navigation attribute in the query might not be considered by the database optimizer when the execution plan is created. By indexing the navigation attribute in the respective master data table, the index can be considered in the execution plan.

Indices on master data tables

For the 0COMP-CODE InfoObject (company code), let us assume the time-constant navigation attributes are 0COMPANY (company) and 0COUNTRY (country). For the 0COMPANY navigation attribute, an additional index has to be created. The /BI0/XCOMP_CODE table (for time-dependent navigation attributes, the /BI0/YCOMP_CODE table) contains the S__0COMPANY column for the 0COUNTRY navigation attribute. Using Transaction SE11, an additional index can be created on this column.

In Transaction SE11 (see Figure 9.27), the respective master data table is called ❶, for which an additional index is created on the columns of the underlying master data table using the **Indexes** button ❷. For this purpose, the columns are selected in a selection box ❸.

When creating an index—depending on the database system—you can choose whether an index defined in the ABAP Dictionary will be created on the database. If you select the **Index on all database systems** setting, the index is always created on the database.

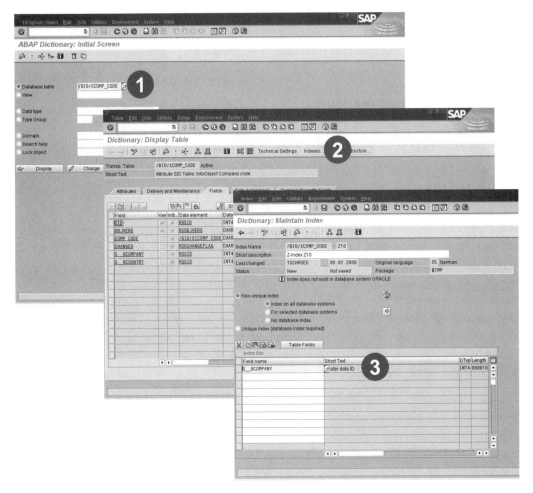

Figure 9.27 Creating Additional Indices on Master Data Tables

If you select the **For selected database systems** setting, you must specify in a selection list on which databases the index will be created; otherwise, you must use an exclusion list to specify the database systems on which the index will not be created.

If you select the **No database index** option, the index is not physically created on the database. If this option is chosen for indices already existing on the database, these indices will be deleted from the database when it is activated.

A unique index must always be created on the database, because it prevents the insertion of duplicate data records. To ensure data consistency, a unique index may not be deleted from the database.

9.5   Database Optimizer

The SQL statement of a query describes which database objects are to be read when the query is executed; however, it cannot describe the optimal way to find the data on the database. The search strategy required for this purpose is determined by an instance in the database that is referred to as the database optimizer. Using the SQL statement, the database optimizer determines the best search strategy and creates an execution plan. There are two types of database optimizers: the rule-based optimizer and the cost-based optimizer. SAP BW uses the cost-based optimizer exclusively.

As you can infer from the name, the cost-based optimizer evaluates the various search strategies by "cost" and then selects the most favorable strategy. During cost evaluation, the optimizer only considers the number of expected I/O processes if the various possible search strategies were carried out. For evaluating the anticipated hit rate, the optimizer performs sample searches and uses statistical information of the database system that is described in more detail in the following sections.

Cost-based optimizer (CBO)

On the one hand, the decision is made using the fields contained in the WHERE clause of the SQL statement and the available indices of these fields. The most important criterion here is the number of indexed fields that are listed with an equal-to condition in the WHERE clause. For the search process, the database optimizer will use the index that best matches the fields in the WHERE condition.

Another criterion for determining the best search strategy is the table size. For small tables, a full table scan can be a more favorable search strategy than accessing the data via an index, because, in the latter case, the index table needs to be read in addition to the database table.

For an index to be used in the search process, the indexed field should restrict the amount of data to be read to the greatest possible extent. The higher the number of distinct values of a field, the better can the amount of data to be read be reduced when there is a restriction to values of this field.

Another important role when determining the ideal search strategy is that of the physical storage and distribution of the data field values. For this purpose, the optimizer determines the number of blocks or pages,[2] respectively, that must physically be read from the database. If the data is highly fragmented due to a low population grade of the blocks or pages, this affects the use of the index. The distribution of the characteristic values within a table column is considered via using *histograms* or data samples. To determine the search strategy, the database optimizer verifies whether the characteristic values are evenly distributed across a column, or if they are aggregated.

9.6 Database Statistics

To determine the most favorable access path for SELECT, UPDATE, and DELETE statements, the cost-based optimizer requires information about the database tables and indices. Based on these statistics, the access path with the lowest expected cost is selected.

Calculating the costs
The costs of different access paths are calculated by the cost-based optimizer according to an internal algorithm that is not exposed by the database vendor. A measure for the calculated costs is the number of accesses to the blocks or pages to be read that is required to select the data. This is generally referred to as *I/O costs*. The cost calculation is based on the DB statistics that differentiate by different types:

▶ The table statistics contain information about the number of rows (NUM_ROWS) and the number of occupied blocks (NUM_BLOCKS), the average row length as well as the accuracy (SAMPLE_SIZE), or the date of the last analysis (LAST_ANALYZED).

▶ The index statistics contain information about the size of the index tree (BLEVEL), the number of leaf blocks (LEAF_BLOCKS), the number of distinct keys (DISTINCT_KEYS), the clustering factor that represents a measure for the table ranking (CLUSTERING_FACTOR), the accuracy (SAMPLE_SIZE), as well as the date of the last analysis (LAST_ANALYZED).

▶ The column statistics contain information like the number of distinct values (NUM_DISTINCT), the lowest value in the column (LOW_VALUE), the highest value in the column (HIGH_VALUE), the accuracy (SAMPLE_SIZE), and the date of the last analysis (LAST_ANALYZED).

Depending on the database system, you can additionally create histogram information that specifies how the values of a table column are dis-

---

2 The data in a database system is always distributed to blocks or pages. Depending on the database and operating systems, the size of those blocks and pages ranges between 2 and 32 KB.

tributed. Using the histograms, the cost-based optimizer can determine that specific values occur frequently, and other values occur rarely or not at all. Based on this information, the cost-based optimizer can select the optimal access path.

The various statistic parameters are summarized in the following table.

Statistic type	System table[3]	Parameter	Description
Table	DBA_TABLES	NUM_ROWS	Number of rows in a table
		NUM_BLOCKS	Number of used blocks
		SAMPLE_SIZE	Accuracy
		LAST_ANALYZED	Date of the last statistics creation
Index	DBA_INDEXES	BLEVEL	Number of levels of the index tree
		LEAF_BLOCKS	Number of leaf blocks
		DISTINCT_KEYS	Number of distinct keys
		CLUSTERIN_FACTOR	Measure for the table ranking compared to the index
		SAMPLE_SIZE	Accuracy
		LAST_ANALYZED	Date of the last statistics creation
Column	DBA_TAB_COLUMNS	NUM_DISTINCT	Number of distinct values
		LOW_VALUE	Lowest value in the table column
		HIGH_VALUE	Highest value in the table column
		SAMPLE_SIZE	Accuracy
		LAST_ANALYZED	Date of the last statistics creation
Histograms	DBA_TAB_HISTOGRAMS	ENDPOINT_NUMBER	Bucket number. By default, the data values are distributed to 75 buckets.[4]
		ENDPOINT_ACTUAL_VALUE	Bucket end value
		LOW_VALUE	Lowest value
		HIGH_VALUE	Highest value

Table 9.4 Statistic Parameters for the Cost-Based Optimizer

---

3   Table view in an Oracle database system.

The statistical data for tables and indices can be retrieved via the execution plan of a query in the query monitor (Transaction RSRT) using the **Debug** option.

For the tables and indices called in the execution plan, you can display the detailed information for the statistical data described in Table 9.2 (see Figure 9.28).

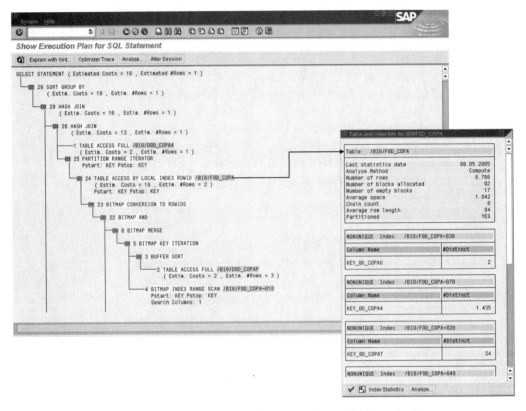

Figure 9.28 Execution Plan and Statistical Data of Tables and Indices

---

4 If many different column values exist, it is almost impossible to make an exact statement on the value distribution. Instead, the system merely stores a maximum number of distribution details. Each piece of distribution information is referred to as a bucket. By default, the system stores a maximum of 75 buckets per column.

9.7 Administration of Database Statistics

The cost-based SQL optimizer uses statistics that are created using the UPDATE STATISTICS statements. Database statistics can be created using different processes. In order for the cost-based optimizer to determine the most favorable access paths, you must ensure that the statistics are always current. The quality of the statistics is not determined by the time of the last analysis. It is more important that the statistics map the current dataset as accurately as possible. New statistics are required whenever the number of data records in a table has changed by more than a specific threshold value. Usually, this threshold value (database parameter STATS_CHANGE_THRESHOLD) is 50%. In general, statistics should be updated whenever large datasets have been changed by database operations (inserts, updates, deletes).

9.7.1 Administration of Database Statistics Using BRCONNECT

BRCONNECT is an SAP utility of the BR*Tools series for administering the database under the Oracle database system. BRCONNECT supports various administration tasks—for example, the collection of system statistics like operating system resources, CPU performance, I/O accesses, and so forth—that are used by the cost-based optimizer to determine the optimal access paths. The system statistics are usually collected using the Oracle DBMS_STATS standard package at a time when the system shows an average usage. In the first step, the tool determines the tables that need new statistics based on the number of table rows. In the second step, new statistics are created for the relevant tables.

SAPDBA is a similar tool for collecting statistical data. As of SAP Basis Release 6.10, BRCONNECT has implemented the statistic functions of SAPDBA, because SAPDBA could no longer create statistics with histograms, nor could it process partitioned tables.

Only an experienced database administrator should execute the statistic runs with BRCONNECT. BRCONNECT is called at database command level using the SYSTEM database user, because the DBA authorization is required for executing the DBMS_STATS.GATHER_SYSTEM_STATS package procedure.

You can view the log data of the BRCONNECT job via the log display for DBA operations (Transaction DB14, see Figure 9.29).

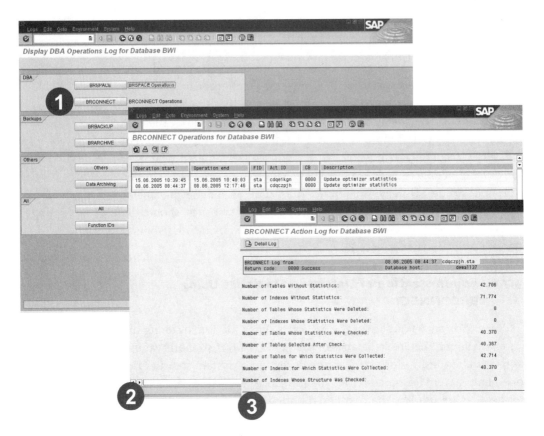

Figure 9.29 Log Display for DBA Operations

Using the **BRCONNECT** button ❶, the corresponding BRCONNECT operations can be called ❷. For BRCONNECT operations, it is required that jobs exist with the function ID (FID) = sta (or, depending on the use of BRCONNECT, with FID = opt or FID = aly). For the BRCONNECT operation, you can retrieve an action log ❸ and a detailed job log.

To keep the statistics up to date, you should schedule BRCONNECT at least once a week. For collecting all DB statistics for SAP BW tables, as of BW 3.0B and higher, SAP recommends that you use BRCONNECT (Release 6.40 or higher). Please note that statistics for BW tables should always be created with histograms, which is only possible with BRCONNECT 6.10, starting at patch level 11!

9.7.2 Statistics for InfoCubes

A high-performing execution of BW queries requires up-to-date statistics of the SAP BW InfoCube tables. For SAP BW InfoCube tables, you must create statistical data using the calculation of histograms (see also Table 9.4). To calculate and update the statistics, various options can be executed.

For older releases of BW systems (up to BW 3.0A), SAP recommends that you run the ABAP report SAP_ANALYZE_ALL_INFOCUBES once a week. This ABAP report is only relevant for BW systems with the Oracle, MaxDB/SAP DB, or IBM DB2/UDB (DB6) database systems.[5]

SAP_ANALYZE_ALL_INFOCUBES enables histogram calculation; however, this is not possible with BRCONNECT 6.10 if older release versions (up to BW3.0A) are used. You cannot run the report during data uploads. The runtime depends on the number and size of the InfoCubes. The volume of data to be analyzed necessary to calculate the statistics can be set by specifying a sample size percentage. For a complete analysis of all data, the sample size is 100%.

SAP_ANALYZE_
ALL_
INFOCUBES

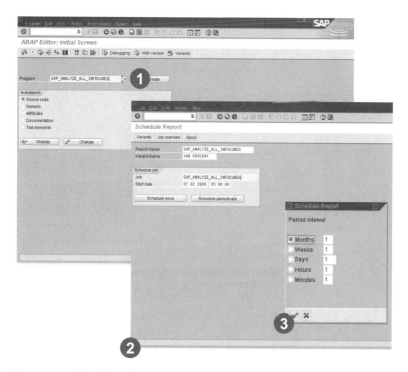

Figure 9.30 Scheduling the Statistics Job SAP_ANALYZE_ALL-INFOCUBES

---

5 You can find more information on this topic at *http://service.sap.com/dbaora*.

The statistics job SAP_ANALYZE_ALL_INFOCUBES can be scheduled as a background job via Transaction SE38 (❶ in Figure 9.30) using **Program · Execute · Background** ❷. Using the **Schedule periodically** button, you can set the job to be run on a regular basis. SAP recommends that you run the report once a week as a batch job. Because the job runtime is partially determined by the number and size of the BW InfoCubes and is almost impossible to forecast, you should start with an initial sample size of 10% to get a general idea of the runtime values.

BRCONNECT As of BW3.0A or higher, the general recommendation is that you use BRCONNECT (Release 6.40 or higher) to calculate the database statistics (see also Section 9.7.1), because this release also enables the creation of histograms for BW InfoCube tables.

Administration during InfoCube maintenance Database statistics for InfoCubes can also be created via the central administration of the InfoCube maintenance. In addition to the administration of InfoCube indices, the **Performance** tab (see Figure 9.31) enables you to manage statistics as well.

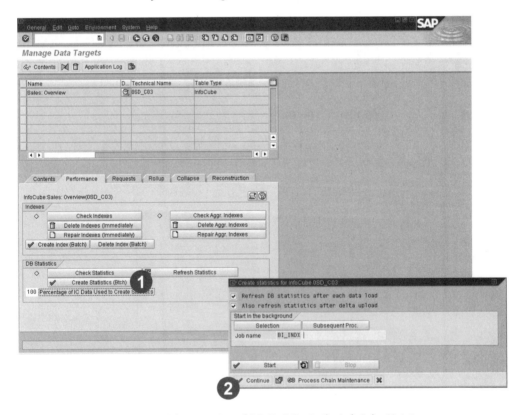

Figure 9.31 Administration of DB Statistics in the InfoCube Maintenance

The **Check Statistics** button retrieves the status of the DB statistics for the InfoCube. For this purpose, it uses the result of the last statistic calculation. The **Refresh Statistics** button starts the creation of new DB statistics for the InfoCube tables in the dialog process. DB statistics for the InfoCube can be scheduled in the background via the **Create Statistics (Btch)** button ❶. If you select this option, a dialog box is displayed ❷ that enables you to automate the DB statistic calculation depending on the load requests of the InfoCube.

> For automatic request processing, please note that the respective settings of the InfoCube are not considered if process chains are used. In this case, the automatic processes must be additionally integrated in the process chain as process types.

The scheduling and execution of statistics jobs of the InfoCube administration can be checked in the job overview using Transaction SM37. The names of all statistics jobs start with BI_STAT.

9.7.3 Administration of Database Statistics Using Transaction DB20

For checking and updating the DB statistics for individual tables, you can use Transaction DB20. An update or check of the DB statistics of individual tables can be required, for example, for diagnostic reasons.

After calling Transaction DB20, you must enter the name of the table to be checked (see Figure 9.32).

After the input has been refreshed (STRG+F1), the results of the last statistic run are displayed: date, time, analysis method (Oracle), and sample size, as well as the number of table rows and the deviation between the old and the new value.

To determine whether you have to refresh the DB statistics, you must check the number of table entries (old and new value) and the deviation. If the deviation between the old value and the new value is greater than 50%, the DB statistics should definitely be updated using the Refresh function (STRG+F2). After the screen information has been refreshed, it displays the result of the new statistic calculation. The log of the corresponding BRCONNECT operation can be retrieved via Transaction DB14 or the **DBA Operations** button (see Figure 9.32 and also Figure 9.25).

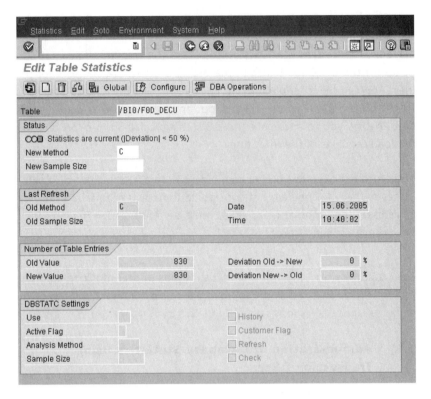

Figure 9.32 Checking Database Statistics Using Transaction DB20

If you create new tables or indices, the table statistics should always be refreshed via Transaction DB20, because the individual analysis of an index (i.e., a newly created or reorganized index) usually results in incomplete statistics, and, consequently, in poor execution plans.

DBSTATC control table

Regardless of the described procedures, the calculation of UPDATE STATISTICS is based on standard settings that are the same for all tables. For tables that require a DB statistics to be handled differently, there is the DBSTATC control table. It contains a list of selected SAP database tables with settings—to update the statistics for the cost-based optimizer—that differ from the standard values. The entries contained in the DBSTATC table are preset by SAP and are delivered with the SAP system. At the time of delivery, the table contains several hundred entries for SAP Basis and application tables. The DBSTATC control table is called via Transaction DB21 (see Figure 9.33).

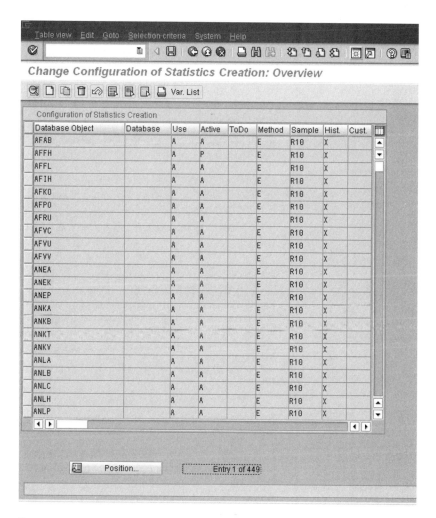

Figure 9.33 DBSTATC Control Table

The DBSTATC table contains various rows, the most important of which are described in Table 9.5:

Column	Value	Description
Database Object	<Name>	Name of the table in capital letters for which you want to specify how to check and update the statistics.
Database	<Name>	Database type (for example, Oracle, Informix, etc.) for which the entry is relevant. An empty entry means that the settings are database-independent.

Table 9.5 Columns and Possible Values in the DBSTATC Table

Column	Value	Description
Use	O	O = Optimizer: Table is relevant for the cost-based optimizer (default setting).
	A	A = Application monitor: Table is relevant for the application monitor; additional statistics will be calculated (Caution: long runtime!).
Active	A	A = Active: Statistics are checked and updated, if necessary (default setting).
	I	I = Ignore: For these tables, no statistics will be updated or deleted.
	N	N = Negative: No statistics will be created, statistics are deleted. Default procedure for all pool and cluster tables.
	P	P = Priority: Tables with this setting are checked before the tables with the default setting "A" and are updated, if necessary. This setting should be enabled if the time-limited statistics update is used (available for Oracle databases as BRCONNECT option) and you want to ensure that the table is preferred.
	U	U = Unconditional: Statistics for this table are always updated without prior checking (Caution: longer runtime!).
	R	R = Restrictive: Statistics are created only temporarily for the application monitor and then deleted immediately.
ToDo	X	For this table, a statistic should be created only once and without checking during the next update. The ToDo flag is then reset.
Method (only relevant for Oracle database systems)	E	Evaluation of statistics (default setting)
	EH	Evaluation of statistics and creation of histograms
	EI	Evaluation of statistics and structure evaluation of the indices
	EX	Evaluation of statistics, creation of histograms, and structure evaluation of the indices
	C	Exact creation of statistics
	CH	Exact creation of statistics and creation of histograms

Table 9.5 Columns and Possible Values in the DBSTATC Table (cont.)

Column	Value	Description
	CI	Exact creation of statistics and structure evaluation of the indices
	CX	Exact creation of statistics, creation of histograms, and structure evaluation of the indices

Table 9.5 Columns and Possible Values in the DBSTATC Table (cont.)

If the DBSTATC table is changed or entries are added, all UPDATE STA-TISTICS runs use these new values for the objects entered in the table! Therefore, changes or additions to the DBSTATC table should be made only after a thorough verification, or after a recommendation from SAP.

9.7.4 Automating the Database Statistics in the DBA Planning Calendar

The DBA Planning Calendar allows you to schedule and execute database administration actions that need to be done on a regular basis. The DBA Planning Calendar is a database administration tool and part of the Computing Center Management System (CCMS) in an SAP system. This tool enables you to administer, schedule, and execute various database actions automatically such as creating data backups, performing database checks, and updating database statistics. The DBA Planning Calendar consists of two transactions that are used, depending on whether the Planning Calendar is implemented centrally or locally: The central DBA Planning Calendar (Transaction DB13C) enables you to view the SAP systems per day, for which DBA actions have been scheduled; the local DBA Planning Calendar (Transaction DB13) displays the DBA actions planned for the local system (see Figure 9.34).

Via Transaction DB13C, the central DBA Planning Calendar is called. Using the **Local Calendar** button ❶ or Transaction DB13 after you selected the system ❷, you can open the local DBA Planning Calendar ❸.

The DBA Planning Calendar can be used for many regular database administration actions that can be automated. For optimizing the database statistics, the actions listed in Table 9.6 should be scheduled in the DBA Planning Calendar:

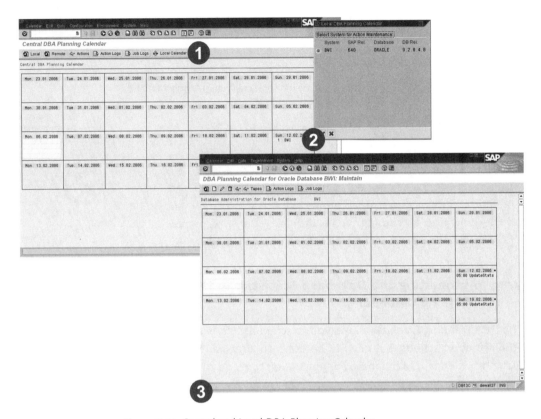

Figure 9.34 Central and Local DBA Planning Calendar

Figure 9.35 shows how to schedule the update statistics in the local DBA Planning Calendar.

Action	Description	Schedule (recommended setting)
Check optimizer statistics: **UPD_CHECK**	Determines the tables that require an update of the SQL optimizer statistics	Weekly
Refresh optimizer/space statistics: **UPD_COND**	Updates the SQL optimizer statistics for those tables determined by UPD_CHECK (restricted update)	Weekly
Create new optimizer/space statistics: **UPD_UNCOND**	Unrestricted update of SQL optimizer statistics	Weekly

Table 9.6 Update of Statistics

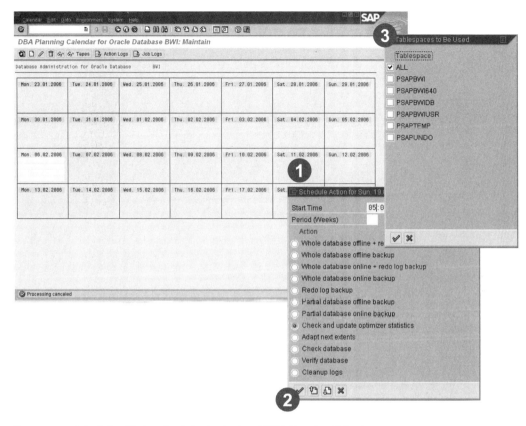

Figure 9.35 Scheduling Update Statistics in the Local DBA Planning Calendar

Double-clicking on the day of the week in the calendar ❶ displays a list of DBA actions ❷ that you can use to select the appropriate DBA actions. For the selected action, you need to pick a start time, the periodic execution, and the calendar type (for example, *US factory calendar*). After confirming the DBA action, you have to specify the tablespaces for which the action is to be executed ❸.

10 Reporting Performance

*This chapter familiarizes you with options for analysis, admin-
istration, and optimization of reporting performance. It introduces the tools contained in SAP BW for analysis and
improvement, and discusses the effects of query design on
performance.*

We've already addressed reporting performance to some extent in Chapter 6, which dealt with data modeling, and we'll discuss it further in
Chapter 11, which focuses on aggregates. Good reporting performance
presupposes the design aspects discussed in data modeling and creating
appropriate aggregates. This chapter describes the various monitoring
tools of SAP Business Information Warehouse (SAP BW) that help you
with analysis during the running of queries. SAP BW also features tuning
tools that will help you to optimize the query performance.

You can use the tools described in this chapter for a detailed analysis of
running queries, the parameterization of query properties, and for tuning
the query performance. As we did in Chapter 6, we'll also discuss various
aspects of performance during the creation of queries.

10.1 OLAP Processor

To access the data stored in SAP BW, the end user doesn't need to know
which database tables store the key figures and characteristics. Nor does
the end user need to call specific aggregates in a query, or pay particular
attention to the changed status of data in an InfoCube.

Data access does not occur directly on the data stored in the database;
instead, data is accessed with the *online analytical processing (OLAP) processor*. The OLAP processor is a query management tool that translates
the query defined by the end user into a language specific to the database. Then, it returns the data stored in the InfoProviders to the frontend
in a multidimensional and formatted view.

Data access occurs with the analysis tools provided by the SAP Business
Explorer (BEx), for example, BEx Analyzer, or with third-party query tools.

You can use the following interfaces to connect the frontend tools of
third parties (see Figure 10.1):

▶ OLE DB for OLAP (ODBO)

▶ OLAP BAPI (Business Application Programming Interface)

▶ XML for Analysis (XML/A)

The interfaces are based on MDX (*MultiDimensional Expressions*) Processor, a query language developed by Microsoft for queries on multidimensional data.

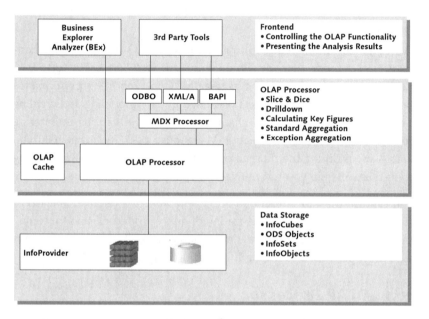

Figure 10.1 Integrating the OLAP Processor in SAP BW

Table 10.1 lists the essential functions of the OLAP processor:

Function	Description
Navigation	▶ Dicing according to characteristics and removing dices ▶ Drilldown into hierarchy nodes and drillup.
Filtering	▶ Limit and slice selection on characteristic values (individual values, value areas, and hierarchy values)
Presentation	▶ Display and hide results ▶ Display key values and texts
Calculation and Aggregation	▶ Standard aggregation, such as totaling individual values ▶ Exception aggregation (MIN, MAX, and AVG)

Table 10.1 Functions of the OLAP Processor (Selection)

Function	Description
Query Performance	▶ Transparent consideration of aggregates ▶ Reuse of query results in memory (OLAP caching)
Data Status	▶ Transparent consideration of status changes in data (the display of correct and consistent load requests) ▶ Transparent consideration of change runs and rollups
Interface	▶ Translation of MDX commands from third-party interfaces into OpenSQL ▶ Translation of queries from analysis tools of the business explorer

Table 10.1 Functions of the OLAP Processor (Selection) (cont.)

Analysis of the data is not only determined by the definition of the query, but also by the configuration of the OLAP processor, as described in more detail in the following sections.

10.2 OLAP Cache

The OLAP processor has a memory area that stores the result of every query in the main memory of the application server, or in tables or files. By storing the query results, new calls of the query with the same selection criteria, or subsets of the query, don't require another selection in the database—instead, they can be answered from the faster cache memory of the application server. The OLAP cache is therefore an efficient performance tool to use for optimizing query runtimes.

The OLAP cache distinguishes between the *local cache* and the *global cache*. The local cache stores the results calculated by the OLAP processor for a session specifically by a user in the roll area. It is used when it is impossible to store the query result in the cross-transaction, global cache. Such a situation can arise when the global cache has been deactivated or turned off on the InfoProvider, or on the query. You cannot use the local cache in multiple sessions or by multiple users.

Local cache

The global cache is a cross-transaction application buffer that stores the results and navigation status of a query in the main memory of the application server. As long as the OLAP processor needs the objects, they are stored in the roll area. All query sessions and query users can use the global cache.

Global cache

Only the local cache was available up to SAP BW 2.0B. As of SAP BW 3.0B, both the global cache and the local cache are available. All users can call objects buffered in the global cache unless using it is impossible, in which case the local cache is used.

When the OLAP processor uses data from the cache during a query run, the response time of the query is improved, because the read process of the cache is much, much faster than another selection of data in the database.

But a query can use the OLAP cache only if a previous query call used the same selection criteria, or if the new query calls a subset of a selection that has already run. The OLAP cache cannot be used with other selection criteria in a second call of the same query. In this case, the query results are stored in the cache and are available for a repetition of the identical call.

Invalidating the OLAP cache A query may not use the OLAP cache if the data in the InfoCube has changed (inserted, updated, or deleted). For BasicCubes, non-transactional operational data store (ODS) objects, and master data providers, SAP BW automatically sets a timestamp in Table RSDINFOPROVDATA when the data is changed. When a query is run, the OLAP processor compares this timestamp with the timestamp of the cache package. The cache package is ignored if the timestamp is older than the timestamp in Table RSDINFOPROVDATA.

A query cannot use the OLAP cache in the following cases:

▶ Activation of master data

▶ Use of navigation attributes or numeric variables with replacement data from attributes

▶ Activation of hierarchies used in the query as a selection or presentation hierarchy

▶ Modification of the query definition and regeneration

Up to SAP BW 3.0B, Support Package 17, a query was always regenerated as soon as something in the definition of the query or a reusable element of the query (a variable, structure, or a calculated or limited key figure) changed. At regeneration, the data used by the query in the OLAP cache was automatically invalidated, in other words, deleted. As of SAP BW 3.0B, Support Package 18 or SAP BW 3.1C, Support Package 12, a modification of the query does not automatically trigger the regeneration of the query. Instead, SAP BW compares the old definition of the query with the new definition and all its subobjects.

A regeneration of the query and deletion of the cache data occurs in the following cases:

▶ Modification of InfoProviders or the InfoObjects involved

▶ Modification of the currency translation or currency translation key

▶ Modification of specific variables or some of their properties

The query is regenerated for modifications of text variables and their use; however, the cache data is not invalidated in this case. The query is not regenerated for modification of texts and the exchange of structure elements.

If a query contains virtual characteristics or key figures, the standard settings of the OLAP cache cannot be used, because the OLAP cache manages only the cache objects in its own buffer area and the data targets based on the query. It does not invalidate the cache when data in other database tables is modified—data read using customer exit variables, for example. Nevertheless, if the OLAP cache is to be used, you must explicitly set the **Query Properties** in the corresponding dialog window, so that the data is written to the cache after it is read from the database and run through the customer exit.

Virtual characteristics and key figures

> Note that the OLAP cache is *not* invalidated after a modification of the
> data by the customer exit: therefore, the current data can differ from
> the cached data.

10.3 OLAP Cache Monitor

The OLAP cache monitor is the central monitoring tool for the OLAP cache. You can use the OLAP cache monitor to obtain a view of the global cache parameters, analyze the memory use of the query runtime objects, and analyze the underlying, current cache structure.

You can call the OLAP cache monitor using Transaction RSRCACHE. The **Cache Parameter** button enables you to call the settings for the global cache (see also Section 10.3.2). The **Main Memory** button can be used to call the current memory use of the OLAP cache (see Figure 10.2).

Figure 10.2 OLAP Cache Monitor

In the **Technical Info** submenu ❶, you can call the current parameters of the runtime objects:

OLAP Parameter	Description
Maximum cache size	Maximum size of the cache in MB. Default: 200 MB
Current cache size	Total memory required for all cache objects in KB
Current swap size (for main memory cache mode with swapping or cluster/flat-file cache)	Size of the swap memory (background memory flat file or cluster table) in KB
Cache filled	Percentage of the size of the filled cache of the overall cache
Total current entries	Sum of the current cache entries and current swap entries
Current cache entries	Number of all cache structure elements
Current swap entries	Number of all entries in the background memory

Table 10.2 OLAP Cache Parameters

You can use the **Buffer Objects: Hierarchical Display** submenu ❷ to call a hierarchical view of all buffer objects of a query directory in the OLAP cache. You can use the **Buffer Objects: List Display** submenu ❸ to display the cache objects in chronological sequence or a physical view of how they are stored in the cache.

By double-clicking on the **Query Name and Hierarchies/Variables** level, you can call a detailed display that shows the technical name, the date of the cache entry, the creator of the cache entry (the user who called the query), and information on the use of hierarchies or variables for each query (see Figure 10.3).

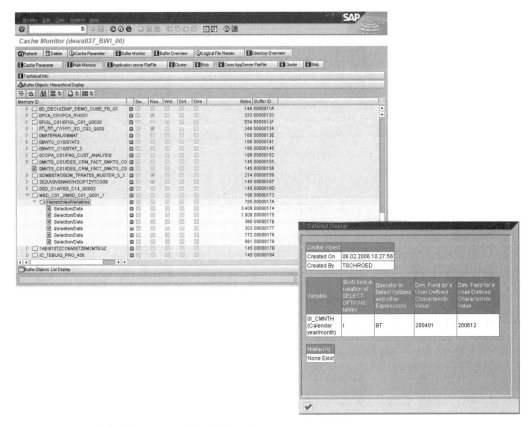

Figure 10.3 Detailed Information on the Cache Objects

You can delete selected buffer objects from the cache (see Figure 10.4) by highlighting the cache element that you want to delete and using the context menu ❶. The **Delete** button removes all the buffer objects in the active view from the OLAP cache ❷.

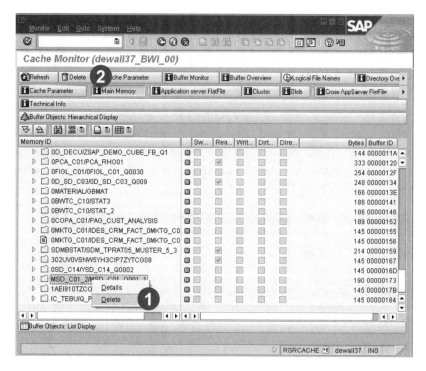

Figure 10.4 Deleting Buffer Objects

10.3.1 Cache Structure

The objects stored in the OLAP cache are stored in a specific cache structure in the buffer area. They can be displayed using the cache monitor.

From a logical viewpoint, the cache objects are structured hierarchically. A query directory is created for each query; the directory contains the structure elements of the cache.

The query directory maps the memory objects contained in the cache in three levels:

Memory Object	Description
Query	Technical name of the query
Hierarchies and variables	Structure for variables requested for the query
Selection and data	Structure for the complete selection for the query

Table 10.3 Memory Objects in the OLAP Cache

As shown in simplified form in Figure 10.5, an entry in the query directory of the OLAP cache is created for each query, depending on the selected selection criteria.

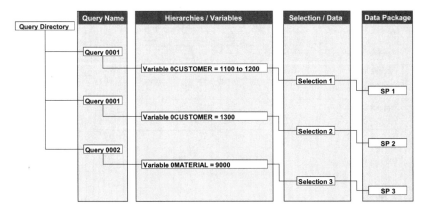

Figure 10.5 Hierarchical Cache Structure

In this example, query 0001 is run with selection variable 0CUSTOMER for value area 1100 to 1200. Query name, selection variable, and hierarchy, and selection data are stored hierarchically in the cache data packages. A new cache entry is generated for another call of query 0001 with input variable 0CUSTOMER = 1300, because the selected value set is not yet present in the cache. If the next call of query 0001 selects the input value 0CUSTOMER = 1500, the query can use the cache, because the subset is already present in the cache (from the first query call).

If a second call of a query cannot read data from the cache, the variable assignment is often the reason. If variables are part of the fixed filter in the query, the OLAP cache must be set up again for each query. The reason is that the key of queries in the OLAP cache consists of "query" + "variables which cannot be changed for navigation" + "selection hierarchies". The cache always stores the value sets (or their subsets) calculated by the OLAP processor and can find the stored subsets or value sets for reuse only if the key of the subset is also a subset of the key of the previously calculated value set.

If you select the **Can be changed in query navigation** setting for a variable, the variable is no longer part of the **Hierarchy/Variable** key. It becomes part of the selection condition that is one level lower in the cache hierarchy. The same **Hierarchy/Variable** subtree is selected for variable selection if the entry has been calculated and stored.

You activate the **Can be changed in query navigation** setting in the SAP BW Variables Editor (see Figure 10.6).

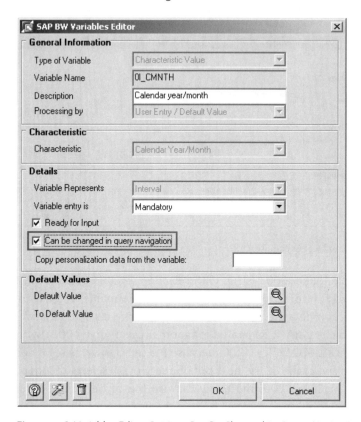

Figure 10.6 Variables Editor Setting: Can Be Changed in Query Navigation

To enable the greatest possible reusability of the cache objects, you should allow queries to be changed in query navigation. But please note the following when reusing cache objects. Only subsets of previously selected sets can be read from the cache, because the OLAP processor examines the relationships between the subsets. It does not combine different cache entries into a new subset.

10.3.2 Global Cache Parameters

You can set the global cache parameters via the SAP BW customizing menu using Transaction SPRO: **SAP Customizing Implementation Guide · SAP NetWeaver · SAP Business Information Warehouse · Reporting-relevant Settings · General Reporting Settings in Business Explorer · Global Cache Settings** (see Figure 10.7).

Figure 10.7 Configuring the OLAP Cache

Storing the query results in the OLAP cache requires additional memory in the main memory of the application server. The size of the OLAP cache must be appropriate to manage the frequency of query calls and the number of users. The size of the global cache depends on the size of the local cache. Cache objects that are no longer used are deleted from the roll area when the size of the local cache is exceeded—for both types of cache objects.

You can configure the cache parameters using Transaction RSCUSTV14 (see ❷ in Figure 10.7):

▶ **Cache Inactive**
Activation of this configuration deactivates the cross-transaction cache. A query can no longer use the global cache—the local cache is used instead.

▶ **Local Size MB**
This parameter sets the size of the local OLAP cache (in MB).

► **Global Size MB**

This parameter sets the maximum value of memory use of all objects in the cross-transaction cache (in MB). The memory use is based on the memory requirements of the objects in the shared memory buffer. The memory usage in the shared memory buffer is generally greater, because it stores the OLAP cache runtime objects in compressed from in the application buffer, along with additional administrative data.

When setting the size of the global cache, note that the actual size of the cross-transaction cache is determined by the minimum value of the **Global Size MB** parameter and the actual memory available in the shared memory buffer (profile parameter `rdsb/esm/buffersize_kb`). You should therefore use Transaction ST02 to check whether the size of the export/import buffer is appropriate. The default setting of 4,096 KB is often too small. SAP recommends the following settings:

► `rsdb/esm/buffersize_kb` = 200000

► `rsdb/esm/max_objects` = 10000.

Persistence mode The persistence mode sets whether and in what form cache data is to be stored and how the data is used when the maximum memory size has been reached. The following modes are available. You can set the modes in the OLAP cache parameters (Transaction RSCUSTV14).

► **Inactive**

The data is deleted from the memory when the memory available for caching has been consumed.

► **Flat file**

The data is swapped out into a file when the memory available for caching has been consumed. A repeated call of the cache object loads it into the cache memory.

► **Database table**

The data is stored in a non-transparent cluster table or in a transparent table with BLOB[1] (binary large object) in the database when the cache memory has been consumed. A repeated call of the cache object loads it into the cache memory.

---

1 BLOB (*Binary Large Object*) is a special type of data that can hold character strings of variable length (up to L+2 bytes, where L < 2^16). It is therefore suitable for storing large data quantities.

The persistence mode is closely related to the cache mode. The cache mode determines how query results and navigation statuses are stored in the cache as compressed files. The persistence mode determines how the cache objects are to be stored when the cache memory has been consumed. You can set the cache mode in Customizing for an InfoProvider as a default value for all queries on the InfoProvider in the SAP BW Customizing menu (Transaction SPRO): **SAP Customizing Implementation Guide · SAP NetWeaver · SAP Business Information Warehouse · Reporting-relevant Settings · InfoProvider Properties** or selectively for a query in the query monitor (Transaction RSRT). See also Section 10.4 on this topic.

Cache mode

Table 10.4 provides an overview of the cache mode and the persistence mode:

		Cache Mode	
		Main memory cache with and without swapping	**Persistent cache per application server or across several application servers**
Persistence Mode	**Inactive**	Data is purged from the cache when the cache memory has been consumed (corresponds to the main memory cache without swapping mode).	
	Flat file	Data is stored in a flat file when the cache memory has been consumed (corresponds to the main memory with swapping mode).	Cache objects are stored as files in a directory on the application server or across several application servers on a network.
	Cluster table	Data is stored in a non-transparent cluster table when the cache memory has been consumed (corresponds to the main memory with swapping mode).	Data is stored as a non-transparent cluster table in the database (depends on the cache mode with or without application server in the key).
	BLOB table	Data is stored in a transparent table with BLOB when the cache memory has been consumed (corresponds to the main memory with swapping mode).	Data is stored as a transparent table with BLOB in the database (depends on the cache mode with or without application server in the key).

Table 10.4 Relationship Between Cache Mode and Persistence Mode

If you don't select an entry for the persistence mode (initial value), the system sets the persistence mode to inactive.

You should check which persistence mode is selected for the queries. For larger result sets, the transparent table (BLOB) can provide better performance, because of its more efficient database operations. For smaller result sets, the cluster table can be advantageous, because the BLOB fields in the database require more administrative effort.

To store cache objects in files (cache modes: **Main Memory with Swapping**, **Flat File Cache per Application Server**, and **Flat File Cache Across Application Servers**), you must first define the logical file path, the physical file path, and the file name. You can maintain the parameters using Transaction FILE, or via the **Logical File Names** menu in the OLAP cache monitor (see Section 10.3 and Figure 10.8).

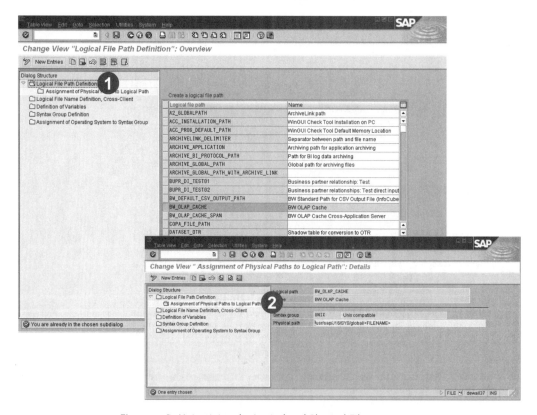

Figure 10.8 Maintaining the Logical and Physical File Names

First, you must define the logical file path of the flat file (Step 1: **Logical File Path Definition**). The platform-independent, logical file path is analyzed at runtime to determine the platform-dependent, physical path. The physical file path is defined in the next step (Step 2: **Assignment of Physical Paths to Logical Paths**). Table 10.5 provides an overview of the parameterization of the logical file path:

Logical File Path	Cache Mode	Description
BW_OLAP_CACHE	Main Memory Cache with Swapping	Logical file path to store the data to be swapped
	Persistent cache for each application server	Logical file path to store all data if the cache data is to be stored in one file. The application server is an element of the file name.
BW_OLAP_CACHE_SPAN	Persistent cache across application servers	The flat file name indicates the logical file path for storing all data. The application server is not an element of the file name.

Table 10.5 Parameterization of the Logical File Path

The physical path is platform-independent and must be set according to the system configuration. The file should be located as close to the application server as possible so that it can be found and read quickly. The physical path is set up according to the following structure: /usr/<SYSID>/global/<FILENAME>. Except for the <FILENAME> parameter, you can select the path per your requirements, as long as it conforms to the configuration of the system. The <FILENAME> parameter must be replaced with the physical file name. The complete, platform-specific file name is actually created automatically only at runtime: it consists of the physical path and the physical file name. A specific schema is stipulated for the definition of the physical file name.

▶ To store the file on the application server, you must use the syntax CACHE_<HOST>_<SYSID>_<PARAM_1>

▶ For cross-application server storage, you must use the syntax CACHE_<SYSID>_<PARAM_1>

The <HOST> parameter specifies the name of the computer or server. The variable is unnecessary if the data is stored across application servers. The <SYSID> parameter differentiates the systems when two SAP BW systems run on one application server. The <PARAM_1> parameter is a sequential number in HEX.

10.3.3 OLAP Properties for InfoProviders

You can use the SAP BW Customizing menu to make global settings for the OLAP cache and to parameterize the default settings of an InfoProvider regarding its read and cache modes. Use Transaction SPRO and menu path **SAP Customizing Implementation Guide · SAP NetWeaver · SAP Business Information Warehouse · Reporting-relevant Settings · General Reporting Settings in Business Explorer · InfoProvider Properties** to call the maintenance dialog (see ❶ in Figure 10.9).

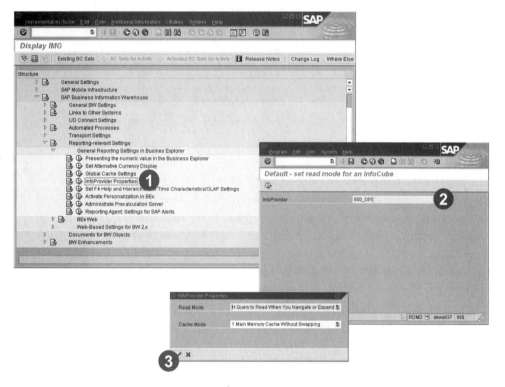

Figure 10.9 OLAP Properties for InfoProviders

After you select the InfoProvider ❷, you can set the OLAP properties, **Read Mode** and **Cache Mode** for the InfoProvider ❸.

The settings apply to all queries that will be created for the InfoProvider. You can make OLAP default settings for existing queries using the query monitor (see Section 10.4).

The read mode of the InfoProvider determines how the OLAP processor retrieves the data during navigation. New queries are then created with the default read mode of the InfoProvider. If no default read mode is set for the InfoProvider, the read mode is set to **Hierarchical Reread**.

You can use the cache mode of the InfoProvider to set the type of storage for query results calculated by the OLAP processor. You can select from the options listed in Table 10.6:

Cache Mode in InfoProvider	Description
Cache is inactive	The cross-transaction cache is switched off for the selected InfoProvider.
Main memory cache with/without swapping	The cross-transaction cache is switched on for the selected InfoProvider (default value). Cache data is stored in a background cache once the memory available for caching has been consumed (with swapping).
Persistent cache per application server or across application servers	The cache data is stored persistently in a cluster table or in flat files for each application server or across application servers. Unlike the case with the main memory cache mode, no swapping takes place.

Table 10.6 Cache Mode of the InfoProvider

The cache modes, **Persistent Cache per Application Server** and **Persistent Cache Across Application Servers** are available as of SAP BW 3.0B, Support Package 13, or SAP BW 3.1C, Support Package 07.

For specific InfoProviders, for which the SAP BW system does not control data changes (RemoteCubes and transactional ODS objects, for example), the query results calculated by the OLAP processor cannot be stored, by default, in the cross-transaction application buffer (cache validity = 0 seconds). You can maintain the cache validity, that is, the retention period of the cache objects, for queries of such InfoProviders in the customizing settings of the InfoProvider. The cache validity of queries of other InfoProviders is automatically determined with the timestamp of the last change of their metadata, master data, and transaction data.

10.3.4 Cache Purging and Swapping

When the memory capacity of the OLAP cache is exhausted (when the maximum cache size has been reached), cache objects must be purged (deleted) or stored elsewhere so that additional data can be written to the cache. Depending on the cache mode selected, you have two options here:

▶ **Main Memory Cache Without Swapping**
Data is purged from the cache (deleted).

▶ **Main Memory Cache With Swapping**
Data is swapped from the cache to a background memory.

You can view the status of the cache objects using the status flag in the OLAP cache monitor (**Main Memory · Buffer Objects: Hierarchical Display or Buffer Objects: List Display**, see Figure 10.10).

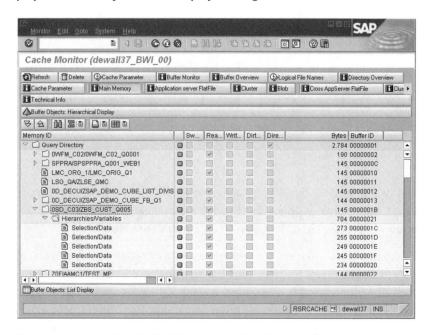

Figure 10.10 Status of the Buffer Objects in the Main Memory of the OLAP Cache

The **Write** flag is set when a cache element is written to the cache for the first time and the cache mode is persistent. No **Write** flag is set for the new cache elements if the cache mode is not persistent. The **Read** flag is set when the cache object is called again. Cache objects with a **Read** flag have been read from the OLAP cache. Cache objects that have been swapped from the cache to background memory are marked with the **Swapped** flag. The **Dirty** flag is set when the data is written to background memory before being purged and the cache mode is persistent. The **Dirty** flag corresponds to the **Write** flag with purging. The **Directory** flag marks the highest node of the content directory of the queries.

10.4 Query Monitor

The query monitor is the administration, testing, and monitoring tool for SAP BEx queries. You can use the query monitor to generate, test, and run SAP BEx queries and to configure general properties of queries. You can call the query monitor using Transaction RSRT (see Figure 10.11).

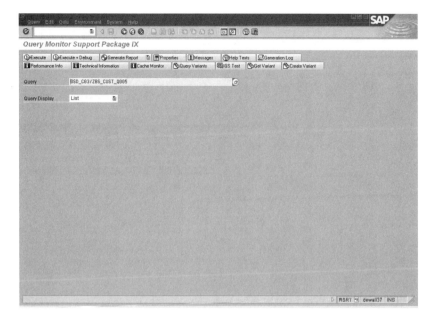

Figure 10.11 Query Monitor (Transaction RSRT)

From the viewpoint of performance, the settings for query properties, the performance information, and the test functions of a query (debugging) are especially important. The following sections describe these points in more detail.

10.4.1 Query Properties

In the **Query Properties** dialog window of the query monitor (see Figure 10.12), you can configure settings for the Read Mode, Cache Mode, and Optimization Mode of the query.

The read mode of a query determines how often the OLAP processor retrieves data from the database during query navigation. The query definition tells the OLAP processor which data it must select. The query definition is determined by the InfoObjects of the query, with a distinction between the InfoObjects in rows (key figures + characteristics), the InfoObjects in columns (key figures + characteristics), the free characteristics, and the filter characteristics. As early as the first navigation step of the query, the InfoObject data in the rows, columns, and filter is read from the database. The data of the free characteristics, however, doesn't need to be read until the dicing of the free characteristics in the query occurs.

Read mode

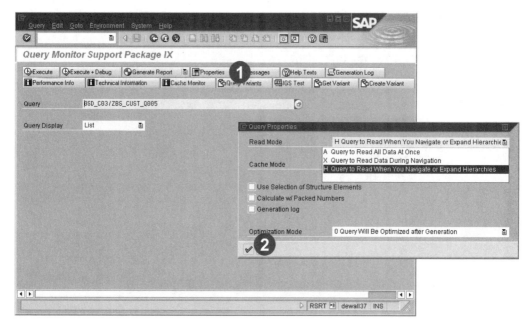

Figure 10.12 Configuring the Query Properties in the Query Monitor

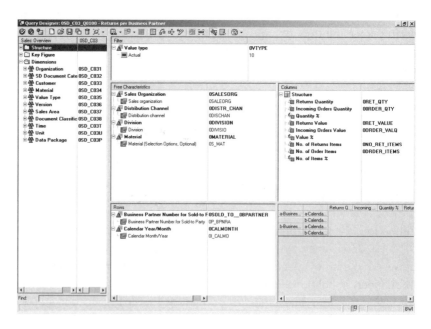

Figure 10.13 Query Definition

The read mode distinguishes between three types of read processes:

▶ Read all data (setting **A: Query to Read All Data At Once**)
▶ Reread the data (setting **X: Query to Read Data During Navigation**)
▶ Reread the data when expanding a hierarchy (setting **H: Query to Read When You Navigate or Expand Hierarchies**)

The default setting for a new query is Read Mode **H: Query to Read When You Navigate or Expand Hierarchies** or the setting made using Transaction RDMD in Customizing for the underlying InfoProvider. In the query monitor, you can change the default settings of the read mode for existing queries. The read mode settings made in the query monitor over-rule the settings of the InfoProvider underlying the query. You can define the cache validity of the cache objects only in Customizing for InfoProviders.

The **Read all Data** read mode includes only one read procedure. All the data needed by the query is read from the database in the first step and loaded into the main memory of the OLAP processor. For all additional navigation steps, including the navigation through the free characteristics, the data is aggregated and calculated from the main memory. Another read access to the database is not required.

Read mode: Read all Data

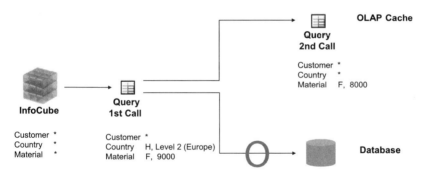

Figure 10.14 Read Mode: Read all Data

The example shown in Figure 10.14 selects hierarchy level 2 for the *Country* object in query call 1 and the fixed value of 9000 for the *Material* object. Additional navigation steps do not limit *Country* any further and select the fixed value of 8000 for *Material*. Despite the changed query selection, query call 2 does not read from the database, because all the selection data of the query is present in the OLAP cache with the first call as the result of navigation.

Once all the data of the query has been loaded into the main memory of the OLAP processor, all additional navigation steps of the query are quite fast, because they don't need to access the database again. However, the first call of the query is very slow, because all the data, including the data of the free characteristics, must be retrieved from the database in a read step. The read process can last quite a long time for queries with many free characteristics.

The **Read all Data** read mode should be used for only very small Info-Cubes. Because this read mode also reads all the free characteristics of the query in the first step, it provides the least support for the concept of aggregates to store preaggregated subsets of data (see also Chapter 11). Queries that contain many free characteristics also require a great deal of cross-transactional memory for the OLAP cache.

Read mode: Reread the Data In the **Reread the Data** read mode, the OLAP processor requires only the necessary data for each navigation step. The data of the free characteristics is read only when it is needed for a dice. Data is read from the OLAP cache when the navigation results have already been selected once. Unlike the **Reread the Data when Expanding a Hierarchy** read mode, this read mode always reads external hierarchies completely at the leaf level, even if a query selects a higher level.

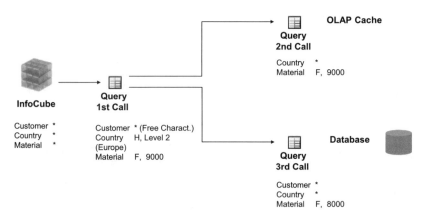

Figure 10.15 Read Mode: Reread the Data

The example shown in Figure 10.15 handles the second query call with *Country* * completely from the OLAP cache. The first query call selected the fixed value of 9000 for *Material* and the entire external hierarchy for *Country* was read into the OLAP cache. The third query call must once again access the database, because the OLAP cache does not yet contain the navigation result with the fixed value of 8000 for *Material*.

The **Reread the Data** read mode navigates more slowly than the **Read all Data** read mode, because it must access the database for every navigation step if the navigation result is not yet present in the OLAP cache. However, this read mode is best suited for the use of aggregates, even when the query uses a large number of free characteristics.

The **Reread the Data When Expanding a Hierarchy** read mode selects the smallest amount of data. This is why this mode requires the most reads on the database. Where the **Reread the Data** read mode reads the expanded hierarchy completely in the first step, the **Reread the Data When Expanding a Hierarchy** read mode reads only the data up to the selected hierarchy level in the first step. If a deeper level of the hierarchy is required in another navigation step, the database must be accessed again.

Read mode: Reread the Data When Expanding a Hierarchy

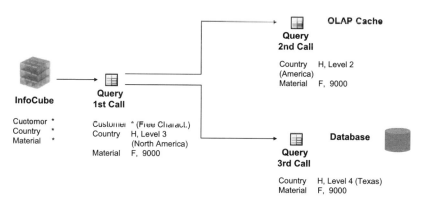

Figure 10.16 Read Mode: Reread the Data When Expanding a Hierarchy

The second query call with hierarchy level 2 in the example shown in Figure 10.16 can use the OLAP cache from *Country*, because the first call already selected the deeper query hierarchy level, Level 3, of *Country*. The third query call must access the database, because hierarchy level 4 of *Country* is not yet present in the OLAP cache as a navigation result.

When you use hierarchy aggregates, you must set the read mode of the query to **Reread the Data When Expanding a Hierarchy**; otherwise, you can't use the hierarchy attributes. You should use this read mode for large hierarchies (from about 500 hierarchy nodes). If you don't, the first call in the **Reread the Data** read mode can result in long waits.

Table 10.7 provides an overview of all three read modes.

In most cases, the **Reread the Data When Expanding a Hierarchy** read mode provides the best response times, because each navigation step has to read only the required data.

Read Mode	Advantages	Disadvantages	Recommendation
Read all data	▶ Very fast query navigation after the first call, because all the data is present in the OLAP cache.	▶ First call is slow ▶ Significant limitations on the use of characteristic aggregates ▶ Requires more memory in the OLAP cache	▶ Use this read mode only with small InfoCubes ▶ Use this read mode only in queries containing few free characteristics.
Reread the data	▶ The first call is very fast, because only the required data is selected. ▶ Good hit rate for characteristic aggregates ▶ Rapid response time for small hierarchies	▶ Requires waiting for additional calls if the selection is not identical to the first call.	▶ Use this read mode for small hierarchies. ▶ Use this read mode with large quantities of results.
Reread the data when expanding a hierarchy	▶ The first call is very fast, because only the required data is selected.	▶ Selects the smallest amount of data in the first call, so that changes to navigation require read accesses to the database.	▶ The use of this read mode is required for hierarchy aggregates.

Table 10.7 Comparison of the Read Modes of the InfoProvider

The read mode of an InfoCube defined via Transaction SPRO in the Customizing Guide is stored in Table RSDCUBE. The read modes of a query defined in the query properties via Transaction RSRT are stored in Table RSRREPDIR. Both tables provide a quick overview of the read modes for an InfoCube and for a query.

You can select the tables using the table browser (Transaction SE16). Figure 10.17 shows Table RSDCUBE. To view only active and usable Info-Cubes, you should limit the selection to **OBJVERS** = "A" and **OBJSTAT** = "ACT".

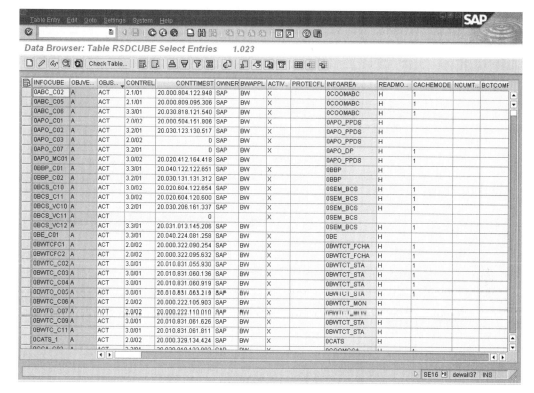

Figure 10.17 Table RSDCUBE

The **READMODE** column indicates the read mode of the InfoCube:

▶ A = query reads all data at once

▶ X = query to read data during navigation

▶ H = query to read data when you navigate or expand hierarchies

The **CACHEMODE** column indicates the cache mode of the InfoCube:

▶ 0/Blank = cache is inactive

▶ 1 = main memory cache without swapping

▶ 2 = main memory cache with swapping

▶ 3 = persistent cache for each application server

▶ 4 = persistent cache across application servers

Buffer objects are chronologically stored flat in the OLAP cache as data packets. After the first run of a query and every 31 days after the last optimization, the OLAP processor determines the optimal initial size of the

Optimization mode

Storage Package (SP) cache packages. You can set the time of the optimization of the memory structure of cache packages in the query properties.

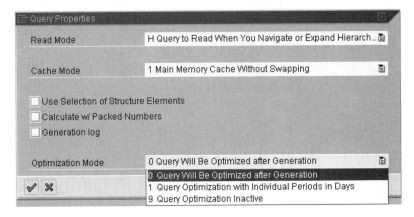

Figure 10.18 Query Optimization Mode

You can set the optimization mode of the query in the dialog shown in Figure 10.18:

▶ **Option 0**
Query Will Be Optimized after Generation. The query is optimized after generation in this optimization mode.

▶ **Option 1**
Query Optimization with Individual Periods in Days. This mode is identical to option 0, but you can also select the period of optimization in days.

▶ **Option 9**
Query Optimization Inactive. In this mode, the memory structure of the table is not optimized after generation of the query.

10.4.2 Debugging Options

To enable specific examination of individual queries, SAP BW provides a query monitor that you can call using Transaction RSRT (see Figure 10.19). The query monitor enables the execution of individual queries with various debugging options.

After you select a query, it can be executed via the **Execute + Debug** button ❶ with a selection of various debugging options ❷. The debugging options provide various ways for you to display or examine specific elements of a query. For example, you can select the **Display SQL/MDX Query** option to display the SQL statement of the query.

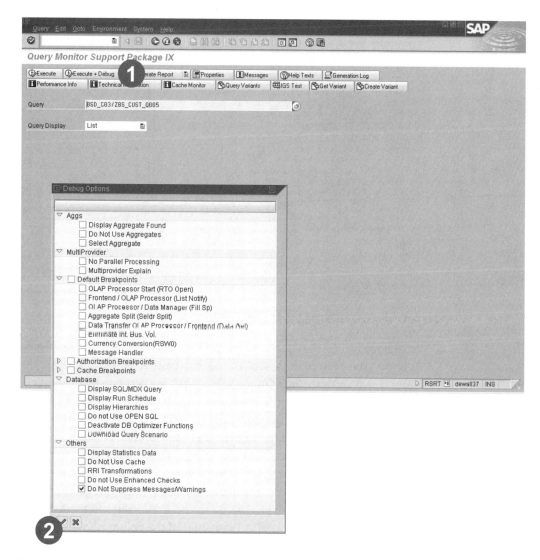

Figure 10.19 Debugging Options in the Query Monitor

For complex queries, the **Display Aggregate Found** option enables you to display the aggregate in use. Queries on MultiProviders display the aggregates with their technical names for all the InfoProviders involved, one after the other. If an aggregate cannot be used, the InfoCubes involved are displayed along with all the InfoObjects and filter settings used in the query. When displaying an aggregate with its six-digit ID, you can use Table RSDCUBE to determine the InfoCube assigned to the aggregate.

"Display Aggregate Found" option

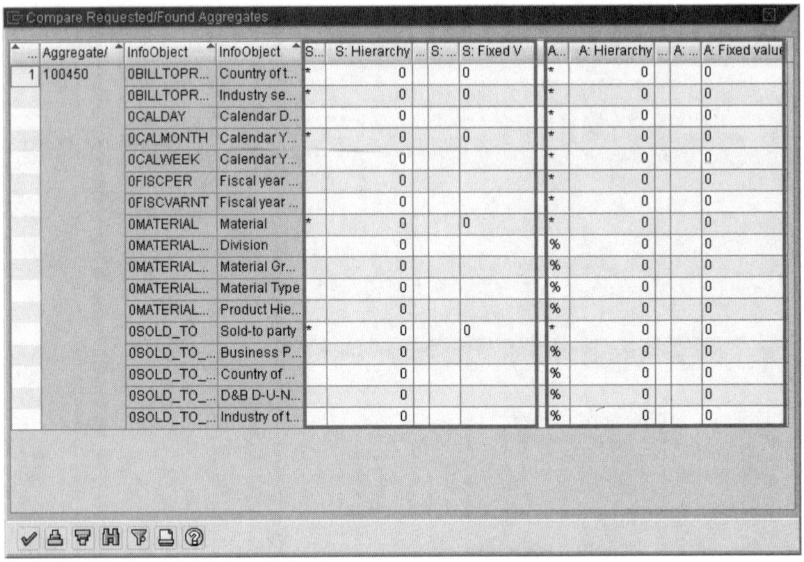

...	Aggregate/	InfoObject	InfoObject	S...	S: Hierarchy	...	S: ...	S: Fixed V	A...	A: Hierarchy	...	A: ...	A: Fixed value
1	100450	0BILLTOPR...	Country of t...	*	0			0	*	0			0
		0BILLTOPR...	Industry se...	*	0			0	*	0			0
		0CALDAY	Calendar D...		0				*	0			0
		0CALMONTH	Calendar Y...	*	0			0	*	0			0
		0CALWEEK	Calendar Y...		0				*	0			0
		0FISCPER	Fiscal year ...		0				*	0			0
		0FISCVARNT	Fiscal year ...		0				*	0			0
		0MATERIAL	Material	*	0			0	*	0			0
		0MATERIAL...	Division		0				%	0			0
		0MATERIAL...	Material Gr...		0				%	0			0
		0MATERIAL...	Material Type		0				%	0			0
		0MATERIAL...	Product Hie...		0				%	0			0
		0SOLD_TO	Sold-to party	*	0			0	*	0			0
		0SOLD_TO_...	Business P...		0				%	0			0
		0SOLD_TO_...	Country of ...		0				%	0			0
		0SOLD_TO_...	D&B D-U-N...		0				%	0			0
		0SOLD_TO_...	Industry of t...		0				%	0			0

Figure 10.20 "Display Aggregate Found" Debugging Option

In Figure 10.20, the query executes a database access on Aggregate 100450. The first column lists all the database accesses, one after the other. The **Aggregate/InfoCube** column lists the aggregate by its six-digit, internal SAP BW ID, or the InfoCube. The **InfoObject** columns list all InfoObjects required in the query access with their technical names or semantic descriptions. Some entries are listed in two separate, marked boxes, because in this way, help you to better understand their function. The first box whose column names begin with "S" contains suggested values for the aggregation type, the hierarchy used (if the aggregation type is H; otherwise, it's 0), the hierarchy level, and fixed values (if the aggregation type is F; otherwise, it's 0). The names of the columns in the second box begin with "A". This box contains the corresponding entries for the aggregate found.

The aggregation type can have the following properties:

- *: all values
- F: fixed value
- H: hierarchy level
- %: navigation attribute
- Blank

As shown in Figure 10.20, the aggregate found contains many InfoObjects, including 0CALDAY, 0CALMONTH, 0CALWEEK, 0FISCPER, and 0FISCVARNT, where no fixed values or hierarchy level is set for any of these objects.

> Note that the results column of the fixed values in the query monitor RSRT shows only the SID values, not the characteristic values themselves. You can identify the corresponding fixed value with the SID key in SID table /BI0/S<InfoObject> or /BIC/S<InfoObject>.

If aggregates are already present but are not used, you can use the **Select Aggregate** debugging option to see why the available aggregates have not been used (see Figure 10.21). The InfoObjects that lead to the non-use of an aggregate are listed for all aggregates of the InfoCube. This lack of use always occurs when the corresponding InfoObject is not contained in the aggregate, or an inappropriate fixed value is defined for the InfoObject in the aggregate, or the query requires a lower degree of detail than exists in the aggregate.

"Select Aggregate" option

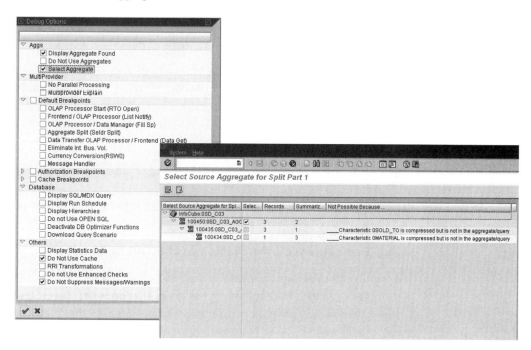

Figure 10.21 "Select Aggregate" Debugging Option

Query results display When you display the results of the query in the query monitor, you can choose from the following options: **List**, **BEx Analyzer**, and **HTML** (see Figure 10.22). If you want to check various query navigation steps for the use of aggregates, you should select the **HTML** display option, because it provides the full scope of query navigation. The selected debugging option is executed at each query navigation step.

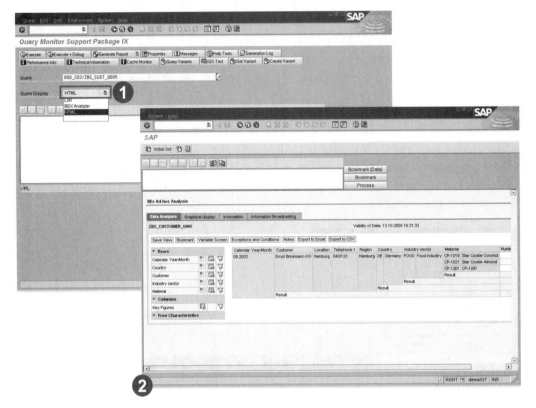

Figure 10.22 Query Results in HTML in the Query Monitor with Complete Navigation Options

10.4.3 Performance Information in the Query Monitor

You can use the **Performance Info** button shown in Figure 10.11 to call performance-relevant information on the query that does *not* correspond to the system recommendations. The information refers to the following areas:

Performance Info Area	Message
Query Definition	Query cannot use the aggregates (corresponds to the information provided in **Technical Information** under **OLAP-relevant Data**)
	Read mode X or A (see read mode, Section 10.4.1)
	Query cannot use the cache (corresponds to the information provided in **Technical Information** under **Cache-relevant Data**)
	Query uses customer exits (see also Section 10.2)
	There are non-cumulative values with AVi (corresponds to the information provided in **Technical Information** under **Non-cumulative flags**)
InfoProvider	The InfoProvider is a MultiProvider (see also Section 10.8.6)
	DB statistics require checking (see also Section 9.6)
	DB index requires checking (see also Section 9.4)

Table 10.8 Performance Information in the Query Monitor

10.5 Query Trace

The query trace is another option for logging individual query steps during the execution of a query. The trace must be switched on separately for each user for whom you want to record a trace. You can activate a trace using Transaction RSRTRACE or SAP BEx Analyzer by selecting the **Trace** option (see Figure 10.23).

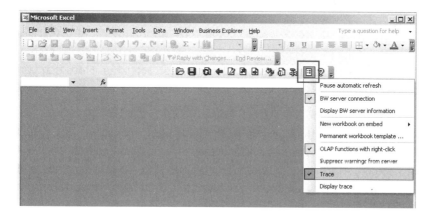

Figure 10.23 Switching on the Query Trace via SAP BEx Analyzer

You can configure the trace for a specific topic when you activate the query trace using Transaction RSRTRACE (see Figure 10.24). You must add individual users with the Plus (+) button and can remove them from the trace by clicking on the Minus (–) button. You can use the Configure user button to configure the trace for specific users.

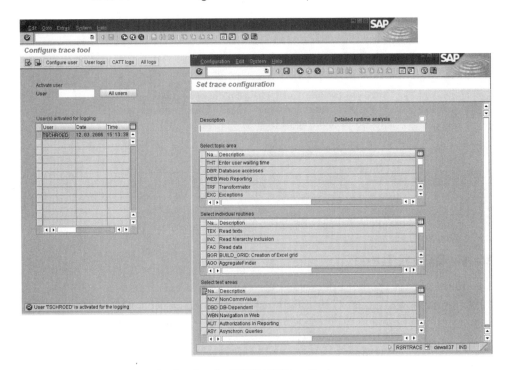

Figure 10.24 Configuring the RSRTRACE Trace Tool

Whether you activate the trace via the Trace option in SAP BEx Analyzer or by using the trace tool RSRTRACE, the trace only goes into effect when the user logs on again, after the trace has been activated. Note that you should activate the trace only for specific analyses, because the logs that result from the trace can affect the performance negatively.

After you execute the query steps that you want to analyze, you should turn off the trace, because constant trace recording demands a great deal of system performance. The log recordings are stored in a trace log and can be called at any time. You can use the DB Debugging button to go through individual steps of the trace at a later time.

Analyzing trace logs You can list the recorded trace logs via the All logs button (see Figure 10.25). Double-click on one of the trace logs in the list to display the recorded trace (see Figure 10.26).

Figure 10.25 Trace Logs

You can use the **Analyze Trace** button to call Transaction RSRCATTTRACE (see Figure 10.27).

Call	SUB	Function module	Parameter	InfoCube	ReportName	CPU time [micro s]
1		SESSION_INIT				60.844
2		RZX0_CONTROL_TEXTS_G				296.065
3		RZX2_OPEN_OBJ_GET				1.295.839
4		RRMX_WB_READ				22.033.380
5	X	REPORT_OPEN		0SD_C03	0SD_C03_Q0100	191.077
6	X	VARIABLES_FLUSH		0SD_C03	0SD_C03_Q0100	62.503
7	X	CMD_PROCESS	STRT	0SD_C03	0SD_C03_Q0100	12.678.609
8	X	CMD_PROCESS	WAIT	0SD_C03	0SD_C03_Q0100	1.092.008
9	X	TXT_SYM_GET		0SD_C03	0SD_C03_Q0100	29.220
10	X	CMD_PROCESS	PING	0SD_C03	0SD_C03_Q0100	86.452
11	X	TXT_SYM_GET		0SD_C03	0SD_C03_Q0100	32.957
12	X	REPORT_CLOSE		0SD_C03	0SD_C03_Q0100	49.108
13	X	RZX2_OPEN_OBJ_GET				123.607
14	X	RRMX_WB_READ				82.342.330
15	XX	REPORT_OPEN		0SD_C14	YSD_C14_Q0003	30.112
16	XX	VARIABLES_FLUSH		0SD_C14	YSD_C14_Q0003	68.832
17	XX	CMD_PROCESS	STRT	0SD_C14	YSD_C14_Q0003	12.798.200
18	XX	CMD_PROCESS	WAIT	0SD_C14	YSD_C14_Q0003	1.508.844
19	XX	TXT_SYM_GET		0SD_C14	YSD_C14_Q0003	30.978
20	XX	CMD_PROCESS	PING	0SD_C14	YSD_C14_Q0003	50.724
21	XX	TXT_SYM_GET		0SD_C14	YSD_C14_Q0003	31.761

Figure 10.26 Log Steps of Trace Recording

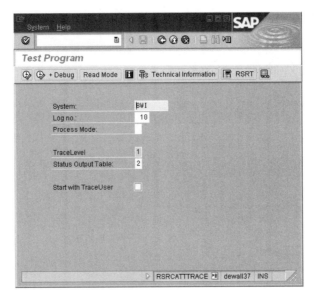

Figure 10.27 Test Program RSRCATTTRACE

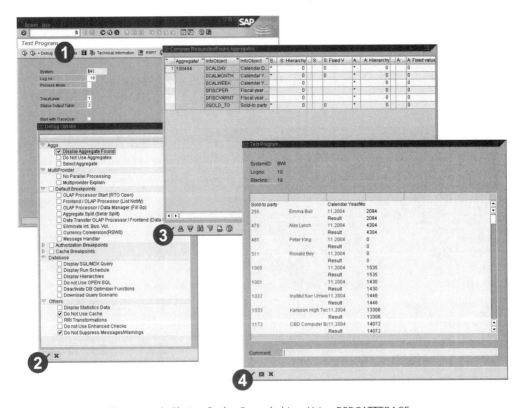

Figure 10.28 Playing Back a Recorded Log Using RSRCATTTRACE

You must enter the log number of the trace log and the system in the initial view of test program RSRCATTTRACE. You can then use the **Execute + Debug** function to rerun the recorded log, just as it was recorded at the time of logging. The system displays the dialog box familiar from Transaction RSRT once again. Here you can select functions to display the SQL statement, or the aggregates found (see Figure 10.28).

Transactions RSRTRACE and RSRCATTTRACE are particularly well suited to generating suggested aggregates for the first navigation step and all additional navigation steps of a query.

10.6 SAP BW Reporting Agent

The reporting agent in SAP BW enables the execution of various reporting functions in the background. For example, you can automatically print queries in the background or precalculate web templates. In addition to other functions of the reporting agent, these two procedures are especially appropriate for warming up (populating) the OLAP cache with the results of the report precalculation, in order to enable faster live access to data from the OLAP cache with identical query navigation.

10.6.1 Printing Queries

You can make the settings required for printing queries in the Reporting Agent menu of the Administrator Workbench. In the **Print** submenu, first select the InfoCube and the query for which you want to generate automatic batch printing.

If no reporting agent settings exist for a query, you must first create them (see ❶ in Figure 10.29). In the subsequent screen ❷, you must enter a technical name for the query-specific reporting agent settings in the **General** tab. You can use the **Print settings** tab to set the printing process. The **Print layout** tab enables you to configure the design of the InfoObjects of the query in print. If you want to use the batch printing function of the reporting agent only to populate the OLAP cache in batch, you do not need to specify the print settings and print layout in any more detail.

Creating reporting agent settings

If you want to schedule a query with input variables for batch printing, you must first create a variant for the input of the variable (see ❶ in Figure 10.30).

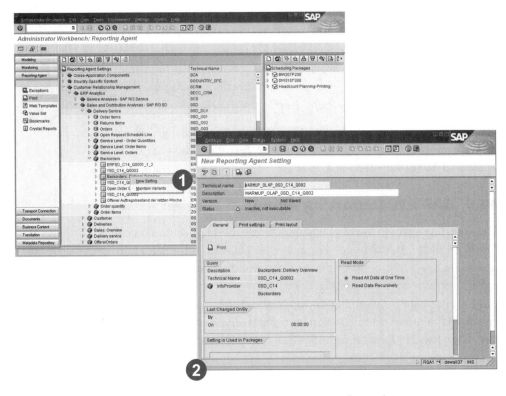

Figure 10.29 Creating New Reporting Agent Settings for Batch Printing

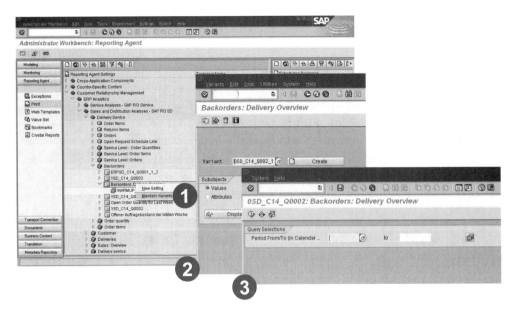

Figure 10.30 Creating Variants for Input Variables in the Reporting Agent

With the creation of a variant ❷, the values for the input of the variables at runtime are already preselected to use for printing in the background ❸.

After you create the reporting agent settings, you must create a scheduling package for background processing (see Figure 10.31). The scheduling package is used to set the time of background processing for the query. You can combine several reporting agent settings in one scheduling package. The settings are then precalculated in a single job (see also ❶ in Figure 10.32).

Creating a scheduling package

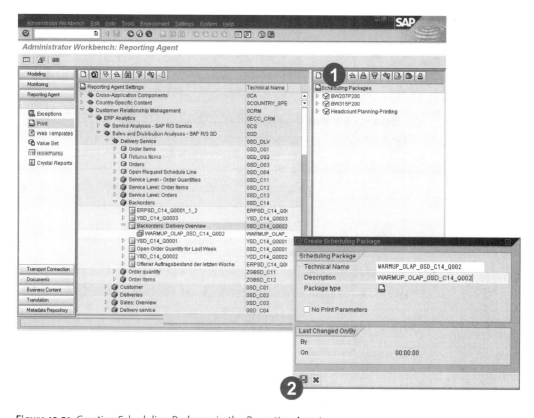

Figure 10.31 Creating Scheduling Packages in the Reporting Agent

In the next step, you use drag and drop to assign a reporting agent setting to a scheduling package (❶ in Figure 10.32). You can then schedule the scheduling package as a job (❷ and ❸) or insert it into a process chain.

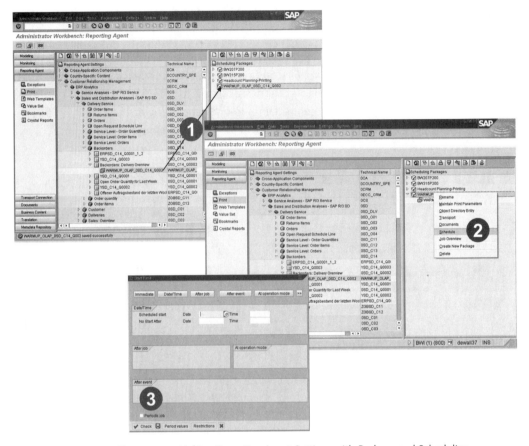

Figure 10.32 Linking Reporting Agent Settings with Package and Scheduling

10.6.2 Precalculating Web Templates

The calculation of web templates is another option for the automatic pre-calculation of query results. Web templates are HTML documents with placeholders specific to SAP BW. The templates display query results in a web browser. You can use precalculated web templates to write query results to the OLAP cache automatically, where they remain available for identical navigation steps, or where they can be called as static web reports, without having to execute an OLAP query.

You must first create a web template to be able to precalculate query results with web templates (see Figure 10.33). Then, you must create the reporting agent settings ❶ for the web template.

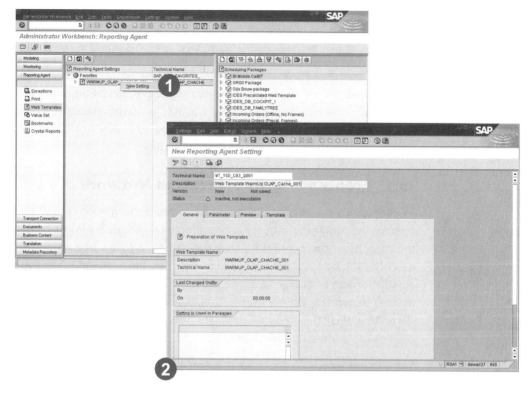

Figure 10.33 Creating New Reporting Agent Settings for Web Templates

You can configure the reporting agent setting in the subsequent screen ❷. Use the **General** tab to define the name of the reporting agent setting and to enter information on the last change (after the first save) and information on the scheduling packages that will use the setting.

You can use the **Parameter** tab to define what is to be precalculated. For the calculation of large result sets, you should select the **Data** option in the **Calculate** menu because the OLAP processor will not have to request the data during later calls of the web template—only the HTML page will have to be generated. When you use workbooks, note that the reporting agent cannot precalculate workbooks. If you want to place the results of a workbook into the OLAP cache, you must schedule each query individually.

If the query uses input variables, you can create a variant that stores the selection values—just as you can use precalculation with background printing.

After you enter the reporting agent settings, you must generate a scheduling package that can be executed via a job or a process chain. The procedure is similar to the configuration of batch printing (see Section 10.6.1).

Both procedures are appropriate for automatic precalculation of a query and making the resulting quantities available as cache elements in the OLAP cache. The procedures differ in the medium used for the query results: static web report, Excel, or batch printing.

10.7 Frontend Performance and Network

In addition to the previous comments on the performance of SAP BW reports, the runtime of a query is also affected by the query frontend and the capacity of the network to transmit data. The following section first describes the basics of communication between the frontend PC and the application server. It highlights the differences between frontend performance, depending on the query tool selected (SAP BEx Analyzer and Web Analyzer), the network capacity available, and the optimization options for frontend performance.

SAP BW provides two tools for the execution of reports: SAP BEx Analyzer for reporting in Microsoft Excel, and SAP Web Applications for web reports that you can design in a web browser using SAP Web Application Designer (WAD).

10.7.1 SAP BEx Analyzer

SAP BEx Analyzer is an Excel-based client query tool of SAP BW and is based on an add-in for Microsoft Excel: *sapbex.xla*. Excel add-ins (*.xla* files) are supplemental programs that provide user-defined commands and functions (for data analysis, for example) in Excel.

The SAP BW frontend is a frontend component specific to SAP BW that is installed locally with the SAP GUI on the frontend PC in the ... \SAP\Frontend\BW directory or on a Windows Terminal Server (WTS).

The SAP frontend for Windows (SAP GUI for Windows) has been delivered in *compilations* since July 1999. A new compilation is assembled when the components contained within it (such as the add-on for SAP BW or SAP Supply Chain Management, SAP SCM) have changed. The new compilation contains all the components of the previous version, the patches that have appeared in the meantime, and the new components.

You can download the current compilations from SAP Service Market-place at *http://service.sap.com/installations*.

The execution of an SAP BEx report occurs in two steps. The first phase involves the registration of SAP BEx Analyzer and the authentication of the SAP BW user on the SAP BW application server. The second phase involves the selection of the data and the transfer of the results of the selection to the frontend of SAP BEx Analyzer, where the data is formatted for display in Excel after the transfer.

The communication of the SAP BEx frontend with the application server is based on the DIAG protocol developed by SAP for communication between the SAP GUI and the application server. During a connection between the application server and the frontend with the protocol, a dialog step generates several communication steps called *roundtrips*. A roundtrip transfers data via a synchronous *remote function call* (RFC) from the application level to the GUI frontend. Accordingly, roundtrips represent the number of communication steps taken between the application server and the frontend during a dialog step.

The accumulated total time of communication in the frontend and on the network within a dialog step is referred to as the *GUI time* (see also Section 8.1.1). In addition to the GUI time, you must consider the *frontend network time*, which is not contained in the GUI time. The frontend network time is the time needed on the network during a dialog step—from the first data transfer from the frontend to the application server, until the last data transfer from the application server back to the frontend.

GUI time and frontend network time

The following factors primarily determine the time needed to transfer data from the application server to the frontend:

▶ The bandwidth of the network, that is, the maximum quantity of data transferred per time unit

▶ The number of protocol roundtrips

▶ The latency period of a protocol roundtrip, that is, the time it takes to transfer an information package from the sender to the recipient and back again

▶ The quantity of data being transferred

The network bandwidth determines the maximum quantity of data that can be transferred per time unit. The latency period of a roundtrip—and therefore the response time for a report—also depends on the available data transfer rate. Particularly for WAN connections, the latency period of

Network bandwidth

a protocol roundtrip can last several hundred milliseconds, which means that many roundtrips during a query call can cause a bottleneck to occur.

Table 10.9 summarizes the relationship between the available bandwidths and the expected latency periods of a protocol roundtrip:

Network Technology	Bandwidth (Kbit/s)	Latency Period [ms]
56k modem	56	~ 250
WAN (Wide Area Network)	128–2.,048	~ 250
100 Mbit LAN	100,000	< 10

Table 10.9 Bandwidth and Latency Period

Protocol roundtrips

The DIAG protocol used by SAP BEx Analyzer compresses data well, but also requires many roundtrips. For example, each execution of an SAP BEx query requires 16 roundtrips (without fixed costs for logging in or working with reusable metadata in the same Excel session) and an additional roundtrip for each 200 cells in Excel. Up to 30 KB of data can be transmitted with each roundtrip. An SAP BEx query also requires a multitude of RFC connections.

You can use Transaction STAD to analyze individual statistical records on the number of roundtrips, the required GUI time, and the amount of data being transmitted (see Figure 10.34).

Call Transaction STAD to reach the overview screen. Use the **Sel. fields** button ❶ to add additional fields to the analysis. Select the **No. of Roundtrips**, **GUI time**, **Terminal in-message**, and **Terminal out-message** fields from the selection screen ❷. The analysis displayed in Figure 10.34 shows the call of an SAP BEx query; the transaction steps relevant to the analysis are marked in the box. Some 18 roundtrips are required. The overall GUI time of the query call is 7.4 seconds. The total quantity of data transferred from the application server to the frontend before compression is 15,225 bytes (**Terminal out-message**); 5,823 bytes were transferred from the frontend to the application server (**Terminal in-message**). The average transfer rate from the application server to the frontend is 2.1 KB per second (**Terminal out-message/GUI time**). The data transfer rate to the frontend should achieve an average value of 1 KB per 100 ms, but not go below 1 KB per second.

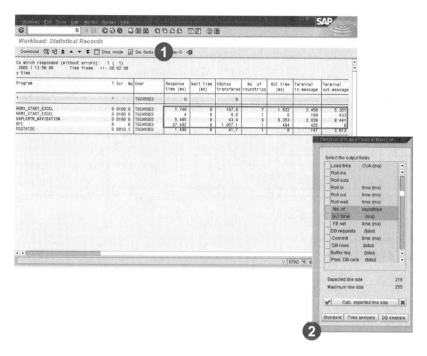

Figure 10.34 Individual Statistical Records Displaying GUI Time and Roundtrips

After the results of the query selection have been transferred to the frontend, the data is formatted in Excel. The time needed to format the data in Excel depends, to a great extent, on the number of cells to be displayed in Excel and on the memory (RAM) available on the client computer (see also Section 10.7.3). If a workbook of SAP BEx Analyzer has many Excel formulas on the ResultSet of the embedded queries, an update of the query in the workbook can take a very long time. You can usually tell that this situation applies if the query runtime will be very long even for repeated cache calls and the frontend runtime will be over 90%.

Data formatting in the Excel frontend

The reason is that the update of a query in the workbook of SAP BEx Analyzer triggers a recalculation for all dependent formulas if the calculation mode for Excel formulas is set to **Automatic** (Excel menu: **Extras · Options · Calculation · Automatic**). During an update of an SAP BEx query in a workbook, SAP BEx Analyzer reads the metadata from the repository sheets, transmits the request to the SAP BW application server, updates the repository sheet with the updated metadata from the SAP BW server, deletes the old ResultSet of the query, and renders the new ResultSet.

A new Excel calculation causes a performance weakness in the workbooks of the analyzer that contain the formulas. If you don't want automatic recalculation when the workbooks are updated for performance reasons, you can turn it off with the **Manual** option.

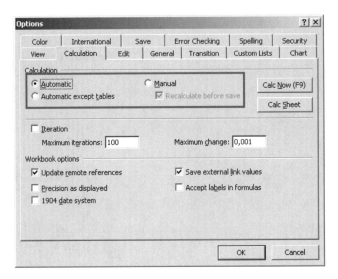

Figure 10.35 Automatic Calculation Mode in Excel

If you turn off automatic calculation, you would then trigger recalculation with the **Calc Now** button (F9). If you select the **Manual** option, you automatically activate the **Recalculate before save** option, so that the dependent Excel formulas are recalculated before the workbook is saved. See the Appendix for additional information on the use of Excel formulas in workbooks and options for optimizing performance.

10.7.2 Web Reporting

In web reporting, you use a web browser to log on and call queries. The selection result is generated as an HTML page on the SAP Web Application Server (SAP Web AS) and displayed in the web browser. Data transfer occurs with HTTP or HTTPS. Unlike the case with SAP BEx Analyzer, the selection result here is transferred to the frontend with a single roundtrip for all the data, regardless of the number of data cells. Each graphic element to be transferred (button, graphics, and so on) requires an additional roundtrip. The graphic elements are cached on the client computer and don't need to be transferred again when the query is updated.

In a wide area network (WAN) with high latency periods for each roundtrip (see Table 10.9), a web query provides clear advantages, because only one protocol roundtrip is usually required to transfer data. A query call in a web browser can therefore be more efficient in a WAN than a query call using SAP BEx Analyzer.

The frontend network time—the time scheduled on the network between the application server and the frontend—cannot be accessed when executing web queries. To examine the performance of the frontend, you can use IEMon (Internet Explorer Monitor) program, which you can download at *http://service.sap.com/bi* under Performance.

Analysis of the web frontend network time

IEMon.exe (see Figure 10.36) is a simple web browser with an additional function for recording logging steps. You can enter any URL address in the web browser. To analyze a web query, you must enter the complete URL of the reporting web page in IEMon. You can use the **Navigate** button to call the web page. The program creates a log file, *iemon.txt*, that records every browser event in milliseconds.

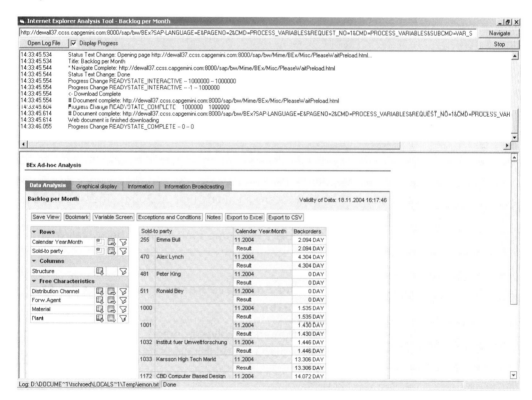

Figure 10.36 Analysis Tool IEMon.exe

Check the **Display Progress** box to display the sequential recording of the log steps. You can use the **Open Log File** button to open the log recording, *iemon.txt*, in Editor. Figure 10.37 shows a log file created by log recording with IEMon.

```
16:26:46.052    x Before Navigate: http://dewall37.ccss.capgemini.com:8000/sap/bw/Mime/BEx/Misc/PleaseWaitPreload.html -- SAP_BW_SNIPPET
16:26:46.062    Status Text Change: Opening page http://dewall37.ccss.capgemini.com:8000/sap/bw/Mime/BEx/Misc/PleaseWaitPreload.html...
16:26:46.062    Title: Auftragsrückstand pro Monat
16:26:46.072    * Navigate Complete: http://dewall37.ccss.capgemini.com:8000/sap/bw/Mime/BEx/Misc/PleaseWaitPreload.html
16:26:46.102    Status Text Change: Done
16:26:46.102    Progress Change READYSTATE_INTERACTIVE -- 1000000 -- 1000000
16:26:46.102    Progress Change READYSTATE_INTERACTIVE -- -1 -- 1000000
16:26:46.102    <- Download Complete
16:26:46.102    # Document complete: http://dewall37.ccss.capgemini.com:8000/sap/bw/Mime/BEx/Misc/PleaseWaitPreload.html
16:26:46.132    Progress Change READYSTATE_COMPLETE -- 1000000 -- 1000000
16:26:46.142    # Document complete:
http://dewall37.ccss.capgemini.com:8000/sap/bw/BEx?cmd=ldoc&infocube=OSD_C14&query=YSD_C14_Q0002&sap-language=DE
16:26:46.142    Web document is finished downloading
16:26:46.603    Progress Change READYSTATE_COMPLETE -- 0 -- 0
```

Figure 10.37 IEMon Log File

You must monitor three types of events to measure the frontend response time:

▶ **Before Navigate**
Event that transmits the HTTP request to the web server

▶ **Navigate Complete**
Response of the web server and the return transmission of the requested HTML page (report page)

▶ **Document Complete**
End of the rendering of the web page by the web browser

In the example shown in Figure 10.37, the HTTP request to execute the web query was transmitted at 16:26:46.052 and the browser responded at 16:26:46.072. That means a loading time of 20 ms. The web browser rendered the HTML code of the report between 16:26:46.072 and 16:26:46.142. Accordingly, rendering took 70 ms. The overall frontend response time therefore took 90 ms.

10.7.3 Hardware and Software Recommendations for the SAP BW Frontend

Because the SAP BW frontend involves frontend components specific to SAP BW—components that must be installed locally, in addition to components that must be installed in the SAP GUI, on the PC, or the WTS—the frontend performance also depends on the hardware resources of the frontend computer.

The hardware requirements for the SAP BW frontend essentially correspond to those hardware requirements for the SAP GUI (SAP Note 26417). The SAP GUI and the SAP BW frontend are downwardly compatible, but the version of the SAP GUI must be at least as high as the lowest SAP R/3 Basis release.[2]

The amount of main memory (RAM) has a direct influence on the time necessary to process queries in the frontend computer. For larger queries (queries with over 3,000 rows), 128 MB is the minimum amount. The processor speed on the client computer has less of an influence on the time necessary to process queries. In short, the speed can lead to bottlenecks only if the computer does not have enough memory.

Table 10.10 provides an overview of the minimum recommended hardware resources for the SAP BW frontend (depending on the operating system in use):

Operating System	Component	Minimum and Recommendation
Win95	Processor	Minimum: Pentium 133 MHz
		Recommendation: Pentium 300 MHz (or faster)
	RAM	Minimum: 64 MB
		Recommendation: 64 MB
	Disk	27 MB for SAP BW frontend component (without SAP GUI 4.5B)
	Graphics card	Minimum: 800x600, 256 colors, 2 MB memory
		Recommendation: 1,024x768, 32,768 colors, 4 MB memory
Windows 98 and Windows NT 4.0	Processor	Minimum: Pentium 133 MHz
		Recommendation: Pentium 300 MHz (or faster)
	RAM	Minimum: 64 MB
		Recommendation: 128 MB (or more)
	Disk	27 MB for SAP BW frontend component (without SAP GUI)

Table 10.10 Hardware Recommendation for the SAP BW Frontend

---

2 Refer to SAP Note 309461 to see which Basis release serves as the foundation of which SAP BW release. For the SAP BW 3.0B frontend, SAP GUI 6.20 or higher is required. The SAP BW 3.5 frontend requires SAP GUI 6.20, SAP GUI 6.40, or a higher release.

Operating System	Component	Minimum and Recommendation
	Graphics card	Minimum: 800x600, 256 colors, 2 MB memory
		Recommendation: 1,024x768, 32,768 colors, 4 MB memory
Windows 2000	Processor	Minimum: Pentium 133 MHz
		Recommendation: Pentium 500 MHz (or faster)
	RAM	Minimum: 128 MB
		Recommendation: 192 MB (or more)
	Disk	27 MB for SAP BW frontend components (without SAP GUI)
	Graphics card	Minimum: 800x600, 256 colors, 2 MB memory
		Recommendation: 1,024x768, 32,768 colors, 4 MB memory
Windows XP	Processor	Minimum: Pentium 133 MHz
		Recommendation: Pentium 500 MHz (or faster)
	RAM	Minimum: 192 MB
		Recommendation: 256 MB (or more)
	Disk	27 MB for SAP BW frontend component (without SAP GUI)
	Graphics card	Minimum: 800x600, 256 colors, 2 MB memory
		Recommendation: 1,024x768, 32,768 colors, 4 MB memory

Table 10.10 Hardware Recommendation for the SAP BW Frontend (cont.)

10.8 Performance Aspects Relevant to SAP BEx Queries and Excel Workbooks

The design of queries and workbooks can have a significant impact on the reporting performance. SAP BEx Query Designer allows you to work with the most flexible reporting requirements for function and layout. When you create queries, you should look beyond function and layout to examine aspects of performance. Long query runtimes are not always the result of large quantities of data. They can also result from complex user functions. The following section gives you an overview of design decisions that are critical to performance when you create queries and workbooks.

10.8.1 Using Cell Editors (Exception Cells)

If a query defines selection criteria and formulas for structural elements, generic cell definitions are implicitly created at the intersection of the structures when a query has two structures. The generic cell definitions set the value in the cell. In addition to this implicit cell definition, you can also define selection conditions in the intersections of cells to override the implicit cell values. These types of exception cells can be defined only with queries with two structures.

Using cell editors

When you use exception cells with the cell editor, note that each defined cell corresponds to a separate query execution during the running of the query, and that the separate execution uses up a dialog process. The definition of several exception cells multiplies the query load on the system accordingly.

10.8.2 Using Formulas in Excel Workbooks

You can store queries in Excel workbooks to use the comprehensive functions of Excel to format or calculate SAP BEx queries. Excel functions in workbooks are therefore frequently used as a variant method of processing an SAP BEx query in additional steps. The use of Excel formulas can have a significant impact on the runtime of workbooks. Because all calculations in Excel run on the client computer, optimization measures used on the application server are inappropriate when trying to improve the runtime of workbooks. But, the configuration of the client can result in performance bottlenecks if the CPU and the memory are insufficient for comprehensive calculations in Excel.

When you create workbooks, you should therefore pay close attention to the use of Excel formulas to calculate data. The effect on the runtime of workbooks depends on the number of cells that require the calculation of a formula in Excel.

If a workbook of SAP BEx Analyzer has many Excel formulas on the ResultSet of the embedded queries, an update of the query in the workbook can take a very long time, the reason being that during the update of the workbook, SAP BEx Analyzer deletes the old ResultSet and must render the new results area in the workbook again. If the calculation mode in Excel is set to **Automatic** (Excel menu: **Extras · Options · Calculation · Automatic**), a new calculation is triggered for all dependent formulas. The repeated Excel calculation causes a performance weakness in the workbooks of the analyzer that contain the formulas. If your workbook contains many Excel formulas, you should set the calculation of formulas to **Manual**.

Because the runtime of the workbook depends on the number of Excel formulas in the workbook, workbooks that require an Excel calculation for many rows can be critical in terms of runtime. For such workbooks, you should avoid static prepopulation of the Excel formulas for a large number of rows (a few thousand and more), because the Excel formulas must be calculated, even when the reference cells are not populated with data. See the Appendix for a technical solution for generating Excel formulas dynamically, depending on the rows selected at the runtime of the query.

10.8.3 Using Restricted Key Figures, Filters, and Selections in Queries

When you use filters, restricted key figures, or selections, you should always include the filter characteristic in the selection and not exclude it from the selection (see Figure 10.38).

The reason is that only characteristics included in the selection can use a database index. Characteristics in the exclude condition cannot use a database index.

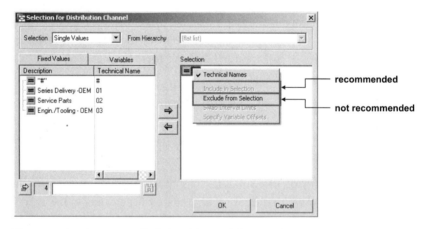

Figure 10.38 Selecting and Excluding Filter or Selection Characteristics

10.8.4 Query Read Mode

Query read mode The read mode of the query should always be set to **Reread the Data** or **Reread the Data When Expanding a Hierarchy** because the first call of this read mode selects only the required data and looks for an appropriate aggregate with each navigation step. When you use hierarchy aggregates, the read mode must be set to **Reread the Data When Expanding a Hierarchy** so that hierarchy aggregates can be used (see also Section 10.4.1).

10.8.5 Calculated Key Figures in Queries

When you use calculated key figures in queries, ensure that the Time of Calculation is set to **After Aggregation** in the extended maintenance for calculated key figures (see Figure 10.39).

The **Before Aggregation** option usually results in poor performance, because it must deal with a large amount of data (individual records). The need to calculate before aggregation exists when all individual records of the key figure are required for the calculation. Such a situation exists, for example, with currency translations in SAP BEx Analyzer, or with formula calculations that must be executed before aggregation, such as sales = price × quantity.

Figure 10.39 Calculation Time for Calculated Key Figures

10.8.6 Queries on MultiProviders

A MultiProvider is a special type of InfoProvider. It summarizes data from multiple InfoProviders to make it available for reporting. As of SAP BW 3.0, MultiProviders can link the following InfoProviders:

▶ Basic InfoCubes

▶ Remote InfoCubes

▶ InfoSets and InfoObjects

▶ ODS objects

The number of InfoProviders is unlimited, but a MultiProvider should not contain more than ten InfoProviders for performance and administration reasons (see Figure 10.40). The MultiProvider itself does not physically contain any data, since it simply joins data targets. The data of the objects involved is not summarized using a JOIN operation (an intersection of sets), but via a UNION operation (set union).

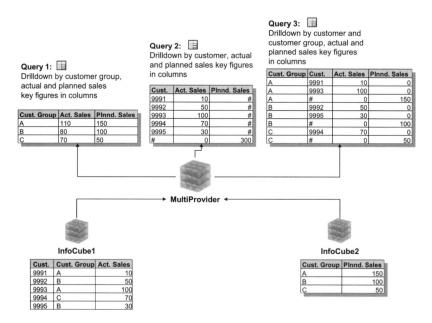

Figure 10.40 Linking InfoProviders via a MultiProvider

When a query is run on a MultiProvider, the OLAP processor splits the query into several subqueries. Depending on the definition of the Multi-Provider, the key figures contained in the query definition are supplied from one InfoProvider so that the key figures determine the InfoProvider to be selected by the OLAP processor. At least one subquery is generated per InfoProvider involved in the process.

MultiProviders can be subdivided into two categories:

1. *Homogeneous MultiProviders* consist of identical InfoProviders in terms of their modeling. The InfoProviders are InfoCubes with the same characteristics and key figures. For example, one InfoCube would hold data for fiscal year 2004, and another InfoCube would hold data for fiscal year 2005. This division of the InfoCubes corresponds to a partitioning at the application level so that the OLAP processor can exclude Info-Cubes according to the fixed values defined in the query when the InfoCubes don't contribute to the result of the query. The number of required accesses of the database is therefore reduced, which can lead to a better-read performance. Setting up this kind of fixed value partitioning is available only for InfoCubes. It must be set when modeling the BasicCubes (see also Section 12.2.2).

Homogeneous MultiProviders

2. *Heterogeneous MultiProviders* consist of InfoProviders with only some identical characteristics and key figures. Other characteristics and key figures are distributed separately across the InfoProviders. These MultiProviders are well suited for linking InfoProviders that map various business views. For example, a MultiProvider can summarize revenue accounting (e.g., actual and plan data) when one InfoCube contains the actual data and another InfoCube contains the plan data.

Heterogeneous MultiProviders

The subqueries split by the OLAP processor are executed in parallel by default. Each subquery (generally one subquery for each InfoProvider) uses a dialog process. After execution of a subquery, the results are summarized in the main memory of the application server and transferred to the frontend.

Parallel and sequential processing

Sequential processing allows for redirecting partial results to the OLAP processor. Parallel processing requires that the overall result must first be collected in the main memory.

As a rule, parallel processing of the subqueries of a MultiProvider is faster than sequential processing. Sequential processing works through one query after the other and can begin working on the next query only when the result of the previous query has been established. The system load from one query can be quite high for MultiProvider queries with large result sets, many subqueries, or long runtimes. When the intermediate result of a parallel MultiProvider query is too large (exceeding 30,000 data records), parallel processing is aborted to avoid a memory overflow.

The MultiProvider query is then automatically restarted and processed sequentially. The termination of parallel processing in these cases means a loss of performance, because the runtime that has been used cannot contribute to the query result and processing must begin again sequentially.

 Note that each additional InfoProvider in a MultiProvider requires additional I/O capacities in the database. The degree of parallelization of subqueries in SAP BW 3.x is limited to the number of free dialog processes minus 2.

Changing the maximum size of intermediate results of Multi-Providers

As of SAP BW 3.0B SP14 and SAP BW 3.1C SP08, you can parameterize the SAP BW system so that the effect described above for an intermediate result of more than 30,000 rows occurs instead for an intermediate result of more than x KB. A precondition here is sufficient memory on the application server.[3] To parameterize the size of the intermediate result of the MultiProvider, use Table RSADMIN and enter for **OBJECT** = MPRO_MAX_RESULT and enter for **VALUE** the maximum size of the intermediate result in KB. To enter the values in table RSADMIN, you can use ABAP program SAP_RSADMIN_MAINTAIN.

Identifying queries with aborted parallel processing

You can use SAP BW statistics data to examine queries that have aborted. You can study MultiProviders—for which you have created SAP BW statistics for queries—by using Transaction SE16 to search Table RSDDSTAT for queries on MultiProviders with a value of 30,000 or higher in Column QDBTRANS.

You can also use the query monitor (Transaction RSRT) to check if the MultiProvider query can be run in parallel. For this purpose, you must activate the **MultiProvider Explain** option in the **Execute + Debug** button (see Figure 10.41).

The results screen, which also shows the query results, displays various messages after execution of the **MultiProvider Explain** debugging option. If the message *DBMAN146* is displayed, parallel processing was aborted and sequential processing restarted for the query. In these cases, we recommend that you first increase the threshold value MPRO_MAX_RESULT in Table RSADMIN before parallel processing for the MultiProvider is turned off completely.

---

3 According to observations of typical OLAP queries, the default setting of a maximum of 30,000 results corresponds to a main memory usage of 3.5 to 4.5 MB. These values are only approximate.

To turn off parallel processing of the MultiProvider, you must create a new data record for the MultiProvider in Table RSADMIN using ABAP program SAP_RSADMIN_MAINTAIN (Transaction SE38).

Turning off parallel processing

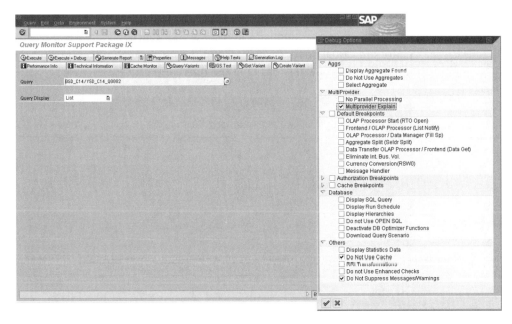

Figure 10.41 "MultiProvider Explain" Option

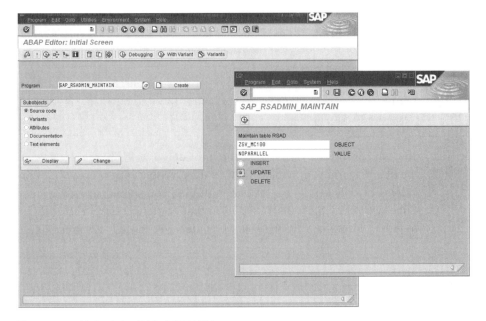

Figure 10.42 Maintaining Table RSADMIN

Select the menu path **Program · Execute · Direct** and enter the technical name of the MultiProvider in the **OBJECT** field and NOPARALLEL in the **VALUE** field in the dialog screen that displays (see Figure 10.42).

Once you make this setting, note that all queries on this MultiProvider will be processed sequentially. If you want to deactivate parallel processing for individual queries, you must set the **no parallel processing** option in the Query **Properties** dialog in the query monitor (see Figure 10.43).

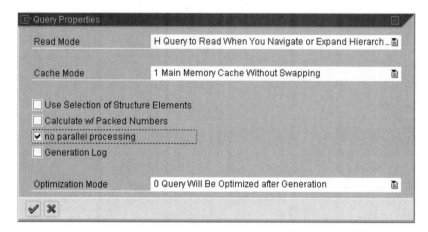

Figure 10.43 Setting Parallel Processing in the Query Properties

In the results screen of the query monitor, you can use the **MultiProvider Explain** debugging option shown in Figure 10.41 to check the sequential processing of the query on the MultiProvider (see Figure 10.44).

Note that all queries on MultiProviders that contain at least one Info-Provider with non-cumulative key figures (non-cumulative values) are executed sequentially.

InfoObject
0INFOPROV

You can control the selection of the InfoCube of a MultiProvider used in the query by using InfoObject 0INFOPROV. When a query on a MultiProvider uses only key figures of one InfoCube, you should select the Info-Cube with InfoObject 0INFOPROV so that no unnecessary read accesses to other InfoCubes of the MultiProvider are carried out (see Figure 10.45).

Figure 10.44 Sequential Processing of a MultiProvider Query

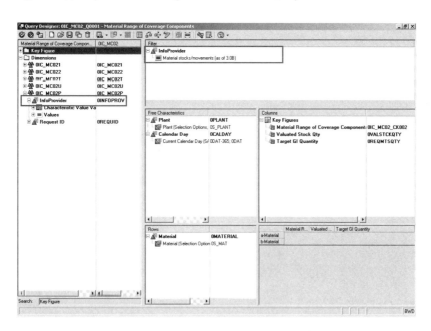

Figure 10.45 InfoObject 0INFOPROV in MultiProvider Queries

11 Aggregates

Aggregates are one of the most important performance opti-
mization components in SAP BW. This chapter provides infor-
mation on the structure, creation, and administration of
aggregates.

Aggregates store data redundantly for the basic InfoCube, but the data
that is contained in the aggregate has a lower level of detail, or is a subset
of the data contained in the basic InfoCube.

This means that aggregates are materialized subsets of the fact table data
of the BasicCubes and are physically stored in the database. Technically,
aggregates and InfoCubes are not configured identically. Although aggregates contain a fact table and dimension tables, they store the InfoCube
data at a higher level of aggregation. Because of the resulting smaller
number of data records to be read, the query performance is improved;
however, aggregates require additional memory and system resources for
the periodic load management that handles the data updates. Figure 11.1
illustrates the difference between the data transfer of a read access from
an InfoCube and the data transfer of a read access from an aggregate for
an aggregation on the *Region* characteristic.

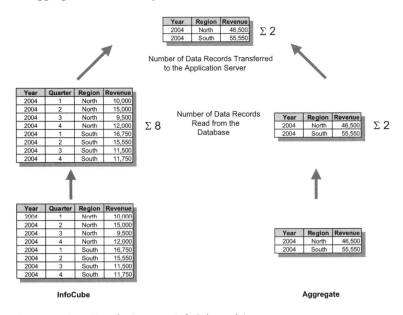

Figure 11.1 Data Transfer Between InfoCube and Aggregate

Aggregation in the aggregate

When accessing data in the InfoCube, eight data records must be read in the database and then be aggregated into two data records, which are transferred to the application server. In this case, accessing the aggregate is preferable. The aggregate already contains the totals for the "North" and "South" regions, so that only two data records must be read in the database. The results, which are transferred to the application server, are identical in both cases, irrespective of whether the data was accessed through the aggregate or the InfoCube.

Usability of aggregates

When running a query, the user doesn't need to specifically select the aggregate, because the OLAP processor automatically recognizes the usability of an aggregate. But, during the execution of a query, the OLAP processor can use an aggregate only if the query requires data that has either the same level of detail as the aggregate data, or a higher level of detail. If data with a higher level of detail is required, which is not contained in the aggregate, the OLAP processor cannot use the aggregate and accesses the detail data of the BasicCube automatically. The selection of an appropriate aggregate and the differentiation between using an aggregate or the BasicCube is handled automatically by the OLAP processor and is transparent to the user.

Aggregates can optimize the query runtimes for only basic InfoCubes and cannot be used for queries on operational data store (ODS) objects, InfoSets, RemoteCubes, and InfoObjects that are declared as InfoProviders.

When analyzing large data quantities, you should ensure that the data is stored in BasicCubes so that you can fully utilize the optimization options of aggregates.

Aggregates for MultiProvider queries

For queries that access MultiProviders, you must create aggregates for those BasicCubes of the MultiProvider whose data is required by the respective queries. The reason for this is that MultiProviders exist only as a logical definition, while the data is stored in the InfoProviders that they are based on.

When an aggregate is newly structured, the data of the BasicCube is aggregated according to the level of detail that exists in the aggregate. Data that is added to the BasicCube is then also stored in the aggregate during the rollup process.

Table RSDDSTAT provides information on whether aggregates can improve the runtime performance of queries. Aggregates should improve the runtime of a query if

▶ The DBSEL/DBTRANS relationship is > 10

▶ The number of selected data records (DBSEL) is > 10,000

▶ The share of database runtime is > 30% of the entire runtime

▶ The database runtime is > 3 seconds

If these conditions exist, you should try to improve the runtimes of the relevant queries by using aggregates; however, please note that too many aggregates require storage space and resources during the running operation. It is therefore advisable to define aggregates that have a high hit ratio and meet the requirements of most queries.

11.1 Basic Principles

You can define aggregates in different ways. What all types of SAP BW aggregates have in common is that the number of data records is reduced by an aggregation or summation. The aggregation is based either on a decrease in the data granularity, or on the storage of data subsets. The data granularity is determined by how many InfoObjects are used in the aggregate—fewer InfoObjects in the aggregate entail a lower data granularity.

You can create aggregates at different aggregation levels of the contained InfoObjects. The different aggregation levels, which we'll describe in more detail in the following sections, are *Characteristic values*, *Hierarchy level*, and *Fixed values*.

11.1.1 Aggregates on Characteristics

Aggregates on characteristics or on the characteristic attribute values involve the reduction and aggregation of data records by reducing the characteristics used in the aggregate. Figure 11.2 shows that the *Customer* characteristic is dropped during the aggregation of data on the *Region* characteristic: The *Revenue* key figure for the *Region* characteristic is totaled across all characteristic values in the aggregate. The result of this summation is stored in the fact table of the aggregate, which contains less data records than the fact table of the BasicCube, on which the aggregate is based. The aggregation within the aggregate is determined by the characteristics available in the aggregate. In our example, this process involves a loss of information, insofar as the aggregate doesn't contain any revenue figures at the customer level. For this reason, a query for customer revenue figures cannot be run on that aggregate, but on the BasicCube instead.

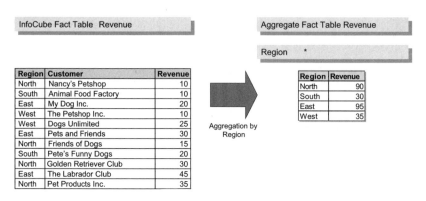

Figure 11.2 Aggregation on Characteristic Values

Structure of aggregates Technically speaking, the aggregate is a separate InfoCube that contains its own fact table and dimension tables. When an aggregate is created, the system automatically generates a six-digit number to identify the aggregate. This number always begins with 1. The table descriptions are similar to those used for an InfoCube:

▶ /BIC/E1XXXXX and /BIC/F1XXXXX for the fact tables

▶ /BIC/D1XXXXP, /BIC/D1XXXXT and so on for dimension tables

Since SAP BW 2.0B, two different types of fact tables are generated—the E fact table and the F fact table. During an upload of the aggregate, the data is first loaded into the uncompressed F fact table. The aggregate can be compressed, if necessary. If the aggregate is compressed, the load request IDs are deleted and the data is moved from the F fact table into the E fact table. The F fact table is empty if compressed aggregates are used. If, in turn, the aggregates are uncompressed, the E fact table is empty.

The dimension tables can be commonly used by the fact tables of the InfoCube and of the aggregate, provided that all characteristics of the InfoCube dimension are also contained in the aggregate dimension. If that's not the case, separate dimension tables are created for the aggregate (see Figure 11.3).

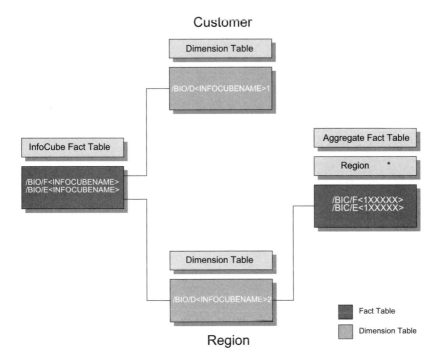

Figure 11.3 Characteristics Aggregate—Technical View

For time-related InfoObjects such as 0CALMONTH, all those InfoObjects are automatically included in the *Time* dimension, which can be derived from that InfoObject. For example, when the InfoObject 0CALMONTH is included in an aggregate, the InfoObjects 0CALQUARTER and 0CALYEAR are automatically included also, because these InfoObjects can be derived as higher levels of aggregation from the InfoObject 0CALMONTH.

InfoCubes and aggregates can share dimension tables, if all InfoObjects contained in the InfoCube dimension are also used in the aggregate and if the aggregate contains more than 13 InfoObjects. The aggregate can then generate its line item dimensions (see also Section 11.1.6).

You can use Transaction LISTSCHEMA to call the structure of fact and dimension tables for InfoCubes and aggregates (see Figure 11.4).

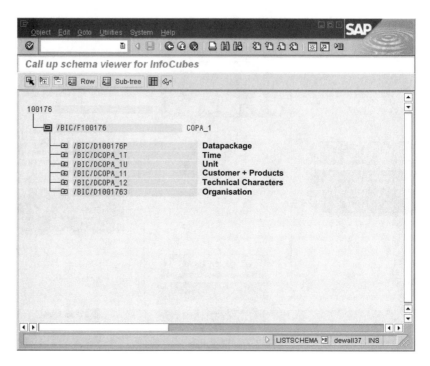

Figure 11.4 Transaction LISTSCHEMA—Aggregates View

Figure 11.4 displays an aggregate that uses four dimensions of the basic InfoCube "COPA_1". The *Organization* dimension is modeled as a separate aggregate dimension. For this reason it contains the system-internal six-digit aggregate description, 100176, and the number counter of the dimension (/BIC/D1001763). The Data package dimension is always modeled as a separate dimension in an aggregate (/BIC/D100176P).

The level of detail of the aggregate is determined by the characteristics included in the aggregate: The inclusion of fewer characteristics in the aggregate than in the BasicCube causes the aggregation. If compounded characteristics exist, the compounded object is automatically included in the aggregate. In general, all key figures that also exist in the BasicCube are included in the aggregate. Key figures with exception aggregation represent a special case here. In that case, the reference characteristics are also included in the aggregate (see also Section 11.1.5).

11.1.2 Aggregates on Navigation Attributes

You can define aggregates on navigation attributes of characteristics. If a basic InfoCube contains navigation attributes, you should only include the navigation attribute in the aggregate if possible. The concurrent inclusion of a characteristic and its navigation attribute in an aggregate is only possible in the Expert mode (menu path **Extras · Switch Expert Mode On/Off** in the aggregate maintenance, see Figure 11.5). The aggregate that contains the navigation attribute has the same granularity as the aggregate that contains the characteristic; however, it must be adjusted using the hierarchy/attribute change run if master data is changed. Due to a join with the master data table, the attribute information is contained in the characteristics aggregate.

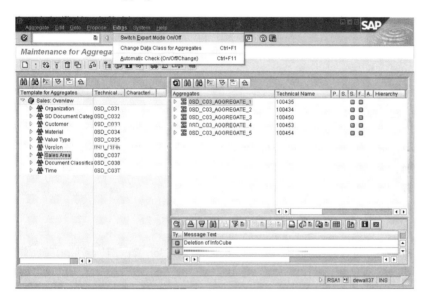

Figure 11.5 Expert Mode in the Aggregate Maintenance

It can be useful to structure an aggregate only with the required navigation attributes if the corresponding basic characteristic isn't needed. Those aggregates can have a better performance because typically the number of attribute values is smaller than the number of basic characteristic values. For example, usually there are more material numbers 0MATERIAL than the number of values for the corresponding navigation attribute, *Material group*, 0MATERIAL—0MATL_GROUP.

Technically speaking, the navigation attribute becomes a characteristic, because it is stored in a corresponding dimension table. During a query access to the navigation attribute in the aggregate, it is not the corresponding SID master data table /BIO/X* that's accessed, but the aggregate dimension table /BIO/D<1XXXXX>1. Due to the decrease in the number

Time-constant navigation attributes

of table joins, this type of access shows a better performance than the join via the master data table.

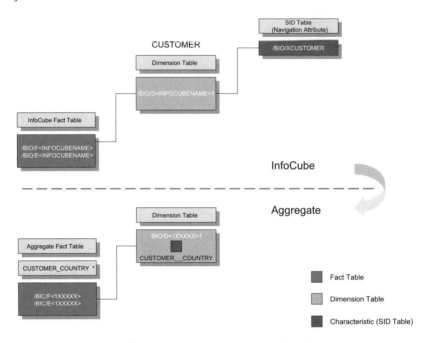

Figure 11.6 Navigation Characteristics in Aggregates — Technical View

When an aggregate is created, a new dimension table is generated that contains the navigation attribute 0CUSTOMER__0COUNTRY. The technical names of navigation attributes contain two underscores that are placed between the name of the characteristic and the attribute name: Navigation attribute = characteristic__attribute. The name of the database table of the new dimension is /BIO/D<1XXXXX>1, 1XXXXX being the six-digit number of the system-internal aggregate name. As shown in Figure 11.6, the aggregate dimension contains only the navigation attribute 0CUSTOMER__0COUNTRY, but not the basic characteristic 0CUSTOMER. For this reason, there is no connection between the aggregate fact table and the dimension table of the BasicCube.

Time-dependent navigation attributes In addition to modeling time-constant attributes, you can also include time-dependent navigation attributes in an aggregate. Time-dependent navigation attributes have different characteristic attributes on different key dates; however, an aggregate cannot store the different values of time-dependent navigation attributes. Therefore, when modeling time-dependent navigation attributes in aggregates, you must take into account the restriction that the aggregate must be calculated for only a specific key date. This means that when the aggregate is filled with data, only the time-dependent attributes and hierarchies for that specific key date are calculated.

Master Data Table: Region

Region	Sales Manager	Valid from	Valid to
North	Harrison	04/01/2003	07/31/2005
North	Smith	08/01/2005	12/31/9999
South	Smith	02/03/2003	07/31/2005
South	Williams	08/01/2005	12/31/9999
East	Roberts	02/03/2003	07/31/2005
East	Harrison	08/01/2005	12/31/9999
West	Roberts	08/01/2005	12/31/9999

Fact Table: Revenue

Region	Customer	Revenue
North	0815	10,000
North	0816	15,000
South	0817	35,000
South	0818	12,000
East	0819	20,000
West	0820	12,000
West	0821	5,000

Aggregate: Revenue

Sales Manager   *
Key Date: 07/10/2005

Sales Manager	Revenue
Williams	0
Harrison	25,000
Smith	47,000
Roberts	20,000

Figure 11.7 Time-Dependent Master Data in Aggregates

The aggregate shown in Figure 11.7 summarizes the revenues for the sales managers of the respective regions that are valid on the key date.

For this reason, you must specify a key date when defining an aggregate. You can use the aggregate if the key dates of the query and the aggregate are identical.

When you include time-dependent navigation attributes or hierarchies, you can select the key date for the aggregate by using a variable or the calendar day (see Figure 11.8). If you use variables, the key date is calculated by using a variable in the query. This variable uses the SAP exit or customer exit processing types for the calculation of the key date ❶. If you use the calendar day, a fixed date is selected in the **Calendar** dialog that opens when you use the CALENDAR object ❷.

Figure 11.8 Selecting a Key Date for Time-Dependent Navigation Attributes

Time-dependent navigation attributes can dramatically increase the administration effort required for aggregates, because an appropriate aggregate must be created for each key date. Depending on the number of values for the key dates (end of a period, end of a month, daily, and so on), it may become impossible to create adjusted aggregates. You should therefore determine whether you actually need time-dependent aggregates, and, if so, how many key date aggregates you'll need.

11.1.3 Aggregates on Hierarchy Nodes

If you use external hierarchies in aggregates, you can either include the entire characteristics hierarchy in the aggregate, or only a specific level of a hierarchy node. You can use aggregates that contain hierarchies for queries, which use a hierarchy node as a filter or as a presentation hierarchy.

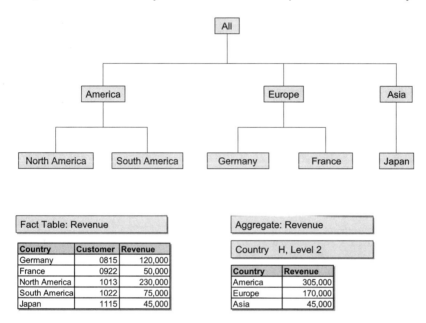

Figure 11.9 Using Hierarchies in Aggregates

The aggregate shown in Figure 11.9 summarizes the revenues to the Level 2 hierarchy nodes. Such an aggregate can be used by queries that contain a hierarchy level that's smaller than (e.g., Level 1 = All), or equal to Level 2. Consequently, you must specify the hierarchy level when creating hierarchy aggregates (see Figure 11.10).

You can select the hierarchy level in the aggregate maintenance menu by opening the context menu for the hierarchy object ❶. You can then select a hierarchy from a list of available hierarchies ❷, and finally select the hierarchy node you want to include in the aggregate ❸.

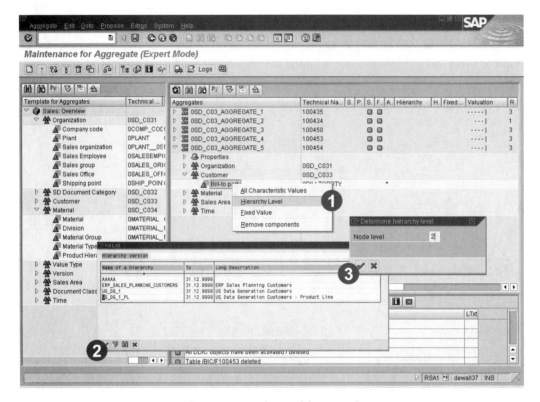

Figure 11.10 Selecting a Hierarchy Level for Hierarchy Aggregates

Technically speaking, the Level 2 hierarchy attribute becomes a character-istic, because it is stored in a corresponding dimension table. During a query access to the hierarchy node in the aggregate, it is not the corresponding hierarchy inclusion table /BI0/I* (hierarchy node structure) that is actually accessed, but the aggregate dimension table /BI0/D<1XXXXX>1 (see Figure 11.11).

The use of hierarchies in aggregates involves specific requirements that must be met so that a query can use the aggregate: A hierarchy aggregate can be used only if the read mode of the query is set to **Read upon navigation/hierarchy drills** (Transaction RSRT, **Read mode**). Moreover, you must ensure that the query is not restricted to other hierarchy levels in the columns.

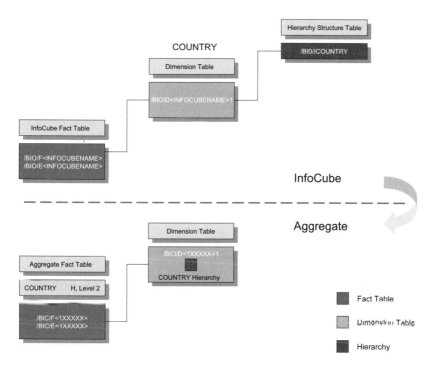

Figure 11.11 Hierarchies in Aggregates — Technical View

Since SAP BW 2.0B, you can create hierarchies without "remaining nodes." If you use such a hierarchy in an aggregate, you can't calculate the total by adding up the individual nodes, because the values of the remaining nodes are missing. The root node is automatically included in the dynamic filter in the query definition if these hierarchies are used. The query can use the aggregate only if the dynamic filter contains the root node. If the hierarchy-defining characteristic is defined as a free characteristic in the query, the query cannot use the aggregate.

11.1.4 Aggregates on Fixed Values

In addition to the processes for creating aggregates described so far, you can also use fixed values of characteristics to reduce the data volume of an aggregate. Here, the aggregation of data is based on the creation of data subsets. This aggregate variant involves the specification of constant values or *fixed values* for one or more characteristics contained in the aggregate. The fixed values determine the data subset contained in the aggregate.

When you create fixed value aggregates, you can only include data records in the aggregate that has the relevant fixed value. You can define only one fixed value per InfoObject, since the definition of intervals or multiple fixed values is not supported. A fixed value aggregate can be used by queries that use identical filter values.

Based on the fixed value setting "Country = Germany," the aggregate shown in Figure 11.12 contains a subset of the InfoCube data. Such an aggregate can be used by queries that have the same fixed value in their filters.

Fact Table: Revenue

Country	Customer	Revenue
Germany	0815	120,000
France	0922	50,000
North America	1013	230,000
South America	1022	75,000
Japan	1115	45,000
Germany	0816	35,000

Aggregate: Revenue

Country   F, Germany
Customer *

Country	Customer	Revenue
Germany	0815	120,000
Germany	0816	35,000

Figure 11.12 Using Fixed Values in Aggregates

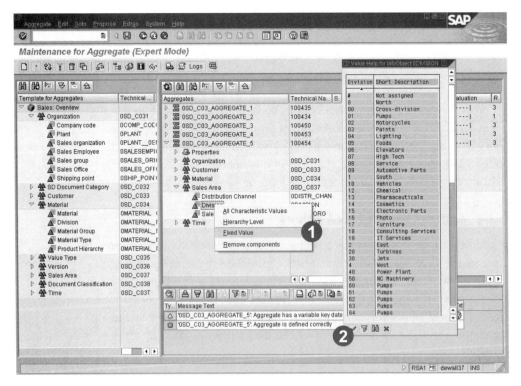

Figure 11.13 Selecting a Fixed Value for Fixed Value Aggregates

You can select the Fixed Value in the aggregate maintenance menu by opening the context menu for the InfoObject (see ❶ in Figure 11.13). Then, you can select the fixed value from a list of values ❷.

11.1.5 Exception Aggregations in InfoCubes

The regular standard aggregation process consists of totaling or determining the MIN/MAX values; however, more complex aggregation processes may be required. The exception aggregation is an example of such a process. This aggregation process comprises different types of aggregation, such as SUM, MAX, MIN, AVG, COUNT, FIRST, LAST, VARIANCE. Typical examples of using an exception aggregation include the calculation of the number of deliveries per month and the average revenue per customer.

These types of key figures require the specification of an InfoObject as a reference value. The InfoObjects can be both time-related and non-time-related characteristics

Figure 11.14 illustrates the calculation of an exception aggregation based on a sample average value calculation for the number of purchase orders per day. The calculation of the *Orders* key figure is based on the standard aggregation process, *Summation* (SUM). This step is carried out in the database. Moreover, the key figure also contains the exception aggregation, *Average* (AVG). The calculation of the key figure *Average number of orders per day* is handled by the OLAP processor.

When you use key figures with exception aggregation in the InfoCube, the reference characteristics of the key figure are automatically included in the aggregate. In the example shown in Figure 11.14, the aggregate must contain the time characteristic 0CALDAY because 0CALDAY represents the reference characteristic for the exception aggregation.

The automatic inclusion of reference characteristics in exception aggregations can affect the size and therefore the performance of the aggregate. You can remove the reference characteristic via the Expert mode (menu path: **Extras · Switch Expert Mode On**). But, in that case, the OLAP processor can use the aggregate only if the query does not contain the corresponding key figure.

Calendar Day	Ø Orders
01/17/05	40
01/18/05	29

 Exception Aggregation AVG (OLAP)

Calendar Day	Customer	Orders	
01/17/05	0815	30	Ø 40
01/17/05	0816	50	
01/18/05	0815	22	Ø 29
01/18/05	0816	36	

 Standard Aggregation SUM (Database)

Calendar Day	Customer	Material	Orders	
01/17/05	0815	AAA	14	Σ 30
01/17/05	0815	BBB	16	
01/17/05	0816	AAA	50	
01/18/05	0815	CCC	22	
01/18/05	0816	DDD	18	Σ 36
01/18/05	0816	AAA	18	

Figure 11.14 Standard Aggregation and Exception Aggregation

Calculation before/after aggregation
For calculated key figures that use only operands of the same aggregation, you can define the time of calculation in the query definition. In the Properties of the Calculated Key Figure dialog, you can define whether the key figure should be calculated before or after the standard aggregation. For example, this may be necessary for the calculation of a multiplication (e.g., revenue = price x quantity), because the aggregated revenue does not result from the product of the total of all quantities.

When selecting the Time of Calculation (see Figure 11.15), you should note that the **Before Aggregation** option often affects the query performance, because it's always necessary to read the individual records of the fact table. For this reason, queries containing calculated key figures that are calculated before the aggregation cannot use aggregates. You should therefore carefully check whether it's really necessary to create a calculated key figure before using the **Before Aggregation** option, or if it makes more sense to create the key figure during the update process.

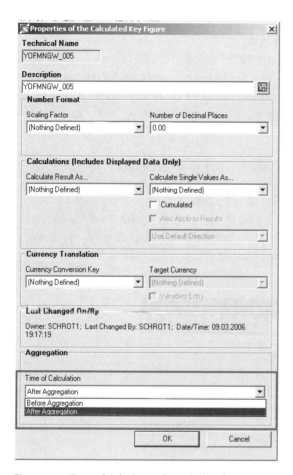

Figure 11.15 Time of Calculation for Calculated Key Figures

11.1.6 Line Item Aggregates (Flat Aggregates)

When defining an InfoCube, you can model its dimensions as line item dimensions. If a line item dimension is used, the SID keys of a dimension table characteristic are directly included in the fact table, which indicates that the dimension table is no longer needed. But, you can only model a line item dimension if the dimension contains exactly one characteristic. Basically, you should model line item dimensions in the InfoCube only if the number of characteristic values of the InfoObject corresponds to approximately 20% or more of the number of data records in the fact table (see also Section 9.3.5).

An aggregate usually contains fewer characteristics than the corresponding InfoCube. For this reason, SAP BW automatically tries to model all characteristics contained in the aggregate as line item dimensions when an aggregate is being created. As is the case with InfoCubes, you can freely define 13 dimensions for an aggregate. The technical dimensions *Data package*, *Unit*, and *Time* are already predefined by the system. An aggregate shouldn't contain more than 13 characteristics or attributes, so that it's possible to create all dimensions of the aggregate as line item dimensions.

Aggregates that consist only of line item dimensions are filled with data from only the database. This results in a higher performance during the filling and rollup processes. Characteristics of the unit and data package dimensions are never modeled as line item dimensions. Line item dimensions of the basic InfoCube are shared with the corresponding aggregate dimension.

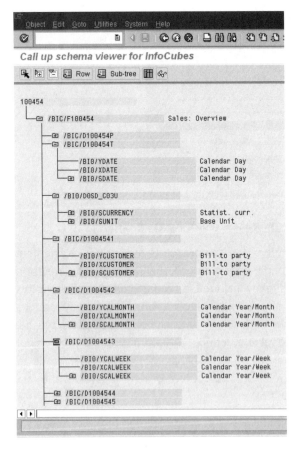

Figure 11.16 Structure of Fact and Dimension Tables in an Aggregate

The structure of the aggregate tables can be called using Transaction LISTSCHEMA. Figure 11.16 shows Aggregate 100454. The naming of the tables occurs in accordance with the schema described in Section 11.1.1.

Fact table /BIC/F100454 is assigned eight dimension tables. Let's look at the first six tables:

▶ /BIC/D100454P: Package dimension

▶ /BIC/D100454T: Time dimension

▶ /BIC/D0SD_C03U: Unit dimension of the corresponding InfoCube 0SD_C03

▶ /BIC/D1004541: Line item dimension *Bill-to party*

▶ /BIC/D1004542: Line item dimension *Calendar Year/Month*

▶ /BIC/D1004543: Line item dimension *Calendar Year/Week*

11.2   Automatic Creation of Aggregates

The SAP BW system can automatically propose aggregates. For this purpose, the system uses the statistical data of BW statistics already described earlier in this book, because this data consistently logs the entire query behavior. There are several ways in which SAP BW can make aggregate proposals.

For example, you can use Transaction RSDDV or the aggregate mainte nance menu in the Administrator Workbench to obtain an aggregate proposal from the system (see Figure 11.17).

Several options exist for aggregate proposals. The following table provides an overview (see Table 11.1):

#	Type of proposal	Description
1	Propose (Statistics, Usu-ally Query)	Proposal is based on log data from SAP BW statistics or on the query definition.
2	Propose from Query	Proposal is based on the query definition.
3	Propose from Last Navi-gation	Proposal is based on the last entry in the transparent tables RDDDSTAT/RSDDSTATAGGRDEF for the current user.

Table 11.1 Types of Proposals for Automatic Aggregate Creation

#	Type of proposal	Description
4	Propose from BW Statistics (Tables)	Proposal is based on the transparent tables RSDDSTAT/RSDDSTATAGGRDEF.
5	Propose from BW Statistics (InfoCube)	Proposal is based on the BW statistics of the InfoCube.

Table 11.1 Types of Proposals for Automatic Aggregate Creation (cont.)

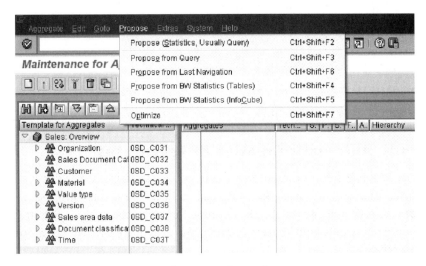

Figure 11.17 Automatic Creation of Aggregate Proposals

BW statistics vs. query

For each navigation step that leads to a database query, the statistical OLAP data stores information on the characteristics, navigation attributes, and hierarchies that have been involved in the respective step. The advantage of using proposals from the SAP BW statistics (processes 1, 3, 4, 5) over using proposals from queries (process 2) is that the former takes into account the actual user behavior. Process 2, on the other hand, uses the query definition of the characteristics and key figures in columns and rows, as well as the characteristics in the filter and the free characteristics, as a basis for the aggregate proposal. Note that representative user behavior data should be available for the proposal types that are based on the statistical data.

When using the proposal process based on statistical data, you can generate the aggregate proposals for specific maximum query runtimes and for a specific period in which query calls are executed (see Figure 11.18).

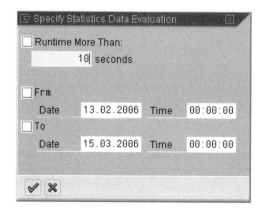

Figure 11.18 Specifying the Evaluation of Statistics Data

The following sections describe the creation of aggregate proposals for different types of proposals, as listed in Table 11.1, in further detail.

11.2.1 Proposing Aggregates from BW Statistics

You can use the proposal type **Propose (Statistics, Usually Query)** to generate aggregate proposals based on the SAP BW statistics. If no statistics data is available, the aggregate proposal will be based on the query definition.

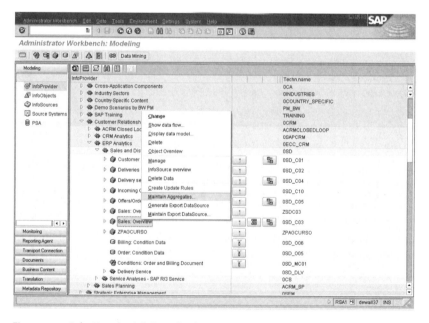

Figure 11.19 Selecting the InfoProvider for Aggregate Maintenance

1. Select the InfoCube to be optimized via the aggregate maintenance menu by using Transaction RSDDV or from the Administrator Workbench (see Figure 11.19).

2. Launch the aggregate proposal by selecting **Propose · Propose (Statistics, Usually Query)** in the aggregate maintenance menu (see Figure 11.17).

3. Specify the evaluation of the statistics data (see Figure 11.18).

4. The system proposes several aggregates that have the name STAT<number> (see Figure 11.20).

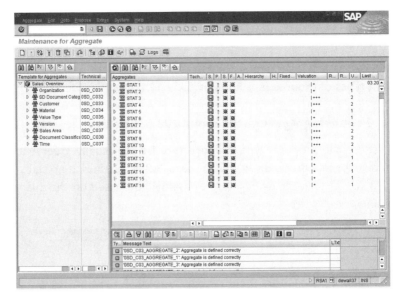

Figure 11.20 Aggregate Proposal Based on SAP BW Statistics

At that moment, the proposals are not yet filled with data and are still inactive. The traffic lights for **Status Filled/Switched off** are red.

5. If the system generates many aggregates, you can reduce the number of aggregate proposals using the **Optimize** function (Ctrl+Shift+F7) in the **Propose** menu. If you do that, SAP BW summarizes several aggregates into larger aggregates. The resulting aggregates can be less efficient than the previous aggregate proposals, but the performance of the aggregates should always correspond to the number of aggregates and the administration effort made necessary by them (see also Section 11.4.3).

6. You can save the aggregate proposals without activating them (Ctrl+S), and you can activate and fill them with data (F6).

11.2.2 Proposing Aggregates from the Query Definition

Aggregate proposals based on the query definition can be generated for queries that have already been defined. You should select this option, if no statistical data is available for the execution of the query. If, on the other hand, statistics data is available, you should proceed according to the descriptions in Section 11.2.1, because the statistics also contain information on the frequency of the query execution as well as on individual navigation steps.

You should proceed as follows to create aggregate proposals based on queries:

1. Launch the aggregate proposal by selecting **Propose · Propose from Query** in the aggregate maintenance menu (see Figure 11.17).

2. Select one or more queries for analysis from the selection menu that opens (see Figure 11.21).

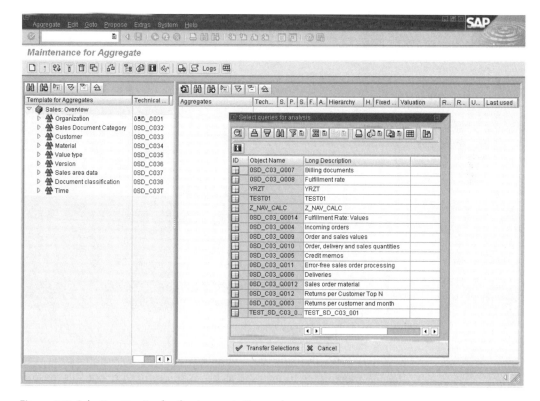

Figure 11.21 Selecting Queries for the Aggregate Proposal

3. The system proposes two aggregates with the name MIN<number> and MAX<number> for each query:

  ▶ *MIN* describes the smallest possible aggregate for the first execution of the query with a minimum drilldown. The query must be set to hierarchical reading or reading upon each navigation step in the Query Properties (Transaction RSRT).

  ▶ *MAX* describes the aggregate for all navigation steps of the query. This aggregate proposal is based on the assumption that all characteristics contained in the query (including free characteristics) are used in the drilldown, which means that the aggregate can be used for all navigation steps of the query.

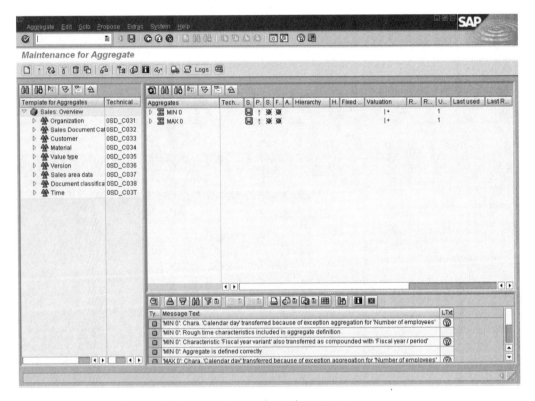

Figure 11.22 Aggregate Proposal Based on Queries

4. If a query contains many free characteristics, the data volume can cause the MAX aggregate to become as big as the InfoCube. For this reason, you should verify whether you really need this aggregate.

5. If a query doesn't contain any free characteristics, the MIN and MAX aggregates are identical.

6. If the system generates many aggregates, you can reduce the number of aggregate proposals using the **Optimize** function (Ctrl+Shift+F7) in the **Propose** menu. If you do that, SAP BW summarizes several aggregates into larger aggregates. The resulting aggregates can be less efficient than the previous aggregate proposals, but the performance of the aggregates should always correspond to the number of aggregates and the administration effort that results because of them.

7. You can save the aggregate proposals without activating them (Ctrl+S), and you can activate and fill them with data (F6). You can also modify or delete the aggregate proposals.

8. The name of the aggregate can be changed at a later stage by using the **Change description** context menu. The name change does not affect the system-internal six-digit number.

11.3 Manual Creation of Aggregates

In addition to having aggregate proposals automatically created by the system, you can also manually create aggregates for queries and recurrent evaluation requirements.

The InfoObjects used in a query are needed by the OLAP processor as evaluation criteria for the use of aggregates. It is therefore critical that you make a distinction between the different InfoObjects, such as filtering characteristics, characteristics/key figures In rows, characteristics/key figures in columns, and free characteristics. The first time a query is run, the database reads the InfoObjects in filters, rows, and columns. The free characteristics are read at a later time, namely, when the user performs additional navigational steps to include the free characteristics into the analysis.

A query can use an aggregate only if the aggregate contains the filtering characteristics of the query, as well as the InfoObjects contained in the rows and columns of the query. Depending on the read mode of the query (Transaction RSRT, **Query Properties**), you can also include free characteristics and hierarchy levels when selecting an aggregate. But, it is not advisable to include too many free characteristics in the query, because if the option **Read all data** is set in the Query Properties dialog, the system generally won't be able to find any appropriate aggregates.

You should also note that the aggregates are specific to the respective read mode, so that you must set the correct read mode prior to starting the search for the necessary aggregates.

Procedure for
manual aggregate
creation The following section describes a procedure that uses the analysis tools described in Chapter 10. This procedure is recommended for the systematic definition and creation of aggregates. If you must optimize several queries, for example, several queries of a workbook, you should apply this procedure to each query:

1. Analyze the query using the Query Monitor (RSRT)

2. Create the aggregate

3. Check and evaluate the aggregate

4. Check the aggregate tree

5. Summarize aggregates

11.3.1 Analyzing the Query Using the Query Monitor (RSRT)

Section 10.4 described the Query Monitor, which enables an exact analysis of a query. The Query Monitor provides two debug options that produce the information required for creating an aggregate.

An aggregate can always be used by a query, if it contains the characteristics contained in the query in the required granularity. The Query Monitor can analyze the configuration of a query for a specific navigation step.

The following sections describe two debug options for analyzing the query so that you can create appropriate aggregates.

Debug option
"Display
Aggregate Found" The debug option **Display Aggregate Found** enables you to display the characteristics and characteristic values required for a query navigation step, as well as the aggregate and InfoProvider used. You can use this debug option particularly if no aggregates are available yet and you still have to determine the query characteristics and characteristic values required for creating the aggregate. Section 10.4.2 describes the procedure for using this option. Figure 11.23 shows the result of a query navigation step using the debug option **Display Aggregate Found**.

Figure 11.23 shows that the executed query doesn't use any aggregate yet as the **Aggregate/InfoCube** column does not contain a six-digit aggregate name, except the name of the InfoCube on which the query is based.

...	Aggregate/	InfoObject	InfoObject	S...	S: Hierarchy	... S: ...	S: Fixed V	A...	A: Hierarchy	... A: ...	A: Fixed value
1	0SD_C03	0CALMONTH	Calendar Y...	*	0		0		0		
		0DEB_CRED	Credit/debit...	*	0		0		0		
		0DOC_CLASS	Document ...	*	0		0		0		
		0SOLD_TO	Sold-to party	*	0		0		0	.	
		0VTYPE	Value Type ...	F	0		10		0		

Figure 11.23 Results List for the Debug Option "Display Aggregate Found"

The query executes a database access, which is indicated by the sequential numbering in the first column. Each database access listed in that column must be checked against the InfoObjects listed. The InfoObject column lists all InfoObjects that have been used in the query access with their technical names or semantic descriptions. The column names that begin with the letter "S" contain suggested values for the aggregation type, the hierarchy used (if the aggregation type is "H," otherwise "0"), the hierarchy level, and fixed values (if the aggregation type is "F," otherwise "0").

If MultiProviders are used, a separate results window is displayed for each basic InfoCube. You can call the results windows sequentially using the F3 key.

Regarding the aggregation types, you should always determine whether a fixed value has been set through a filter in the query, or, if a specific fixed value has been selected in the selection dialog during the query startup (for example, hierarchy nodes of a customer hierarchy). A fixed value can cause a high degree of compression and therefore is a good means of evaluating the aggregate. However, it restricts the usage frequency for the aggregate if a different selection value—such as a different customer hierarchy node—is selected in another query. You should therefore always consider the navigation and selection steps of the query user when creating aggregates.

For this reason, it is imperative that you find the right relationship among the number, size, and quality of the aggregates in the planning and development phase. Many aggregates require system resources in the regular change run, while a few large aggregates can never improve the query runtimes. Moreover, you should note that the aggregate proposals determined by Transaction RSRT are always based on a query. Consequently, if you want to optimize the runtimes of several queries or workbooks that contain several queries, you must inspect every additional query in accordance with the procedure that we have outlined here.

In addition to the characteristic values used in the query, you can also display the *SQL run schedule* for the query. To do that, you must select the debug option **Display Run Schedule** in the Query Monitor RSRT.

It is possible to read out the fact table of the basic InfoCube ("F") and the characteristics of the involved dimensions ("D") from the SQL statement shown in Figure 11.24. The characteristics to be included in the aggregate can be derived from the GROUP BY statement. The WHERE condition describes the required JOIN operations that contain restrictions based on fixed values, among other things.

Figure 11.24 SQL Run Schedule

 If you use complex queries, you should always take into account the run schedule, because it lists all aggregates, InfoProviders, and InfoObjects involved in the query.

11.3.2 Creating the Aggregate

Based on the query definition determined with the help of the Query Monitor, you can now define the aggregate.

To do that, you must call the aggregate menu by using Transaction RSDDV or via the **Maintain Aggregates** command in the context menu of the InfoProvider, which the query Is based on (see ❶ in Figure 11.25). If there is no aggregate available yet for the InfoCube, the system generates a warning message, which you must confirm by clicking the **Create by Yourself** button ❷.

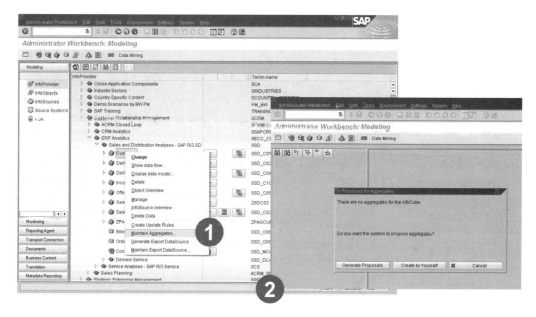

Figure 11.25 Creating Aggregates (I)

The left-hand pane in Figure 11.26 displays the configuration of the InfoCube including its dimensions and characteristics. You can drag and drop the characteristics or attributes to be included in the aggregate into the empty field on the right ❶. If no aggregate exists, or if you drop the object that is to be included in the aggregate onto the empty field, you must define the aggregate name in the window that opens next. You can choose any aggregate name that meets your requirements and even assign the same name multiple times. When the aggregate is activated, the system assigns an internal six-digit number to it which begins with a "1": 1XXXXX.

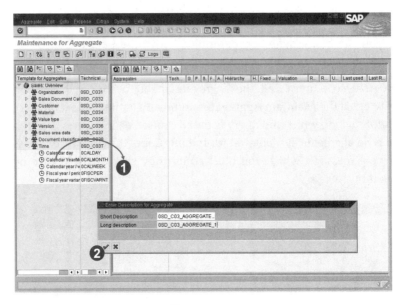

Figure 11.26 Creating Aggregates (II)

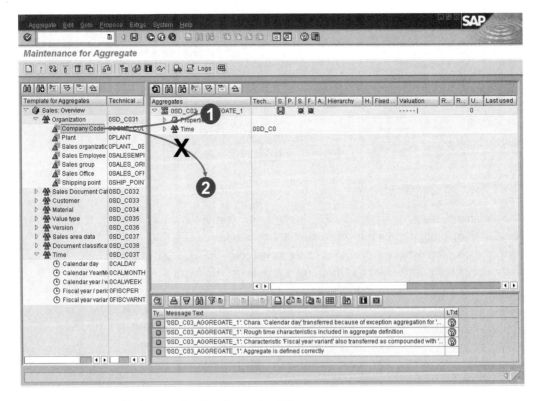

Figure 11.27 Creating Aggregates (III)

You can include additional characteristics by dragging objects from the left and dropping them into the right-hand field (see Figure 11.27). You must drop those additional objects on the aggregate to be defined ❶. Otherwise, you would have to define a new aggregate ❷. After completing the configuration, the aggregate is not yet activated and doesn't contain any data. Therefore, you must activate it and fill it with data (F6).

11.3.3 Checking and Evaluating Aggregates

SAP BW provides an automatic evaluation function for aggregate proposals and for aggregates that already contain data and are active (see Figure 11.28).

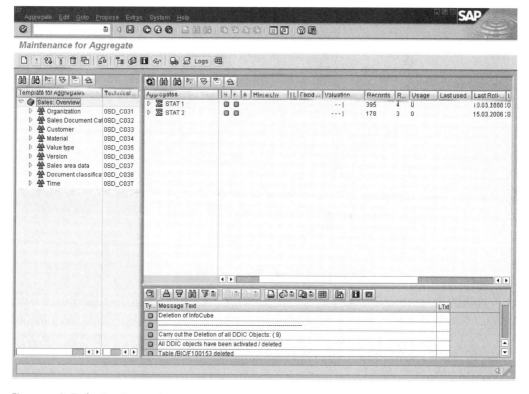

Figure 11.28 Evaluating Aggregates

Table 11.2 provides an overview of the most important evaluation categories in Figure 11.28:

Column	Content
Valuation	Each aggregate is assigned an evaluation in the form of + and—symbols. The scope of the evaluation ranges from five minus signs to five plus signs. The higher the number of aggregated data records, the better the evaluation. Aggregates ▶ that have a similar size as the InfoCube ▶ that aren't used ▶ that haven't been used for a long time ▶ that have a bad compression factor get a bad evaluation result.
Records	Number of records in the aggregate. The number of records in the aggregate should always be considered in relation to the number of records in the InfoCube. The smaller the number of records with regard to the InfoCube, the better the level of aggregation.
Records aggregated	The number of aggregated records indicates the number of records read in the InfoCube, or in the parent aggregate, in order to store a record in the aggregate. The number of aggregated records determines the compression factor of the aggregate. The higher the number of aggregated records, the better the evaluation of the aggregate.
Usage	This figure indicates the frequency at which the aggregate is used and thus enables a quality evaluation for the "hit precision" of the aggregates. Here you can check whether new aggregates are being used. The usage figure is reset every time an aggregate is restructured.
Last used	Date of the last access by a query. Here you can check whether new aggregates are being used.

Table 11.2 Evaluation Categories for Aggregates

11.4   Maintaining Aggregates

To keep the data contained in aggregates up-to-date for reporting, it must be adjusted and modified regularly. These processes include the rollup of aggregates and the adjustment of aggregates as they pertain to hierarchy and attribute changes.

11.4.1 Aggregate Rollup

As soon as new data has been updated in an InfoCube, the data in the corresponding aggregates of the InfoCube must be adjusted as well so that the data used in reporting is current. The process of filling new data into an aggregate is referred to as *rollup*. The aggregate rollup cannot start until the data has been successfully updated in the associated InfoCube.

During the period of time that passes between the updating of the data in the InfoCube and the aggregate rollup, the InfoCube already contains the new data, whereas the aggregate still contains the old dataset. For this reason, the new data is not available for reporting until the aggregate rollup has successfully completed. Therefore, during the rollup process, reporting can be carried out only on the basis of the old dataset.

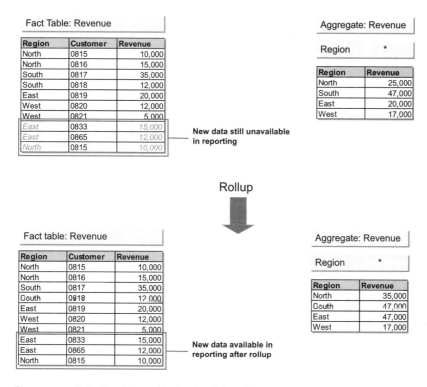

Figure 11.29 Data Consistency During the Rollup Process

If activated aggregates are available for an InfoCube and new requests are loaded into the InfoCube, that data must also be rolled up into the aggregates. Only then is the data that is contained in the InfoCube or in the aggregates available for reporting. Therefore, you should always determine whether you need all aggregates of an InfoCube, since the aggregate rollup requires additional system resources after each loading process.

Figures 11.30 through 11.32 illustrate the different steps involved in a rollup process.

In Status 1, the InfoCube and the aggregate contain the same data packages. The data is available in reporting up to and including the maximum request ID. When data is loaded into an InfoCube, each request is assigned a separate request ID that is stored in the package dimension in the fact table.

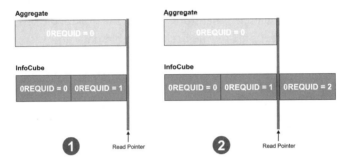

Figure 11.30 Rollup—Technical View (I)

In Status 2, a new request is updated in the InfoCube. A new request ID for the load request is written into the fact table of the InfoCube. The new request is not available in reporting until the read point is updated to the last value of the new request ID.

InfoObject 0REQUID You can use the request ID (InfoObject 0REQUID in the *Data package* dimension) for managing individual loading processes. The read pointer functions like a filter for the request ID and guarantees that only complete and correctly updated load requests are released for reporting. All new requests, which haven't been successfully updated in the InfoCube or rolled up into active aggregates, won't be released for reporting. Load requests that have been correctly updated are automatically assigned the quality status "free of errors" (green traffic light) by the system. Alternatively, you can manually define the request status.

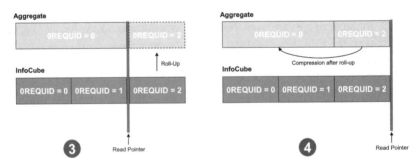

Figure 11.31 Rollup—Technical View (II)

Once the data has been successfully updated in the InfoCube, the request can be rolled up into the aggregate ❸. Not until the data package has been successfully rolled up into all aggregates will the read pointer be updated to the value of the last data package ❹. The data in the InfoCube and aggregate is now consistent and can be used in reporting ❺.

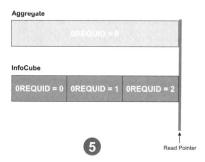

Figure 11.32 Rollup—Technical View (III)

Reporting unreleased requests

It may become necessary to release requests for reporting, which do not yet have a green request status or haven't been rolled up into an aggregate. You can release such requests by using certain variables for the technical characteristic OREQUID. Since SAP BW 3.0B Support Package 21, SAP BW 3.1 Content, Support Package 15, and Support Package 03, SAP Business Content provides three variables for the OREQUID characteristic that enable reporting based on unreleased requests:

▶ The OS_RQMRC variable can be used to report data that hasn't been rolled up into aggregates yet. However, you can only report data up to the first erroneous request; transactional InfoCubes are read completely.

▶ The OS_RQTRA variable can only be used for transactional InfoCubes. For all other InfoCubes, only those requests are read that are also contained in the aggregates, as in the usual read mode.

▶ The OS_RQALL variable applies to all InfoCubes. A query that contains this variable reads the entire set of data from the InfoCube, regardless of whether the requests contain errors.

If MultiProviders are used, the variables only affect non-compressed Info-Cubes and sub-InfoCubes. All other types of providers (ODS objects, InfoSets, master data) are read in the usual mode. Requests that have already been successfully rolled up into aggregates are read from the aggregates; all other requests are read from the InfoCubes.

Like InfoCubes, aggregates contain two fact tables—the E fact table and the F fact table—since SAP BW Release 2.0B. During an upload of the aggregate, the data is first loaded into the uncompressed F fact table. In addition, the aggregate can be compressed ❺. The aggregates are automatically compressed when the InfoCube is filled with data, or when the rollup of data packages has completed. When the aggregate is compressed, the load request IDs are deleted and the data is moved from the F fact table into the E fact table. The deletion of the request ID corresponds to a summation of the data based on the request ID.

The default system setting is that the aggregates are compressed. You can deactivate the aggregate compression in the **Rollup** tab in the **Manage Data Targets** dialog (see Figure 11.33). If you deactivate the aggregate compression, the aggregates won't be compressed until the InfoCube is compressed. You should select this setting, however, if requests must be deleted frequently from the InfoCube. Note that if a request is deleted from the InfoCube, it can also be deleted from the aggregates.

You should use only aggregates that keep all requests, if this is specifically required, because those aggregates require a bigger data volume that can affect the system performance.

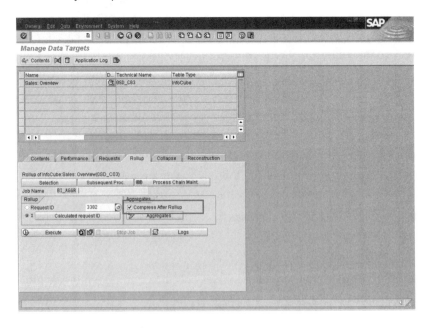

Figure 11.33 Compressing Aggregates

The compression of aggregates has the same effects as the compression of InfoCubes: You cannot delete compressed requests from the InfoCube or from the aggregate. If you want to delete a data package (request) from the InfoCube, which has already been rolled up into the aggregates, you must deactivate and regenerate the aggregates.

You can trigger the aggregate rollup both manually and automatically after each load request (see Figure 11.34).

Rolling up aggregates

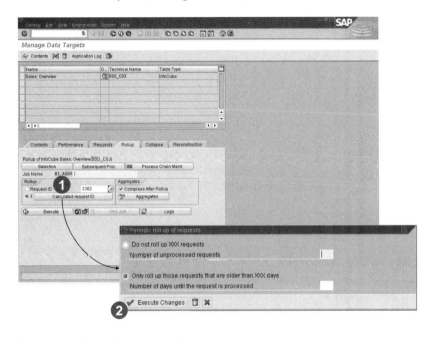

Figure 11.34 Manual Aggregate Rollup

In a manual rollup, you can schedule specific requests to be included in the rollup ❶, or calculate a set of requests to be rolled up ❷. In addition, for the calculated request ID, you can specify the number of non-processed requests, or the number of days until the requests will be processed. The number of non-processed requests indicates how many requests should always remain unaggregated or uncompressed in the InfoCube. The system checks after each loading process if more than XXX requests of the InfoCube are uncompressed. If there are too many requests, they will be aggregated or compressed. The number of days until the requests are processed indicates how many days will pass until a request is aggregated or compressed. After each loading process, the system checks whether a request is older than XXX days, based on the date it was loaded the last time. The requests are not compressed until they have exceeded that specific number of days.

To configure the automatic rollup of requests, you can set the parameters in the **Environment · Automatic Request Processing** menu (see Figure 11.35, ❶).

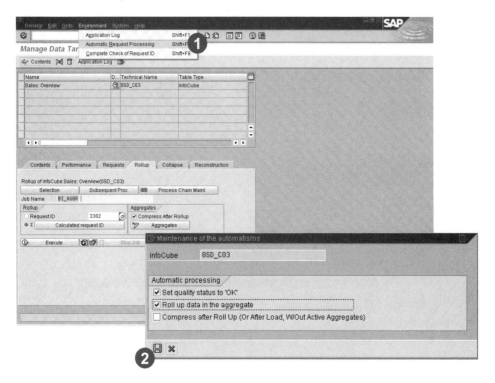

Figure 11.35 Settings for an Automatic Aggregate Rollup

In the window that opens ❷, you can select several options for the automatic processing:

▶ **Set quality status to 'OK'**
You can use this option to define that the quality status is automatically set to **green** once the data has been loaded into the data target. You should always set this status unless you want to check the data before releasing it. Data in ODS objects cannot be activated until the request has the status **OK**.

▶ **Roll up data in the aggregate**
This option triggers the automatic rollup of data into the aggregates once it has been successfully loaded into the InfoCube. You should select the automatic rollup only if the requests are loaded into the

InfoCube in such a way that the loading, rollup, and other processes don't interfere with each other.

▶ **Compress after Roll Up (Or After Load, W/Out Active Aggregates)**
This option causes the InfoCube contents to be automatically compressed once the rollup has completed. If aggregates exist, only those requests are compressed that have already been rolled up. If no aggregates exist, all requests that haven't been compressed yet will be aggregated. Compressed requests can no longer be selectively deleted from the InfoCube.

The automatic processing of requests can sometimes result in system locks and terminations, especially if large data quantities are loaded simultaneously. For this reason, you should pay attention to the chronological sequence of the processes and the lock logics when configuring the automatic processing. The processes and logics are listed in the table below.

Lock logics

If the automatic processing of requests is not possible, you should schedule the jobs in a process chain.

	During the load process	During the creation of indices	During the creation of statistics	During rollup	During the compression process	During the deletion process	During the update process
Loading data						☹	
Deleting data	☹						
Archiving data	☹	☹	☹		☹		☹
Creating indices	☹		☹	☹	☹	☹	
Deleting indices	☹	☹	☹	☹	☹	☹	
Creating statistics		☹		☹	☹	☹	
Filling aggregates		☹	☹	☹	☹	☹	
Rolling up requests into aggregates		☹	☹		☹	☹¹	
Updating requests into other data targets		☹	☹		☹	☹¹	

Table 11.3 Lock Logics in Data Management

---

1 In certain cases.

	During the load process	During the creation of indices	During the creation of statistics	During rollup	During the compression process	During the deletion process	During the update process
Compressing requests		☹	☹	☹		☹¹	☹
Performing a change run		☹	☹	☹	☹	☹¹	

Table 11.3 Lock Logics in Data Management (cont.)

11.4.2 Checking the Aggregate Tree (Rollup Hierarchy)

If several aggregates are created on an InfoCube, SAP BW checks the rollup hierarchy of all aggregates of the InfoCube and arranges them in a hierarchical tree structure. Figure 11.36 illustrates the organizing principle.

The aggregate hierarchy is based on the characteristics contained in the aggregate. New aggregates are inserted under existing aggregates if they contain a subset of the characteristics of the parent aggregate. For example, aggregates 1.1 and 1.2 are CHILD aggregates of the superordinate BASIS aggregate 1, because they contain a subset of the characteristics contained in aggregate 1. On the other hand, aggregate 2.1 cannot be included under aggregate 1, because it contains the 0MATERIAL characteristic, which can be found in aggregate 2, but not in BASIS aggregate 1.

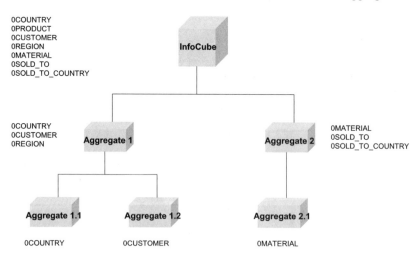

Figure 11.36 Aggregate Hierarchy

The hierarchy of the aggregates is a critical factor for the aggregate rollup. You should avoid creating too many BASIS aggregates on an InfoCube, because all data records of the InfoCube must be read for each basis aggregate, and large InfoCubes would require sufficient system performance and rollup times. For the CHILD rollups, the system does not read the data from the InfoCube, but from the parent aggregate, which may reduce the rollup times due to the aggregation factor of the aggregate. For this reason, the aggregate tree can be used to identify aggregates that should be summarized.

To avoid reading all data records in the InfoCube multiple times, you can create larger basis aggregates, which can be used for the creation of child aggregates. The child aggregates must not contain any navigation attributes and hierarchies; otherwise, they would have to be adjusted during a change run.

Figure 11.37 displays a sample aggregate tree that contains three BASIS aggregates and two CHILD aggregates.

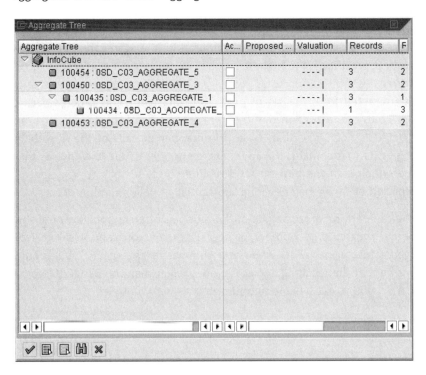

Figure 11.37 Aggregate Tree (Shift+F6)

11.4.3 Summarizing Aggregates/Optimization

If many aggregates have been created on the basis of automatic proposals, it does not always make sense to activate all aggregates. For this very reason, the SAP BW system provides an option that allows you to summarize the aggregates of an InfoCube so you can optimize the total number of aggregates. Although this can result in longer query runtimes, you should factor the number of aggregates, the memory requirement, and the time required for the rollup, in addition to the runtimes.

Optimizing aggregates
If many aggregates exist, you should verify whether it's worth summarizing them. SAP BW provides the **Optimize** function (Ctrl+Shift+F7) in the **Propose** menu precisely for this reason. This function enables you to summarize similar aggregates into larger aggregates. The optimization process is based on the rule that the number of aggregates should be reduced. For this purpose, the system selects only those aggregates that were rarely called and add up to only 20% of all calls. These aggregates are referred to as *poor aggregates*. The system verifies whether the poor aggregates can be integrated in other aggregates that contain exactly one additional component. If several aggregates with exactly one additional component can be used for the optimization, the aggregate that has the best-hit precision—the highest number of calls—will be selected. Those aggregates are referred to as *good aggregates*. The analyzed aggregate is then deleted from the set of poor aggregates. But, this process occurs only with the restriction that the number of calls of the aggregate to be deleted is not larger than twice the number of calls of the absorbing aggregate that contains the additional component. This rule ensures that the principle of the best-hit ratio is adhered to, so that no aggregate is replaced by an aggregate with a substantially smaller number of calls.

You can perform an aggregate optimization as often as you like, until you obtain the required number of aggregates, or you cannot summarize aggregates further. But, when you summarize aggregates, you should ensure that the resulting aggregates are smaller than the BasicCube; otherwise, you won't be able to optimize the query runtimes.

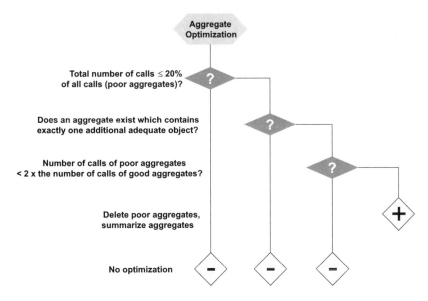

Figure 11.38 Aggregate Optimization

You should always summarize aggregates if:

▶ The number of records contained in the aggregates is identical

▶ You can summarize several small aggregates to a bigger one at a tolerable deterioration of the runtime (factor 10 smaller than the Basic-Cube)

▶ Too many basis aggregates exist that must read too many data records from the InfoCube during the rollup process

▶ Aggregates that are used infrequently can be integrated in other aggregates at a tolerable deterioration of the runtime (factor 10 smaller than the BasicCube)

11.4.4 Switching Off Aggregates

Aggregates that are no longer used can be disabled for being used by queries. You don't need to delete those aggregates, because you can switch them off individually (see Figure 11.39).

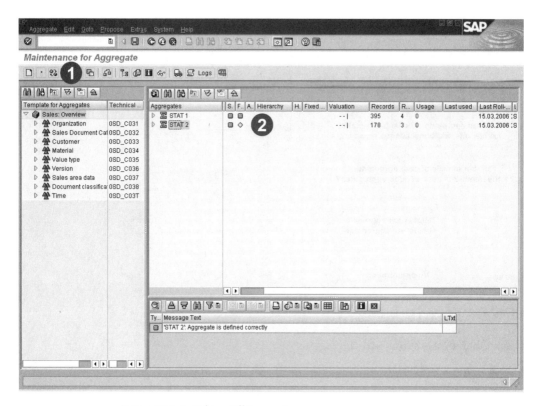

Figure 11.39 Switching Off Aggregates

The **Switch On/Off** function **❶** enables you to switch off aggregates so that they are no longer considered for reporting purposes. As a matter of fact, a disabled aggregate is not deleted, because its definition and data remain in the aggregate (**green** status). Moreover, the change run and rollup processes for the aggregate continue to be performed, however, the aggregate is no longer included in the queries (filled/switched off status = **gray**).

11.4.5 Analyzing and Monitoring the Filling and Rollup of Aggregates

The filling of aggregates and the rollup of data requests from the InfoCube or from basis aggregates can be monitored with regard to the time at which the processes are started and the time required for the execution. You can use Transaction SM37 to analyze the respective background jobs.

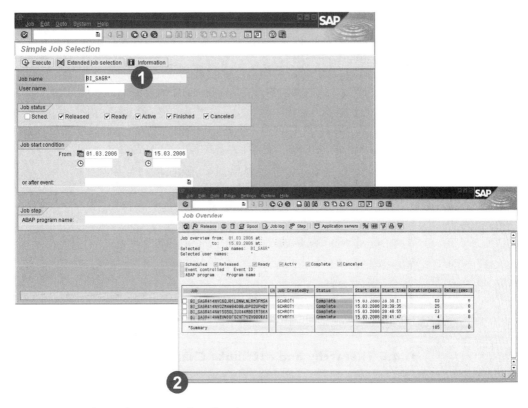

Figure 11.40 Analyzing the Runtimes for Filling Aggregates

The names of all rollup jobs begin with "BI_AGGR" ❶. The job overview ❷ provides information on the start and end times, as well as the runtime of a job. The job log then enables you to calculate the runtimes of the change run jobs.

Monitoring aggregate rollups

In addition, the runtimes for the creation of aggregates are collected in Table RSDDSTATAGGR if the collection of OLAP statistics data is activated for the respective InfoCube (**Tools · BW Statistics for InfoProviders**). You can analyze the table using the data browser (Transaction SE16). The most important fields in Table RSDDSTATAGGR are displayed in Table 11.4.

Table RSDDSTA-TAGGR

Field	Description
AGGRCUBE	Name of the aggregate
INFOCUBE	InfoCube on which the aggregate is based
PARENICUBE	Name of the InfoCube from which the data was read (this can also be an aggregate)
UNAME	Name of the user who executed the action
CHANGEMODE	Editing mode (N = new creation; R = rollup; D = delta).
TIMEREAD	Time required for reading the data
TIMEINSERT	Time required for saving the data
TIMEINDEX	Time required for the index creation
TIMEDBANALYZE	Time required for analyzing the database statistics
REC_READ	Number of records read
REC_INSERTED	Number of inserted records

Table 11.4 Fields of Table RSDDSTATAGGR

11.4.6 Hierarchy and Attribute Changes

Aggregates that contain navigation attributes or hierarchies are subject to the hierarchy and attribute change run. When master data is changed, the aggregates that use the relevant attributes or hierarchies must be adjusted.

Change run

Due to the change run, the master data is updated, whether or not the aggregates contain attributes or hierarchies. The new, updated master data is not available for reporting until the change run has completed.

In the example shown in Figure 11.41, some contents of the *Sales employee* attribute (SALESEMPLY) are changed in InfoObject ZREGION_1. At first, sales employee 2015 is responsible for the SOUTHERN region ❶. Then, the responsibility for the SOUTHERN region is transferred to sales employee 1623. For this reason, an additional data record is inserted in the master data table before the change run starts: The new status is assigned the object version M (modified) and is not yet available for reporting. This data record is marked with the change flag I (= insert). Prior to the change run, the previous status of the master data is still available in reporting.

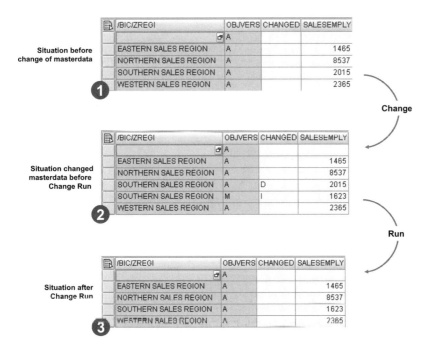

	/BIC/ZREGI	OBJVERS	CHANGED	SALESEMPLY
	▣ A			
	EASTERN SALES REGION	A		1465
	NORTHERN SALES REGION	A		8537
	SOUTHERN SALES REGION	A		2015
	WESTERN SALES REGION	A		2365

Situation before change of masterdata ❶

Change

	/BIC/ZREGI	OBJVERS	CHANGED	SALESEMPLY
	▣ A			
	EASTERN SALES REGION	A		1465
	NORTHERN SALES REGION	A		8537
	SOUTHERN SALES REGION	A	D	2015
	SOUTHERN SALES REGION	M	I	1623
	WESTERN SALES REGION	A		2365

Situation changed masterdata before Change Run ❷

Run

	/BIC/ZREGI	OBJVERS	CHANGED	SALESEMPLY
	▣ A			
	EASTERN SALES REGION	A		1465
	NORTHERN SALES REGION	A		8537
	SOUTHERN SALES REGION	A		1623
	WESTERN SALES REGION	A		2365

Situation after Change Run ❸

Figure 11.41 Change Run Process (I)

Those data records are assigned the object version A (active) and are marked for being deleted by the change run (change flag D, delete) ❷. The newly added data records are activated after the change run so that the updated, modified set of master data becomes available for reporting ❸.

All aggregates that are affected by the navigation attribute or hierarchy changes are adjusted during the master data activation. During that process, all aggregates, InfoCubes, and master data objects are locked for a rollup. To make them available for reporting during a change run the system generates a temporary aggregate fact table, /BIC/E2XXXXX, with XXXXX being the system-internal five-digit number of the aggregate fact table E1. Once the aggregate fact table /BIC/E2XXXXX has been generated, it is copied to E1XXXXX, and Table E2XXXXX is deleted.

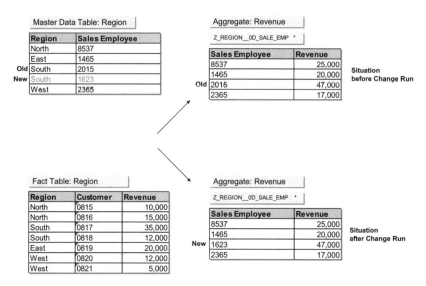

Figure 11.42 Change Run Process (II)

11.4.7 Parameterizing the Hierarchy and Attribute Change Runs

Depending on the number of changed master data objects and aggregates to be adjusted, the runtime of the change run can take a very long time. When creating the aggregates, you should therefore always check whether navigation attributes or hierarchies are required in the aggregate, or whether you can define the aggregate with the basic characteristics, which would omit the need for a change run for those aggregates. At the time you schedule a change run, you often don't know which aggregates must be adjusted. A monitoring function is available for this purpose since SAP BW 2.0B Support Package 14 and SAP BW 2.1C Support Package 06. ABAP Report RSDDS_CHANGERUN_MONITOR and Transaction RSATTR enable you to generate a list of characteristics and hierarchies that are activated and of the aggregates involved (see Figure 11.43).

You can trigger the hierarchy and attribute change run manually in the Administrator Workbench via the following menu: **Apply Hierarchy/Attribute Change**. The screen, which is opened by this command, displays the InfoObjects ❶ and hierarchy lists ❷ in which you can see which InfoObjects and hierarchies have been scheduled for the hierarchy and attribute change run.

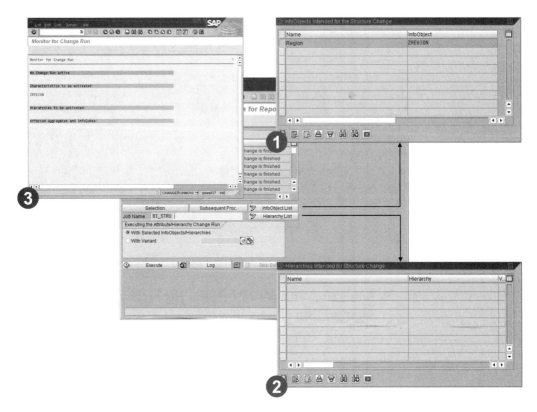

Figure 11.43 Change Run Monitor

The two dialog boxes are configured in such a way that all those InfoObjects and hierarchies are highlighted whose master data has been changed. You can select the objects and hierarchies to be activated from these lists. If nothing gets changed, the system activates all objects and hierarchies that are contained in the lists. You can also start the change run using the ABAP program RSDDS_AGGREGATES_MAINTAIN (Transaction SE38, see Figure 11.44).

The program can be assigned a list of InfoObjects and hierarchies to be adjusted by the change run. You can save the lists as variants and schedule them as periodic runs for an event in a process chain. As of SAP BW 2.0B Support Package 16 and SAP BW 2.1 Support Package 08, you can separately schedule and start the hierarchy and attribute change run in the Administrator Workbench. Once the run, which has been scheduled using the ABAP report, is completed, it is displayed in the list of completed hierarchy and attribute change runs in the Change Run Monitor.

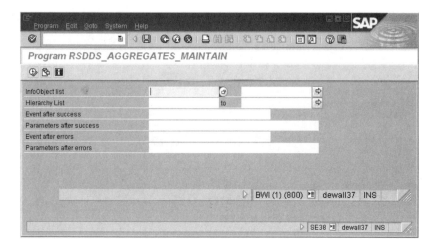

Figure 11.44 ABAP Report RSDDS_AGGREGATES_MAINTAIN

11.4.8 Analyzing and Monitoring a Hierarchy and Attribute Change Run

Each change run job can be analyzed with regard to its runtime. To do this, you can select the change run job in Transaction SM37 (see Figure 11.45).

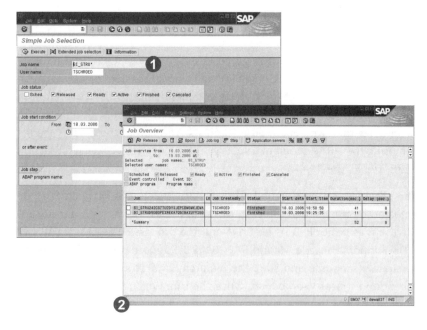

Figure 11.45 Analyzing the Runtimes of Change Run Jobs

The names of all change run jobs begin with "BI_STRU". In the Job Overview ❷ you can determine the start and end times, as well as the runtime of the job. The job log then enables you to calculate the runtimes of the change run jobs.

11.4.9 Delta Process/Rebuild

After a change run, the aggregates must be adjusted so that the changed data can be displayed. Previous versions of SAP BW required a complete rebuild of all aggregates that were involved, which affected the system performance, particularly in cases where only a few master data changes had been carried out.

For this reason, two strategies are available to adjust the aggregates—the rebuild and the delta process. In the delta process, the old records of changed master data are updated negatively, whereas the new data records are updated positively. In a rebuild, on the other hand, the entire aggregate is recalculated. If only a few changes to an aggregate exist, the delta process is the most appropriate way to adjust an aggregate; however, with a specific number of changes, the delta process becomes more time-consuming and costly than a rebuild, which is why the system automatically carries out an aggregate rebuild when a certain threshold value has been reached. If you want to modify the threshold value, you can do that in the SAP Customizing Implementation Guide (Transaction SPRO) in the following menu: **SAP Business Information Warehouse · General BW Settings · Parameters for Aggregates** (Transaction RSCUSTV8, see Figure 11.46).

The threshold value is defined as a percentage of changed master data and is set to 20% by default. This means that if more than 20% of all master data was changed, all involved aggregates are rebuilt and not adjusted in a delta process. If you don't specify a value, the aggregates will always be rebuilt. When you choose a value, you should consider the number and size of the aggregates and the frequency with which master data changes occur. The best way to find the ideal threshold value is to perform several test runs with different value settings. A threshold value that lies between 15% and 20% is a good starting point for optimizing the system's performance.

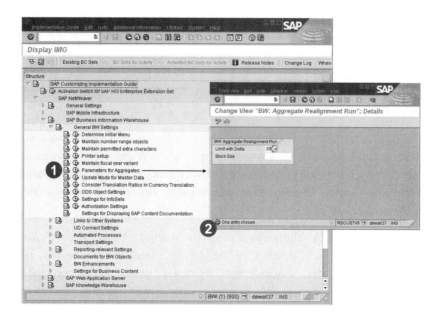

Figure 11.46 Maintaining Change Run Parameters

 The delta process is used only for aggregates whose basic InfoCubes contain key figures or non-cumulatives that can be summarized. If a basic InfoCube contains key figures with the *MAXIMUM* or *MINIMUM* aggregations, you must carry out a complete rebuild of the corresponding aggregates.

11.4.10 Aggregate Block Sizes

During an aggregate rollup, the data is read from a basic InfoCube, or, if an appropriate rollup hierarchy exists, from a basis aggregate, and is written to the F fact table of the aggregate. When the aggregate is compressed, the data records are written to the E fact table and deleted from the F fact table.

If aggregates are filled with data from very large InfoCubes, the process requires a great deal of memory (up to several hundreds of megabytes) and temporary tablespace in the database. Prior to the release of Support Package 21 for SAP BW 2.0B and Support Package 13 for SAP BW 2.1C, aggregates were filled by aggregating the entire source (InfoCube or basis aggregate). This process caused the database to read, sort, and aggregate large quantities of data, which resulted in high resource consumption.

Since SAP BW 2.0B Support Package 21, the data is read, sorted, and aggregated in blocks when an aggregate is filled. You can specify the size of the blocks, which indicates the number of data records to be processed simultaneously. The default setting for the block size is 10,000,000 data records.

The block size you choose must be related to the size of the temporary tablespace in the database. If the block size is too small, many database read accesses are required, which may affect the runtime of the change run. If the block size is too big, the memory size of the tablespace can be exceeded, which terminates the operation (overflow of TEMP tablespace).

Choosing the block size

You can change the block size using the program RSDDK_BLOCKSIZE_SET, which is available only in SAP BW Releases 2.0B as of SP 21 and 2.1C as of SP 13. From SAP BW 3.0A onward, you can modify the block size in the SAP Customizing Implementation Guide (Transaction SPRO) in the following menu: **SAP Business Information Warehouse · General BW Settings · Parameters for Aggregates** (Transaction RSCUSTV8, see Figure 11.46).

11.4.11 Parallel and Serial Change Runs

Change runs can be subdivided into parallel and serial change runs. In a serial change run, the aggregates to be updated are calculated sequentially in a background work process. As of SAP BW 2.0B Support Package 28, SAP BW 2.1C SupportPackage 20, and SAP BW 3.0B Support Package 05, the change run can be parallelized. Parallel change runs are especially advantageous if you have to update aggregates of several InfoCubes.

In a parallel change run, the background work process starts one dialog work process per InfoCube. The adjustment of aggregates is distributed to several work processes that run in parallel. A separate dialog work process is started per InfoCube, during which the aggregates that correspond to the InfoCube are updated. The parallelization of the change run can lead to a runtime improvement if the aggregates are equally distributed across several InfoCubes. But, if only a few InfoCubes dominate the runtimes of the aggregate adjustments, the parallelization won't result in any significant performance improvement (see Figure 11.47).

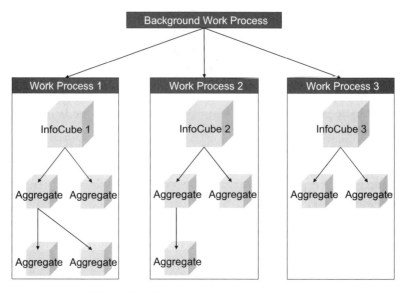

Figure 11.47 Parallelizing the Change Run

The default setting for the change run is the serial change run in a batch process. If you want to change to parallel operation, you should set up a new RFC server group in Transaction RZ12. Once you have set up the RFC server group, you must use ABAP Report SAP_RSADMIN_MAINTAIN (Transaction SE38) to change the following object entries in Table RSAD-MIN (see Figure 11.48):

▶ CR_RFCGROUP = name of the RFC server group (optional)

▶ CR_MAXWPC = maximum number of work processes to be used

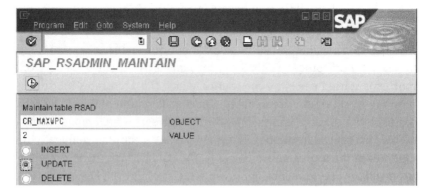

Figure 11.48 ABAP Report SAP_RSADMIN_MAINTAIN

The number of work processes depends on the number of InfoCubes whose aggregates are to be updated. The maximum number of work processes that are started is determined by using the object entry CR_MAX-WPC.

Note that when you parallelize the change run, the memory usage increases due to the parallel use of the dialog processes. If a memory of CPU bottleneck already exists in the system, you should not configure parallel change runs, as that can cause a dramatic increase in paging processes.

Because the dialog work process won't be released until all aggregates of an InfoCube have been updated, you must set the profile parameter rdisp/max_wprun_time of the respective application servers to a value that prevents the work process from terminating due to a timeout.

If aggregates are rebuilt in a parallel change run, you must also ensure that adequate storage space is available in the temporary tablespace of the database.

12 Compression and Partitioning

The ability to compress and partition InfoCubes in SAP BW is an efficient optimization measure that reduces the data volume of the fact table. This chapter describes the basic principles and the parameterization of these tuning activities.

The optimization measures described in this chapter are based on the goal of reducing the number of data records contained in the fact table of an InfoCube. Contrary to creating aggregates, which are another compressed type of data storage in the InfoCube, the compression and partitioning processes here involve a reduction of the data volume in the InfoCube, without generating any additional data storage object.

12.1 Compressing InfoCubes

The *package* dimension, which stores the request ID, is part of every InfoCube.

The request ID is automatically generated with each loading process so it can identify the loading process when an InfoCube is filled. When data is loaded into the InfoCube, complete requests are inserted.

Request ID

One advantage of the request ID concept is that you can delete individual, complete requests from the InfoCube after the loading process has finished; for example, if the data loaded last is erroneous.

Alternatively, the request ID enables you to store identical data records (i.e., all characteristics except the request ID are identical) multiple times in the fact table. This causes an unnecessary increase of the data volume. Moreover, you must create aggregates based on the request ID every time a query is run. Both factors can lead to a needless loss in reporting performance.

When data is transferred into SAP BW, the data records of each loading process are dispatched in packages of different sizes. You can set the package size in BW Customizing. If you don't enter any value here, the data is transferred with a default setting of 10,000 KB per data package. You can increase this setting to 40,000 KB or higher. When an InfoCube is filled, the data is aggregated only within a data package, but not across different data packages, so that the fact table contains a high level of detail, which, from an analysis viewpoint, is extraneous (see Figure 12.1).

Data packages

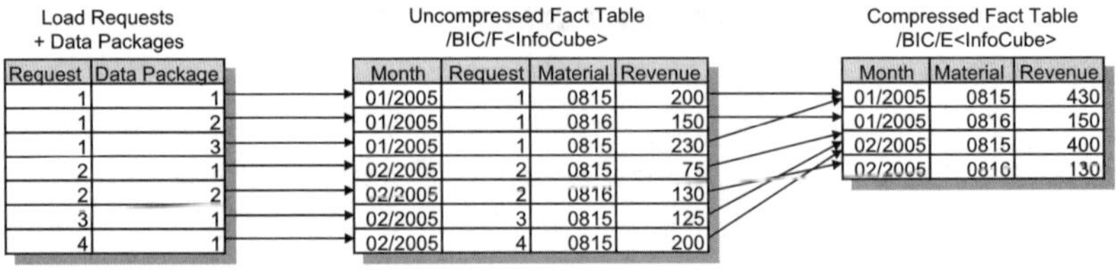

Figure 12.1 Compressing the Fact Table

Depending on the level of detail applied to the data in the InfoCube and on the frequency of loading processes, the data volume of the InfoCube can grow rapidly which may affect the reporting performance.

F and E fact tables Since SAP BW Release 2.0B, each InfoCube has two fact tables. The F fact table contains uncompressed data including the request IDs of the loading processes. The E fact table contains the compressed data records without the request IDs. In the standard version, the uncompressed F fact table is filled, while the E fact table is left empty. During a compression of the InfoCube, the request IDs are deleted from the F fact table, and the compressed load requests are moved to the E fact table. You can either compress the entire fact table, or move some of the older requests to the E fact table. During a data analysis, the OLAP processor automatically includes the requests of both fact tables, which is transparent to the user.

An essential drawback of the InfoCube compression is that the compression cannot be undone. Therefore, you can't delete individual loading processes based on their request IDs; for example, when you discover that the data contains errors. For that reason, before you compress an InfoCube, you should ensure that the data you want to load is free of errors.

Except for Oracle-based SAP BW systems, data cannot be analyzed during the data compression process. The time required for compressing a request is approximately 2.5 ms per data record to be compressed, and approximately 5 ms per data record of non-cumulative cubes to be compressed. What accounts for this difference is that for non-cumulative InfoCubes, the marker of the non-cumulative must be updated as well. Consequently, you should not carry out a compression and an analysis at the same time.[1]

---

1 For non-cumulative InfoCubes, you can ensure that the non-cumulative marker is not updated by setting the **No Marker Updating** indicator. You must use this option if you're loading historic non-cumulative value changes into an InfoCube after an initialization has already taken place with the current non-cumulative. Otherwise, the results produced in the query won't be correct. For performance reasons, you should compress subsequent delta requests.

The compression of an InfoCube occurs in the **Collapse** tab of the Basic-Cube administration (see Figure 12.2). Loading requests can be selected by specifying the request ID up to and including which data of the Info-Cube is to be compressed. Then, all the requests of the InfoCube that have a request ID, which is smaller than or equal to the specified request ID, are compressed.

Requests can also be compressed automatically within specific periods. For this purpose, the system calculates the requests to be compressed. You can use the **Calculated request ID** button to define the number of requests that you don't want to compress, or to compress only those requests that are older than *n* days.

Periodic compression

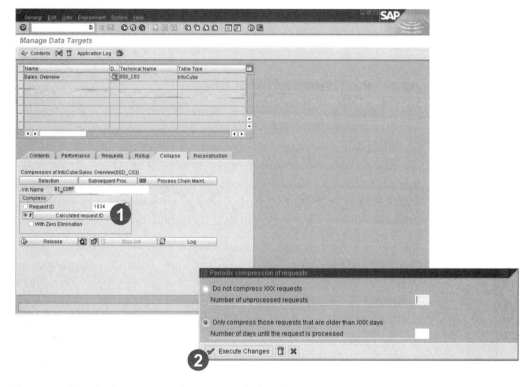

Figure 12.2 Periodic Compression of Requests (Calculated Request ID)

You can use the option **Do not compress XXX requests** to specify the number of requests that you want to keep permanently uncompressed or unaggregated in the InfoCube. In that case, the last requests in an Info-Cube remain uncompressed. After each loading process, the system checks whether more than XXX requests of the InfoCube are uncompressed. If there is a surplus of requests, they will be compressed or aggregated.

You can use the option **Only compress those requests that are older than XXX days** to specify after how many days a request should be compressed. After each loading process, the system checks whether a request is older than XXX days, based on the date it was loaded the last time. The requests are compressed only when they have exceeded that number of days.

Before compressing an InfoCube, you should verify whether the E fact table contains the P index (Transaction DB02, **Detailed Analysis**). If that index is not available, it is almost impossible to compress the InfoCube, or, at least, the compression will take a very long time. If there is no index, you can create one by reactivating the InfoCube.

12.2 Partitioning InfoCubes

Partitioning is another optimization measure that you can use to improve the reporting performance. Unlike the compression of InfoCubes, in a partitioning process, although the dataset is not modified because it's already compressed, it is distributed to several small, physically independent and redundancy-free units in the database. This distribution of data helps to improve the performance in reporting, as well as the performance during the deletion of data from the InfoCube.

Technically, the fact table of the InfoCube is physically distributed to several tables in the database on the basis of a time-related partitioning characteristic. The performance advantage is that, in reporting, several read processes can search the individual partitions simultaneously, instead of just having one read process search through the entire fact table. Moreover, in reporting, you can restrict the read process to the partitioning characteristic that reduces the amount of data to be read.

Types of partitioning There are two types of partitioning an InfoCube:

▶ Partitioning at the database level
▶ Partitioning at the application level

What both types have in common is that they separate the dataset of the InfoCube into smaller datasets. The partitioning process is part of the data modeling process and is possible only as long as no data has been loaded into the InfoCube.

12.2.1 Partitioning at the Database Level

Partitioning at the database level means that the database system is responsible for administering the partitions, that is, the database system distributes the data to the individual partitions and it creates new partitions.

This type of partitioning requires that the database, which the SAP BW system runs on, can be partitioned. With the exception of MaxDB, most database systems support partitioning.

Requirements

The following two types of partitioning must be differentiated in an SAP BW system:

Partitioning types

▶ Range partitioning for IBM DB2/390, Informix, and Oracle database systems

▶ Hash partitioning for the IBM DB2/UDB database system

Range partitioning includes data from a specific value range. For example, Partition 1 ranges from 01/01/2005 through 03/31/2005; Partition 2 ranges from 04/01/2005 through 06/30/2005; Partition 3 ranges from 07/01/2005 through 09/30/2005; and so on.

With hash partitioning, the data records are distributed to the individual partitions via a hash algorithm. Hash partitioning is completely transparent to the SAP BW system. Therefore, all fact tables in IBM-UDB-based BW systems are automatically partitioned and the partitions don't need to be configured by the user.

Since SAP BW Release 2.0B, the F fact table is automatically partitioned via the package dimension according to the field "key_<InfoCube>p" in Oracle-based BW systems. When the InfoCube is activated, the fact table is created including a partition with "high value" = 0. With each loading process, an additional partition is created in which the request is written. When the InfoCube is compressed, the corresponding partitions of the compressed requests are deleted. Therefore, the partitions of the F fact table are dynamic as new partitions are created at runtime with each loading process, while older partitions are deleted upon the compression of requests. Figure 12.3 illustrates the partitioning procedure for the F fact table (Transaction SE14, **Storage parameters**).

F fact table

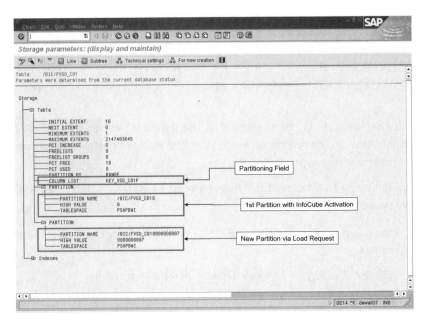

Figure 12.3 Partitioning Procedure for the F Fact Table

When an InfoCube is compressed, the partition that corresponds to the request is deleted and no new partition with the same name is created. Moreover, the package dimension table entry that corresponds to the request is deleted. You can also remove data of entire requests by selectively deleting requests from the InfoCube and keeping the corresponding partitions. Consequently, you would either end up with empty partitions that don't contain any data, or with unusable partitions that do contain data, but have no entry in the package dimension table of the InfoCube, if the compression run doesn't complete successfully. As of SAP BW 3.x, you can identify and remove empty or unused partitions from the F fact table of an InfoCube by using ABAP report `SAP_DROP_EMPTY_FPARTITIONS`.

E fact table   In Oracle-based SAP BW systems, the E fact table is statically partitioned. This means that no changes to the configured partitioning procedure occur at runtime. If aggregates for an InfoCube have been defined, the E fact table adopts the partitioning property of the BasicCube, provided that the partitioning characteristic is not aggregated. Partitioning on the basis of a time characteristic integrates an additional field in the fact table, which serves as a partitioning field (SID_0CALMONTH or SID_0FISCPER). Figure 12.4 illustrates the partitioning procedure for the E fact table (Transaction SE14, **Storage parameters**).

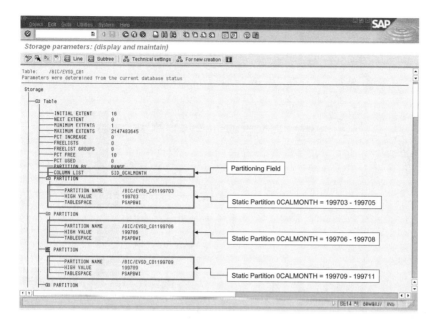

Figure 12.4 Partitioning Procedure for the E Fact Table

A partitioning based on the time characteristic OCALMONTH has the effect that when you run a query for a selected period of time, for example, June 1997, only the relevant partition 06/1997 through 08/1997 must be read, because the optimizer excludes non-relevant partitions, which, in turn, results in an improvement of the reporting performance as fewer data records are to be read.

The type of partitioning must be defined once during the data modeling process so that the database system knows how the data is to be distributed to the individual partitions. Then, the data distribution doesn't need to be considered any further during the data staging process.

Partitioning can occur in the InfoCube maintenance on the basis of the time characteristics *Calendar month* (OCALMONTH) or *Fiscal year/period* (OFISCPER). At least one of the two characteristics must be contained in the InfoCube. If you want to partition the InfoCube on the basis of the *Fiscal year/period* characteristic, you must first set the *Fiscal year variant* (OFISCVARNT) characteristic to the *constant* value, because the two characteristics are compounded.[2]

Partitioning characteristics

---

2 See SAP Note 375871 for more information on partitioning InfoCubes from the OFISCPER characteristic.

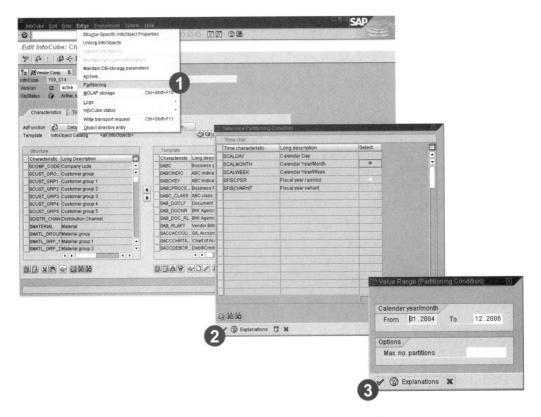

Figure 12.5 Partitioning the InfoCube at Database Level

The partitioning process can be configured in the InfoCube maintenance menu by using the following path: **Extras · Partitioning** (see ❶ in Figure 12.5). If the InfoCube does not yet contain any data, you can carry out the partitioning using the time characteristics 0CALMONTH and 0FISCPER ❷. When selecting the time characteristic, you must define the value range for the partitioning condition ❸, because when the InfoCube is activated in the database, the fact table is created with a number of partitions that corresponds to the value range. In addition, you can define the maximum number of partitions for the fact table of the InfoCube.

Example:

You select the partitioning condition 0CALMONTH and define the value range from 01/2003 through 12/2006. Then

4 years × 12 months + 2 = 50 partitions

are created in the database.[3]

In addition, you choose **20** as being the maximum number of partitions. This maximum number of partitions means that one partition must contain several months. The selected value range produces 50 individual values. The system summarizes three months into each partition so that

   4 years × 4 partitions/year + 2 marginal partitions = 18 partitions

are created in the database.

When parameterizing the partitions, you should ensure that the partitions have an adequate size. If the time range you choose is too short, the partitions will become too big and therefore result in many individual time values, for example, months, which will have to be summarized into one partition. If the time range you choose is too long and extends far into the future, a large quantity of partitions will be created in the database. You should therefore first try to create a partition with a restricted time range, for example, for one year. You can then repartition the Info-Cube when that year has expired. The option of repartitioning InfoCubes that have already been filled with data is available from SAP NetWeaver 2004s on. The repartitioning of InfoCubes is currently supported for the following databases:

- ▶ UDB for Unix/Windows
- ▶ DB2 for z/OSDB2/OS390
- ▶ DB2/AS400
- ▶ Oracle
- ▶ MS SQL

If the repartitioning option is technically not yet available to you, you can proceed as follows to create new partitions in a filled InfoCube:

1. Create a copy of the InfoCube.

2. Create a new, extended partitioning in the new InfoCube.

3. Load data from the old InfoCube into the new InfoCube via the Data-Mart interface.

---

3 Two partitions are created for values outside of the range: < 01/2003 and > 12/2006.

12.2.2 Partitioning at Application Level

If a partitioning at the database level isn't possible; for example, because the database system that serves as a basis for the SAP BW system cannot be partitioned, or because the requests in the InfoCube should not be compressed, you can carry out the partitioning process at the application level.

This type of partitioning does not depend on the partitioning technique of the database system. The separation of the data volume of an InfoCube into several partitions requires the definition of a separate InfoCube for each partition. A MultiProvider merges the data of the individual sub-InfoCubes for reporting purposes. The MultiProvider partitioning concept therefore represents a way to implement a logical partitioning with specific characteristics, in addition to the technical partitioning according to time characteristics.

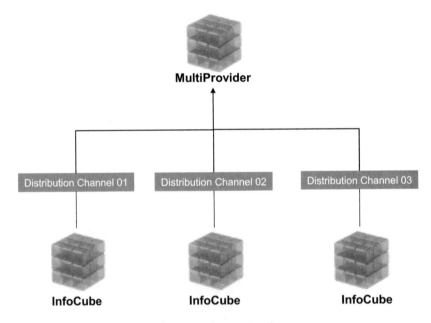

MultiProvider

Distribution Channel 01   Distribution Channel 02   Distribution Channel 03

InfoCube   **InfoCube**   **InfoCube**

Figure 12.6 Partitioning InfoCubes at Application Level

The read accesses to the BasicCubes, which the MultiProvider is based on, usually occur simultaneously, if no other settings that affect the OLAP processor have been configured (see also Section 10.8.6 on this topic). Moreover, you can determine that individual BasicCubes are excluded from the read access by defining fixed values in the query, or by restricting the 0INFOPROV characteristic. The example in Figure 12.6 shows that a fixed value is defined by the restriction to one specific distribution channel.

To separate the data across the different basic InfoCubes of the MultiProvider, you must define the structure-specific properties of each InfoCube, as well as the distribution of the data in the loading processes.

Structure-specific properties of an InfoCube

By maintaining the structure-specific properties of the partitioning characteristic in the InfoCube, you can selectively exclude individual basic InfoCubes from the read process during a data analysis. For example, you can configure an InfoCube in such a way that the partitioning characteristic *Distribution channel* (ODISTR_CHAN) contains only the constant "01". Therefore, the InfoCube is not included in the read process of a query on the corresponding MultiProvider, if the selection does not contain distribution channel "01". This setting improves the query performance, because the system doesn't need to search for data in that InfoCube.

You must define the setting for the partitioning characteristic during the creation of an InfoCube in its structure-specific properties (see Figure 12.7), which is only possible, if the InfoCube does not yet contain any data. Up until SAP BW Releases 3.0B SP8 and 3.1C SP2, you could use only non-compounded InfoObjects as partitioning characteristics. This restriction was eliminated by the service packs mentioned.

In the structure specific properties settings, you should only use those characteristics as partitioning characteristics that are not subject to constant changes; otherwise, an additional basic InfoCube would have to be created for each new characteristic value (for example, month/year).

In addition to maintaining the partitioning characteristics, you must also configure the separate distribution of data to the basic InfoCubes, as that cannot be done automatically via the structure-specific properties of the InfoCube. There are two possible ways to carry out the data distribution:

Data distribution

▶ Distribution via InfoPackages
▶ Distribution during the InfoCube update

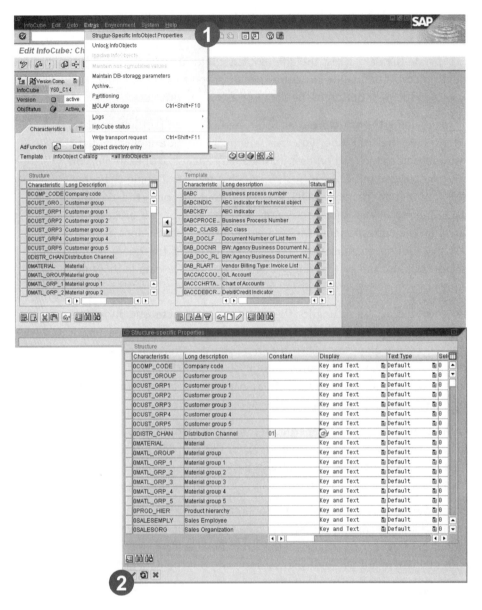

Figure 12.7 Maintaining Partitioning Characteristics in the Structure-Specific Properties of the InfoCube

Data Distribution via InfoPackages

For the data distribution via InfoPackages, you must select the data update of the DataSource for each basic InfoCube (❶ in Figure 12.8). The restriction of the data to be extracted is configured in the data selection via the corresponding constant of the partitioning characteristic ❷.

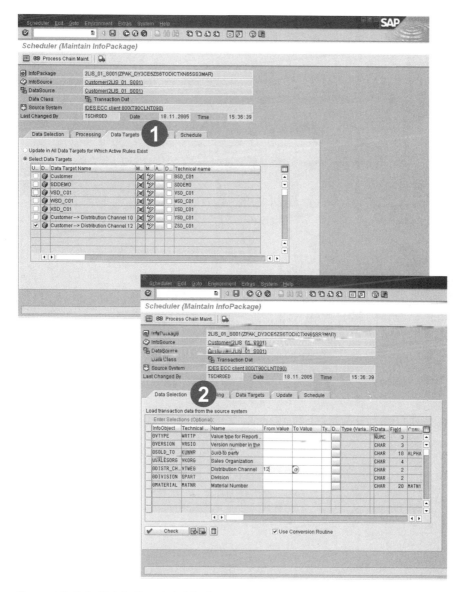

Figure 12.8 Data Distribution via InfoPackages

Data Distribution During an InfoCube Update

You can also configure the data distribution in the update process for an InfoCube. In that case, the distribution is carried out by using an ABAP routine to "filter" the correct values for each basic InfoCube in the update rules of the partitioning characteristic. Figure 12.9 shows a corresponding sample code.

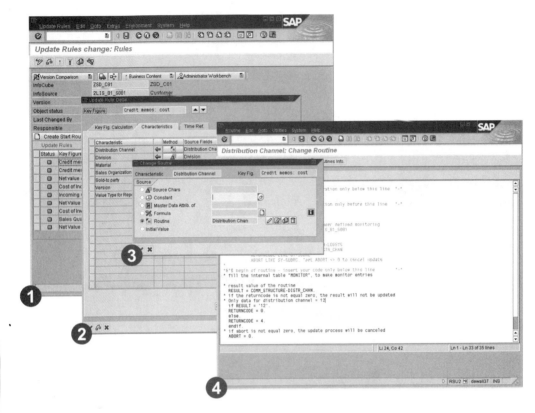

Figure 12.9 Data Distribution During an InfoCube Update

13 Extraction and Load Performance

One of the most important processes in SAP BW is the data extraction and load process. This chapter describes the basic technical principles and performance aspects of this data staging process.

Data acquisition, which consists of the data extraction, transformation, and load processes (often also referred to as the *ETL processes*), is one of the most important data warehousing processes that is used for a periodic and up-to-date retrieval of data from the source systems.

SAP Business Information Warehouse (SAP BW) provides several different communication interfaces and transfer techniques to help you retrieve data from heterogeneous source systems. The following sections describe the types of data sources that you can integrate with SAP BW, and the corresponding transfer techniques that are available. The ETI compo-nents of the SAP BW data flow are also Introduced, along with their related terminology.

The data to be loaded into SAP BW should be up-to-date and must be available for analysis for periodic intervals, usually on a daily basis, but sometimes, even for shorter intervals. The extraction of data from the source systems and its staging can require a large portion of the available processing time, particularly when the data volume is big and the data structures and transformation procedures are complex. In addition to the extraction of source system data and its transformation, the data staging process in SAP BW includes other warehouse management processes such as the filling of data targets—Persistent Staging Area (PSA), Operational Data Store (ODS), and InfoCubes—the updating of master data and hierarchies, the calculation of aggregates, and the updating of indices and database statistics. All those processes require time, during which the data cannot be used for reporting purposes. After the description of the basic principles for data staging in SAP BW, this chapter introduces you to the various performance-monitoring options for extraction and load processes, as well as the different procedures for optimizing the warehouse management processes.

13.1 Data Sources and Their Integration

SAP BW supports the acquisition of data from nearly any data source. Depending on the source system, it uses different communication interfaces for the data acquisition process. Table 13.1 provides an overview of the source system types and the corresponding communication techniques used:

Source System Type	Examples	Interface
SAP systems	SAP R/3, SAP CRM, SAP APO	Application-specific extractors
Relational databases	IBM DB2, Teradata, Oracle	DB Connect
Multidimensional databases	Hyperion	UD Connect
Flat files	CSV files, ASCII	Flat file InfoSource
XML data	SAP NetWeaver	SAP XI, SOAP, web service
Third-party systems	Oracle Financials	BAPI

Table 13.1 Data Sources and Communication Interfaces in SAP BW

Data extraction from SAP systems
For the integration of data from SAP systems, you have to use extractor programs that must be installed as plug-ins into the source systems. In addition to the data extraction programs, the plug-ins also contain preconfigured extraction structures for various modules. Those structures are provided by SAP as business content. To meet customer-specific requirements, you can extend the extraction structures and also develop customized extractors.

The SAP BW system can also serve as a source system and provide data for other systems, such as other BW systems as well as SAP and non-SAP systems. From a technical point of view, the data extraction options are identical to the processes of extracting data from SAP systems in this context, which means that you can use both existing extractors in BW, or develop your own extractors for the data extraction. The distribution of data from InfoProviders of an SAP BW system to other InfoProviders can be carried out through the DataMart interface. You can distribute the data of the InfoProvider (InfoCube, ODS object, InfoObject) across several SAP BW systems, to other SAP systems, and even within the same SAP BW system (*MySelf connection*).

If you want to distribute data from an SAP BW system to SAP and non-SAP systems, you can use the *open hub service* provided by SAP BW. The central object in the data export process is the *InfoSpoke*, which determines from which sources data objects are to be collected and to which data targets they are to be transferred. The open hub service enables you to distribute data from InfoCubes, ODS objects, and InfoObjects (attributes or texts) to database tables and flat files. The open hub service turns SAP BW into an Enterprise Data Warehouse (EDW), which ensures the controlled distribution of data across multiple systems.

With DB Connect, SAP BW provides a flexible way for you to extract data from relational databases. DB Connect enables you to directly transfer data from the tables and views of the database management systems supported by SAP. The data is presented in SAP BW using the DataSources that are generated from the tables and views and is then processed like the data from all other sources.

Data extraction from relational databases

Multidimensional databases store data in a specific data structure and storage format that has been optimized for the purpose of analysis. You can use *Universal Data Connect* (UD Connect) to extract data from almost any relational and multidimensional database. Data that is extracted from multidimensional database systems is converted into a flat format. To use UD Connect, you must install a J2EE Engine including the BI-Java components.

Data extraction from multidimensional databases

SAP BW supports the transfer of data from flat files, as well as from *American Standard Code for Information Interchange* (ASCII) and *Comma Separated Value* (CSV) files. The structure of flat files—the sequence of fields and the field lengths—must match the metadata (transfer structure of the DataSource) defined in SAP BW. The transfer of the data into SAP BW is carried out through a file interface whose parameters can be set in the InfoPackage maintenance.

Flat files

In general, the data transfer from source systems to SAP BW requires a data request, which is sent from SAP BW to the source system (*pull method*); however, you can also send data to SAP BW from outside (*push method*). The transfer of data with the push method is based on XML. SAP provides various transfer technologies for transferring XML data, which include:

XML data

▶ Transferring data through the Simple Object Access Protocol (SOAP) service in SAP Web Application Server (SAP Web AS)

▶ Transferring data through Web services

▶ Transferring data through SAP Exchange Infrastructure (SAP XI)

Each of these scenarios uses transfer mechanisms that are based on SOAP.

Data extraction from third-party systems

SAP BW contains open interfaces that you can use to extract data from applications in non-SAP systems. These interfaces enable you to extract data at application level. The so-called staging *Business Application Programming Interfaces* (BAPIs) are standardized programming interfaces that allow for a connection to various third-party extraction tools, for example, to transfer data from a third-party application.

You can find very detailed additional information on the different options for transferring data into SAP BW in the book *SAP BW – Data Retrieval.*[1]

13.2 Data Flow in SAP BW

DataSources

In general, DataSources are used in the source systems to provide the data. DataSources comprise a set of fields containing logically related data. When SAP BW sends a data request, the DataSources provide the data in a predefined structure to transfer it into SAP BW. Technically speaking, the DataSource is based on the fields of the extract structure, which in the R/3 system is automatically generated from the DataSource. Therefore, the extract structure contains the set of fields that is provided by the DataSource for loading data in the R/3 system. You can expand and alternatively hide the fields of the extract structure during the data transfer. Prior to the data transfer, the DataSource must be replicated into the SAP BW system. You can use DataSources to transfer both transaction data and master data (texts, attributes, and hierarchies). Table ROOSOURCE provides an overview of the DataSources available in the SAP source system and SAP BW, including their extract structures.

Transfer structure

The transfer of data to SAP BW occurs in the transfer structure. The transfer structure is used to transfer fields of data from the extract structure to SAP BW. Table ROOSGEN provides an overview of the DataSources available in the SAP source system and SAP BW, including their transfer structures.

InfoSource

An InfoSource is a set of all objects containing logically related data, for example, the set of all transaction data related to Sales and Distribution (SD) invoices. The InfoSource is therefore a collection of logically related InfoObjects. An InfoSource can contain transaction data and master data. The structure of the InfoObjects is referred to as the *communication structure*. The communication structure (i.e., the InfoSource) is not specific to a source system. You can assign several DataSources to one InfoSource,

---

1 Norbert Egger et al.: *SAP BW—Data Retrieval*. SAP PRESS 2005.

whereas you cannot assign one DataSource to several InfoSources in a source system. The transfer of fields from the transfer structure into the InfoObjects of the communication structure is defined in the transfer rules. The transfer rules determine which DataSources are assigned to an InfoSource, and which fields of the DataSource are assigned to the InfoObjects.

In the update rules, you specify how the data from the communication structure (key figures, time characteristics, characteristics) is updated to an InfoSource in an InfoProvider. The update rules are the link between the InfoSource and the InfoProvider. You must specify an update rule for each key figure and characteristic of the InfoCube.

Update rules

Figure 13.1 shows a simplified illustration of the data flow in SAP BW.

Extractors are programs that—when prompted by a SAP BW request—fill the extract structure of a DataSource with source system data and provide the structure for the load process. We distinguish between application-specific and application-independent extractors.

Extractors

Extractors that extract data from a specific SAP module—such as the controlling (CO), accounting (FI), or sales and distribution (SD) modules—are application-specific. The application-specific extractors can again be subdivided into two types of extractors: On the one hand, there are extractors that are based on a business content DataSource and fill the extract structure of the DataSource with data from specific standard tables and fields of the SAP modules, such as SD and MM (materials management). On the other hand, there are customer-specific extractors that enable you to extract data from SAP components whose tables and fields would not exist without the adjustments made by the customer. For example, those applications include CO-PA—the Profitability Analysis component in SAP.

Application-specific extractors

You can also extract data from any table or database view, or by using SAP queries and function modules, independent of any application. For this purpose, you can develop your own generic extractors that enable you to extract data, for which the business content provides either no extractors, or only those that are inappropriate.

Application-independent extractors

The SAP source system extractors and DataSources are provided as plug-ins that you must install in your source system. You can only establish a communication between SAP source systems and SAP BW if the corresponding plug-in is installed in the source system.

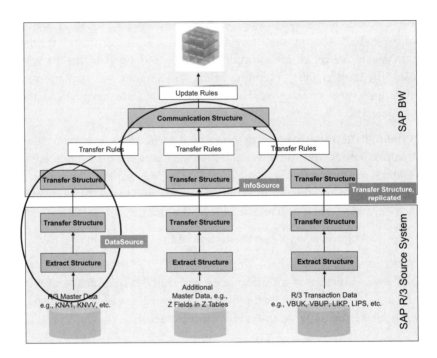

Figure 13.1 Data Flow in SAP BW

13.3 Enabling the Communication Between SAP R/3 and SAP BW

SAP BW employs several communication techniques for transferring data between SAP R/3 (or mySAP ERP) and SAP BW. These techniques are described in greater detail in the following sections. These communication techniques are also used to establish communication between SAP systems and external systems.

Remote Function Call (RFC)

RFC   The remote function call (RFC) is the foundation for almost all interfaces in SAP BW. Basically, the RFC is used to call a program, which runs in a different system than the program that performs the call. You can also call programs and function modules in the same system via an RFC. Remote function calls can be used by SAP systems (e.g., SAP R/3, SAP APO, SAP BW) to communicate with each other and with non-SAP systems. Within an SAP system, the RFC is used to establish a communication between application instances, or between the application and presentation levels, and to make processes parallel when a program launches several RFCs concurrently.

The following four different types of connection are possible for RFCs: synchronous, asynchronous, transactional, and queued RFCs.

The synchronous connection, which is also referred to as "narrow coupling," requires the availability of the communicating systems at the time the function call is executed. An essential characteristic of this type of connection is that at the start of the function, the sending system expects a confirmation of receipt by the target system. If the connection is interrupted, for example, due to a network problem, or because the receiving system is not available, the function that uses the RFC terminates with an error. The read accesses of the data analysis are an example of a synchronous connection in SAP BW. Here, the client computer has to wait for a response from the application server.

Synchronous RFC

The asynchronous connection, also referred to as "loose coupling," does not require the communicating systems to be available at the same time. The receiving system can receive and process a function call from the sending system at a later point in time. If the receiving system cannot be reached, the function call is placed in the outbound queue of the sending system. The call is repeated at regular intervals from here until it can be processed by the receiving system. The extraction of data from source systems is an example of an asynchronous connection in SAP BW.

Asynchronous RFC

A transactional RFC (tRFC) is an asynchronous RFC, which executes the function module called exactly once. During a transactional RFC, all calls are first collected in an internal table, from which they are then processed according to their transactional sequence. A tRFC is used if a function is to be executed as a *logical unit of work* (LUW). An LUW comprises all steps of an operation that can't be subdivided any further into substeps without compromising the data integrity.[2]

Transactional RFC

A queued RFC (qRFC) is a transactional RFC in which the LUWs are processed in the target system in the same sequence as they have been created in the sending system. We recommend using a qRFC if you want to ensure that different transactions are processed in a predefined sequence.

Queued RFC

In an ABAP program, you can recognize RFC calls by the CALL FUNCTION syntax, which is complemented by the function name and the connection name (DESTINATION). The DESTINATION parameter tells the SAP system, which target system currently runs the called function module. You

---

2 In SAP systems, transactions work according to the *ACID principle*, which means they must be "Atomic," "Consistent," "Isolated," and "Durable."

must use Transaction SM59 to uniquely define the target system across the entire system landscape.

13.4 Transfer Techniques

The following sections describe several different transfer techniques that are available for transferring data into SAP BW and for the data exchange between SAP systems and non-SAP systems.

13.4.1 Application Link Enabling (ALE)

Application Link Enabling (ALE) is an integration service that supports the configuration and operation of distributed, but integrated SAP applications. ALE comprises a controlled, business-relevant exchange of messages among distributed applications with a consistent data storage in loosely coupled SAP applications.

ALE enables the distribution and synchronization of master data, control data, and transaction data through an asynchronous connection. It uses synchronous connections to read data. Moreover, ALE provides functions for monitoring the data transfer and for troubleshooting.

13.4.2 Intermediate Document (IDoc)

During a data transfer via ALE, the entire information is transferred as intermediate documents (IDocs). The IDoc is a standard SAP document format that transfers the data as simple ASCII text files between different application systems through a message-based interface. IDocs contain a fixed structure (control record, data record, status record), which is generated by the IDoc interface. For this reason, IDocs produce a bigger overhead than the data transfer via RFC, which may affect the performance of the data transfer. SAP BW still allows for the extraction of mass data using IDocs. However, it is primarily the RFCs that are used for data extractions, while IDocs are mainly used for exchanging messages that contain data requests and receipt confirmations. In this context, the IDocs are also called Info IDocs.

13.4.3 Business Application Programming Interface (BAPI)

The Business Application Programming Interface (BAPI) is a standardized program interface that enables the communication between SAP systems at application level. The program interface is an open interface, which enables third-party applications to communicate with SAP applications via BAPIs. In the SAP system, BAPIs are stored as RFC-enabled function modules in the Function Builder of the ABAP Workbench. They can be called via RFCs, tRFCs, and even by using IDocs.

13.5 Transfer Methods

Two transfer methods are available for transferring data into SAP BW: IDoc and PSA.

If you use the IDoc transfer method, the source system data is placed into IDocs and then sent to the business information warehouse. In SAP BW, the data is stored persistently and intransparently in the IDoc storage. From there, the IDocs can be updated automatically or manually in the InfoCubes. Due to the increased data overhead associated with the IDoc structure, you should not use the IDoc transfer method for transferring mass data into SAP BW, because it would essentially affect the system performance. You often hear the term data IDocs mentioned in connection with the IDoc transfer method, because the IDoc serves as a data container that transports the data to be transferred. Make sure you don't confuse the Data IDocs with the Info IDocs, which are used for exchanging messages containing data requests and receipt confirmations via the ALE interface. Info IDocs are used in both the IDoc and PSA transfer methods to exchange information on the traffic light status during the monitoring of the load requests.

IDoc transfer method

The more appropriate method to be used for transferring mass data into SAP BW is the *Persistent Staging Area* (PSA). If you use the PSA transfer method, the data is sent directly from the source system to the business information warehouse where it is stored in the PSA. The data is transferred into the PSA via a tRFC, and one tRFC is executed per data package.

PSA transfer method

An exception to using the PSA transfer method is the loading of hierarchies, which usually must be loaded using the IDoc transfer method. But, as of SAP BW 3.0, you can also use the PSA transfer method to load hierarchies from DataSources that are specifically enabled for this process. You can also load hierarchies from files using the PSA transfer method.

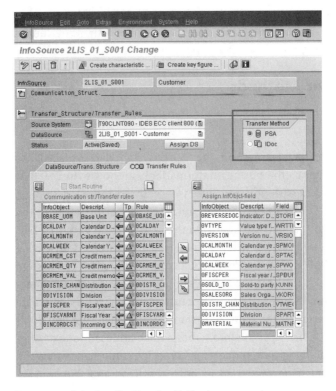

Figure 13.2 Selecting the Transfer Method

You can define the transfer methods in the transfer rules maintenance (see Figure 13.2).

The following section describes the PSA in more detail.

13.6 Persistent Staging Area

The PSA is the inbound storage location for data that comes from source systems. The data is stored in relational database tables of SAP BW, and the transfer structure of the source system is not changed. A transparent PSA table is created for each transfer structure that is activated. Additionally, the PSA tables are assigned a key field for the request ID, the data package number, and the data record number. The data format transferred from the source system remains unchanged so that no aggregation or transformation occurs. From the PSA, you can update the data automatically or manually in the respective data targets.

The temporary storage of the extracted source system data in the PSA enables a separation of the extraction processes in the source system from the time-consuming processing of the data in SAP BW. The PSA therefore improves the load performance, and the operational system is not strained by the data processing tasks performed in SAP BW.

You can store the data as long as you want in the PSA, because it is not Table RSTSODS automatically deleted once it has been updated into the data targets. Since the PSA data exists in the most granular form in which it is extracted from the source system, the PSA tables can grow rapidly. The PSA tables are managed using the transparent table RSTSODS (see Figure 13.3). The technical name of the PSA table is specified in the ODSNAME_TECH field (naming convention: /BIC/B000*). When changing a DataSource, which usually involves changing the transfer structure, you must adjust the PSA table accordingly. During the course of that modification, SAP BW creates a new PSA table with a new validity period so that Table RSTSODS stores all versions of the PSA tables.

To avoid large quantities of data in the PSA, you should delete the data from the PSA on a regular basis, once it has been successfully updated into the data targets.

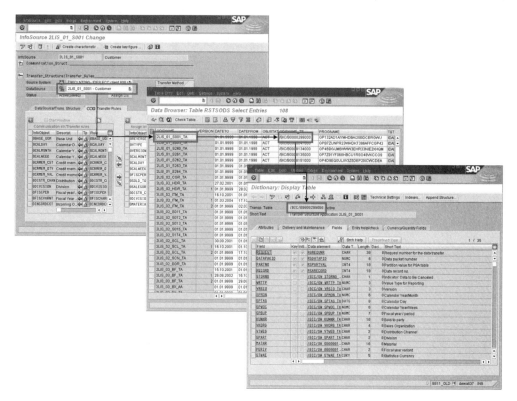

Figure 13.3 Identifying PSA Tables

13.6.1 Partitioning the PSA

To improve the system performance when updating data from the PSA, you can partition the PSA tables so that the dataset of a PSA table is separated into several small, physically independent, and redundancy-free units.

You can use Transaction RSCUSTV6 to make the settings for partitioning the PSA in the Change View **BW: Threshold Value for Data Load** dialog (see Figure 13.4).

The size of a partition defines the number of records that serves as the upper limit for a partition. If that number is exceeded, the system creates a new partition. As of SAP BW 2.0B SP20 and SAP BW 2.1C SP13, the minimum number of data records in a partition is set to 1,000,000. The settings you make in Transaction RSCUSTV6 are applied to all PSA tables of the SAP BW system. However, you can only use partitioning if the database system, on which the SAP BW system is based, supports the partitioning of tables.[3]

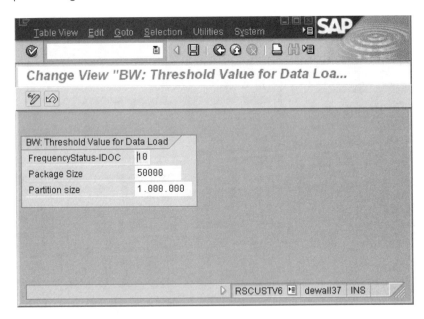

Figure 13.4 Configuring the Size of PSA Table Partitions

---

3 For more information on partitioning PSA tables, refer to SAP Notes 485878 (DB2/390) and 524456 (Informix).

13.6.2 Processing Options for the PSA

When using the PSA transfer method, several options are available for updating data in SAP BW. You can define the type of data update in the **Processing** tab of the InfoPackage maintenance scheduler (see Figure 13.5).

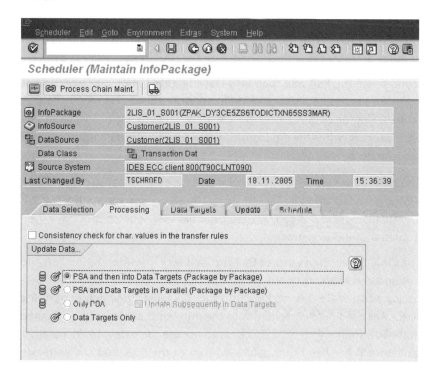

Figure 13.5 Processing Options for the PSA

The following processing options are available:

▶ PSA and then into Data Targets (Package by Package)

▶ PSA and Data Targets in Parallel (Package by Package)

▶ Only PSA

▶ Data Targets Only

If you select the **PSA and Data Targets in Parallel** option, a dialog process is started for each data package to write the data from the data package to the PSA table. Once the data has been successfully updated to the PSA, a second process is started simultaneously in which the data records from the data package are updated to the data targets. The data is updated package by package to the PSA and to the data targets concurrently.

PSA and Data Targets in Parallel

The maximum number of parallel data transfer processes, which are specified in the control parameters for the data transfer (see also Section 13.8.1), does not restrict the number of transfer processes in SAP BW. You can use as many dialog processes to load the data, as there are available. For this reason, the number of processes that you can use to upload data into the PSA is determined by the number of freely available processes in the R/3 source system; whereas, the number of processes that you can use to update the data into the data targets is determined by the number of freely available processes on the SAP BW application server.

PSA and then into Data Targets If you select the **PSA and then into Data Targets** option, a dialog process starts for each data package in order to write the package into the PSA table. Once the data has been successfully updated in the PSA table, the *same* process writes the data into the data targets. The data update occurs *sequentially by package*.

The maximum number of dialog processes used per data package in SAP BW corresponds to the data transfer settings made in the control parameter maintenance. If data is loaded from flat files, a batch process is used instead of the dialog process.

Only PSA The **Only PSA** option ensures that the data is only written to the PSA and not updated to the data targets. In this case, a process is started per data package that writes the package into the PSA table. The number of dialog processes used here corresponds to the number that has been configured in the R/3 source system. If you want to update the data into the data targets once it has been successfully written to the PSA, you can either do that manually, or activate the **Update Subsequently in Data Targets** option. A background process is then started for the request, so it can write the data packages that were successfully updated to the PSA into the data targets one by one. The data update occurs *sequentially upon request*.

Data Targets Only If you select the **Data Targets Only** option, the data is not updated in the PSA, but is written directly into the data targets. The number of dialog processes used here corresponds to the number that is available in the R/3 source system. Since no updating process occurs through the PSA, this processing option is very fast in terms of load performance; however, data can be lost when erroneous data must be updated again.

13.7 Monitoring the Load Processes

SAP BW provides a wide range of analysis tools that you can use to monitor the loading and data transfer processes in general, and the ETL processes in particular. Each load process initiates the creation of a loading log for the underlying request, which is stored in the system. You can call the load monitor using Transaction RSMO, via the **Monitoring · Monitor** menu in the Administrator Workbench, or from the scheduler in the Info-Package maintenance by pressing the **Monitor** function key (F6).

As shown in Figure 13.6, you can use the **Monitor · Maintain Tree Display** menu to adjust the display of the tree structure according to your requirements ❶. You can select the load request logs to be analyzed according to different filtering options via the **Monitor · New Selections** menu ❷.

Each load request log contains *header data*, *status information*, and *detail information*, and can be called by selecting the load request

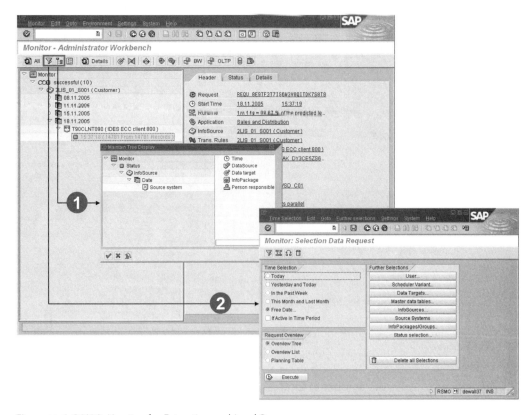

Figure 13.6 RSMO Monitor for Extraction and Load Processes

13.7.1 Header Data of the Load Request

The header data of a request (see Figure 13.7) contains various pieces of information that describe the load request with regard to its identification, scheduled execution, and type of processing.

The most important information on the load request provided by the header data is displayed in the RSMO monitor. Figure 13.7 shows a load request that was used to load 14,781 data records. The runtime of the request was 1m 14s; the transaction data of InfoSource 2LIS_01_S001 (Customer) was updated to InfoCube VSD_C01 using the **PSA and data targets parallel** option.

Request ID The request ID is created during the start of the load process and it uniquely identifies the stored monitoring log across the entire system landscape. An SID key is generated for each request ID and is written in the package dimension of the InfoCube during the update of the data.

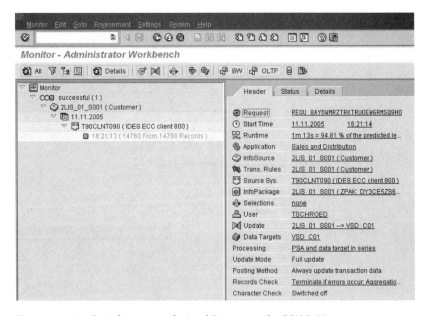

Figure 13.7 Header Information of a Load Request in the RSMO Monitor

Start time and runtime The start time indicates the date and time at which the monitor received the Info IDoc, along with the command to start processing the corresponding InfoPackage. The runtime is calculated by the system and indicates the amount of time required by the data request in absolute figures. It also shows how this runtime compares with other data requests by the same InfoPackage with the same selection options. The runtime is measured until the request is updated to the point where it is considered technically correct in the data target (green traffic light), or until the request has been set as such by a Quality Management (QM) action, or until it has reached the maximum amount of time allowed.

The categorization information identifies all the components that make up the entire dataflow— namely, the application, the InfoSource, the transfer rules, the source system, the InfoPackage, the data targets, and so on.

Categorization information

The processing information indicates how the load request should be processed within SAP BW. This information includes details on the PSA transfer method (see Section 13.6.2), the update mode, the posting method, and the records and character checks.

Processing information

13.7.2 Status Information for the Load Request

The status information for the load request contains details on the technical status of the request processing and the overall status of the load request in the data targets. This Information is indicated by traffic lights.

The processing of a request consists of several processing steps. The technical status of the request is considered to be free of errors (traffic light = green) only if all steps have been processed successfully.

Technical status

A yellow traffic light indicates that the processing either hasn't completed, or that it has completed, but it contains warning messages. In the standard setting, a request is also assigned a yellow traffic light if warnings occur during the actual processing.

A red traffic light indicates that the request contains errors, or that the maximum wait time has been exceeded. The wait time for the entire system is configured using Transaction RSCUSTV2. It represents the period of time during which the system waits for the last IDoc of the request. If the point in time at which the last IDoc was received lies outside of the period defined as the maximum wait time, the traffic light in the monitor is set to red.

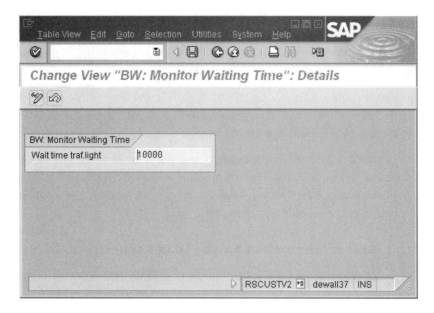

Figure 13.8 Defining the Monitor Wait Time (Transaction RSCUSTV2)

If a request is rated as being erroneous because the wait time has been exceeded, the system does not consider the request processing as terminated. If the monitor receives additional IDocs after the wait time has been exceeded, the traffic light is set back to yellow and the processing continues. The wait time is specified as <hhmmss>.

You should configure a sufficiently long wait time if you plan to transfer large data quantities. In addition to the system-wide configuration via Transaction RSCUSTV2 (see Figure 13.8), you can also use the **Scheduler · Timeout time per InfoPackage** menu to define the maximum wait time, after which a request should be set to red in the monitor. This overrules the system-wide setting.

Overall status

The overall status indicates the status of the request with regard to the data processing in the data targets. By default, the overall status is determined by the technical status. You can change the overall status using the so-called QM action. For example, this can be useful if a request that didn't provide any data is considered technically erroneous, but the overall status is rated as error-free. If you set the overall status manually, however, the technical status won't change.

13.7.3 Detail Data of the Load Request

The Details tab of the monitor displays comprehensive information on process steps and statuses for all actions of the request that have been performed in a tree structure. Each intermediate step of a process step is displayed, including the traffic light status and the time the processing took place. The **footer** of the monitor provides additional information on the process step, such as the **calling program** that indicates which process step caused the generation of a message.[4] The potential calling programs for each step are listed in the Appendix.

The processing steps are divided into the following areas:

▶ Data basis

▶ Requests

▶ Extraction

▶ Transfer

▶ Processing

▶ Post-processing

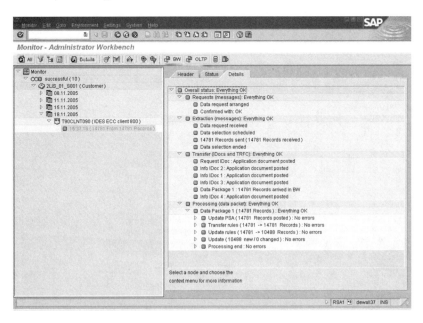

Figure 13.9 Detail Data for a Load Request in the Monitor

---

4 You can use the F4 input help to find out what each number means.

Data basis If the data source for the extraction of data is an InfoCube or an ODS object, all those requests are listed under **Data basis** that have been originally loaded into the data target. The requests are then summarized into one new request and updated into the data target.

Requests The **Requests** step contains messages on the creation of the data request for the extraction in the source system, as well as the receipt confirmation of the source system indicating the confirmation status.

Extraction The **Extraction** step contains those messages from the source system that have been sent in an Info IDoc (see Figure 13.10). There are several different types of messages from the source system, which can be differentiated by the Info IDoc status. The messages are displayed in the footer of the monitor.

Table 13.2 contains a list of the Info IDoc status messages. You should pay special attention to the Info IDoc with status 2, which describes the number of records that have been extracted in the source system and sent to SAP BW. The number of records received by SAP BW is verified based on this information in order to calculate the runtime of the request.

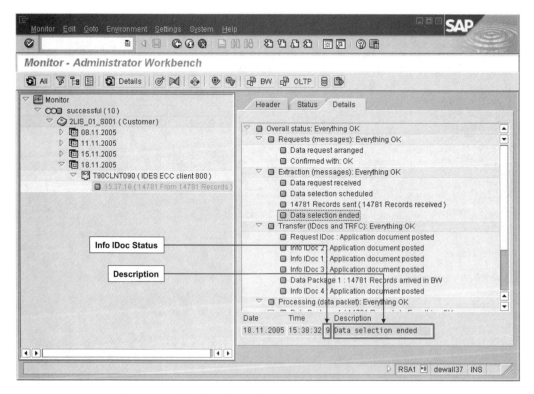

Figure 13.10 Info IDoc Status for a Processing Step

Info IDoc status	Description
0	Data request received
1	Data selection started
2	Data selection running
5	Error in data selection
6	Transfer structure obsolete, regenerating transfer rules
8	No data available, data selection ended
9	Data selection ended

Table 13.2 Info IDoc Status

The **Transfer** step displays information on the transfer of data and mes- Transfer
sages between SAP BW and the source systems. All messages sent by the
source system in an Info IDoc are listed here. In addition, the footer of
the monitor displays the IDoc numbers of the SAP BW system and of the
source system that correspond to each IDoc message.

To monitor the processing, the communication between the source system and the BW system is carried out using an IDoc status for each Info
IDoc, which consists of two digits. The IDoc status is set by the IDoc
interface in the source system and target system when a new IDoc is created. The statuses for outbound IDocs range between "01" and "49,"
while the statuses for inbound IDocs begin with "50." The IDoc status is
set by the function module EDI_DOCUMENT_CLOSE_CREATE in the
IDoc interface when a new IDoc is created. All subsequent status records
are then written explicitly by the function module EDI_DOCUMENT_
STATUS_SET.

The number of Info IDocs that are transferred per Data IDoc must be
defined in the data transfer control parameters in the SAP BW Customizing Guide (**Data Transfer to the SAP Business Information Warehouse ·
General Settings · Maintain Control Parameters for Data Transfer**). You
can find more information on maintaining the control parameters in Section 13.8.1.

The Frequency column specifies for each source system after how many
Data IDocs an Info IDoc must be transferred; in other words, how many
Data IDocs are described by one Info IDoc.

You should generally choose a frequency between 5 and 10 here, but not
more than 20.

The bigger the package size of a Data IDoc, the smaller the frequency you should choose. In this way, you can ensure that you receive information on the relevant data loading status at relatively short intervals when uploading the data. You can define the size of the data packages per source system in the **Max. (kB)** column. SAP recommends that the data package size range between 10 and 50 MB (see also Section 13.8.1).

Processing

The **Processing** step involves the actual processing of the transferred data packages in SAP BW. This includes the updating of data in the PSA, the processing of the data in the transfer and update rules, the update in the data targets, and the end of the processing. Due to the comprehensive process steps, **Processing** represents that part of the data processing that affects the runtime to the largest extent.

Because all messages are sent per data package, the process steps involved in **Processing** must be executed for each data package.

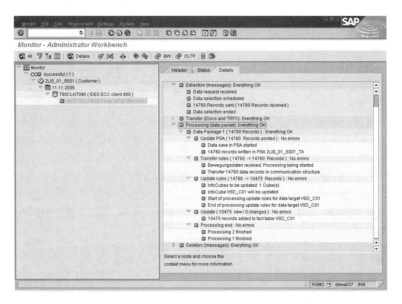

Figure 13.11 The Processing Step in the RSMO Monitor

Post-processing

The **Post-processing** step involves additional steps for processing master data, texts, and external hierarchies.

For external hierarchies, the individual data packages are first collected in a table. Provided the hierarchies are marked for automatic activation, they are activated in the post-processing step. If automatic activation of the hierarchy is not set, the hierarchy is marked for activation and then activated during the hierarchy and attribute change run.

For master data and texts, the update lock, which has been previously set during the load process, is deleted.

13.8 Performance Aspects for Data Extraction

The following section describes some of the performance aspects that are relevant to the extraction and load processes. It provides useful recommendations regarding the parameterization of the system and the options available for optimizing the data extraction process.

13.8.1 Maintaining the Control Parameters for the Data Transfer

Depending on the number of data records to be extracted, the requests are divided into several data packages during the extraction. The subsequent processing in SAP BW then occurs at the level of those data packages. The bigger the data packages, the bigger the memory requirement for the data extraction in the source system and for the transfer and update of the data in the SAP BW system.

You can maintain the control parameters for data extraction for the entire system in the Customizing Implementation Guide (Transaction SBIW) in the following menu: **Data Transfer to the SAP Business Information Warehouse · General Settings · Maintain Control Parameters for Data Transfer** (see Figure 13.12). Alternatively, you can do that in the transparent table ROIDOCPRMS.

System-wide maintenance of data package size

To transfer data from SAP R/3, you must maintain the control parameters for the data transfer directly in the R/3 source system. For the data transfer from SAP BW, for example, when updating data from DataMarts, you must maintain the control parameters for the data transfer in SAP BW.

The data package size setting specifies the size of a data package in terms of kilobytes, or in terms of the number of data records per data package. During the data extraction process, a new data package is created as soon as one of the two limits is reached. SAP recommends that the data package size range between 10 and 50 MB. You should keep in mind that the smaller the data package size, the smaller the main memory requirement; however, this means that the data extraction process is very slow due to the internal administration requirement. So, to improve the extraction and load performance, you should therefore choose as large a data package size as possible.

Figure 13.12 Maintaining the Control Parameters for the Data Transfer

The size of a data package is determined by the number of data records and the record width of the extract structure. If no entries for the control parameters for the data transfer have been maintained, the default setting for the number of data records per data package is 100,000 rows (**Max. lines**), while the default setting for the data package size is 10,000 KB per data package (**Max. (kB)**). You can use the following formula to calculate the data package size for the source system:

Package size (KB) = MAXSIZE × 1000 / transfer structure size (bytes)

The package size cannot be larger than MAXLINES; if MAXLINES is smaller than the result of the formula, the MAXLINES value will be entered into SAP BW.

You can determine the extract structure that corresponds to the active DataSource in Table ROOSOURCE using the data browser (Transaction SE16, ❶ in Figure 13.13). Its size can be determined in the ABAP Dictionary (Transaction SE11) ❷ via **Utilities · Runtime Object · Display** ❸.

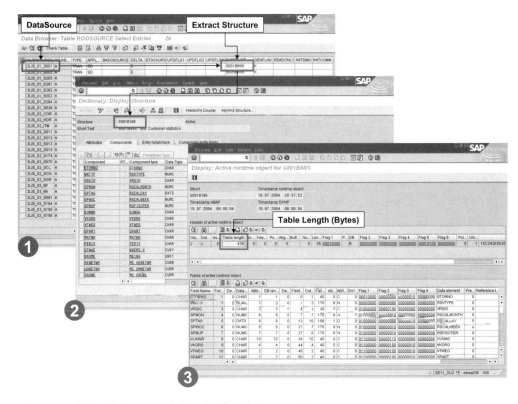

Figure 13.13 Determining the Table Length of an Extract Structure

Table 13.3 lists some examples of the package size for generic extractors with an extract structure table length of 250 bytes.

Example	BW	OLTP
Scenario 1		
MAXSIZE	–	10,000
MAXLINES	–	100,000
Calculated package size = MAXSIZE (OLTP) *1000 / 250 = 40,000 MAXLINES = 100,000 > 40,000 → The package size is 40,000.		
Scenario 2		
MAXSIZE	–	20,000
MAXLINES	–	20,000
Calculated package size = MAXSIZE (OLTP) *1000 / 250 = 80,000 MAXLINES = 20,000 < 80,000 → The package size is 20,000.		

Table 13.3 Calculating the OLTP Data Package Size

Example	BW	OLTP
Scenario 3		
MAXSIZE	10,000	20,000
MAXLINES	–	20,000
Calculated package size = MAXSIZE (BW) *1000 / 250 = 40,000		
MAXLINES = 20,000 < 40,000 → The package size is 20,000.		

Table 13.3 Calculating the OLTP Data Package Size (cont.)

The actual package size that is set by the R/3 source system also depends on the extractor.[5]

Maintaining the data package size in the scheduler

In the InfoPackage maintenance of SAP BW, you can also maintain the size of individual data packages. The settings that you select in the scheduler (see Figure 13.14) override the system-wide settings for a Data-Source; however, you can only reduce the data package size in the Info-Package maintenance to the data package size that is valid across the entire SAP BW system.

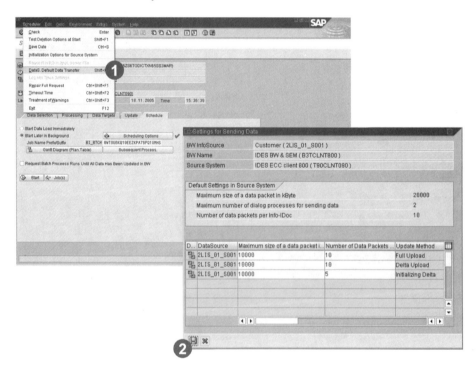

Figure 13.14 Maintaining the Data Package Size in the Scheduler

---

5 For more information, see SAP Note 417307.

You should schedule several InfoPackages concurrently when transferring very large data quantities. You can do that by using the data selection to divide the InfoPackages.

You cannot set the data package size for the transfer of data from flat files in the source system, because you must enter that setting directly in SAP BW (see Figure 13.15). To do that, you must use Transaction RSCUSTV6. The setting applies to all flat file systems in SAP BW.

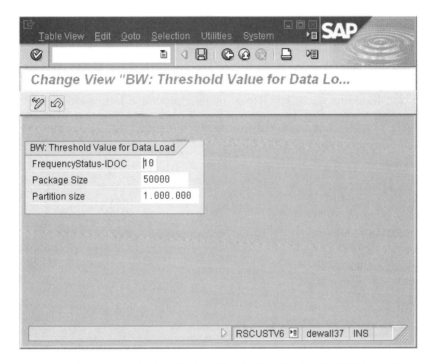

Figure 13.15 Maintaining the Data Package Size for Flat Files in SAP BW (Transaction RSCUSTV6)

For the transfer of large data quantities via a flat-file upload, you should provide the flat file on the SAP BW application server instead of filling it from the client computer, so you can avoid having to deal with an unnecessary network load.

The number of work processes that can be used simultaneously during the data extraction process can be defined in the control parameters maintenance for the data extraction, or via the **Max. proc.** parameter in the control table ROIDOCPRMS. If the **Max. proc.** value is > 0, the data

Maintaining the work processes

packages are always transferred simultaneously to SAP BW. The number of parallel work processes defined in the source system determines the degree of parallelization for the data transfer into the PSA, whereas the setting does not affect the update of the data in SAP BW. The data update process uses as many dialog processes as are available in SAP BW (see also Section 13.6.2).

Since SAP Release 3.1I, you can use parallel processes, which is why this parameter (**Max. proc.**) is ignored by earlier releases.

Frequency of the Info IDocs

The frequency at which an Info IDoc is transferred per Data IDoc can be defined using the **Frequency** parameter, which is contained in the control parameters for the data transfer (see Figure 13.15). The value indicates for how many Data IDocs an Info IDoc is to be transferred. If you don't enter a value in this field, the default setting is 1, which means that an Info IDoc is transferred for each Data IDoc. The recommended setting is 5 to 10.

Table 13.4 contains a summary of the recommended settings for the control parameters for the data transfer.

Parameter	Content	Recommended setting
Max. (kB)	Maximum size of a data package in KB	20,000–50,000 KB
Max. lines	Maximum number of lines in a data package	50,000–100,000 data lines
Frequency	Frequency at which Status IDocs are transferred	5–10
Max. proc.	Maximum number of parallel processes for the data transfer	2–5

Table 13.4 Recommended Settings for Control Parameters for the Data Transfer

13.8.2 Main Memory Requirements for the Data Extraction

Depending on the data package size, BW extractors can have a strong memory requirement in the source system.

During the extraction from the R/3 source system, the size of the transferred data packages corresponds to the settings in the control parameters for the data transfer (**IMG · Data Transfer to the SAP Business Information Warehouse · General Settings · Maintain Control Parameters for Data Transfer**) or to the settings stored in control table ROIDOCPRMS (see Figure 13.16).

If you haven't specified any parameter values, the data is transferred with a default setting of 10,000 KB or 100,000 data records per data package.

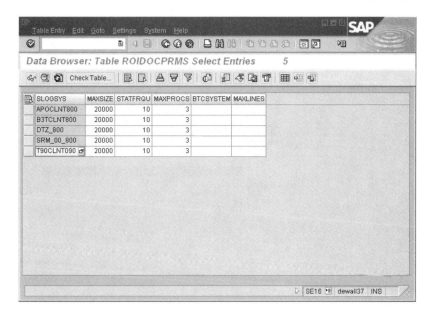

Figure 13.16 Control Table ROIDOCPRMS in the R/3 Source System

If you use large data packages, the main memory requirement in the R/3 source system depends primarily on the number of data records contained in the data package. You can roughly calculate the main memory requirement of an extractor using the following formula:

Main memory requirement = 2 × "Max. lines" × 1,000 bytes

This means that if you use the default settings for a data package (100,000 lines), the main memory requirement of the internal table is approximately 200 MB.

13.9 Performance Aspects Relevant to Data Transformation

This section describes some of the performance aspects that are relevant to the data transformation process. It provides useful recommendations regarding the parameterization of the system and the options available for optimizing the data transformation process.

To transfer data from the transfer structure to the communication structure, you must define transfer rules for each InfoSource. The transfer rules enable you to consolidate and cleanse the data. You can apply the data transformation to transaction and master data, and configure it in the InfoSource maintenance (see Figure 13.17).

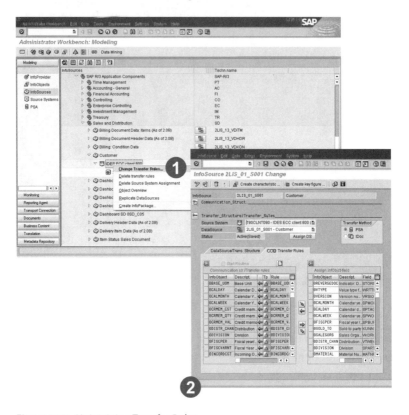

Figure 13.17 Maintaining Transfer Rules

Per DataSource, you must define transfer rules for each field or InfoObject of the communication structure (see also Sections 13.2 and following) in order to determine the transformation of the objects from the DataSource to the communication structure. The transfer rules can be defined by an exact mapping, by determining constants, or by using formulas or ABAP routines.

You should pay special attention to the definition of transfer rules when analyzing the load performance, because complex transformation processes can substantially affect the load performance.

The following sections describe how you can identify "expensive" transfer rules and the performance aspects you should consider when designing the transfer rules.

13.9.1 Simulating the Update

Before you update the data to a data target, you can simulate the data update. The update simulation helps you to find errors in the transfer rules if you cancel the update. For this purpose, the request to be examined must exist in the PSA.

To simulate the update, go to the Details tab of the RSMO monitor and under **Transfer**, select a data package whose update you want to simulate (see Figure 13.18).

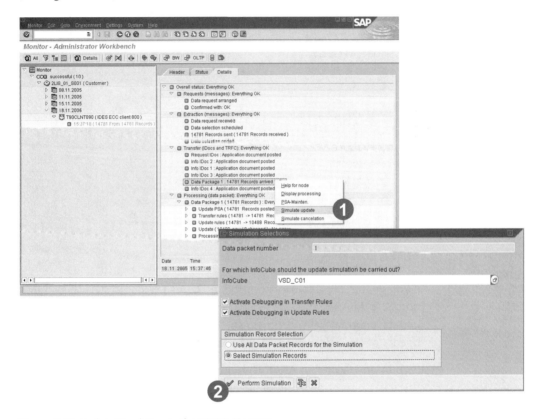

Figure 13.18 Update Simulation in the RSMO Monitor

Using the **Simulate update** menu option of the context menu ❶, you can first isolate the data records to be updated, and then determine whether the simulation of the update should be performed in the transfer rules or the update rules by activating the respective debugging option ❷. Using the **Select Simulation Records** option (see Figure 13.19), you can specifically select data records from the data package the update of which you want to check.

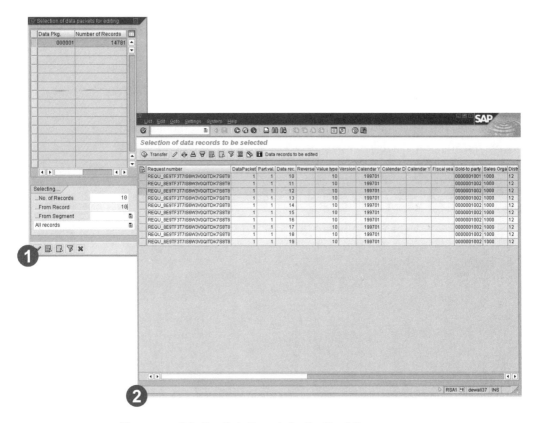

Figure 13.19 Selecting Data Records for the Simulation

If you enable the debugging option in Figure 13.18 and start the simulation, the ABAP Debugger jumps to an interruption of the transfer or update program several times, so that you can specifically analyze the update of the data records step by step.

If you don't want the ABAP Debugger to run, you don't have to enable the selection options. The debugging process can also be disabled in the debugging window (Figure 13.20) via the **Debugging · Debugging off** menu. Once the update simulation has been started, the selected data records can be called as they are passed from the transfer structure to the communication structure (see ❶ and ❷ in Figure 13.21). The structure used for storing the data in the InfoCube after the update can be retrieved via the data target view (Shift + F6) ❸.

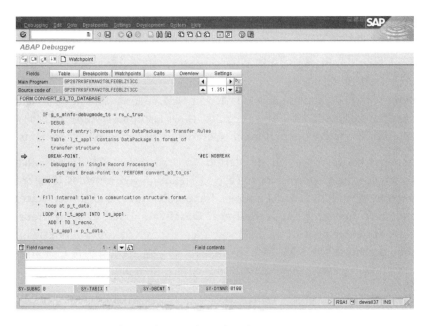

Figure 13.20 ABAP Debugger for Transfer and Update Routines

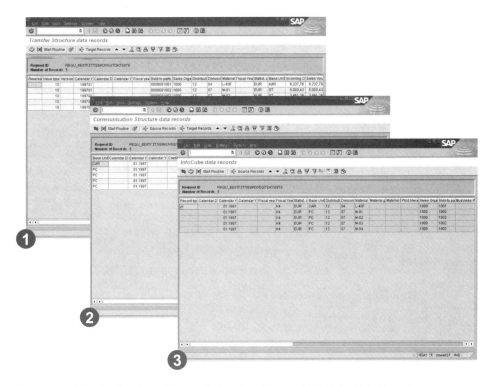

Figure 13.21 Transfer Structure, Communication Structure, and InfoCube Data Records

13.9.2 ABAP Source Code in Transfer and Update Rules

The implementation of transfer or update rules via ABAP source code provides a flexible option of data transformation, but it often leads to a poor load performance. The performance of ABAP programs is largely determined by database accesses. If you observe long runtimes during a data transfer or update, and if you're using customized ABAP routines, you should analyze the performance of the programmed SQL statements.

Performance trace A performance trace can be started via Transaction ST05. The initial screen for the performance trace (see Figure 13.22) provides different trace modes (**SQL Trace**, **Enqueue Trace**, **RFC Trace**, and **Buffer Trace**) and trace functions (**Activate Trace**, **Deactivate Trace**, **Display Trace**, etc.). For an analysis of the SQL statements stored in your routines, you should activate the SQL Trace. By default, the trace is activated for your user; however, you can also activate the trace for a different user.

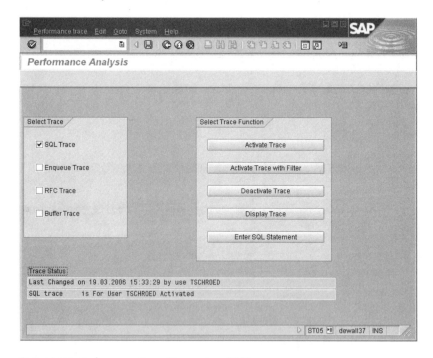

Figure 13.22 Performance Trace (Transaction ST05)

To keep the trace simple, you should activate it only for the action to be analyzed, like data updates.

For analyzing the trace, you should first deactivate the trace recording and retrieve the recorded trace log using the **Display Trace** button. The basic trace list is displayed first (see Figure 13.23), which you can compress via the **Trace List · Summarize Trace by SQL Statement** menu.

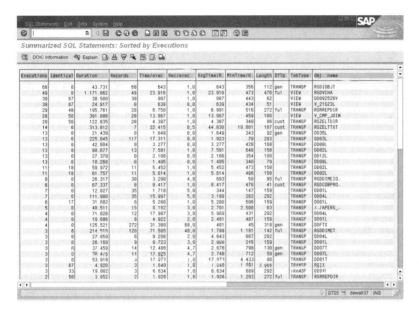

Figure 13.23 SQL Trace List

Performance-intensive SQL statements stand out due to long runtimes and frequent database accesses. Therefore, you should sort the list of summarized SQL statements in descending order by **Executions** and **Duration** to identify SQL selects with long runtimes.

13.9.3 Optimization Measures in SQL Programming

When creating your ABAP routines with SQL statements, you should follow some rules that serve as the basis for highly performing SQL statements. This book is not intended to replace an ABAP tuning manual, and there are many good books available on that topic. You can also find comprehensive information on and examples of high-performing SQL programming in the runtime analysis of the SAP system (Transaction SE30) under the **Tips and Tricks** menu item

You should try to keep the amount of data transferred from the database to the application server as small as possible. For this purpose, you must add a WHERE clause to the SQL statement to set limits to the hitlist. By using the WHERE clause, you can avoid selecting unnecessary data records and thereby reduce the I/O load and the CPU utilization of the database server.

Keeping transferred data quantities small

If it's necessary to load entire tables, you should load them into the main memory first, so that the data records required for the subsequent data operations can be read individually from the main memory instead of the database. Note that accesses to the main memory are a hundred times faster than database read accesses.

If you use internal tables or global variables that are required for updating the data packages, ensure that you include a start routine in the transfer or update rule. A start routine is executed for the entire data package at the beginning of the transfer or update rule. If a request contains several data packages, the start routine is executed multiple times. Unlike transfer and update rules, a start routine does not contain any return value. Instead, it is used for a preliminary creation of internal tables or global variables, which are then accessed in the transfer and update rules.

13.10 Performance Aspects Relevant to the Update of InfoCubes

This section describes some of the performance aspects that are relevant to the data update process in InfoCubes. In this context we'll provide some recommendations regarding the parameterization of the system and optimization options.

13.10.1 Deleting Secondary Indices

In the fact table of an InfoCube, the columns that contain the foreign key of a dimension table (prefix KEY_) are assigned an index. The indices on the dimension keys of the fact table are required in order to increase the performance of read accesses performed by queries and aggregate rollups.

When filling an InfoCube with data, those indices must be adjusted by the database system, which may result in a decrease in performance. When you update data quantities into an InfoCube, you can improve the load performance by previously deleting the secondary indices in the fact table and recreating them once the data update is completed.

If you plan to carry out delta uploads of large data quantities, for example, more than one million data records or more than 10 to 15% of new data, you should delete the indices prior to the data upload. Since the indices are relevant to the reporting performance, you should ensure that you delete and regenerate the indices during those times when no analysis of the system operation is being carried out.

Indices are examined and deleted via the **Performance** tab in the Administrator Workbench in the InfoCube administration. For more information on the administration of indices, see Section 9.4 and the following section.

13.10.2 Increasing the Number Range Buffer of Dimension Tables

During the update of transaction data into an InfoCube, new keys are generated in the foreign key columns of the dimension tables, which are contained in the fact table, in order to establish a relationship between the transaction data records and the dimension tables. The SAP BW system uses *number ranges* to establish the key relationships. Number ranges are used to complete the key for an object, because the number range contains a number range interval that consists of a defined set of characters. The number range interval consists of numbers or alphanumeric characters within the interval limits "From number" and "To number."

The number ranges are mapped as number range objects in the SAP system. For example, for each dimension table, SAP BW contains a number range object whose set of number ranges serves as a basis for the creation of the dimension ID keys.

When updating the data of an InfoCube, you should store the number range of the relevant number range object for large dimension tables, which contain many attributes in the main memory. By storing the number range, you can ensure that the system doesn't have to retrieve a number from the number range table for each data record to create the fact table keys during the filling of an InfoCube. The process of storing the numbers of a number range object is referred to as *number range buffering*.

You can determine the number range object of a dimension table using the function module, RSD_CUBE_GET. To do that, call the function module RSD_CUBE_GET in Transaction SE37 using the **Test · Single Test** option and enter the name of the InfoCube into the I_INFOCUBE field. Then, enter the object version (= A) into the I_OBJVERS field, and the value X into the I_BYPASS_BUFFER field (see ❶ in Figure 13.24).

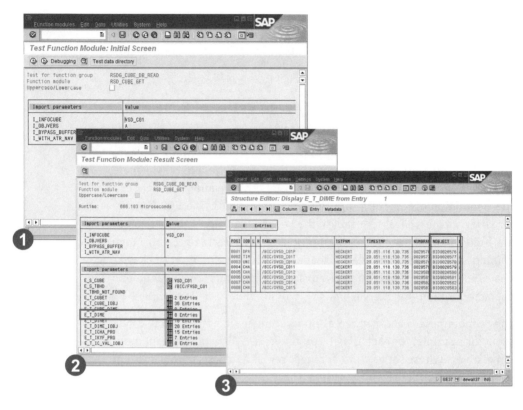

Figure 13.24 Determining Number Range Objects

The number range objects of the dimension tables are contained in Table E_T_DIME ❷, in column NOOBJECT ❸. For dimension tables, the names of the number range objects begin with BID*; for master data tables, they begin with BIM*.

You can then use Transaction SNRO to call the number range object maintenance (see Figure 13.25).

Enter the name of the number range object of the dimension table into the **Object** field (e.g., BID0028579) ❶, and then go to **Change**. In the subsequent screen ❷, select the **Edit · Set-up buffering · Main memory** menu to go to the maintenance screen that enables you to change the number range object. In the **No. of numbers in buffer** field, you can specify the number of numbers that is to be stocked in the buffer of the application server when the number range intervals are buffered. SAP recommends a value, which ranges between 50 and 500 numbers, that is to be stocked in the buffer. The value depends on the quantity of data expected for both the initial and future (delta) uploads.

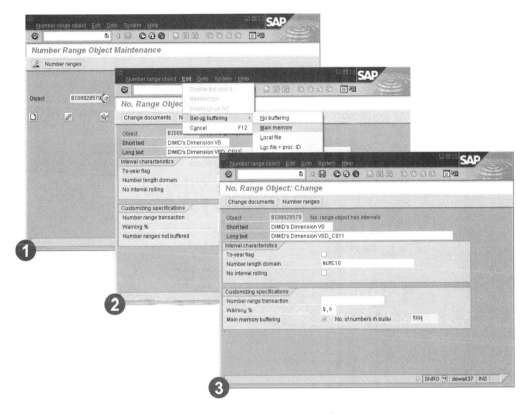

Figure 13.25 Number Range Object Maintenance (Transaction SNRO)

 Note that you must never buffer the number ranges for the package dimension and for InfoObject 0REQUID.

13.10.3 Uploading Transaction Data

When uploading transaction data, you should ensure that all related master data is first loaded in the SAP BW system.

During the update of an InfoCube, the system reads the SID table of a characteristic for each value of the characteristic in the transaction data. For example, if the value "BP-100" is provided for the characteristic 0MATERIAL in the transaction data record, the corresponding SID key is determined in SID table /BIO/SMATERIAL during the upload of the transaction data. If no SID is available for the characteristic value that has been transmitted along with the transaction data, a new entry is generated in the SID table.

In the subsequent step, the SID key of the characteristic value is used to determine the DIM-ID key in the corresponding dimension table /BIC/D<InfoCube><X> or /BIO/D<InfoCube><X> respectively. If no entry exists for the SID ID in the dimension table, a new entry is generated.

In the third step, the data record is entered into the fact table, including the corresponding key combination of the DIM ID.

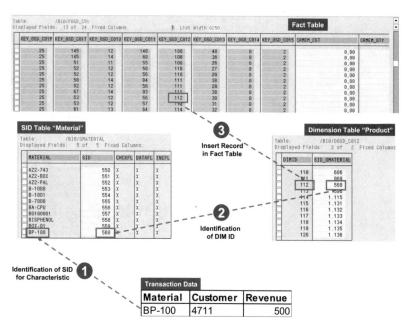

Figure 13.26 Updating Transaction Data in the InfoCube

If you update transaction data, without having previously uploaded the corresponding master data, the SAP BW system generates new master data on the basis of the uploaded transaction data by extracting SID keys and inserting new data records in the SID table. You can upload the master data later, however, the texts and attributes and hierarchies, if available, remain unknown until that point in time. Accordingly, uploading transaction data—without having previously uploaded master data by extracting SID keys—can take longer. For this reason, you should verify that the master data has been correctly loaded, before you update transaction data into an InfoCube.

You can configure the update process for transaction data in the **Update** tab in the InfoPackage maintenance screen (see Figure 13.27). By selecting a data update type in the data targets, you can define whether transaction data will be updated without master data.

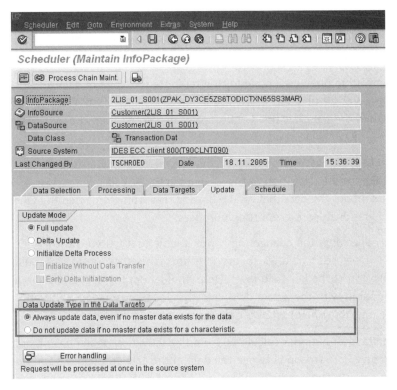

Figure 13.27 Configuring the Data Update in the InfoPackage Maintenance

13.11 Performance Aspects Relevant to the Update of Standard ODS Objects

For a better understanding of the performance optimization options, regarding the data update and the activation of ODS objects, we'll first describe the structure of a standard ODS object. Then, we'll introduce some optimization options.

13.11.1 Structure of a Standard ODS Object

In the database, an ODS object is represented by three transparent tables:[6]

---

6 In Release SAP NetWeaver 2004s, the term "standard ODS object" was replaced by "standard DataStore object." However, due to the widespread use of the former term, we use ODS object in this book. Note that there's a difference between the standard ODS object and the transactional ODS object, which can be filled with data outside of the SAP BW data update process by using other tools, for example, planning tools.

- ▶ The activation queue

- ▶ The active data

- ▶ The change log

Activation queue The activation queue is a table for the temporary storage of data records, which are to be updated in the ODS object but haven't been activated yet. Once the data has been activated, it is deleted from the activation queue.

Active data The active data is represented by the A table. The table is structured according to the definition of the ODS object (key fields and data fields) and it contains the data that can be used for reporting, provided the ODS object was enabled for reporting purposes.

Change log Strictly speaking, the change log is not a table that belongs to the ODS object, because it belongs to the PSA and is used to determine delta information at the key field level. Here, the data of the activation queue is compared with the active data, and the delta information is stored in the change log when the ODS data is activated.

The delta information is calculated from the activation of an ODS object, based on a comparison between the data of the activation queue and the active data. In the example shown in Figure 13.28, Request 1 is loaded with the amount 10; Request 2 is loaded with the amount 15; and Request 3 is loaded with amount 20.

When the ODS object is activated, the system calculates the change log by comparing the data with the active data. The old record in the active table is stored with a negative algebraic sign in the change log (-10), while the new record is assigned a positive sign (+15).

Due to the activation step, the data is transferred to the table that contains the active data, and at the same time, it is deleted from the activation queue. The amount 10 is replaced by 15 (provided the **Overwrite** option has been selected as update type), and the amount 20 is newly inserted.

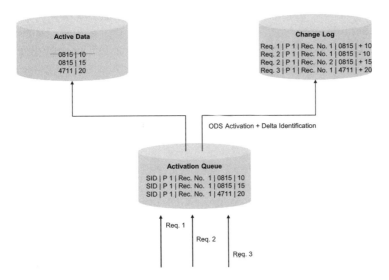

Figure 13.28 Updating ODS Data

13.11.2 Options for Optimizing the Activation Runtime

Large data quantities can cause a substantial increase of the runtime required for activating ODS data, which can be optimized by the following influencing factors:

▶ The size of the activation queue

▶ The SID determination

▶ Simultaneous upload and activation

If possible, the table of the activation queue should not contain more than 1 million data records. During the activation of the data of a standard ODS object, the data of the activation queue is stored in the main memory, and the check for existing records of active data is carried out in a common request. The limit for the main memory is approximately 1 million data records in the activation queue. For larger data volumes, the activation is carried out by individual selections, which may increase the load time.

Size of the activation queue

To keep the number of data records in the activation queue as small as possible, you should activate the ODS object on a regular basis. If you use very large requests that contain more than a million data records, you should distribute the data packages into several requests, which are uploaded more frequently.

SID determination For ODS objects that are used for data analysis purposes, you must make certain that SID keys exist, which correspond to the characteristic values contained in the ODS object. If an ODS object is enabled for reporting, the ODS data is checked against the SID tables of the characteristics during the activation. If the characteristic values contained in the ODS data do not exist in the master data, new SID keys must be created. The verification of the SID keys and the creation of new SID keys require a substantial portion of the time allotted to the data update process.

If you don't need the ODS data for reporting purposes, don't release the ODS object for Business Explorer (BEx) Reporting. Instead, you can activate an ODS object for reporting in the ODS object settings (see Figure 13.29).

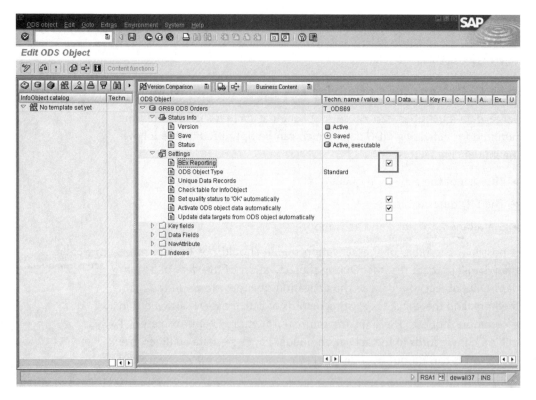

Figure 13.29 Activating ODS Objects for Reporting

Alternatively, rather than activate an ODS object for reporting, you can create an InfoSet query on the ODS that enables reporting on ODS data. You don't need to activate the ODS object for BEx Reporting to do that.

In SAP NetWeaver 2004s, SAP introduces a new type of DataStore object—the *write-optimized* DataStore object. The write-optimized DataStore object provides data for reporting, even without a prior determination of the SID, because the SID values are determined at reporting runtime.

As of SAP BW 3.x, you can upload and activate the ODS data in parallel work processes so you can optimize the load performance. If you activate the requests of an ODS object in parallel, the data of the activation queue is read and packaged. The data packages are then processed in several concurrent dialog processes. You can set the maximum number of dialog processes in the maintenance view for ODS fields (Transaction RSCUSTA2) in the **No. of Par. Proc.** field (see Figure 13.30).

Simultaneous upload and activation

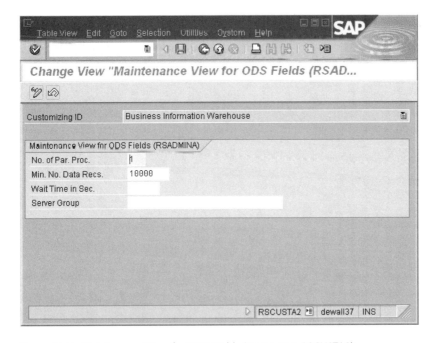

Figure 13.30 Maintenance View for ODS Fields (Transaction RSCUSTA2)

In the **Server Group** field, you can specify a server group or a server that you want to use for the activation of the ODS data.

14 Appendix

14.1 Transparent Tables of SAP BW Statistics

This section contains a description of the transparent tables of SAP BW statisics for logging activities of the OLAP processor and the staging engine.

14.1.1 Table RSDDSTAT: Statistical BW Data for Aggregate Selection and Accounting

Field	Description
STATUID	Primary table key, link in RSDDSTAT_V view
SESSIONUID	Identification of the frontend call. All data of a frontend session between the start and end of the frontend (e.g., BEx Analyzer) is compounded using this unique GUID.
NAVSTEPUID	Number of a navigation step in a frontend session
INFOCUBE	Technical name of the InfoCube the query is run on
HANDLE	Sequential number (ID) of an embedded query in the frontend. If web queries are run, the ID "9999" is set.
QUERYID	Technical name of the query that is run
PAGEID	Technical name of the web query HTML page
UNAME	System name of the user
QAGGRUSED	Name of the aggregate used by the OLAP processor. It is left blank, if no aggregate was used.
QNACHLESEN	Read mode of the query: ▶ H = query reads upon navigation or expansion of the hierarchy ▶ X = query reads upon navigation ▶ A = query reads all data at once

Table 14.1 Fields of Table RSDDSTAT

Field	Description
OLAPMODE	Operation mode of the OLAP processor: ▶ 000 = no OLAP activity ▶ 001 = run query or navigation step ▶ 002 = batch printing ▶ 003 = rolling up an aggregate ▶ 004 = warehouse management ▶ 005 = Tensor interface ▶ 006 = query on the web ▶ 007 = database interface (ListCube)
DBSELTP	Database read mode ▶ 000 = not assigned ▶ 001 = cumulative value ▶ 002 = non-cumulative value, reference points ▶ 003 = non-cumulative value, delta
QNAVSTEP	Sequential numbering of navigation steps within a query session
QDBSEL	Number of records that had to be read from the database
QDBTRANS	Number of records transferred from the database to the server
QNUMCELLS	Number of cells transferred to the frontend
QNUMRANGES	Number of formats transferred to the frontend
RECCHAVLREAD	Quantity of master data to be read
QRUNTIMECATE-GORY	Time needed for a navigation step (QTIMEOLAPINIT + QTIM-EOLAP + QTIMEDB + QTIMEEXCEL + QTIMECHAVLREAD), rounded up to the next decimal power (1,10,100,1000, ... seconds). As of Release 1.2B rounded to 1,2,3,...10,20,30,...,100,200,300, ... and so on in seconds
QNUMOLA-PREADS	Number of read processes per navigation step in the OLAP processor.
QTIMEOLAPINIT	Time needed for initializing the query. To load the query in OLAP for compilation, if necessary, for example
QTIMEOLAP	Time used by the OLAP processor to run the query
QTIMEDB	Time used by the database and network to select and transfer the transaction data
QTIMEVARDP	Time needed by the user for entering the variables ("time to think it over" for the user)
QTIMEUSER	Time needed by the user between the navigation steps

Table 14.1 Fields of Table RSDDSTAT (cont.)

Field	Description
QTIMECLIENT	Time needed for data preparation in the frontend. This time value includes the transport of data through the network and the output in the frontend.
TIMECHAVLREAD	Time needed for reading master data
TIMEAUTHCHECK	Time needed to perform an authorization check
TALERTMON	Time needed to read the alert monitor
TIMEREST	Remaining time, without any specific assignment
DMTDBBASIC	Time needed to read data from a BasicCube
DMTDBREMOTE	Time needed to read data from a RemoteCube
DMTDBODS	Time needed to read data from an ODS object
STARTTIME	Long form of UTC timestamp
TIMEFRONTPROC	Time needed for the processing in the frontend

Table 14.1 Fields of Table RSDDSTAT (cont.)

14.1.2 Table RSDDSTATAGGR: Statistical BW Data for Aggregate Selection and Accounting

Field	Description
STATUID	Primary table key
AGGRCUBE	Name of the aggregate (system-internal six-digit number)
INFOCUBE	InfoCube based on which the aggregate was created
PARENTCUBE	Name of the SourceCube or aggregate from which the data has been read
UNAME	User name that executed the action
CHANGEMODE	Editing mode (N = new creation; R = roll-up; D = delta). For a new creation, you can only use the N mode; for a roll-up, you can only use the R mode. If you use the delta procedure during a change run, you can use all three modes, otherwise, only the N mode is possible.
TIMEREAD	Read time
TIMEINSERT	Time needed for storing the data in the aggregate
TIMEINDEX	Time needed for the index creation
TIMEDBANALYZE	Time needed for analyzing the database statistics

Table 14.2 Fields of Table RSDDSTATAGGR

Field	Description
TIMECONDENSE	Time needed for condensing
STARTTIME	Long form of UTC timestamp
REC_READ	Number of records read from the InfoCube
REC_INSERT	Number of records inserted into the aggregate

Table 14.2 Fields of Table RSDDSTATAGGR (cont.)

14.1.3 Table RSDDSTATWHM: Statistical BW Data for Warehouse Management

Field	Description
RSSID	Master data ID
IPAKID	Request ID for the data package
ACTION	Type of processing step in WHM: ▶ 010 = processing in source system ▶ 011 = data dispatch ▶ 012 = extractor ▶ 020 = conversion of the communication structure ▶ 030 = data backup in PSA ▶ 039 = read from PSA ▶ 050 = conversion of update rules ▶ 060 = insert in InfoCube ▶ 065 = change InfoCube ▶ 200 = delete InfoCube contents ▶ 210 = delete request from InfoCube ▶ 220 = reversal posting ▶ 300 = entire process including saving the data in SAP BW (ALE/ODS) ▶ 600 = new creation of InfoCube ▶ 900 = entire process
INFOCUBE	Name of the InfoCube
ISOURCE	Name of the InfoSource
LOGSYS	Logical name of the source system
UNAME	User name that executed the action

Table 14.3 Fields of Table RSDDSTATWHM

Field	Description
MANUAL	Specification as to whether data has been updated manually or automatically (X = manually)
TFMETHOD	Transfer method: IDOC/TRFC
RECORDS	Number of data records
Time	Runtime
STARTTIME	Short form of UTC time stamp (YYYYMMDDhhmmss)

Table 14.3 Fields of Table RSDDSTATWHM (cont.)

14.2 Job Prefixes in SAP BW

This section of the Appendix contains the most important prefixes of job-driven processes in SAP BW. All jobs can be analyzed using Transaction SM37, Job overview, for example, start time and runtimes.

Job Prefix	Content
BI_BTCH	Data request
BI_PROCESS_	Job chains
RIRFQU	Source system extraction (for flat file, DataMart, and BAPI → job runs in SAP BW)
BI_PSAD	Deletion of PSA tables
BI_ODSA	Activation of ODS data
BI_EVEN	Event collector
BI_INDEX	Creation of indices
BI_HIER	Post-processing hierarchies
BI_STAT	Calculation of InfoCube statistics
BI_NEW	New creation of an InfoCube
BI_COMP	Compression of an InfoCube
BI_STOR	Deletion of requests
BI_SAGR	Initial filling of aggregates
BI_AGGR	Rollup of aggregates
BI_STRU	Hierarchy or attribute change run
BI_REQD	Preliminary check, if request must be deleted

Table 14.4 Job Prefixes in SAP BW

Job Prefix	Content
BI_BOOK	Data upload from PSA to InfoCube
BI_DELR	Deletion of request from InfoCube
RA	Creation of reporting agent packages

Table 14.4 Job Prefixes in SAP BW (cont.)

14.3 Transactions in the SAP BW System

Transaction	Description
BAPI	BAPI Explorer
CMOD	Project administration of SAP enhancements (customer exits)
FILE	Creation of logical file paths
LISTCUBE	List viewer for displaying data contents (BasicCubes, ODS objects, InfoObjects)
LISTSCHEMA	Schema viewer for InfoCubes and aggregates
PFCG	Role maintenance
RRC1	Create definition for currency translation
RRC2	Modify definition for currency translation
RRC3	Display definition for currency translation
RRMX	Start SAP Business Explorer Analyzer
RS12	Display and delete table lock entries
RSA1	Administrator Workbench (→ Modeling)
RSA3	Extractor checker
RSA4	Generate DataSources
RSA5	Import Business Content
RSA6	Post-process DataSources
RSA7	Maintain delta queue
RSA8	Repository of DataSources
RSA9	Import application components from Business Content
RSA11	Administrator Workbench (→ InfoProvider)
RSA12	Administrator Workbench (→ InfoSources)

Table 14.5 Transactions in SAP BW

Transaction	Description
RSA13	Administrator Workbench (→ Source systems)
RSA14	Administrator Workbench (→ InfoObjects)
RSBBS	Maintain jumps for the Report-to-Report Interface (RRI)
RSCDS	Schedule InfoCube compression
RSCUSTV1	Change settings for flat files
RSCUSTV2	Change monitor wait time
RSCUSTV3	Change user default value for ALE connections in the source system
RSCUSTV4	Change BEx values
RSCUSTV5	Change currency translation for external systems
RSCUSTV6	Change threshold values for data loads
RSCUSTV7	Change basic settings
RSCUSTV8	Change settings for an aggregate change run
RSCUSTV9	Change update mode for master data
RSCUSTV10	Generate server-side URL
RSCUSTV11	Change standard web template
RSCUSTV12	Change MS Analysis Services settings
RSCUSTV13	Change RRI settings for web reporting
RSCUSTV14	Change OLAP cache parameters
RSD1	Edit InfoObjects of the "characteristic" type
RSD2	Edit InfoObjects of the "key figures" type
RSD3	Edit InfoObjects of the "units" type
RSD4	Edit time characteristics
RSD5	Edit technical characteristics (request ID, hierarchy ID, and so on)
RSDCUBE	Edit InfoCubes
RSDDV	Maintain aggregates
RSDIOBC	Edit InfoObject catalog
RSDMD	Maintain master data for a characteristic
RSDMD_TEST	Test master data

Table 14.5 Transactions in SAP BW (cont.)

Transaction	Description
RSDMPROM	Edit MultiProviders
RSDODS	Edit ODS objects
RSDV	Maintain validity period (BasicCube with non-cumulative key figures)
RSFH	Testing tool for transaction data extractors
RSIMG	BW Customizing Guidelines
RSISET	Maintain InfoSets
RSKC	Maintain additional characters allowed in BW
RSMD	Testing tool for master data extractors
RSMON	Administrator Workbench (→ Monitoring)
RSMONCOLOR	Evaluate requests
RSO2	Maintain generic DataSources
RSO3	Set up delta extraction for attributes and texts
RSOR	Administrator Workbench (→ Metadata Repository)
RSORBCT	Administrator Workbench (→ Business Content)
RSPC	Maintain process chains
RSRCATTTRACE	Run CATT-Trace
RSRT	Query Monitor
RSRTRACE	Query trace
RSRV	Analysis and repair of BW objects
RSSM	Maintain reporting authorization objects
RSU1	Create update rules
RSU2	Change update rules
RSU3	Display update rules
SARA	Archiving tool
SBIW	Implementation Guide (→ extractor customizing)
SCAL	Maintain factory calendar
SE03	Transport Organizer tools
SE09	Organizer Workbench requests

Table 14.5 Transactions in SAP BW (cont.)

Transaction	Description
SE10	Organizer customizing requests
SE11	ABAP Dictionary
SE16	Data browser
SE37	ABAP Editor: Maintain function modules
SE38	ABAP Editor: Maintain ABAP programs
SE80	Object Navigator
SICF	Maintain Internet Communication Framework (ICF)
SM04	Display user list
SM12	Select lock entries
SM21	Online evaluation of the system log
SM30	Table maintenance
SM37	Job overview
SM38	Job definition
SM50	Process overview
SM59	Display and maintain RFC destinations
SM62	Display and maintain events
SM66	Global overview of work processes
SPAM	SAP Support Package Manager
SMX	System → own jobs
SPRO	Call customizing guidelines
SQ02	Maintain SAP Query/InfoSets
SQ10	Assign Query/InfoSets to user and role
SQLR	SQL-Trace Interpreter
ST03	Call system load monitor (BW statistics)
ST05	SQL-Trace
ST22	ABAP dump analysis
SU01	User maintenance
SU24	Role template maintenance

Table 14.5 Transactions in SAP BW (cont.)

Transaction	Description
SU53	Resolve error codes at authorization level
TRSA	Testing tool for service API

Table 14.5 Transactions in SAP BW (cont.)

14.4 Transactions Relevant to BW in the SAP R/3 System

Transaction	Description
LBWE	Customizing cockpit for logistics extract structures
RSA3	Extractor checker SAP 3.0
RSA5	Transfer DataSources from Business Content
RSA6	Post-process DataSources
RSA7	Maintain delta queue
RSA8	DataSource Repository
RSA9	Transfer application components
RSO2	Maintain generic DataSources
RSU7	Maintain control parameters for data extraction
SBIW	Display Implementation Guide (customizing extractors)
SM50	Process overview
SM59	Display and maintain RFC destinations

Table 14.6 Transactions in the SAP R/3 System

14.5 Processing Steps and Calling Programs in the RSMO Monitor

Processing Step	Calling Program	Description
Request	01	Start of data request
	02	End of data request
	09	Info IDoc (RQSTATE)

Table 14.7 Processing Steps and Calling Programs in the RSMO Monitor

Processing Step	Calling Program	Description
Transfer rules	20	Start of processing in SAP BW
	29	Data has been written to the communication structure
Update to PSA	30	Writing to ODS has started
	32	Writing to ODS has ended
	36	Reading from ODS has started
	39	Reading from ODS has ended
Update Rules	50	Update of transaction data has started
	51	Number of InfoCubes to be updated
	52	Update of InfoCube
	55	Start of aggregation
	57	Notification message from update routine
	58	Notification message from update routine
	59	End of aggregation
Update	60	Insert/update to transaction data database
	61	Insert/update to text database
	62	Insert/update to master data database
	63	Insert/update to hierarchies database
	66	Error during insert/update of transaction data database
Post-processing	70	End of processing
	80	Start of second step for master data, texts, hierarchies
	84	End of intermediate step for hierarchies
	89	End of second step for master data, texts, hierarchies

Table 14.7 Processing Steps and Calling Programs in the RSMO Monitor (cont.)

14.6   SAP R/3 and BW System Tables

This section contains some important SAP R/3 and BW system tables.

Table	Description
DBSTATC	Configuration of statistics creation
DD02L	SAP tables
E070	Transport system: request and task headers
E071	Transport system: object entries for requests and tasks
E07T	Transport system: short descriptions for requests and tasks
EDIDC	Control record (IDoc)
EDIDOT	Short description of IDoc types
INSTVERS	Documentation of installation status and history
PAT03	Patch directory
RODELTAM	SAP BW delta process
RODELTAMT	SAP BW delta process (texts)
RODIOBJCMP	SAP BW: InfoObjects/compounding
RODKYF	SAP BW: key figures
ROEXSOURCE	ABAP source code for SAP BW extractors
ROIDOCPRMS	Control parameters for transferring data from the source system
ROOSOURCE	Header table for SAP BW OLTP sources (relevant as of 2.0)
ROOSPRMS	Control parameters per DataSource
RSADMIN	Data import for administration settings
RSADMINA	Customizable control table
RSADMINC	General SAP BW customizing table
RSADMINS	System settings
RSAFORM	SAP BW formulas—check table
RSAFORMT	SAP BW formulas—text table
RSALLOWEDCHAR	Additional characters in SAP BW allowed by the customer
RSAREACUBE	InfoAreas of a cube

Table 14.8 SAP R/3 and BW System Tables

Table	Description
RSBASIDOC	Assignment of source systems to SAP BW systems including IDoc types
RSDDSTAT	Statistical BW data for aggregate selection and accounting
RSDDSTATAGGR	Statistical BW data for aggregate selection and accounting
RSDDSTATAGGRDEF	Statistical OLAP data: navigation step/aggregate definition
RSDDSTATBCACT	BW statistics: SAP Business Content activation
RSDDSTATCOND	BW statistics: data on InfoCube compression run
RSDDSTATDELE	Data on data deletions in the InfoCube
RSDDSTATEXTRACT	BW statistics extractor: time of last delta load
RSDDSTATLOG	BW statistics: sequence of events for DEBUG user
RSDDSTATWHM	BW statistics data for warehouse management
RSDMDIMTAB	Model table: dimension table
RSDMFACTAB	Model table: fact table
RSDRHLRUBUFFER	LRU buffer for hierarchy processing
RSTSODS	Operational data store (ODS) for the transfer structure
RSZCALC	Definition of a formula element
RSZCEL	Query Designer: directory of cells
RSZCOMPDIR	List of reusable components
RSZELTATTR	Attribute selection per dimension element
RSZELTDIR	Directory of reporting component elements
RSZELTXREF	Directory of query element references
RSZGLOBV	Global variables in reporting
RSZRANGE	Selection definitions for an element
RSZSELECT	Selection properties of an element
SDBAC	DBA action table
T006	Measurement units
TBTCO	Job status overview table
TEDS2	Short description of IDoc status values
TLOCK	Change and Transport System (CTS): lock table

Table 14.8 SAP R/3 and BW System Tables (cont.)

Table	Description
TPFET	Table of profile parameters
TSTC	SAP transaction codes
TSTCT	Transaction code texts
USR02	Logon data (kernel-based usage)
USR04	User master for authorizations
USR06	Additional data per user

Table 14.8 SAP R/3 and BW System Tables (cont.)

14.7 SAP Notes

This section contains some important SAP Notes relevant to performance. You can download all SAP Notes from SAP Service Marketplace at *http://service.sap.com*.

14.7.1 Database Settings

SAP Note	Title
567745	Composite note BW 3.x performance: DB-specific setting
632427	Oracle 8.1.7* database parameterization for BW
632556	Oracle 9.2.0* database parameters for BW
565075	Recommendations for BW systems with Oracle 8.1.x
181945	Performance guide: BW on Informix
327494	Configuration Parameters for SQL Server 2000
28667	Microsoft SQL Server Specific Profile Parameters
374502	DB6: DB2 UDB—BW Performance—Overview of notes
390016	DB2/390: BW: DB settings and performance.
546262	DB6: Administration & Performance on SAP BW, SAP SCM, SAP SEM
307077	iSeries: Performance Optimization for BW Systems
501572	iSeries: EVI stage 2 support
541508	iSeries: Checking the system parameters for BW
351163	Creating Oracle DB statistics using DBMS_STATS

Table 14.9 SAP Notes on Database Settings

SAP Note	Title
428212	Update of statistics of InfoCubes with BRCONNECT
725489	SAP DB (MaxDB) performance analysis tools
767635	MaxDB-Version 7.5 parameter settings for OLTP/BW
820824	FAQ: MaxDB

Table 14.9 SAP Notes on Database Settings (cont.)

14.7.2 System Settings

SAP Note	Title
31395	System parameters: Defined where? Displayed how?
39412	How many work processes to configure?
88416	Zero administration memory management from 4.0A/NT
97497	Memory Management Parameter (3.0/3.1)
192658	Setting basis parameters for BW systems
373986	Overflow of the export/import buffer

Table 14.10 SAP Notes on System Settings

14.7.3 Aggregates

SAP Note	Title
159485	Familiar problems with the aggregate setup
166433	Options for finding aggregates
198568	On the use of aggregates with hierarchies
202469	Using aggregate check tool
356732	Performance Tuning for Queries with Aggregates

Table 14.11 SAP Notes on Agregates

14.7.4 Composite SAP Notes and FAQs

SAP Note	Title
557870	FAQ: BW Query Performance
567746	Composite note BW 3.x performance: Query & Web applications
567747	Composite note BW 3.x performance: Extraction & loading
588668	FAQ: Database statistics

Table 14.12 Composite SAP Notes and FAQs

14.8 SAP Online Resources

This section provides information on some useful SAP websites that you can refer to for more information. Those sites marked with an "R" require a user registration.

SAP Online Resource	Address	Description	Type
SAP Help Portal	http://help.sap.com	Online documentation for all SAP solutions, PDF files, SAP Best Practices	
SAP Service Marketplace	http://service.sap.com	Internet portal for various online resources such as support, education, help portal, partner portal, and so on	
SAP Training Catalog	http://service.sap.com/trainingcatalog	Finding and registering for SAP trainings	R
SAP Developer Network	www.sdn.sap.com	Website for SAP developers that contains mainly technical information, web logs, and downloads	R
SAP Partner Portal	http://service.sap.com/partnerportal	Marketing and sales information, events, ramp-ups, testing and demo licenses for partners	R
SAP Support Portal	http://service.sap.com/notes	Search for SAP Notes	R

Table 14.13 SAP Online Resources

SAP Online Resource	Address	Description	Type
SAP Business Communities	www.sap.com/community	Community site containing online events, discussion forums, information on SAP customers, web logs of the executive board, and communities for innovative topics	R
DSAG	www.dsag.de	German-speaking SAP user group	R
SAP Info	www.sap.info	Online version of the SAP INFO magazine. Personalization is possible via registration.	
SAP Software Distribution Center	http://service.sap.com/swdc	Software distribution center of SAP; provides downloads of current support packages, among other things	R
SAP Quick Sizer	http://service.sap.com/quicksizer	Quick link to information and online application of SAP Quick Sizer	R
SAP Business Intelligence	http://service.sap.com/bi	Quick link to all topics related to the SAP Business Intelligence area	R

Table 14.13 SAP Online Resources (cont.)

14.9 Optimizing the Performance of Workbooks Containing Excel Formulas

This section describes a technical solution that enables you to avoid having to perform a static and performance-critical preassignment of Excel formulas in a large quantity of rows in a workbook, and instead generate Excel formulas dynamically at query runtime based on a selection of rows.

The following example uses a workbook to which data from a BEx query result is added by using the Excel formula VLOOKUP. The Excel formula VLOOKUP enables the system to search for a value within a column, and to return a value from a different column that matches the search criterion in the same row.

The VLOOKUP formula has the following syntax:

```
VLOOKUP(lookup_value;table_array;col_index_num;range_
lookup)
```

- ▶ `lookup_value` is the value located in the first column of the matrix.

- ▶ `table_array` is the table that contains the data. You can use a reference to an area or area name.

- ▶ `col_index_num` is the column number within the table from which the searched value is to be returned. A col_index_num 1 returns the value of the first column in the table; col_index_num 2 returns the value of the second column in the table, and so on.

- ▶ `range_lookup` is a logical value that specifies whether VLOOKUP is to return an approximate or exact value. If this parameter is not used, or if it is TRUE, an approximate value is returned. If it is FALSE, only exact values are returned.

Figure 14.1 illustrates the functionality of the VLOOKUP formula.

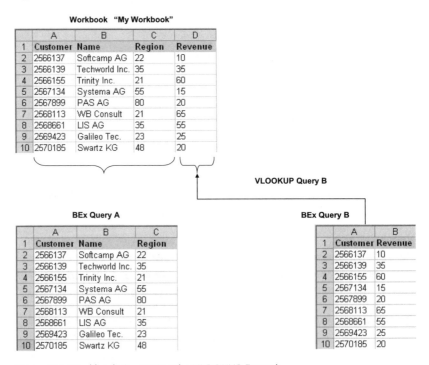

Figure 14.1 Workbook Containing the VLOOKUP Formula

Example: "My Workbook"

Suppose "My Workbook" contains two BEx queries. BEx Query A provides the *Name* and *Region* characteristics for the customer number. BEx Query B provides the sales figures for the customer number. The connection of both result areas using VLOOKUP is useful, if the result set of Query A is not the same as the result set of Query B, so that the data of one query can be added to the data of the other query. In the example shown in Figure 14.1, the VLOOKUP formula is used to add the sales figures from Query B to the customers in Query A. For this purpose, VLOOKUP enables the integration of data from query B in the sales figures column in "My Workbook:"

```
Cell value = VLOOKUP(A1;BEx-Query B;2;FALSE)
```

You should read the formula as follows: For the customer number found in Column A Row 1, the exact value must be found in the "BEx-Query B" area in Column 2. We'll proceed accordingly for the other rows.

Figure 14.2 displays the runtimes measured for the workbook, depending on the number of cells that have been preassigned the VLOOKUP formula.

Test series	No. Columns	No. Rows	No. Cells with VLOOKUP	1. Execution [s]				2. Execution (OLAP Cache			
				Time complete [s]	DB Time [s]	Frontend Time [s]	Frontend [%]	Time complete [s]	DB Time [s]	Frontend Time [s]	Frontend [%]
1	8	1,000	8,000	112.5	23.1	88.5	78.7%	92.0	0.0	81.8	99.0%
2	8	2,500	20,000	238.9	23.6	214.4	89.7%	209.7	0.0	208.9	99.6%
3	8	5,000	40,000	446.2	24.1	420.7	94.3%	427.4	0.0	426.6	99.8%
4	8	7,500	60,000	653.5	17.7	634.9	97.2%	621.5	0.0	620.3	99.8%
5	8	10,000	80,000	882.5	35.5	845.2	95.8%	843.8	0.0	842.2	99.8%
6	4	10,000	40,000	446.9	20.4	423.4	94.7%	451.3	0.0	450.4	99.8%

Figure 14.2 Evaluation of Workbook Runtimes (Static VLOOKUP) (I)

In measurement rows 1 to 5, the workbook was formatted in such a way that a VLOOKUP formula was assigned to a different number of rows (1,000, 2,500, 5,000, 7,500, 10,000) in 8 different columns. A VLOOKUP formula was stored in 4 columns and 10,000 rows in measurement row 6.

Static preassignment of Excel cells with formulas

The runtime analysis of the workbook shows that most of the runtime is needed in the frontend (client computer) due to the number of cells that contain the VLOOKUP formula. The total runtime increases as the number of VLOOKUP cells increases; and the frontend runtime portion of the total runtime is usually above 90% in the initial call. In the second call of the query result from the OLAP cache, the runtime is almost completely utilized in the frontend. Although the query is responded to completely from the OLAP cache (DB runtime = 0), the measured runtimes of the workbook are only insignificantly smaller than they are in the initial call.

Calculations affecting the frontend runtime

An analysis of the CPU utilization at query runtime shows that the frontend runtime is utilized by the Excel calculations of the VLOOKUPs (client computer configuration: MS Windows 2000 Service Pack 4, Intel Pentium 4 1.60 GHz, 500 MB RAM).

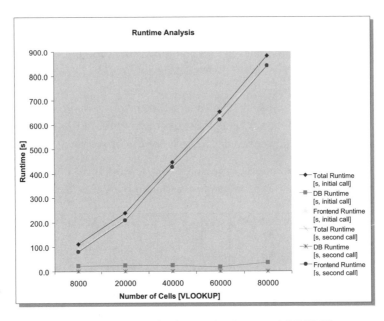

Figure 14.3 Evaluation of Workbook Runtimes (Static VLOOKUP) (II)

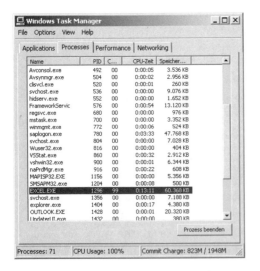

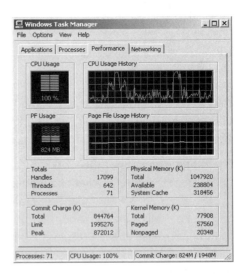

Figure 14.4 CPU Utilization During Execution of BEx Workbook Containing VLOOKUP Cells

A decisive factor for the use of VLOOKUPs is the absolute number of cells that contain a VLOOKUP formula, irrespective of whether those cells are actually filled with data from a BEx query. For this reason, you should not preassign many rows of your workbooks with VLOOKUP formulas.

Frequently, you can assume that the number of rows expected in the result area of a query—with regard to the specified selection criteria—is unknown. In other words, you cannot determine the number of rows to which you must assign a VLOOKUP formula in the relevant columns. Therefore, you should refrain from using the static preassignment of a sufficient number of rows with VLOOKUPs (e.g., 10,000 rows, if you predict that the result set won't exceed 10,000 rows). Instead, you should determine the number of rows in the results area dynamically, by using a VBA table pointer. Then, you can generate the necessary VLOOKUP formula for the columns at query runtime, which is based on the number of rows in the results area, by using a VBA copy command. For this purpose, you must store the VLOOKUP formula in the first row of the results area of a column. Then, you must copy the formula, which is based on the number of rows in the executed BEx query.

Dynamic preassignment of Excel cells with formulas

The following sample VBA code illustrates the functionality:

```
Sub SAPBEXonRefresh(queryID As String, resultArea As
Range)
    Dim RANGE1 As String
    Dim Rows1   As Integer
If queryID = "SAPBEXq0001" Then
    If Not resultArea.Resize(1, 1).Value = "No
    matching data found" Then
    A1 = "D2"
    Z9 = "D" & 2 + resultArea.Rows.Count
    RANGE1 = A1 & ":" & Z9
    Sheets("Result").Select
    Range("D2").Select
    Selection.AutoFill Destination:=Range(RANGE1),
    Type:=xlFillDefault
    End If
  End If
End Sub
```

To determine the number of assigned rows in the results area, you must first generate the two variables RANGE1 and Rows1. RANGE1 contains the range of the column that is to be filled with the VLOOKUP formula; Rows1 stores the number of preassigned rows. If data is found for Query SAPBEXq0001, the range of the column is identified, to which data is to be added by using the VLOOKUP formula. In the example above, this is column D from row 2 to row 2 + the number of rows contained in the results area of BEx Query SAPBEXq0001. The number of preassigned rows in the results area of the BEx query is determined by using the table pointer `resultArea.Rows.Count`. The local variables A1 and Z9 are used to fill the range object RANGE1. For example, if the results area of the BEx query comprised 128 rows, the range object would be `RANGE1 = D2:D128`.

This range is filled in the next step using the VLOOKUP formula. For this purpose, the actual VLOOKUP formula has been previously stored in row 2 of column D in the results sheet. Using the command

```
Selection.AutoFill Destination:=Range(RANGE1),
Type:=xlFillDefault
```

it is then copied to as many rows as have been determined by the table pointer Rows1. In the preceding example, this means that the VLOOKUP formula is stored in only 128 rows of column D.

Therefore, you do not have to preassign the VLOOKUP formula to 10,000 rows, because the formula is generated dynamically at runtime on the basis of the assigned cells.

The workbook measured above was restructured correspondingly and extended by the VBA code. Figure 14.5 shows the measurement results after the restructuring.

The comparison of runtimes shows that the frontend runtime of the workbook, which now contains a dynamic VLOOKUP formula, is only 7% of the workbook runtime with a static VLOOKUP formula and 1,000 preassigned rows. Of course, the frontend runtime for the dynamic workbook also depends on the number of VLOOKUPs to be created. If the VLOOKUP formula must be created for many rows in the results area, the total runtime of the workbook might increase accordingly.

	1. Execution [s]			2. Execution (OLAP Cache)		
	Time complete [s]	DB Time [s]	Frontend Time [s]	Time complete [s]	DB Time [s]	Frontend Time [s]
Dynamic VLOOKUP (8 X 128 Rows)	41.2	33.2	6.5	7.6	0.0	6.6
Static VLOOKUP (8 X 1,000 Rows)	112.5	23.1	88.5	82.6	0.0	81.8

Figure 14.5 Comparison of Workbook Runtimes (Static and Dynamic VLOOKUP)

The Author

Thomas Schröder is a managing consultant in the Finance Transformation—Application Consulting area at Capgemini Deutschland GmbH, Germany. He has many years of project experience in designing and implementing business intelligence solutions. His consulting work focuses on business intelligence strategies, business analytics, data modeling, data warehousing architectures, and SAP BW.

Index

Expert advice to implement key ETL processes

Complete coverage of master data, transaction data and SAP Business Content

Step-by-step instruction and field tested solutions

552 pp., 2006, US$ 69,95
ISBN 1-59229-044-2

SAP BW
Data Retrieval

www.sap-press.com

N. Egger, J.-M. Fiechter, R. Salzmann, R.P. Sawicki, T. Thielen

SAP BW Data Retrieval

Mastering the ETL process

This much anticipated reference makes an excellent addition to your SAP BW Library. Read this book and you'll discover a comprehensive guide to configuring, executing, and optimizing data retrieval in SAP BW.

The authors take you, step-by-step, through all of the essential data collection activities and help you hit the ground running with master data, transaction data, and SAP Business Content. Expert insights and practical guidance help you to optimize these three factors and build a successful, efficient ETL (extraction, transformation, loading) process. This all-new edition is based on the current SAP BW Release 3.5, but remains a highly valuable resource for those still using previous versions.

Comprehensive overview of the functions of SAP BI

Extensive descriptions of all new features

Includes details on Visual Composer and High Performance Analytics

approx. 600 pp.,US$ 69,95
ISBN 1-59229-082-6, Aug 2006

SAP Business Intelligence

www.sap-press.com

N. Egger, J.-M. Fiechter, R.P. Sawicki, S. Weber

SAP Business Intelligence

This book provides information on all the important new BI features of the SAP NetWeaver 2004s Release. Essential subjects like data modeling, ETL, web reporting, and planning and covered along with all of the newest functions making this book an unparalleled companion for your daily work. Real-life examples and numerous illustrations help you hit the ground running with the new release. Plus, useful step-by-step instructions enable the instant use of new features like Visual Composer, and many more.